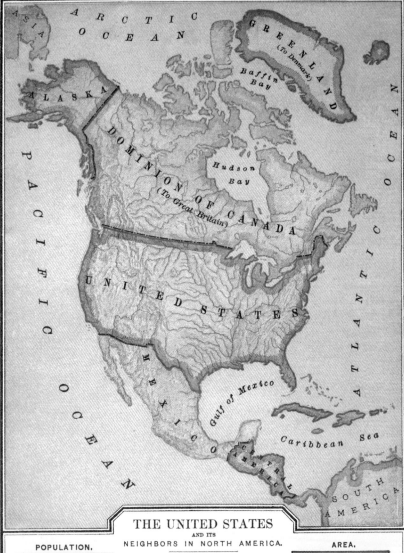

THE UNITED STATES
AND ITS
NEIGHBORS IN NORTH AMERICA.

NOTE—*The colored diagrams show the relative population and the relative areas in the North American possessions of the several powers on the continent, including Greenland and the West India islands. The colors in the squares are the same as those used for the several divisions of the map to which they refer.*

POPULATION.

AREA.

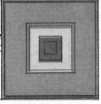

POPULA'N.	POSSESSIONS OF	AREA, SQ. MI.
62,982,244	UNITED STATES	3,668,167
11,395,712	MEXICO	751,584
5,027,698	GREAT BRITAIN	3,777,550
3,010,324	CENTRAL AMERICAN STATES	179,730
2,323,400	SPAIN	46,770
113,208	DENMARK	889,874

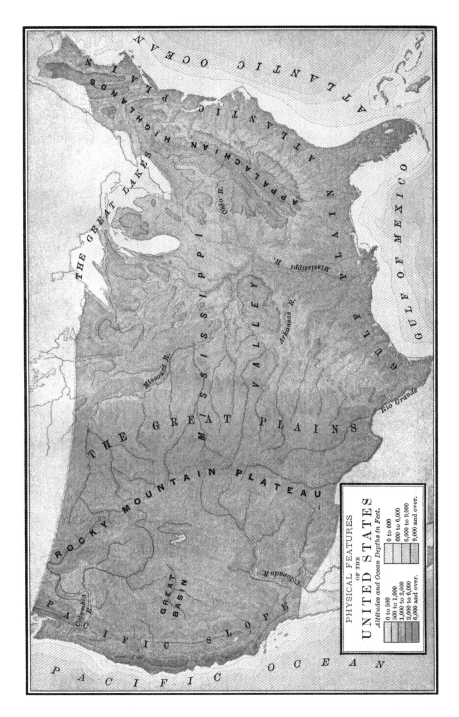

PHYSICAL FEATURES
OF THE
UNITED STATES
Altitudes and Ocean Depths in Feet.

0 to 500
500 to 1,000
1,000 to 2,000
2,000 to 6,000
6,000 and over.

0 to 600
600 to 6,000
6,000 to 9,000
9,000 and over.

PACIFIC OCEAN

ATLANTIC OCEAN

ATLANTIC OCEAN

GULF OF MEXICO

ATLANTIC PLAIN

ATLANTIC PLAIN

APPALACHIAN HIGHLANDS

THE GREAT LAKES

THE GREAT PLAINS

ROCKY MOUNTAIN PLATEAU

PACIFIC SLOPE

GREAT BASIN

MISSISSIPPI VALLEY

Ohio R.

Mississippi R.

Arkansas R.

Missouri R.

Rio Grande

Colorado R.

Columbia R.

Colonial Costumes

EARLY PURITAN COSTUME	A GOVERNOR IN THE 17TH CENTURY	A PURITAN DIVINE
A DIGNITARY IN THE 18TH CENTURY	AN OFFICER IN THE REVOLUTION	A GENTLEMAN ABOUT THE TIME OF THE
A GENTLEMAN IN THE 18TH CENTURY	A GENTLEMAN ABOUT THE TIME OF THE	REVOLUTION
A MERCHANT IN THE 18TH CENTURY	REVOLUTION	A COLONIAL GOVERNOR IN THE 18TH CENTURY

A History of
The United States
and Its People

A History of The United States and Its People

By

EDWARD EGGLESTON

Lost Classics Book Company
Publisher
Lake Wales
Florida

Publisher's Note

—+—

Recognizing the need to return to more traditional principles in education, Lost Classics Book Company is republishing forgotten late 19th and early 20th century literature and textbooks to aid parents in the education of their children.

This edition of *A History of the United States and its People* was reprinted from the 1888 copyright edition. The text has been updated and edited only where necessary. Some of the quotes and expressions in the book reflect the attitudes of their time and do not necessarily reflect today's attitudes.

© Copyright 1998
Lost Classics Book Company

Library of Congress Catalog Card Number: 98-85397
ISBN 0-9652735-8-X

Cover Image:
Spirit of '76
by Archibald McNeal Willard

The original painting hangs in the Selectmen's Meeting Room, Abbott Hall, Marblehead, Massachusetts

EDWARD EGGLESTON

———+———

Edward Eggleston was born December 10, 1837 in Vevay, Indiana into a Methodist family. He was educated at the local high school in Vevay where he discovered his gift for writing. His militant opposition to slavery, however, caused him to refuse an offer to attend the University of Virginia. Ill health prevented his attending any college. In 1858 Edward Eggleston became a Methodist preacher. In 1866 he left the ministry to pursue his career as a writer. He began as an editor of the *National Sunday School Teacher* in Evanston, Illinois. In 1870 he moved to New York and began working on the *Independent*, for which he'd been a Western correspondent for some time. In 1871 he began his career as a popular novelist with the publishing of the *Hoosier Schoolmaster*. His subsequent fiction had an important influence in turning American literature towards realism.

Eventually Eggleston's main literary interest shifted from fiction to history. He had come to look upon the novel as a means of making "a contribution to the history of civilization in America." His school histories and other minor historical and biographical publications were merely by-products of his work on an ambitious plan for a history of life in the United States, which he did not live to complete. As president of the American History Association in 1900, he set forth his conception of the ideal history as primarily a record of the culture of a people, not merely or even chiefly a record of politics and war.

His last years, like his early life, were troubled with serious illness. He died in September of 1902.

PREFACE

———+———

ONE of our American humorists has said that it is better The first requirement not to know so much than to know so many things that are not true. Errors accepted in childhood become articles of faith, and are not easily dispelled. The absence from this book of certain well-worn fables, which have served more than one generation of American schoolchildren for historic facts, will be regretted, perhaps, on sentimental grounds. It does not seem worthwhile, however, to keep current in elementary books statements which every sound historical scholar rejects. No work of history ever yet escaped error, but I have at least tried to make this a genuine history, in harmony with the best historical scholarship of the time. Many laborious years passed in the critical study of original printed and manuscript authorities for the history of American institutions and American life have perhaps given the author of this book some right to speak with assurance on questions relating to our early history.

Next to correctness the most important feature in a Clarity and interest book for the young is clarity. To achieve this one must not treat more subjects than can be handled with sufficient fullness for comprehension. Attempts to write a little about everything are fatal to lucidity. The writer for the young finds all his skill taxed to be clear and to be interesting, and the two things lie close together. One of the highest benefits that a good textbook in the hands of a good teacher can confer is to leave the pupil with a relish for historical reading.

The order in which the various topics are treated has Arrangement of topics much to do both with the clearness and the interest of a history. In the strictly chronological history the reader skips from theme to theme, resuming under several dates the broken thread of now this and now that story. The relation of cause and effect is almost entirely lost, and history becomes a succession of events with little logical connection. The understanding is benumbed, the attention is but feebly roused, imagination slumbers, and memory gets small hold on occurrences that are presented like beads unstrung. The rigid grouping of a history by epochs is fatal to a truly logical arrangement. One of the most important of the novel features of the present history is its arrangement. Discoveries, settlements, Indians and Indian wars, colonial life, the French wars, government in colonial time and the rise of the Revolution, and other kindred topics, are severally grouped together, so that, for instance, the pupil learns about the nature of Indian life, the chief Indian wars, and the means of attack and defense used by white men and Indians in successive chapters, pursuing this general subject until it is finished. Cause and effect are thus clearly set before his mind, and history becomes a reasonable science.

Position of the reviews

The reviews are not placed at regular intervals, according to a stiff mechanical rule, but these also follow in the main the same rule of grouping as the chapters. When a chief topic is completed, there is a review, whether the chapters be many or few.

The history of civilization

The "proper knowledge of mankind is man," and the real importance of history lies in the light that it throws upon humanity. For this reason liberal attention has been here given to the domestic and social life of the people, their dress, their food, their modes of thought and feeling, and their ways of making a livelihood. The succession of events in minor wars would only weary the attention, but the modes of attack and defense and the character of the arms of the various belligerents are essential facts in the history of man in this New World. And the story of the progress of civilization, as marked by the introduction of new inventions and by changes in modes of living, is of primary importance in any history written in the modern spirit.

This is from first to last a schoolbook. No other aim has been in view in its preparation than that of making the best possible teaching book of American history. The length and arrangement of the chapters, the questions, topical and geographical studies, and skeleton outlines, as well as the reviews, are all arranged with reference to the needs of teacher and pupil. An effort has here been made to apply to history in a thorough and practical way the great Pestalozzian principle of teaching through the eye. The suggestions for blackboard illustrations, the diagrams, the abounding illustrations, and the little maps scattered through the pages, are all part of a plan to make the facts of history visible, and by that means to render the study easily comprehensible and therefore delightful. *A teaching book*

Instead of a few large maps in various colors and confused with many names, among which the pupil must grope painfully for the places that pertain to the events under consideration, there are in this history more maps than chapters, and every one of the smaller maps is arranged to bear upon one fact, or at most upon two or three in close relation. Only so many names are put upon each map as are necessary to make clear the event under consideration. Not only is the pupil saved from *The maps* much needless toil by this plan, but maps thus arranged serve the double purpose of elucidating the narrative and impressing it on the memory at the same time, by giving it form to the eye. Each little map becomes a local diagram of some historical fact, and the form of the map will remain in the memory inseparably associated with the event to which it belongs—a geographical body to an historical soul. Educational writers have said much about the importance of teaching geography and history together. There is not, perhaps, any better device for teaching the two branches in unison than these simple and perspicuous maps, each immediately associated on the page with the single event to which it pertains.

The illustrations   Though the illustrations are by some of the best artists and engravers of the time, and are many of them of high artistic merit, and though they are far more abundant than is usual in books of this kind, there has been no thought of making this a mere picture book. The illustrations are part and parcel of the teaching apparatus; their primary use, like that of the maps, diagrams, and blackboard exercises, is to make the history visible. A very considerable body of historical knowledge of the most important kind might be acquired from these cuts alone. Illustrations of costumes, manners, implements, arms, jewels, vehicles, and inventions are valuable in proportion to their truthfulness. Those here given have been made under the author's personal supervision, and they have cost quite as much labor and study as the text itself. Many are founded on rare prints, others are from ancient original drawings not before printed, and a few have been carefully drawn from descriptions of contemporary writers. The device of placing many of the smaller cuts in the margin serves to make the page more pleasing to the eye, while it has rendered it possible to illustrate abundantly without unduly increasing the size and cost of the book. The author cannot forbear expressing his appreciation of the liberality with which the publishers have availed themselves of so many of the resources of the modern art of illustration to enhance the value of this history. The illustrations have been made under the artistic supervision of Mr. John A. Fraser.

In *English as She is Taught*; a definition is cited from a schoolboy's exercise book to the effect that "the Constitution of the United States is that part at the back of the book which nobody reads" Since no schoolboy or schoolgirl ever does read it, and since it is not a document meant to be construed by children, it seemed better to utilize the space for other things than to reprint the Constitution for mere claptrap. The same remark applies to the Declaration of Independence. But I have, instead, explained the purport of the Declaration of Independence in its place, and I am sure the pupil will get far more from the account given in this work of the various departments of our government, their origin, and their operation under the Constitution, than from reading the letter of the Constitution itself. *The study of the Constitution*

One of the main difficulties the writer of a school history has to meet is in the treatment of recent history, many particulars of which are still matters for difference of opinion. Real historic judgment on these things must be deferred to a generation that had no part in them. Manifestly a schoolbook, since it is frequently prescribed by public authority, should be free from partisanship. I have tried, *Treatment of controverted points* however, to state admitted facts frankly, without offensive terms or a premature judgment on disputed points.

Marginal titles By omitting the numbers usually placed at the beginning of paragraphs, the book has been relieved of stiffness; by printing the subject of each paragraph in the margin, a means of reference far more convenient is provided. This feature is part of the general design of the book, which aims to keep before the minds of teacher and pupils the salient features of the topic under discussion, and thus to discourage mere rote study.

E. E.

Suggestions Regarding the Use of the Book

———+———

"Questions for Study" follow each chapter. These are intended, in the first place, to guide the pupil in mastering his lesson, to make him test his understanding of the subject by analyzing and reasoning about his facts, and by associating them with related facts. The teacher will also find these questions helpful to him in preparing and hearing a recitation.

The "Study by Topics" which follows the questions is meant chiefly to aid the teacher in conducting a recitation, or, at least, a review of a recitation. The topical method of recitation develops the pupil's power of grasping and holding each branch of a subject in its entirety. But it can not be used to the exclusion of the use of questions and answers without danger of its degenerating, on the one hand, into an inadequate statement, or, on the other, into a mere repetition of the words of the text-book.

Some teachers will use now one and now the other method, testing the pupil's understanding of the subject at one recitation by questions, at the next developing his power of synthesis and his mastery of language by giving him a division of the subject to be stated in his own way and with his own words, and then, when he has completed his statement, pointing out his omissions or misapprehensions.

Other teachers will prefer to combine the two plans in the same recitation. This may be done—1. By a thorough examination of the subject by questions, followed by a topical review of the whole chapter, each division of the subject being assigned to a pupil in his turn. 2. Another mode of combining the two is by following the recitation of each topic by questions meant to bring out from the class points forgotten or obscured in the pupil's account of that branch of the subject. No recitation can fully accomplish its purpose without the use of questions at some stage.

Skeleton summary

The "Skeleton Summary" appended to many of the chapters will suggest its proper use. It may be copied on papers or on slates and filled in by each pupil, or the teacher may have it written on the blackboard and then have the blanks filled by suggestions from the class.

Geographical study

The geographical facts connected with each event should be brought out distinctly. When larger or fuller maps than those in this book are needed, the atlas or the school wall-map can be easily referred to. The small maps accompanying the text may be sketched on the blackboard, as further described, or they may be used from the page.

Blackboard

In general, the blackboard should be used wherever possible. In particular:

1. The Study by Topics may be written on the blackboard with advantage in almost every recitation. The subject under consideration is thus displayed in a natural order. This may be done before the recitation begins, or each topic may be added as the recitation proceeds, thus constructing a visible table of the subject before the eyes of the class.

2. When diagrams are given in the book, they may be put on the board, to give a visible illustration to some proportion of size or number.

3. Word-diagrams are often useful. See, for example, pages 13 and 121. In these the location of the words or phrases helps the mind to group and the memory to hold important facts.

4. It is an excellent plan to sketch the small map on the blackboard. This should not be done elaborately or with too much attention to detail. The most useful maps of all are mere diagrams of location sketched by a pupil rudely but readily, as he might do in explaining a fact in conversation.

The cuts, especially those illustrating life and manners, are a part of the history, and the teacher should, by remark or question, draw attention to the facts illustrated by them. — Pictures

The "Reviews" which close each group of chapters may be treated as a briefer topical recitation, developing rapidly the salient points of the chapters reviewed. The review may also be put upon the blackboard, in sections, if not as a whole. — Reviews

In the prevailing movement to lighten the labors of the pupil in school, history is sometimes taught by using the textbook for a reader. In such cases, there should be a line of comment or question maintained by the teacher sufficient to make sure that the chapter read is fully understood, and sufficient to impress what has been read on the memory. By writing the "Study by Topics" on the blackboard, a habit of thoughtful reading will be promoted. The abundant illustrations of customs and the little special maps in this book will prove of the greatest advantage to teachers using this as a reading-book. — The school history as a class reading-book

Topics for school composition are now and then suggested from the subjects treated in the current chapter.

There is a double advantage in these: The puzzled pupil is helped to a topic for writing, while the best results of historical study are secured by giving him occasion to exercise his thoughts upon the subjects studied. The teacher will easily suggest other topics; particularly may the pupil write upon the several actors in our history in those schools where access can be had to works of biography or books of reference.

CONTENTS

—✦—

THE SHIPS OF COLUMBUS

CHAPTER I

How Columbus Discovered America

IT is now about five hundred years since Columbus discovered America. Before that time people in Europe knew
nothing of any lands on the western side of the Atlantic.
Trade with India was carried on by caravans, and travelers
who had gone to China and Japan brought back wonderful
stories of the riches of their cities, and of the curious people
who lived in those faraway countries. In order to reach
these lands of wonder and to open a trade with India by
sea, the Portuguese had been for a long time pushing their
discoveries down the western coast of Africa. But the seamen of that time sailed mostly in the Mediterranean, and
they were timid in the Atlantic Ocean. The Portuguese
sent out expedition after expedition, for seventy years,
before they succeeded in discovering the Cape of Good
Hope, and they had not yet got around that cape when Columbus offered to find a new and shorter way to India.

As learned men already believed the world to be round,
Columbus asked: Why try to get to In-
dia and China by going around Africa? Why not sail straight to the

Trade with
India in the time
of Columbus

A SAILOR OF
THAT TIME

PROW OF
ANCIENT
WARSHIP

COLUMBUS

west around the world to Asia? He did not know that America was in the way, and he thought that the world was smaller than it is, and he believed that he could reach the rich lands of gold and spices in Asia by sailing only two or three thousand miles to the westward. So Columbus discovered America as a result of two mistakes.

False notions in the way

He first offered to make this discovery for the city of Genoa in which he was born.

Christopher Columbus was born in Genoa, in Italy. The date of his birth is uncertain. His father was a humble wool-comber, but Columbus received a fair education. He knew Latin, wrote a good hand, and drew maps exceedingly well. He sometimes supported himself by making maps and charts. He was well informed in geography as it was then understood. At fourteen he went to sea, and before he sailed on his great voyage he had been almost all over the known world. He had gone some distance down the newly discovered coast of Africa, with the Portuguese, and north as far as Iceland. Columbus married the daughter of a Portuguese navigator and came into possession of his charts. He was a man of great perseverance, and he held to his idea of sailing to the west through many long years of discouragement. He made four voyages to America, setting out on the first in 1492, the second in 1493, the third in 1498, and the fourth in 1502. Though a great navigator, he was not a wise governor of the colonies he planted, and he had many enemies. In 1500 he was cruelly sent home to Spain in chains. But Ferdinand and Isabella, as well as the people, were shocked at this degradation, and he was at once set free. His last voyage was unfortunate, and when he returned to Spain, in November, 1504, the monarchs paid little attention to him. Queen Isabella died soon after his return, while Columbus lay sick, and when the great navigator came to court the king was deaf to his petitions. Worn out with fatigue exposure, and anxiety, the great admiral died on the 20th of May, 1506.

Then he offered his plan to the King of Portugal. But a voyage on the great Atlantic Ocean seemed a dreadful thing in those days. It was called the

STERN OF
ANCIENT WARSHIP

"Sea of Dankness," because no one knew anything about it, and people believed that it was inhabited by hideous monsters. As the world was round, some thought that, if a ship sailed *down* the sides of it, it would find it impossible to get back *up* again. They said that people could not live on the other side of the world because they would be upside down.

The King of Portugal was an enlightened man, and the ideas of Columbus made an impression on him after a while. But he did not like to grant the great rewards demanded by the navigator if he should find land; so he secretly sent out a ship under another commander to sail to the westward and see if there was any land there. The sailors on this ship were easily discouraged, and they returned laughing at Columbus and his notions. When Columbus found that he had been cheated, he left Portugal to offer his idea to the King and Queen of Spain, the celebrated Ferdinand and Isabella. The Spanish monarchs were very busy in their war with the Moors, and Columbus, who was poor and obscure, spent about seven years in trying to persuade them to furnish him ships and sailors. At length, after he had waited so long, they refused his terms, and he set out for France, but certain officers of Queen Isabella, who believed in Columbus' theory, persuaded her to call him back and to send him on his own terms.

Columbus sailed from Spain, with three small vessels, on the 3d of August, 1492, and was more than two months on the voyage. The sailors were more and more frightened as they found themselves going farther and farther out of

A ship sent out secretly

Columbus goes to Spain

His departure on his great voyage, and his discovery of land

THE PART OF THE WORLD KNOWN WHEN COLUMBUS SAILED IS IN WHITE

the known world. They sometimes threatened to pitch Columbus overboard and return. He kept their courage up by every means he could think of, even by concealing from them how far they had come. One night Columbus saw a light, and at two o'clock the next morning, which was the 12th of October, 1492, a sailor on one of the vessels raised the cry "Land!" There was the wildest joy on the ships. Those who had hated Columbus, and wished to kill him, now reverenced him.

What he had found   Instead of finding the rich cities of Asia, Columbus had come upon one of the smallest of the West India islands, which was inhabited by people entirely naked, and living in the rudest manner. He afterward discovered larger islands, and then sailed homeward.

His return to Spain   He carried with him some gold and some of the inhabitants of the islands. He was received by Ferdinand and Isabella with the greatest honor. They even made him

Discoveries before Columbus— There is some reason to believe that America may have been visited from Europe before the time of Columbus. The inhabitants of Scandinavia (the country now divided into Denmark, Sweden, and Norway) were known as Norsemen. In the old romantic tales of Scandinavia there are stories which go to show that these Norsemen, under the command of Leif, the son of Eric, in the year 1001, and afterward, probably explored the coast of America from Labrador southward for some distance. Fanciful theories have been built on these stories such as the notion that the old stone windmill at Newport, R. I., is a tower built by the Norsemen. There is also a tradition in Wales that one Madoc, a Welsh prince, in the year 1170, discovered land to the west of Ireland, and took a colony thither which was never heard of afterward. If these stories of Leif and Madoc represent real voyages, the discoveries which they relate would probably never have been recalled to memory if Columbus had not opened a wide door at the right moment.

sit down in their presence, a favor never shown except to the greatest grandees. The people who had believed him a fool when he went away, followed him with cheers as he walked along the street.

Columbus in his second voyage to America, planted a colony on the island of Hispaniola, or Haiti. In this and in two other voyages he discovered other islands and a portion of the coast of South America, which he first saw in 1498. He never knew that he had found a new world, but lived and died in the belief that the large island of Cuba was a part of the mainland of Asia.

Later voyages of Columbus

1. *Who discovered America?*
2. *How long is it since Columbus discovered America?*
3. *What did people in Europe know about America 500 years ago?*
4. *What did they know about the roundness of the world?*
5. *How was the trade with Asia carried on?*
6. *What stories were told in Europe at this time by travelers?*
7. *What shorter route to India from Europe has been made in our time?*
8. *How did the Portuguese try to get to India at this time?*
9. *Had they reached India by sea when Columbus sailed to America?*
10. *How many years had they spent exploring the coast of Africa before they got to the Cape of Good Hope? Where is the Cape of Good Hope?*
11. *What shorter route to India from Europe has been made in our time? [Ans. The canal through the Isthmus of Suez.]*
12. *How did Columbus propose to get to India?*
13. *In this plan there were two mistakes: what were they?*
14. *What is in the way between Spain and Asia if one sails straight to the west?*
15. *How far did Columbus think it? Is it much farther?*
16. *To whom did Columbus first make his offer?*
17. *To what king did he next offer his plan?*
18. *What was the Atlantic Ocean sometimes called in that day?*
19. *What kind of creatures were thought to live in it?*
20. *What foolish notion of uphill and downhill did men get from the roundness of the earth?*
21. *What did the King of Portugal do to find out whether Columbus' notion was correct or not? Was this fair to Columbus?*
22. *What did Columbus do when he found that he had been cheated?*
23. *What were the names of the King and Queen of Spain at this time?*
24. *In what war were they engaged?*
25. *How long did Columbus have to wait in order to persuade them to let him have ships?*

Questions for study

26. *To what king was he going when Isabella called him back?*
27. *In what year did Columbus start on his voyage? On what day of the month did he sail?*
28. *Leaving on the 3d of August, 1492, he was how long on the voyage?*
29. *How did the sailors feel as they sailed farther and farther into the unknown "Sea of Darkness"?*
30. *What threats did they make against Columbus? How did he deal with them?*
31. *What day of October was it on which Columbus first saw land on this side of the ocean?*
32. *Had Columbus found Asia and its rich cities? What had he found?*
33. *What was the appearance of the people? How did they live?*
34. *What did he discover afterward? What did he take home with him?*
35. *How was he received by the king and queen? How by the people?*
36. *Where did he plant his first colony?*
37. *Did he ever know that he had found a new continent?*
38. *What did he think about Cuba?*

Study by topics

Tell about—
    1. Columbus in Portugal.
    2. Columbus in Spain.
    3. Columbus on his voyage.
    4. Columbus after his return from the first voyage,
a. Mention three false notions which made men oppose Columbus.
    1. That it would be sailing uphill coming back.
    2. That there were monsters in the unknown seas.
    3. That nobody could live on the other side of the world.
b. Tell what you know of two mistaken notions held by Columbus that promoted his voyage.

Skeleton summary

(Fill up the blanks.)—Columbus discovered America about _____ years ago. He wished to reach _____ by sailing to the _____. He offered to make this discovery for the King of _____, who secretly sent out a ship to find out the truth of Columbus' idea. When Columbus saw that he was cheated, he went to _____ to lay his plans before the king and queen, whose names were _____ and _____. He waited in Spain nearly _____ years. He sailed from Spain in August, _____, and discovered land in the month of _____. He first saw the continent of _____ in 1498. But he died supposing that the island of Cuba was part of the continent of _____.

Voluntary work

The pupil may find out what he can of the life of Columbus.

Composition

A subject for composition may be had by the scholar's supposing himself to have just returned with Columbus from his first voyage. Let him write a letter to a supposed friend in England telling him all he can of Columbus, of the ships, of the voyage, of the Indians, and of their reception by the king and queen.

To teachers

The "Study by Topics" may always be written on the blackboard with advantage, especially where there is no other blackboard exercise.

Books for reference and reading

Life of Columbus, by Washington Irving. The latest conclusions of the learned about Columbus and his discoveries, in Winsor's *Narrative and Critical History of America*, vol. ii. For the events of the time, Prescott's *Ferdinand and Isabella*. For a history of the Portuguese discoveries and the Spanish colonies, Helps' *Spanish Conquest of America*.

THIS MAP SHOWS HOW COLUMBUS FOUND AMERICA TO GET TO ASIA. IT ALSO SHOWS THE VOYAGES OF DA GAMA AND MAGELLAN, AS TOLD IN CHAPTER II

CHAPTER II.

Other Discoveries in America

Naming of America

A PART of the glory of Columbus' great discovery was taken away from him by accident. An Italian, Amerigo Vespucci [am-a-ree´-go ves-poot´-chee], whose name in Latin was written Amer´-icus Vespu´-cius, was with an expedition that discovered part of South America in 1499. A false claim was made, indeed, that Americus saw that continent two years earlier, which would be before Columbus discovered it in 1498. Americus Vespucius wrote pleasantly about the new lands which he had seen, and some German geographers were so pleased with his descrip-

Americus Vespucius was born in Florence in 1451. He went into mercantile life at Florence, and afterward removed to Spain a little before Columbus sailed on his first voyage. Vespucius claimed to have made four voyages to the New World, the first in 1497. But it is now believed that this first date is not correct, and that Vespucius was in Spain during all of that year. He undoubtedly went to America several times, both from Spain and Portugal. In 1503 Vespucius built a fort on the coast of what is now Brazil; and he left there a little colony, the first in that part of South America. Ferdinand of Spain made him pilot-major of his kingdom in 1508, and he died in 1512.

AMERICUS

tions that they called the country America, in honor of Americus, supposing him to have first seen the continent. When North America came to be placed on the maps, this name was applied to it also. Thus, nearly half the world goes by the name of a man who had no claim to be called its discoverer.

John Cabot

The voyage of Columbus was undertaken, as we have seen, to open a trade with the Spice Islands of Asia, and the failure to find these was disappointing. There was another great Italian naviga-tor living at the same time as Columbus, whose name was Zuan Cab-ot´-o. He is called in English John Cab´-ot. He had been in the city of Mecca, in Arabia, and had there seen the caravans bringing spices from India. He inquired of the people of these caravans where they got their spices. They said that other caravans brought them to their country, and that the people in those caravans said that they bought them from people who lived yet farther away. From all this John Cabot concluded that the spices so much valued in Europe must grow in the most easterly part of Asia, and that he could reach this part of Asia by sailing to the west, as Columbus had done.

> **John Cabot**, or Zuan Caboto, as he was called in the Venetian dialect, was probably born in Genoa, but he was naturalized in Venice. He was living in Bristol, in England, with his wife and three sons, in 1495, when he laid his plans before Henry VII. He received a charter for discovery from that king in 1496, in which his three sons were named, and he sailed on his first voyage in 1497, and the second in 1498. It is probable that his son Sebastian went with him on both voyages. There is no account of John Cabot's second return, nor do we know any more about him after his sailing to America the second time. His son Sebastian who was a great geographer, and who lived to be very old, seems to have always spoken of the voyages as though he had made them alone, but we now know that it was John Cabot who discovered North America.

HENRY VII

The King of England at this time was Henry VII. While Columbus was trying to persuade Ferdinand and Isabella

CABOT AT MECCA

to send him on a voyage of discovery, he had sent his brother Bartholomew Columbus to make a like offer to the English king. When Bartholomew returned to Spain with King Henry VII's answer, Christopher Columbus had already discovered the New World.

Columbus and Henry VII

But, though Columbus had found what he believed to be a part of Asia, he had not found the region of gold and spices. John Cabot, who was then living in England, believed that he might be more fortunate. He got permission from Henry VII to sail at the expense of certain English merchants, and in May, 1497, nearly five years after Columbus had started on his first voyage, Cabot set sail from Bristol with only one small vessel and eighteen persons. He discovered the continent of North America, which he of course supposed to be a part of

Cabot discovers North America

INDIAN NEEDLES FOR MAKING NETS

Asia. He did not meet any Indians, but he brought to King Henry one of their traps for catching game, and a needle for making nets. He was received with great honor, and he who had gone away a poor Venetian pilot was now called "the Great Admiral," and dressed himself in silks, after the manner of great men of that time.

A GREAT MAN OF THAT TIME

Second voyage
of the Cabots

The next year, accompanied by his son Sebastian, he set sail with a much larger expedition, to find his way to Japan or China. After going far to the north, he sailed along what is now the coast of Canada and the United States as far to the south as North Carolina. But, as he did not find the riches of Asia, the English appear to have lost much of their interest in Western voyages.

Balboa discovers
the Pacific Ocean

After both Columbus and John Cabot were dead, people began to suspect that the newly discovered lands were not part of Asia. In 1513 Vasco Nuñez de Balboa [vas´-co noon-yeth deh bal-bo´-ah] crossed the Isthmus of Panama [pan-ah-mah´] and discovered the Pacific Ocean at the west of America.

Magellan finds
a way around
the world

It now became a question of finding a way through or around America, so as to come to the rich trade of the East Indies, which the Portuguese had reached in 1498, when Vasco da Gama [vas´-co dah gah´-mah] sailed there around the Cape of Good Hope. In 1520 Magellan [ma-jel´-lan], a Portuguese in the employ of Spain, sailed through the straits which bear his name, and so into the Pacific. It was not then known that one could pass around Cape Horn. Magellan lost his life in the Philippine Islands, but one of

MAGELLAN

Fernando da Magalhaens [mah-gal-yah´-ens], as his name is written and pronounced in Portuguese, but who is known in English as Magellan, was born in Portugal. He served the Portuguese government in the East Indies, and was in the expedition that discovered some of the Spice Islands. Having received a slight from the Portuguese government, he publicly renounced his country and entered the service of the King of Spain. He sailed on his famous voyage in September, 1519, with five ships. On the coast of South America he lost one of his vessels and suppressed a mutiny. In October, 1520, he entered the straits that bear his name. His men were very reluctant to go on, and one ship turned back out of the channel and sailed home. With the three ships left he entered the Pacific. At the Philippine Islands he was killed in a battle with the natives. Only one of his ships, the *Victoria*, succeeded in getting around the world, and she had but eighteen men left alive when she got back, and they were sick and almost starving.

his smallest ships succeeded in making the circuit of the earth—the first that ever accomplished that feat.

Magellan's route was too long a course for trade, and many other navigators sailed up and down the American coast, expecting to find some passage by which they could get through the continent to go to China, India, and Japan. They thought America very narrow, and, indeed, they believed that it might prove to be cut through in some places by straits, if they could only find them. Several great English navigators tried to discover what they called the Northwest Passage, by sailing along the coast of Labrador and into the rivers and bays of America.

Other explorers seek the Northwest Passage

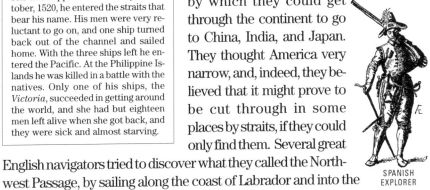

SPANISH EXPLORER

For a long time nobody in England thought it worthwhile to send colonies to North America; it was regarded only as a bar to all attempts to reach Asia by the west. But, the colonists sent from Spain having found gold in great quantities in Mexico and South America, the English at length began to think of settling colonies in North America, to look for gold there also. Frobisher and Sir Humphrey Gilbert, in the time of Queen Elizabeth, proposed to settle such colonies, but it was not until Sir Walter Raleigh undertook it that a hopeful beginning was made.

Colonies proposed

INDIAN'S TRAP

Questions for
study

1. How did our part of the world get the name of America?
2. Who was Amerigo, or Americus? Was he the discoverer of America?
3. Who first proposed to give the name of America to South America?
4. What was the object of Columbus' first voyage?
5. What other great Italian navigator of that time had the notion of finding the trade in spices by going to the west?
6. Where had John Cabot seen the caravans bringing spices?
7. What questions did he ask of the men of these caravans?
8. Where did these men say that they got their spices?
9. What opinion did Cabot form about the country where spices grew? How did he propose to reach the eastern part of Asia?
10. Who was King of England at this time?
11. What had Columbus to do with Henry VII?
12. When Bartholomew Columbus got back to Spain, what had happened?
13. What permission did Cabot get from Henry VII?
14. Who bore the expense of the voyage?
15. How long was this after the sailing of Columbus?
16. How many men did Cabot have when he sailed from Bristol in 1497?
17. How many ships? What did he discover? What did he suppose North America to be?
18. What specimens of Indian work did he bring back with him?
19. How was he received? What was he called? How did he dress?
20. When did he go on his next expedition?
21. What part of the American coast did he see?
22. What seems to have made the English people lose most of their interest in American voyages after this?
23. After Columbus and Cabot were both dead, what suspicion arose about the new western countries?
24. What discovery in 1513 rendered it probable that America was not a part of Asia?
25. Who discovered the Pacific Ocean? In what year?
26. What land did Balboa cross to find that ocean?
27. After the discovery of the Pacific, what new question came up in regard to a way of trading with the East Indies?
28. Who first found a way from the Atlantic to the Pacific?
29. In what year did Magellan make this discovery?
30. By what strait did he pass into the Pacific?
31. Why did he not go around the world?
32. What ship first went the world?
33. Why was the route through the Straits of Magellan not a good one for trade?
34. How did other navigators try to find a way to Asia?
35. What did they think about the width of America?

CAUGHT IN AN INDIAN TRAP

36. *Where did they try to find a northwest passage?*
37. *How was North America regarded by the explorers?*
38. *What effect did the gold found by the Spaniards in Mexico and South America have on the English?*
39. *Who tried to settle colonies to look for gold in North America?*
40. *Who was Queen of England in those times?*
41. *Who made the first hopeful beginning in settling English colonies in America?*

Tell what you can of four famous men: I. Amerigo Vespucci, or Americus Vespucius. 2. John Cabot. 3. Balboa. 4. Magellan.   Study by topics

Tell what you can of—1. The naming of America. 2. The efforts to find a passage through America.

A table showing the order of events in the two chapters. This may be drawn as far as possible from the answers of the scholars. Thus: Blackboard illustration

The Age of Discovery

I. American islands		Columbus, 1492
2. North America		John Cabot, 1497
3. To India by Good Hope	discovered by	Vasco da Gama, 1498
4. South America		Columbus, 1498
5. Pacific Ocean		Balboa, 1513
6. A way around the world		Magellan, 1520

Six great discoveries in twenty-nine years!

The best account of the Cabots is by Charles Deane, LL. D., in *Winsor's Narrative and Critical History*, vol. iii.   Books

CHAPTER III

Sir Walter Raleigh Tries to Settle a Colony in America

SIR WALTER RALEIGH was the first that landed a colony of English people in this country. Having received from Queen Elizabeth a charter which gave him a large territory in America, he sent out an exploring expedition in 1584, ninety-two years after the discovery by Columbus. This expedition was commanded by two captains, named Amidas and Barlowe. They landed on the coast in that part of America which we now call North Carolina. The country pleased them very much. They wondered at the wild   Raleigh sends an exploring expedition grapevines, which grew to the tops of the highest trees, and they found the Indians very friendly. They stayed about six weeks in the New World, and, everything here being strange to their eyes, they fell into many mistakes in trying to describe what they saw and heard. When they got back to England, they declared that the part of America they had seen was the paradise of the world.

The country named Virginia

Raleigh was much encouraged by the accounts

> **Sir Walter Raleigh**, while yet a young man, fought for years on the side of the Huguenots in the French civil wars, and afterward in the war in Ireland. On his return from Ireland, it is said that he won the Queen's favor by throwing his new plush cloak into a muddy place in the road for her to walk on. He fitted out ships and fought against the Great Armada, or fleet, of Spain, when that country tried to conquer England. He was a great statesman, a great soldier, a great seaman, and an excellent poet and historian. He is said to have first planted the potato in Ireland. King James I kept him in prison in the Tower for more than twelve years, and then released him. In 1618 the same king had this great man put to death to please the King of Spain. When Raleigh was about to be beheaded, he felt of the edge of the axe, and said, "It is a sharp medicine to cure me of all my diseases."

Raleigh's first colony

SIR WALTER RALEIGH

which his two captains gave of the new country they had found. It was named Virginia at this time, in honor of Queen Elizabeth, who was often called the "Virgin Queen." But the name Virginia, which we apply to two of our states, was then used for nearly the whole eastern part of what is now the United States, between Maine and Georgia.

In 1585 the year after the return of the first expedition, Raleigh sent out a colony to remain in America. Sir Richard Grenville, a famous seaman, had command of this expedition; but he soon returned to England, leaving the colonists in charge of Ralph Lane. There were no women in Ralph Lane's company. They made their settlement on Roanoke Island, which lies near to the coast of North Carolina, and they explored the mainland in many directions. They spent much time in trying to find gold, and they seem to have thought that the shell-beads worn by the Indians were pearls. Like all

QUEEN ELIZABETH

the others who came to America in that time, they were very desirous of finding a way to get across America, which they believed to be very narrow. They hoped to reach the Pacific Ocean, and so open a new way of sailing to China and the East Indies.

The Indians by this time were tired of the white men, and anxious to be rid of them. They told Lane that the Roanoke River came out of a rock so near to a sea at the west that the water sometimes dashed from the sea into the river, making the water of the river salt. Lane believed this story, and set out with most of his men to find a sea at the head of the river. Long before they got to the head of the Roanoke, their provisions gave out. But Lane made a brave speech to his men, and they resolved to go on. Having nothing else to eat, they killed their two dogs, and cooked the meat with sassafras leaves to give it a relish. When this meat was exhausted, they got into their boats and ran swiftly down the river, having no food to eat on the way home. Lane got back to Roanoke Island just in time to keep the Indians from killing the men he had left there.

Lane tries to find the Pacific Ocean

Sir Francis Drake came to see the colony on his return

from an expedition to the West Indies. He furnished the company on the island with a ship and with whatever else they needed. But, while he remained at Roanoke, a storm arose which drove to sea the ship he had given to Lane. This so discouraged the colonists that they returned to England.

SIR FRANCIS DRAKE

Ralph Lane and his companions were the first to carry tobacco into England. They learned from the Indians to smoke it in Indian fashion, by drawing the smoke into their mouths and puffing it out through their nostrils. Raleigh adopted the practice,

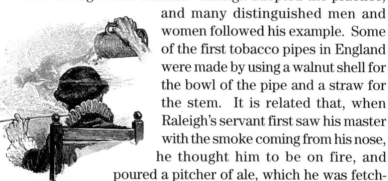

and many distinguished men and women followed his example. Some of the first tobacco pipes in England were made by using a walnut shell for the bowl of the pipe and a straw for the stem. It is related that, when Raleigh's servant first saw his master with the smoke coming from his nose, he thought him to be on fire, and poured a pitcher of ale, which he was fetching, over Sir Walter's head, to put the fire out.

Raleigh set to work, with the help of others, to send out another colony. This time he sent women and children, as well as men, intending to make a permanent settlement. The governor of this company was John White, an artist. Soon after White's company had settled themselves on Roanoke Island, an English child was born. This little girl, being the first English child born in Virginia, was named Virginia Dare.

John White, the governor of the colony, who was Virginia Dare's grandfather, went back to England for supplies. He was detained by the war with Spain, and, when he got back to Roanoke Island, the colony had disappeared. Raleigh had spent so much money already that he was forced to give up the attempt to plant a colony in America. But he sent several times to seek for the lost people of his second colony, without finding them. Twenty years after John White left them, it was said that seven of them were still alive among the Indians of North Carolina.

Raleigh's second colony disappears

INDIAN PIPE DECORATED WITH FEATHERS

PIPE MADE OF THE SHELL OF THE ENGLISH WALNUT

1.   Who gave Raleigh a charter?
2.   Of what country was Elizabeth queen?
3.   What did Queen Elizabeth grant to Raleigh in this charter?
4.   In what year did he send out an exploring expedition?
5.   There were two captains in this expedition; what were their names?
6.   In what part of America did they land?
7.   How long did they stay in America?
8.   What did they think of the country?
9.   When the two captains got back, the country they had explored in America was named what?
10. How large was Virginia at that time?
11. Why was it called Virginia?
12. In what year did Sir Walter Raleigh send out his first colony?
13. Who was left in charge of it?
14. On what island was it settled?
15. What was Ralph Lane looking for when he went up the Roanoke River?
16. What did his men eat when out of food?
17. Who came to see the colony the next year?
18. What put the men on Roanoke Island into the notion of going back to England?

Questions for study

19. What did Lane and his men learn from the Indians?
20. What plant did they first take into England?
21. What kind of pipes were sometimes used?
22. What story is told of Raleigh's smoking?
23. Who was Governor of Raleigh's last colony?
24. Why did John White go back to England?
25. What delayed him there?
26. What was the fate of his colony?

Roanoke Island

Study by topics

Three expeditions are mentioned:

1. Under Amidas and Barlowe, 1584.
2. Under Grenville and Lane, 1585.
3. Under John White, 1587.

Tell what you know of each of these.

Also, tell what you can about—
1. Sir Walter Raleigh.
2. The naming of Virginia.
3. The first use of tobacco in England.

Skeleton summary

(*Write this out or read it, and fill up the blanks.*)—Having received a charter from Queen_____, Raleigh sent an exploring expedition under_____and_____to that part of America which we call_____. On their return the new land was named_____, in honor of_____. In the year_____ Raleigh sent out his first colony, under the command of Sir Richard_____and Ralph_____. This colony was taken back to England by Sir Francis_____. It remained in America_____. In 1587 Raleigh sent another colony, under John_____. The Governor went back for supplies; when he came again to America, the colony had_____. Both of Raleigh's colonies were settled on_____ Island.

Geography

Have each pupil, on a large sheet of paper, make an outline map of the coast of North Carolina and Virginia. On this, mark the place of Raleigh's colonies on Roanoke Island, with the date (1585) of the first colony. Note distinctly on this map the Roanoke River. Preserve the map for use in studying the next chapter. If thought best, the pupil may make an outline map of the whole coast of the United States for use in all the chapters relating to colonization. This map should be made on a piece of Manila paper not less than eighteen inches or two feet square.

Blackboard illustration

We can hardly suppose Lane to have passed over more than about one twenty-fifth of the distance from the Atlantic to the Pacific. Draw a horizontal line say twenty-five inches long. Then mark one inch from the left of the line to show how small a proportion of the way the explorers had traveled. The outline map described above may be drawn on the blackboard for the whole class.

Books

Edwards' *Life of Raleigh*, or Gosse's *Life of Raleigh*. (Note.—The name is spelled in various ways by different writers. We have followed Raleigh's own spelling.)

CHAPTER IV

How Jamestown was Settled

AFTER the total disappearance of Raleigh's second colony, many years passed before another attempt was made. In 1602 Bartholomew Gosnold tried to plant a colony on the island of Cuttyhunk, in Buzzard's Bay. If this had succeeded, New England would have been first settled, but the men that were to stay went back in the ship that brought them. In 1603 Queen Elizabeth died, and her cousin, James VI, King of Scotland, came to the throne of England as James I. In 1606, while Raleigh was shut up in the Tower of London, a company of merchants and others undertook to send a new colony to America. Some of the men who had been Raleigh's partners in his last colony were members of this new "Virginia Company."

JAMES I

The Virginia Company

It was in the stormy December of 1606 that the little colony set out. There were, of course, no steamships then; and the vessels they had were clumsy, small, and slow. The largest of the three ships that carried out the handful of people which began the settlement of the United States was named *Susan Constant.* She was of a hundred tons burden. Not many ships so small cross the ocean today. But the *Godspeed* which went along with her was not half so big, and the smallest of the three was a little pinnace of only twenty tons, called *Discovery.*

Departure of the colony

On account of storms, these feeble ships were not able to get out of sight of the English coast for six weeks. People in that time were afraid to sail straight across the unknown Atlantic Ocean; they went away south by the

A MERCHANT OF THE VIRGINIA COMPANY

The voyage and arrival in Virginia

Canary Islands and the West Indies, and so made the distance twice as great as it ought to have been. It took the new colony about four months to get from London to Virginia. They intended to land on Roanoke Island, where Raleigh's unfortunate colonies had been settled, but a storm drove them into a large river, which they called "James River," in honor of the king. They arrived in Virginia in the month of April, when the banks of the river were covered with flowers. Great white dogwood blossoms and masses of bright-colored redbud were in bloom all along the James River. The newcomers said that heaven and earth had agreed together to make this a country to live in.

PRESENT APPEARANCE OF JAMESTOWN

After sailing up and down the river they selected a place to live upon, which they called Jamestown. They had now pretty well eaten up their supply of food, and they had been so slow in settling themselves that it was too late to plant even if they had cleared ground.

Settlement at Jamestown. Misery of the colonists

One small ladle full of pottage made of worm-eaten barley or wheat was all that was given to a man for a meal. The settlers were attacked by the Indians, who wounded seventeen men and killed one boy in the fight. Each man in James town had to take his turn every third night in watching against the Indians, lying on the cold, bare ground all night. The only water to drink was that from the river, which was bad. The people were soon nearly all of them sick; there were not five able-bodied men to defend the place had it been attacked. Sometimes as many as three or four died in a single night, and sometimes the living were hardly able to bury those who had died. There were about a hundred colonists landed at Jamestown, and one half of these died in the first few months. All this time the men in Jamestown were living in wretched tents and poor little hovels covered with earth, and some of them even in holes dug into the ground. As the sickness passed away, those who remained built themselves better cabins, and thatched the roofs with straw.

One of the most industrious men in the colony at this time was Captain John Smith, a young man who had many adventures, of which he was fond of boasting. He took the little pinnace *Discovery* and sailed up and down the rivers and bays of Virginia, exploring the country, getting acquainted with many tribes of Indians and exchanging beads, bells, and other trinkets for corn, with - which he kept the Jamestown people from starving. In one of these trips two of his men were killed, and he was made captive, and led from tribe to tribe a prisoner. But he managed so well that Powhatan [pow-at-tan´], the head chief of about thirty tribes, set him free and sent him back to Jamestown. It was in this captivity that he made the acquaintance of Pocahontas [po-ka-hun´-tas], a daughter of Powhatan. She was then about

Captain John Smith

A SOLDIER WITH MATCHLOCK AND LIGHTED FUSE

CAPTAIN JOHN SMITH

Captain John Smith was born in England in 1579. While yet little more than a boy, he went into the wars in the Netherlands. He was afterward shipwrecked, robbed at sea, and suffered great want in France. He fought against the Turks and slew three of them in single combat. He was at length made prisoner by the Turks and reduced to slavery. By killing his master he got free; escaping into Russia, after sixteen days of wandering. He got back to England and soon departed with the first company to Jamestown. After leaving Virginia he was the first to examine carefully the coast of New England, and he received the title of "Admiral of New England." He was a bold and able explorer and a brave man, with much practical wisdom. His chief faults were his vanity and boastfulness, which led him to exaggerate his romantic adventures. But without him the Jamestown colony would probably have perished. Like many other worthy men, he died poor and neglected.

ten years old, and Captain Smith greatly admired her. Many years afterward he told a pretty story about her putting her arms about his neck and saving his life when Powhatan wished to put him to death.

Smith leaves the colony

John Smith explored Chesapeake Bay in two voyages, enduring many hardships with cheerfulness. He and his men would move their fire two or three times in a cold night, that they might have the warm ground to lie upon. He managed the Indians well, put down mutinies at Jamestown, and rendered many other services to the colony. He was the leading man in the new settlement, and came at length to be governor. But when many hundreds of new settlers were brought out under men who were his enemies, and Smith had been injured by an explosion of gunpowder, he gave up the government and went back to England.

Questions for study

1. *After Raleigh's failure, how long was it before another colony was tried?*
2. *When Raleigh sent his colonies, Queen Elizabeth was reigning over England: who had taken her place by the time the new colony was sent?*
3. *Where was Raleigh when this new company was formed to send another colony to Virginia?*
4. *In Raleigh's last colony he had some partners: what part did these take in the company?*
5. *In what year did this company send out its colony?*
6. *How many ships were sent?*
7. *What can you tell about the size of these vessels?*
8. *How long did it take the ships to get out of sight of England?*
9. *Did they sail straight for America?*
10. *By what route did they go?*
11. *How long did it take them to get to Virginia from the time they left London?*
12. *How long does it take to cross the ocean in our time?*
13. *Did the new colony settle in the same place as Raleigh's colony?*
14. *What did they call the river into which they sailed? (What is it called to-day?)*
15. *Where is it?*
16. *What city is on its banks?*
17. *How did the country look when they saw it?*
18. *What did they think about it?*
19. *When they had chosen a place for their town, what did they call it?*
20. *Why did they call the river James River, and their town Jamestown?*
21. *What kind of food did they have?*
22. *How much did each man get for a meal?*
23. *What did the Indians do at this time?*
24. *How often did each man have to stand watch at night?*
25. *What kind of water did they have?*
26. *What is said of their sickness?*
27. *How many died in the first few months?*
28. *What sort of houses did they have during the time of their sickness?*
29. *What kind of houses did they build as they grew better?*
30. *Where did Captain Smith sail in the little pinnace "Discovery"?*
31. *What did he buy from the Indians? What did he pay for the corn with?*
32. *What happened to him on one of these trips?*
33. *After he had been led from village to village, he was brought to a head chief: what was the name of this chief?*
34. *He was at the head of how many tribes?*
35. *What did Powhatan do with Captain Smith?*
36. *What is said of Powhatan's daughter?*
37. *What great bay did Smith explore?*
38. *How did it happen that he went back to England?*

Study by
topics

What do you know about—
1. The voyage, and the arrival in Virginia?

2. $\left\{\begin{array}{l}\text{Food} \\ \text{Houses} \\ \text{Sickness}\end{array}\right\}$ at Jamestown?

3. John Smith and what he did in Virginia?

Skeleton
summary

The colonists came from _____. They settled on the River, in the year _____07. They called their town _____. The most active man was _____.

Voluntary work

Scholars who wish to know more than the lesson gives them, may find out what they can of the life of Captain John Smith.

Geography

Let the scholar take the map made for the previous chapter, and extend it so as to include the Chesapeake Bay and James River. Mark 1607 at the site of Jamestown. Write John Smith, 1608, in Chesapeake Bay. Then, in order to get relations with modern times, mark the present site of Richmond with R., of Washington with W., of Baltimore with B.

Books

Life of John Smith, by Charles Dudley Warner. *Life of Pocahontas*, by E. Eggleston and Mrs. Seelye. Bancroft's *United States*.

CHAPTER V

The Starving Time and What Followed

The starving
time

WHEN Captain John Smith went back to England, in 1609, there were nearly five hundred white people in Virginia. But the settlers soon got into trouble with the Indians, who lay in the woods and killed every one that ventured out. There was no longer any chance to buy corn, and the food was soon exhausted. The starving people ate the hogs, the dogs, and the horses, even to their skins. Then they ate rats, mice, snakes, toadstools, and whatever they could get that might stop their hunger. A dead Indian was presently eaten, and, as their hunger grew more extreme, they were forced to consume their own dead. Starving men wandered off into the woods and died there; their companions, finding them, devoured them as hungry wild beasts might have done. This was always afterward remembered as "the starving time."

Along with the people who came at the close of John Smith's time, there had been sent another shipload of people, with Sir Thomas Gates, a new governor for the colony. This vessel had been shipwrecked, but Gates and his people had got ashore on the Bermuda Islands. These islands had no inhabitants at that time. Here these ship- *Sir Thomas Gates wrecked on the Bermuda Islands*

wrecked people lived well on wild hogs. When spring came they built two little vessels of the cedar trees which grew on the island. These they rigged with sails taken from their wrecked ships, and getting their people aboard they made their way to Jamestown.

When they got there they found alive but sixty of the four hundred and ninety people left in Virginia in the autumn before, and these sixty would all have died had Gates been ten days later in coming. The food that Gates brought would barely last them sixteen days. So he put the Jamestown people aboard his little cedar ships, intending *Gates reaches Jamestown* to sail to Newfoundland, in hope of there falling in with some English fishing-vessels. He set sail down the river, leaving not one English settler on the whole continent of America.

Arrival of Lord De la Warr

But before Gates and his people got out of the James River they met a long boat rowing up toward them. Lord De la Warr had been appointed governor of Virginia, and sent out from England. From some men at the mouth of the river he had learned that Gates and all the people were coming down. He sent his long boat to turn them back again. On a Sunday morning De la Warr landed in Jamestown and knelt on the ground a while in prayer. Then he went to the little church, where he took possession of the government, and rebuked the people for the idleness that had brought them into such suffering.

De la Warr's time

During this summer of 1610 a hundred and fifty of the settlers died, and Lord De la Warr, finding himself very ill, left the colony. The next year Sir Thomas Dale took charge, and Virginia was under his government and that of Sir Thomas Gates for five years afterward.

Sir Thomas Dale's government

Dale was a soldier, and ruled with extreme severity. He forced the idle settlers to labor, he drove away some of the Indians, settled some new towns, and he built fortifications. But he was so harsh that the people hated him. He punished men by flogging and by setting them to work in irons for years. Those who rebelled or ran away were put to death in cruel ways; some were burned alive, others were broken on the wheel, and one man, for merely stealing food, was starved to death.

Powhatan, the head chief of the neighboring tribes, gave the colony a great deal of trouble during the first part of Dale's time. His daughter, Pocahontas, who, as a child, had often played with the boys within the palisades of Jamestown, and had shown herself friendly to Captain Smith and others in their trips among the Indians, was now a woman grown. While she was visiting a chief named Japazaws, an English captain named Argall hired that chief with a copper kettle to betray her into his hands. Argall took her a captive to Jamestown. Here a white man by the name of John Rolfe married her, after she had received Christian baptism. This marriage brought about a peace between Powhatan and the English settlers in Virginia.

The capture of Pocahontas. Her marriage

PORTRAIT OF POCAHONTAS

When Dale went back to England in 1616 he took with him some of the Indians. Pocahontas, who was now called "the Lady Rebecca," and her husband went to England with Dale. Pocahontas was called a "princess" in England, and received much attention. But she died when about to start back to the colony, leaving a little son.

Pocahontas in England

Tobacco first raised in Virginia

The same John Rolfe who married Pocahontas was the first Englishman to raise tobacco in Virginia. This he did in 1612. Tobacco brought a large price in that day, and, as it furnished a means by which people in Virginia could make a living, it helped to make the colony successful. But in 1616 there were only three hundred and fifty English people in all North America.

GETTING READY TO GO TO VIRGINIA: SHOWING THE PRESS OF PEOPLE IN THAT TIME

Questions for study

1. How many people were left in the colony in 1609, when John Smith went back to England?
2. How did the settlers get on with the Indians at this time?
3. Why could they not get corn?
4. Mention some of the things eaten by the people in their hunger.
5. What was this time called? What had become of the ship in which Sir Thomas Gates had sailed the year before?
6. What did Gates and his people find to eat on the Bermuda Islands?
7. How did they get away from Bermuda?
8. What state did they find the Jamestown colony in when they came to Virginia?
9. How many days' supply of food for all the people did Sir Thomas Gates have? What did he conclude to do?
10. What happened to Gates before he got out of the river?

11. *Who had sent this long boat?*
12. *What did Lord De la Warr do first when he landed at Jamestown?*
13. *What took place at the church?*
14. *How many of the people died in the sickness of this summer?*
15. *Why did Lord De la Warr leave Virginia?*
16. *What was Dale's profession?*
17. *What kind of a person was he?*
18. *What good effect came from his government?*
19. *But the people hated him: why?*
20. *Mention some of the punishments used by him.*
21. *How did Powhatan and the Indians behave during the early part of Dale's time? What was the name of Powhatan's daughter who had often come to Jamestown? Where was she staying?*
22. *How did Argall get her on board his ship?*
23. *Where did he take her?*
24. *To whom was she married? What effect did this have?*
25. *When Pocahontas went to England, how was she treated?*
26. *What happened to her when she was about to sail to America?*
27. *Who first raised tobacco in Virginia? What effect did this have on the colony?*
28. *How many people were there in Virginia in 1616?*
29. *The colony first reached Virginia in 1607: how long had it been settled when Dale left in 1616? (Subtract 1607 from 1616.)*

Tell about—
1. The starving time.
2. Sir Thomas Gates' shipwreck.
3. Gates' arrival at Jamestown and the departure of the colony.
4. Coming of Lord De la Warr.
Also—a. Dale's government. b. Pocahontas. c. Tobacco in Virginia.

Study by topics

CHAPTER VI

The Great Charter of Virginia and the First Massacre by the Indians

DURING all the early years of the Virginia colony the people were fed and clothed out of a common stock of provisions. They were also obliged to work for this stock. No division was made of the land, nor could the industrious man get any profit by his hard work. The laziest man was as well off as the one who worked hardest, and under this arrangement men neglected their work, and the colony was always poor. The men had been promised that after five

Living and working in common

ENGLISH
COUNTRYMAN
AT THAT TIME

years they should have land of their own and be free, but this promise was not kept. In 1614 Sir Thomas Dale gave to some who had been longest in Virginia three acres of ground apiece, and allowed them one month in the year to work on their little patches. For this they must support themselves and give the rest of their work to the common stock. This arrangement made them more industrious. But the cruel military laws put in force by the governor made Virginia very unpopular.

The Great
Charter of 1618

Argall, who came after Dale, governed very badly, and the colony was almost ruined. In 1618 many new emigrants were sent, and Lord De la Warr was again sent as governor, but he died on the way. The "Virginia Company," of London, which had the government of the colony in November, 1618 granted to Virginia a "Great Charter," under which the people of the colony were allowed a voice in making their own laws. This was the beginning of free government in America. Under this charter the government of Virginia was put into the hands of a governor, a "council of estate," and a "general assembly." The other American colonies afterward took pattern from this threefold government.

Features of the
charter govern-
ment that remain

The government of the United States by a president, a senate, and a house of representatives shows that the ideas put into the Great Charter have left their mark on the constitution of our country. The governments of all our states also show traces of the same idea. Each state has a governor, a senate, and a house of representatives. So that the plan arranged in 1618 for a few hundred people in Virginia was a tiny stream that has spread out into a great river.

Division of land
in Virginia

The Great Charter also gave the people of Virginia the right to divide the land into farms, and to own and work ground each for himself. When the new governor, Sir George

Yeardley, got to Virginia in the spring of 1619 bringing this good news that the settlers were to live under laws of their own making, and were to enjoy the fruits of their own labors, they thought themselves the happiest people in the world.

COUNTRYWOMAN OF THE TIME

About this time it was thought that the colony would be more firmly planted if the colonists had wives. Young women were therefore sent out to be married to the settlers. But, before any man could marry one of these, he was obliged to gain her consent, and to pay the cost of her passage, which was about a hundred and fifty pounds of tobacco. This venture proved very satisfactory to the Virginians, and women were therefore sent for wives from time to time for years afterward. When the colonists had land of their own, they felt themselves at home in America, and no longer thought of going back to England.

Sending of wives to Virginia

Before this there had been a good many small wars and troubles of one kind or other with the Indians. But, as the Indians had few firearms, the white men could easily defend themselves. After 1619 many efforts were made to civilize and convert the savages. Money was given to educate their children, and a college was planned for them. One ambitious Indian brave, whom the white people called "Jack of the Feather," and who was believed to be proof against bullets, was suspected of wishing war. At length he killed a white man. And the white man's servants, in trying to take him to the governor, shot him. The Indians did not show any resentment at his death at first, and O-pe-chan´-ka-no, who had become head chief on the death of Powhatan, said that the sky might fall

"JACK OF THE FEATHER"

sooner than he would break the peace.

But on the 22d of March, 1622, while the men of the colony were in the fields, the Indians suddenly fell on the settlements, killing the white people mostly with their own axes, hatchets, and hoes. Three hundred and forty-seven

men, women, and children were killed in a single day. One Indian lad, living in a white man's house, had given warning during the night before, and some of the settlements had time to prepare themselves for defense. From this time on there was almost continual war with the Indians for many years.

In 1624 the Virginia Company, of London, was dissolved, and the colony was put under the government of the king. But the king, James I, when he put down the company, promised to the colony all the liberties which they then enjoyed. This promise was not well kept by his successors in later years; the Virginians were often oppressed by the governors sent to them, but the right to pass laws in the General Assembly was never taken away.

1. *How were the settlers in Virginia clothed and fed during the early years of the colony?*
2. *What was done with the proceeds of their work?*
3. *How was the land held at first?*
4. *What was the result of this system?*
5. *What encouragement would a man have to work industriously?*
6. *Do you think such a system fair?*
7. *What promise had been made to the colonists?*

8. How was it kept?
9. What arrangement did Sir Thomas Dale make in 1614?
10. What effect did this have on the industry of the colonists?
11. What made Virginia unpopular at this time?
12. What kind of laws did the colony have?
13. What kind of a governor was Argall? Who was sent for governor in 1618?
14. What happened to him?
15. What was the beginning of free government in America?
16. Who granted the Great Charter of 1618?
17. It established three branches of the government in Virginia: what were they?
18. What three lawmaking powers in the government of the United States to-day correspond somewhat to the governor, the council of estate, and the General Assembly of Virginia under the Great Charter?
19. How do the governments of our states resemble this first government?
20. What other rights did the charter of 1618 give to Virginia?
21. When Sir George Yeardley, the new governor, got to Virginia with the Great Charter, how did the people feel about it?
22. In what year did Yeardley reach Virginia?
23. What measures were taken in 1619 to supply the Virginians with wives?
24. What did a man have to pay for his wife?
25. Had there been any Indian wars before this time?
26. What advantage did the white man have over the Indians?
27. What was done for the Indians after 1619?
28. What is said of "Jack of the Feather"?
29. Why and how was he killed?
30. Who was chief in place of Powhatan?
31. What did Opechankano say about the peace?
32. What took place on the 22d of March, 1622?
33. How were the white people killed?
34. Who gave warning the night before?
35. How many of the colonists were killed?
36. What was the relation between the white people and the Indians after this?
37. What change took place in the government of Virginia in 1624?
38. What did the king promise to the colonists when he made this change?
39. Who was king of England at this time? How was his promise, that the Virginians should have all their liberties, kept by his successors?
40. What right was never taken away?

Tell what you know of—   Study by
    1. Common land and common living in Virginia.   topics
    2. The division of the land
    3. The Great Charter and the three branches of government.
Also tell what you can—
    1. Of the sending of wives to Virginia.
    2. Of the Indian massacre.

Blackboard illustration

Idleness and Misery	LAND		Industry and Plenty
	Undivided.	Separately owned.	
	LABOR		
	For a common stock.	Each for himself	
	LIVING		
	From a common store.	From one's own purse.	

HISTORY TEACHES

NOTE—In this and the preceding chapters some statements are made which will be unfamiliar even to those well acquainted with the history of the settlement of Virginia. These are founded, however, on a careful study of the oldest existing manuscript authorities, preserved in the Library of Congress, in the British Museum and in the British Public Record Office.

CHAPTER VII

The Coming of the Pilgrims

The Separatists

IN the seventeenth century (that is, between the year 1601 and the year 1700) there was much religious persecution. In some countries the Catholics persecuted the Protestants, in other countries the Protestants persecuted the Catholics, and sometimes one kind of Protestants persecuted another. There were people in England who did not like the ceremonies of the Church of England, as established by law. These were called Puritans. Some of these went so far as to separate themselves from the Established Church, and thus got the name of Separatists. They were persecuted in England, and many of them fled to Holland.

The Pilgrims in Holland

Among these were the members of a little Separatist congregation in Scrooby, in the north of England. Their pastor's name was John Robinson. In 1607, the year in which

PILGRIM FAREWELL AT DELFT HAVEN

Jamestown was settled, these persecuted people left England and settled in Holland, where they lived about thirteen years, most of the time in the city of Leyden [li´-den]. Then they thought they would like to plant a colony in America, where they could be religious in their own way. These are the people that we call "The Pilgrims," on account of their wanderings for the sake of their religion.

PURITAN OF THE
MIDDLE CLASS

About half of them were to go first. The rest went down to the sea to say farewell to those who were going. It was a sad parting, as they all knelt down on the shore and prayed together. The Pilgrims came to America in a ship called the *Mayflower*. There were about a hundred of them, and they had a stormy and wretched passage. They intended to go to the Hudson River, but their captain took them to Cape Cod. After exploring the coast north of that cape for some distance, they selected as a place to land a harbor which had been called Plymouth on the map prepared by Captain John Smith, who had sailed along this coast in an open boat in 1614.

The voyage to
America in the
Mayflower

All the Indians who had lived at this place had died a few years before of a pestilence, and the Pilgrims found the Indian fields unoccupied. They first landed at this place on the 11th day of December, 1620, as the days were then counted. This is the same as the 21st of December now, the mode of counting having changed since that time. (Through a mistake, the 22d of December is generally kept in New England as " Forefathers' Day.") Before landing, the Pilgrims drew up an agreement by which they promised to be governed.

The landing of
the Pilgrims

The bad voyage, the poor food with which they were provided, and a lack of good shelter in a climate colder than that from which they came, had their natural effect.

PURITAN OF THE
MIDDLE CLASS

Half of the
Pilgrims die

Like the first settlers at Jamestown, they were soon nearly all sick. Forty-four out of the hundred Pilgrims died before the winter was ended, and by the time the first year was over half of them were dead. The Pilgrims were afraid of the Indians, some of whom had attacked the first exploring party that had landed. To prevent the savages from finding out how much the party had been weakened by disease, they leveled all the graves, and planted Indian corn over the place in which the dead were buried.

First acquain-
tance with the
Indians

One day, after the winter was over, an Indian walked into the village and said in English, "Welcome, Englishmen." He was a chief named Sam-o´-set, who had learned a little English from the fishermen on the coast of Maine. Samoset afterward brought with him an Indian named Squanto, who had been carried away to England by a cruel captain many years before, and then brought back. Squanto remained with the Pilgrims, and taught them how to plant their corn as the Indians did, by putting one or two fish into every hill for manure. He taught them many other things, and acted as their interpreter in their trading with the Indians. He told the Indians that they must keep peace with the white men, who had the pestilence stored in their cellar along with the gunpowder! The neighboring chief, Mas-sa-so´-it, was also a good friend to the Pilgrims as long as he lived.

Myles Standish
and the Indians

Captain Myles Standish was the military commander at Plymouth. He dealt severely with any Indians supposed to be hostile. Finding that certain of the Massachusetts Indians were planning to kill all the whites, he and some of his

Pilgrims at Home—The Pilgrims held their meetings in a square house on top of a hill at Plymouth. On the flat roof of this house were six small cannon. The people were called to church by the beating of a drum. The men carried loaded firearms with them when they went to meeting on Sunday, and put them where they could reach them easily. The town was surrounded by a stockade and had three gates. Elder Brewster was the religious teacher of the Pilgrims at Plymouth; their minister, John Robinson, having stayed with those who waited in Holland, and died there. It is said that Brewster, when he had nothing but shellfish and water for dinner, would cheerfully give thanks that they were "permitted to suck of the abundance of the seas and of the treasures hid in the sand."

men seized the plotters suddenly and killed them with the knives which the Indians wore suspended from their own necks.

The people of Plymouth suffered much from scarcity of food for several years. They had often nothing but oysters or clams to eat for a long time together, and no drink but water. Like the Jamestown people (see page 29), they tried a plan of living out of a common stock, but with no better success. In 1624 each family received a small allotment of land for its own, and from that time there was always plenty to eat in Plymouth. Others of the Pilgrims came to them from Holland, as well as a few emigrants from England. Plymouth Colony was, next to Virginia, the oldest colony of all, but it did not grow very fast, and in 1692, by a charter from King Wil-

PILGRIMS ESCORTING THE GOVERNOR, ELDER
BREWSTER, AND MILES STANDISH TO MEETING

Plymouth united
with Massachu-
setts in 1692
liam III, it was united with Massachusetts, of which its territory still forms a part.

Questions for
study

1. When we say "the seventeenth century," what years do we mean?
2. What is said of persecution in the seventeenth century?
3. What ceremonies did the Puritans dislike?
4. What were those Puritans called who went so far as to separate from the Church of England?
5. What happened to these Separatists?
6. When they were persecuted, where did they go?
7. What is said of the Separatists of Scrooby?
8. What was their pastor's name?
9. Where did they go when they were persecuted?
10. To what city in Holland?
11. How long did they live in Holland?
12. What did they then propose to do?
13. What name is now given to these people?
14. How many of them were to go to America first?
15. How did the rest say farewell to them?
16. What was the name of the ship in which they came to America?
17. What kind of a voyage did they have?
18. Where did they select a place to land?
19. Who had called this Plymouth? (Who was this Captain John Smith?)
20. What had become of the Indians who lived at Plymouth?
21. (What is a pestilence?)
22. What advantage did the Pilgrims get from settling where there had been an Indian village?
23. In what year did the Pilgrims land at Plymouth?
24. In what month?
25. On what day of December?
26. But the "old style" which they used then has been changed since that time: What day of the month now is the same as the 11th of December, 1620?
27. How did the Pilgrims arrange about their government?
28. What four things helped to make the Pilgrims suffer with illness?
29. How many died during the first winter?
30. How many died in the first year?
31. How did the Pilgrims feel about the Indians?
32. Had they seen any of them?
33. What did they do to hide from the Indians the fact that so many of them had died?
34. What did the first Indian say who came into Plymouth?
35. What was his name?
36. Where had he learned these words?
37. What was the name of the Indian that Samoset brought with him afterward?
38. How did Squanto get to England?

39. What did he do for the Pilgrims?
40. What story did he tell to frighten the other Indians?
41. What is said of Massasoit?
42. Who was Captain Myles Standish?
43. How did he deal with hostile Indians?
44. What did he do to the Indians who planned to put all the English to death?
45. What kind of food did the people at Plymouth have to eat?
46. What plan of work and living did they try?
47. What colony had tried this before?
48. How did it work in Plymouth?
49. What change was made in 1624?
50. Which was the oldest of all the American colonies?
51. Which was next?
52. What is said of the growth of Plymouth colony?
53. What happened to it in 1692?

1. The Separatists in England.
2. The Pilgrims in Holland.
3. The voyage to America.
4. The Pilgrims at Plymouth.
5. The Pilgrims and the Indians.

Study by topics

The native country of the Pilgrims was _____. They first settled in _____. In the year _____20 they settled at _____, in America. The captain in their wars was _____.

Skeleton summary

Let the pupil make a sketch map of that part of the coastline of New England from the extreme point of Cape Cod to Plymouth. Mark Plymouth and put the date 1620 there. Leave room on the paper to extend the coast of New England in both directions in future lessons. The relation of Jamestown to Plymouth should be studied. Note how far apart were the first two settlements in our country.

Geography

CHAPTER VIII

The Coming of the Puritans

BEFORE the Pilgrims had become comfortably settled in their new home, other English people came to various parts of the New England coast to the northward of Plymouth. About 1623 a few scattering immigrants, mostly fishermen, traders with the Indians, and timber-cutters,

Settlers along the New England coast

JOHN WINTHROP

began to settle here and there along the sea about Massachusetts Bay, and in what afterward came to be the colonies of New Hampshire and Maine.

We have seen in the preceding chapter that the Pilgrims belonged to that party which had separated itself from the Church of England, and so got the name of Separatists. But there were also a great many people who did not like the ceremonies of the Established Church, but who would not leave it. These were called Puritans, because

The English Puritans

they sought to purify the Church from what they thought to be wrong. They formed a large part of the English people, and at a later time, under Oliver Cromwell, they got control of England. But at the time of the

settlement of New England the party opposed to the Puritans was in power, and the Puritans were persecuted. The little colony of Plymouth, which had now got through its sufferings, showed them a way out of their troubles. Many of the Puritans began to think of emigration.

PURITAN GENTLEMAN

Massachusetts Company sends out its first colony. 1628

In 1628, when Plymouth had been settled almost eight years, the Massachusetts Company was formed. This was a company like the Virginia Company that had governed Virginia at first. The Massachusetts Company was controlled by Puritans, and proposed to make settlements within the territory granted to it in New England. The first party sent out by this company settled at Salem in 1628. Others were sent the next year.

John **Winthrop**, the principal founder of Massachusetts, was born in 1588 He was chosen Governor of the Massachusetts Company, and brought the charter and all the machinery of the government with him to America in 1630. He was almost continually governor until he died in 1649. He was a man of great wisdom. When another of the leading men in the colony wrote him an angry letter, he sent it back, saying that "he was not willing to keep such a provocation to ill-feeling by him." The writer of the letter answered, "Your overcoming yourself has overcome me " When the colony had little food, and Winthrop's last bread was in the oven, he divided the small remainder of his flour among the poor. That very day a shipload of provisions came. He dressed plainly, drank little but water, and labored with his hands among his servants. He counted it the great comfort of his life that he had a "loving and dutiful son." This son was also named John. He was a man of excellent virtues, and was the first Governor of Connecticut.

But in 1630 a new and bold move was made. The Massachusetts Company resolved to change the place of holding its meetings from London to its new colony in America. This would give the people the colony, as members of the company, a right to govern themselves. When this proposed change became known in England, many of the Puritans desired to go to America. John Winthrop, the new governor, set sail for Massachusetts in 1630 with the charter and about a thousand people. Winthrop and a part of his company settled at Boston, and that became the capital of the colony. No colony was settled more rapidly than Massachusetts. Twenty thousand people came between 1630 and 1640, though the colony was troubled for a while by bitter disputes among its people about matters of religion and by a war with the Pequot Indians.

The great migration to Massachusetts. 1630

PURITAN LADY

Some of the Puritans in Massachusetts were dissatisfied with their lands. In 1635 and 1636 these people crossed through the unbroken woods to the Connecticut

Connecticut settled, 1636. New Haven Colony settled, and afterward united with Connecticut

REVEREND JOHN DAVENPORT

River, and settled the towns of Windsor, Wethersfield, and Hartford, though there were already trading posts on the Connecticut River. This was the beginning of the Colony of Connecticut. Another colony was planted in 1638 in the region about New Haven. It was made up of Puritans under the lead of the Rev. John Davenport. In 1665 New Haven Colony was united with Connecticut.

Roger Williams lays the foundations of Rhode Island, 1636

In 1636 Roger Williams, a minister at Salem, in Massachusetts, was banished from that colony on account of his peculiar views on several subjects, religious and political. One of these was the doctrine that every man had a right to worship God without interference by the government. Williams went to the head of Narragansett Bay and established a settlement on the principle of entire religious liberty. The disputes in Massachusetts resulted in other settlements of banished people on Narragansett Bay, which were all at length united in one colony, from which came the present State of Rhode Island.

New Hampshire

The first settlement of New Hampshire was made at Little Harbor, near Portsmouth, in 1623. The population of New Hampshire was increased by those who left the Massachusetts Colony on account of the religious disputes and persecutions there. Other settlers came from England. But there was much confusion and dispute about land-titles and about government, in consequence of which the colony was settled slowly. New Hampshire was several times joined to Massachusetts, but it was finally separated from it in 1741.

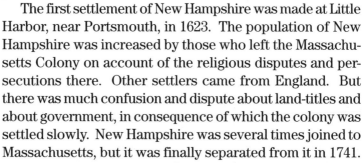

MERCHANT'S
WIFE IN 1620

As early as 1607, about the time Virginia was settled, a colony was planted in Maine; but this attempt failed. The first permanent settlement in Maine was made at Pemaquid in 1625. Maine submitted to Massachusetts in 1652, but it afterward suffered disorders from conflicting governments until it was at length annexed to Massachusetts by the charter given to that colony in 1692. It remained a part of Massachusetts until it was admitted to the Union as a separate state, in 1820. (See Chapter XLIII.)

The New England colonies were governed under charters, which left them, in general, free from interference from England. Plymouth, Massachusetts, Connecticut, New Haven, and Rhode Island were the only colonies on the continent that had the privilege of choosing their own governors. In 1684 the first Massachusetts charter was taken away, and after that the governors of Massachusetts were appointed by the king, but under a new charter given in 1692 the colony enjoyed the greater part of its old liberties.

Government in the New England colonies

1. *What took place along the coast to the northward of Plymouth?*
2. *What occupations did the first few settlers follow?*
3. *To what religious party did the Pilgrims belong?*
4. *There were people who disliked the ceremonies of the Church of England, but were unwilling to separate from it: what were they called?*
5. *How strong were the Puritans?*
6. *Which party was in power at the time of the settlement of New England?*
7. *Who were suffering persecution at this time?*
8. *What made the Puritans think of emigrating to New England?*
9. *In what year was the Massachusetts Company formed?*
10. *What kind of a company was this? By whom was it controlled? What did it propose to do?*
11. *In what year did it send out its first party? Where did they settle?*
12. *What new bold move was made in 1630?*
13. *Why did the leaders of the company wish to change their government to America? What effect did this have?*
14. *Who was the new governor that brought over the charter?*
15. *In what year did Winthrop come over?*
16. *How many people came at the same time?*
17. *Where did Winthrop make his home?*
18. *What town became the capital?*
19. *How many people came in the next ten years?*
20. *From what troubles did the colony suffer in that time?*

Questions for study

21. What cause of dissatisfaction led to the settlement of Connecticut?
22. In what year did the people go to Connecticut from Massachusetts?
23. What towns in Connecticut did they settle first?
24. What other colony was planted within what is now Connecticut?
25. Who was the leader of the New Haven Colony?
26. In what year was the New Haven Colony united with Connecticut?
27. In what year was Roger Williams banished from Massachusetts?
28. For what cause was he banished?
29. What was one of the opinions held by him?
30. Where did Williams go when he was banished? What town did he establish?
31. On what principle did he found his colony?
32. What caused other settlements in Narragansett Bay? What became of these settlements?
33. By what were the little settlements on the coast of New Hampshire increased?
34. But what made this region settle slowly?
35. With what colony was New Hampshire sometimes united?
36. In what year was the first attempt made to plant a colony in Maine?
37. How did the real settlement begin?
38. What caused disorders in the Maine settlements?
39. With what colony was Maine at length united?
40. How was it at last separated from Massachusetts in 1820?
41. How were the New England colonies governed?
42. Which colonies had the privilege of choosing their own governors?
43. How were the Massachusetts governors appointed after 1684?
44. But what is said of the liberties of Massachusetts under its new charter of 1692?

Study by topics

Tell about—I. The settlers along the coast.
    II. The coming of the Puritans.
       1. The Puritans in England.
       2. The Massachusetts Company.
       3. The settlement of Massachusetts.
    III. Other New England colonies.
       1. The settlement of Connecticut and New Haven.
       2. The settlement of Rhode Island.
       3. The development of Maine and New Hampshire.
    IV. The liberties of New England.

Composition

A good subject will be "The Founding of New England," as told in this and the preceding chapter.

Geography

Let the pupil extend his sketch-map used in the preceding lesson so as to represent the whole coast of New England, then mark the sites and dates given in the little map on the preceding page. If preferred, the map may be drawn on the blackboard.

Books

On the Pilgrims and Puritans, besides the general histories before referred to, Palfrey's *History of New England*, a large work of great learning. Drake's *The Making of New England*, interesting to children.

CHAPTER IX

The Coming of the Dutch

THE *HALF-MOON*
IN HUDSON
RIVER

WHILE Captain John Smith was in Virginia (see Chapter IV), he had a notion that there was a passage into the Pacific Ocean somewhere to the north of the Virginia Colony. He may have got this opinion from some old maps, or from misunderstanding something that the Indians told him while he was exploring the Chesapeake Bay. He sent to his old friend Henry Hudson, in England, a letter and a map, which showed a way to go by sea into the Pacific Ocean, a little to the north of Virginia.

Captain John Smith sends a map to Hudson

Henry Hudson was an Englishman already known as a bold explorer. In 1609, soon after getting John Smith's letter and map, Hudson went to Holland and hired himself to the Dutch East India Company. This company sent him out with a little yacht, called the *Half-Moon*, manned by twenty sailors, to find a passage to China, by going around the north coast of Europe. But he found the sea in that direction so full of ice that he was obliged to give up the attempt to get to China in that way. So, remembering John Smith's map, he set sail for America.

Hudson seeks a new route to China

Hudson sailed as far to the south as the entrance to the Chesapeake, and then explored the coast to the northward. He went into Delaware Bay, and afterward into New York Harbor. In hope of finding a way to the East Indies, he kept

Hudson explores Hudson River

on up the river, which we now call Hudson River, for eleven days. But when he had gone nearly as far as to the place where Albany is now, Hudson became satisfied that the road to China did not lie there, and so he sailed down and returned to Europe.

The Dutch establish a fur trade on Hudson River

Though Hudson was an Englishman, he made this voyage for the Dutch, and the very next year the Dutch merchants began a fur-trade with the Indians on this river that Hudson had discovered. In the year that followed (1611) they explored the coast north eastward beyond Boston Harbor, and to the southward they sailed into the Delaware River, claiming all this country, which was then without any inhabitants but Indians. They called this territory New Netherland. Netherland is another name for what we call Holland.

DUTCH WOMEN OF OLD TIMES

The Dutch plant a colony in New Netherland

The Dutch had built a trading post, called a "fort," at what is now Albany, and perhaps others like it elsewhere, but they did not send out a colony until 1623. Then two principal settlements were made, the one at Albany, the other at Wallabout, now part of Brooklyn. But the island of

Henry Hudson—The time of Hudson's birth is not known. Nor is anything known of the early voyages by which he became famous. In 1607 in the employ of an English company he undertook to find the much-desired route to China by sailing straight across the north pole. He failed, of course, though he got farther north than any other voyager had done. In the next year, 1608, for the same company, he tried to find a passage to the East Indies by sailing to the northeast. He did not succeed, but he sets down in his journal that some of his company saw one day a mermaid, with a body like a woman and a tail like a porpoise. Intelligent people believed in such monsters in that day. In the next year Holland and France both tried to secure Hudson's services. It is told in the text how, in this voyage in the *Half-Moon*, he discovered the great river of New York for the Dutch. In the year following he tried to find a way to China by the northwest but, while sailing in what is now called Hudson Bay, part of his crew rose against him, and, putting Hudson and some of his men into an open boat, sailed away, leaving them to perish.

Manhattan, on which New York now stands, had been the center of their trade, and it soon became the little capital of the colony. The town which grew about the fort that stood at the south end of what is now New York city, was called by the Dutch New Amsterdam, after the principal city of Holland, their own country.

The Dutch also had settlements on the Connecticut River and on the Delaware River. But on the Connecticut River they got into trouble with the English settlers, who claimed the whole of that country. On the Delaware River the Dutch had trouble with some Swedes, who had planted a colony there in 1638. This colony the Swedes called New Sweden, just as the Dutch called theirs New Netherland, and as the English called their northern colonies New England, while the French named their settlements in Canada, New France. After a great deal of quarreling between the Swedes and Dutch, the Dutch governor, Peter Stuyvesant, in 1655, mustered a little fleet with six or seven hundred men, and, sailing to the Delaware River, captured New Sweden.

Planting of New Sweden, and its conquest by the Dutch

DUTCH COUNTRY PEOPLE OF OLD TIMES

But the English at this time claimed that all the territory between Virginia and New England belonged to England. They said that all that coast had been discovered by Cabot for Henry VII more than a century and a half before. In 1664, in time of peace, four English ships appeared in the harbor of New Amsterdam and demanded its surrender. Stout old Peter Stuyvesant, the lame governor who had ruled in the Dutch colonies for many years, resolved to fight. But the city was weak and without fortifications, and the people, seeing the

The English conquer New Netherland

uselessness of contending against the ships, persuaded Stuyvesant to surrender. The name New Amsterdam was immediately changed to New York, the whole province having been granted to the Duke of York.

New Amsterdam becomes New York

At the time of the surrender New York city had but fifteen hundred people, most of them speaking the Dutch language. Today there are nearly a thousand times as many people in New York city. Many thousands of the people of New York and many in other states have descended from the first Dutch settlers and bear the old Dutch names. The Dutch settlers were generally industrious, frugal, and religious.

STREET IN NEW AMSTERDAM

Questions for study

1. What notion about a passage into the Pacific Ocean did Captain John Smith have while he was in Virginia?
2. How may he have got this opinion about a waterway to the north of Jamestown? To whom did he send word about this?
3. Where was Henry Hudson when Captain Smith sent him this letter and map?
4. Who was Hudson?
5. Where did he go after he got Smith's letter?

6. *In what year did he hire himself to the Dutch East India Company?*
7. *What did they wish him to do?*
8. *What kind of a ship did the company give him?*
9. *What was her name?*
10. *How many seamen did she have?*
11. *How did Hudson first try to sail his ship to China?*
12. *What stopped him?*
13. *What led him to go to America at this time?*
14. *How far south on the American coast did Hudson go?*
15. *What bay to the north of the mouth of the Chesapeake did he explore?*
16. *After leaving Delaware Bay, into what harbor did he sail?*
17. *Up what river did he sail?*
18. *What did he hope to find by sailing up the Hudson River?*
19. *How long was he in going up this river?*
20. *How far up the Hudson River did he go? At the end of eleven days what did he think of the chance of getting to China by this route?*
21. *When he found that there was no way to sail through America at that place, what did he do?*
22. *For whom did Hudson make this voyage?*
23. *What advantage did the Dutch take of his discoveries?*
24. *How far to the northeast did they explore in 1611?*
25. *Were there any settlements in New England in that year? (In what year was the first settlement in New England made by the Pilgrims? (See page 35.)*
26. *How far to the south did the Dutch explore?*
27. *How much country did they claim?*
28. *What did they call this new country?*
29. *Why did they call it New Netherland?*
30. *In what year did the Dutch send out a colony? (How long was this after the settlement of Virginia? Subtract 1607 from 1623. How long was this Dutch settlement after the settlement of Plymouth by the Pilgrims? Subtract 1620 from 1623.*
31. *How long was the settlement of Salem by the Massachusetts Company after the beginning of the Dutch settlement? Subtract 1623 from 1628. How long was the Dutch settlement before the beginning of Boston? Subtract 1623 from 1630.)*
32. *Where were the two principal settlements of the Dutch located at first?*
33. *Where was their principal trading-post?*
34. *What was the village that grew about the fort on Manhattan Island called?*
35. *Why was it called New Amsterdam?*
36. *Where else did the Dutch have settlements?*
37. *With whom did they have trouble on the Connecticut River?*
38. *Who gave them trouble on the Delaware River?*
39. *In what year was the Swedish colony settled on the Delaware? What was it called?*
40. *What Dutch governor conquered New Sweden? In what year?*
41. *But who claimed the whole territory of New Netherland at this time? On what ground?*

42. What happened at New Amsterdam in 1664?
43. When the English ships demanded the surrender of the town, how did the Dutch governor feel?
44. Who was this Dutch governor?
45. What led Stuyvesant to surrender after a while?
46. When New Amsterdam became English, what was it called?
47. How many people were there in New York when the English took it?
48. About how many times as many are there now?
49. What language did the most of the people speak when the English took it?
50. What kind of people were they?
51. What is said of the descendants of the Dutch in New York today?

Study by topics

Tell about—

1. John Smith and his notion of a way to the Pacific Ocean.
2. Henry Hudson's discoveries in 1609.
3. The Dutch settlement in 1623.
4. Conquest of New Sweden in 1655.
5. Conquest of New Netherland by the English in 1664.

Blackboard Illustration

Order of events: Virginia, 1607. > Hudson's voyage, 1609. > Plymouth Pilgrims, 1620. > Dutch settlement, 1623. > Massachusetts, 1628. > Swedish settlement. 1638.

Geography

Let the pupil make a sketch-map (or have one drawn on the blackboard) of the coast from the Connecticut River to the Delaware. Mark the sites of Brooklyn and Albany, with the date 1623. It will be enough to write "Dutch settlement" and "New Sweden, 1638," in the region of the Delaware.

CHAPTER X

The Settlement of Maryland and the Carolinas

How Virginia was cut down

BY the second charter given for planting the "First colony of Virginia," as it was called, its breadth was cut down to four hundred miles along the seacoast. Virginia had formerly included all that the English claimed in America. Part of the four hundred miles was occupied by the Dutch in New Jersey and Delaware. And the territory of Virginia was, at length, further cut down by the taking of another part of it to form Maryland for Lord Baltimore.

George Calvert, afterward Lord Baltimore, was a Secre- Lord Baltimore's first colony fails
tary of State to James I. In 1621 he planted a colony
in Newfoundland, which he called Avalon. In 1627 he
went to his colony in Newfoundland, but the climate was
so cold that in 1629 he went to Virginia. Before going to
Virginia he wrote to the king, begging for territory to plant
a colony there. Lord Baltimore had become a Catholic
at a time when there were severe laws in England against
Catholics. Even in the colonies Catholics were not
allowed; and the Virginians took advantage of the

FIRST LORD BALTIMORE

orders given them from England, and insisted that he
must take an oath declaring that the king was the head of
the Church. As a Catholic, he could not do this, and the
Virginians bade him leave the colony.

Lord Baltimore returned to England, and got the king, Maryland granted to Lord Baltimore
Charles I, to give him a slice of Virginia north of the Potomac.
This country King Charles named Maryland, in honor of
the queen, his wife. For this Baltimore was to pay to the
king two Indian arrows every year. But, before Lord Baltimore could send out a colony, he died.

The territory was then granted to Lord Maryland planted by the second Lord Baltimore
Baltimore's son, the second Lord Baltimore. He
was given all the powers of a monarch.
The first settlers were sent out in 1633,
and reached Maryland in 1634. This
company was composed of twenty
gentlemen and three hundred laboring-
men, and the first governor was
Leonard Calvert, the second Lord

SECOND LORD BALTIMORE

Baltimore's brother. Roman Catholic priests were
with them, and at their landing they set up a cross.

CHARLES I

{B u t
there were
also a good
many Protes-
tants in the party, and
Baltimore had resolved
from the beginning that there
should be no persecution of any Christians on account
of religion in his new province. In almost every country
in the world at that time the established religion, of whatever sort it might be, was enforced by law.

Early years of Maryland

The colonists came in two ships called the *Ark* and the
Dove; they settled first at a place which they called St.
Mary's, on the St. Mary's River, not far from the Potomac.
They bought from the Indians living on the place their village and corn-ground, and for the rest of that season they
lived in half of the village with the Indians. The colony had
many troubles and several little civil wars in its first years.

These mostly grew out of the religious differences of the people. But after a while Maryland prospered and grew rich by raising tobacco.

After the settlement of New England by Puritans, and Maryland by Catholics, there was a period of about thirty years in which no new colonies were planted. In this period occurred the Great Rebellion in England, in which Charles I was beheaded, and his son Charles II was kept out of England by the Puritans under Oliver Cromwell. But, after Cromwell's death, Charles II was brought back to the throne of England. This is known as the Restoration. It took place in 1660.

No new colonies for thirty years

After the Restoration there was a new interest in colonies. New York was taken from the Dutch, and new colonies were planned. King Charles II was a very thoughtless, self-indulgent monarch, who freely granted great tracts of land in America to several of his favorites. To some of his courtiers he gave, in 1663, a large territory cut off from Virginia on the south, which had been known before this time as Carolana, but was now called Carolina, from Carolus, the Latin form of King Charles' name. This territory included what we call North and South Carolina. Those to whom this territory was granted were called " The Lords Proprietors of Carolina." There were eight of them.

Carolina granted to eight proprietors

CHARLES II

In the northeastern corner of this territory, on the Chowan River, a settlement had been made by people from Virginia, under the lead of a minister named Roger Green, in 1653. This was ten years before the country was granted to these lords proprietors, and the land belonged to Virginia when they settled there. A settlement was made at Port Royal, in South Carolina, in 1670, but the people after-

Beginning of settlements in North Carolina in 1653

HUGUENOT
MERCHANT'S WIFE

ward moved to where the city of Charleston now stands. The foundation of this city was laid in 1680. A large number of Huguenots, or French Protestants, settled in South Carolina about this time.

The lords-proprietors tried to force on the little settlements in the woods a constitution which they had prepared. This constitution provided for three orders of nobility, to be called palatines [pal-a-teens´], landgraves, and caciques [cas-seeks´]. But this system of government worked so badly that it was, after a while, given up.

Failure of the constitution prepared for Carolina

The Carolina colonies grew slowly. But after the introduction of rice culture, in 1696, South Carolina became prosperous. The proprietors, living in England, conducted the government of the colonies in a selfish spirit, and the people disliked their management. In 1719 the South Carolina people rose in rebellion and threw off the yoke of the lords proprietors. In 1729 the king bought out the interest of the proprietors, and after that the governors were appointed by the king. They had already an Assembly elected by the people to pass laws.

Growth of South Carolina, and its change of government

Questions for study

1. How large was the territory of Virginia at first?
2. What part of this territory was taken by the Dutch?
3. How was the territory of Virginia next cut down?
4. Who was George Calvert?
5. Where did he plant his first colony?
6. What did he call it?
7. What was George Calvert called after he had been made a lord?
8. What made Lord Baltimore give up the colony of Avalon in Newfoundland?
9. In what year did he go to Virginia?
10. What did he write to the king before he went there?
11. What was Lord Baltimore's religion?
12. How were Catholics treated in England at that time?
13. Were they allowed to live in the colonies?
14. What oath did the Virginians ask Baltimore to take?
15. Why could he not take it?
16. When he refused, what did they do?
17. When Lord Baltimore got back to England what did he get from the king?

HUGUENOT

18. What name did the king give to Baltimore's new province?
19. In whose honor was it named?
20. What payment did Lord Baltimore have to make to the king for Maryland?
21. What happened to the first Lord Baltimore? To whom did the province go then?
22. What powers were given to Lord Baltimore and his successors?
23. In what year did the first colony reach Maryland?
24. Of what sort of men was it composed?
25. Who are most important in settling a new colony, gentlemen or laboring men?
26. Who was governor of the first colony?
27. What ministers of religion were with them?
28. What did they set up at their first landing?
29. Were all the people who came Catholics?
30. What plan did Lord Baltimore have about persecution for religion? Was religious liberty common at that time?
31. Do you remember the names of the two ships that brought over the Maryland people? (Can you think why they were so named?)
32. Where did the Maryland people settle?
33. How did they get their land?
34. What was the cause of most of the disturbances in the early years of the Maryland colony?
35. What crop did the Maryland colonists raise?
36. After the beginning of New England by the Puritans, and of Maryland by the Catholics, there was a period in which no new colonies were planted: how long was this period?
37. What took place in England during this time?
38. What king was beheaded?
39. Who was the leader of the Puritans in this rebellion?
40. What king was kept out of England while Cromwell lived?
41. In what year was Charles II brought back?
42. What was this bringing back of the king called?
43. After the Restoration what plans about the colonies were set on foot?
44. What kind of a king was Charles II?
45. What tract of land did he give to certain courtiers?
46. What had this southern territory been called before this time?
47. What was it now called?
48. Which two of our states were included in this Carolina grant?
49. What were those to whom this grant was made called?
50. How many lords-proprietors of Carolina were there?
51. Were there any people living in Carolina when this gift was made?
52. Where were they settled?
53. In what year did they settle on the Chowan River? Who was their leader?
54. Where was a settlement made in 1670?
55. Where did these people afterward remove to? In what year was Charleston begun?

56. Who tried to arrange a constitution for the Carolina settlements?
57. How many orders of nobility did this provide for?
58. What were to be their titles?
59. Why was this constitution given up?
60. Did the Carolina settlements grow rapidly at first? What grain was introduced in 1696?
61. What was the effect of rice-culture in South Carolina?
62. In what spirit did the proprietors conduct their government?
63. In what year did South Carolina overthrow the government of the proprietors?
64. What took place in 1729?
65. How were the Carolina colonies governed after that period?

Part I: Maryland. Tell about—
1. The first Lord Baltimore and his colony in Newfoundland.
2. The second Lord Baltimore and his grant.
3. The coming of the colony.

Also: a. What king made the grant?
    b. What was the religion of the Baltimores?
    c. What laws did they make about religion?
    d. Why was the colony called Maryland?

Part II: The Carolinas. Tell about—
1. The lords-proprietors.

Study by topics

2. The first settlement of North Carolina.
3. The first settlement of South Carolina.
4. The constitution.
5. The change of government.

Also: a. What king granted Carolina?
    b. Why was it called Carolina?
    c. What three orders of nobility were established?

Skeleton summary of Part I

George Calvert, afterward Lord _____, planted his first colony, called Avalon, in _____. Finding the climate too cold, he went to _____, in 1629. He got the king to give him a part of _____, north of the river. In the year _____ he sent a colony to this province, which he called _____, in honor of the _____. In religion Lord Baltimore was a _____.

Skeleton summary of Part II

The king gave Carolina to _____ proprietors in _____. But a settlement had been made in North Carolina, in _____, under the lead of _____. Another settlement was made at _____, in South Carolina, in 1670, but these people afterward removed and settled the city of _____, in South Carolina. This city was begun in _____. The cultivation of _____, which was introduced in _____, made South Carolina prosperous.

Geography

The sketch-map prepared for the chapters on the settlement of Virginia may be used. Extend the coastlines, if not previously drawn, to include Maryland. Enter the date 1634 at St. Mary's. Then put the initial A where Annapolis now stands, and B where Baltimore is, in order to fix relative positions. Draw a new sketch-map of the coast of North and South Carolina and Georgia. At Chowan River, in Albemarle Sound, enter the date 1653. At Port Royal, S. C., 1670. At Charleston, 1680. Then draw a line through the figures 1670, at Port Royal, to show that this settlement was given up. These maps may be made on the blackboard.

CHAPTER XI

The Coming of the Quakers and Others to the Jerseys and Pennsylvania

SCOTCH WOMAN

BEFORE the Dutch colony of New Netherland was conquered by the English, in 1664, it was given by Charles II to his brother, the Duke of York, who afterward became King of England as James II. James kept that portion of it that is now called New York to himself. What we call New Jersey he gave to Lord John Berkeley and Sir George Carteret, who, after a few years, sold their interest to others. The colony already contained several settlements of Dutch and Swedes. In 1674 New Jersey was divided into East Jersey and West Jersey.

Conquest of New Jersey, and its division

It was a time of religious persecution. Many people emigrated to the colonies in order to get a chance to be religious in their own way, and the proprietors of the New Jersey colonies promised to all who came liberty to worship in their own way. The people of Scotland, who were Presbyterians, suffered horribly from persecutions after the restoration of Charles II, and East Jersey received many Scotch emigrants, driven out of their own country by the cruelty of the government. Some people from New England also moved into East Jersey.

Persecuted people from Scotland come to New Jersey

The religious sect most severely persecuted in England after the restoration of the king was the Society of Friends, whose members are sometimes called Quakers. Some of these came to East Jersey. West Jersey was bought by cer-

SCOTCHMAN

Quakers come to East and West Jersey tain leading Friends, and a great many members of that society flocked to this province, where they established a popular form of government.

Pennsylvania granted to William Penn Just across the Delaware River from West Jersey was a territory not then occupied except by a few Swedes, who had come over long before to the old colony of New Sweden. Among those who had to do with the management of the West Jersey colony was a famous Quaker minister named William Penn. His father had been a great sea-commander, and William Penn had a claim against the King of England for a considerable sum of money due to his father. The king was in debt, and found it hard to pay what he owed. William Penn therefore persuaded Charles II to settle the debt by granting him a territory on the west side of the river Dela-

William Penn was born in London in 1644, so that he was thirty-seven years old when Pennsylvania was settled. He was the son of Admiral William Penn, who was celebrated for the part he took in the wars between the English and Dutch. Penn first came under the influence of the Friends or Quakers while he was a student at Oxford, and he was expelled from the university, with others, for the resistance they made to certain religious ceremonies introduced at that time. His father sent him to Paris, and he became an accomplished man of the world. He afterward became a Friend, which so mortified his father that the admiral turned him out of his house, but later he became reconciled to him. Penn was repeatedly imprisoned, and he boldly asserted in the English courts the great principle of religious liberty. He traveled into Wales, Ireland, Holland, and Germany, in his preaching journeys, and many of his acquaintances in those countries afterward came to Pennsylvania. Though Penn would never take off his hat in the presence of the king, he had considerable influence at court, which he used to lessen the sufferings of the Quakers and others. Penn died in 1718.

WILLIAM PENN

ware. This the king called Pennsylvania, which means something like Penn's Forest. The name was given in honor of Penn's father, the admiral.

What is now the State of Delaware was also put under Penn's government by the Duke of York. Everything was done with ceremony in those days. When Penn got to New Castle, in Delaware, its government was transferred to him in the following way: the key to the fort at New Castle was delivered to him. With this he locked himself into the fort and then let himself out signifying that the government was his. To show that the land with the trees on it belonged to him, a piece of sod with a twig in it was given to him. Then a porringer filled with water from the river was given to him, that he might be lord of the rivers as well as of the land.

Delaware delivered to Penn

Penn sent his first emigrants to Pennsylvania in 1681. Philadelphia, where they landed, was yet a forest, and the people had to dig holes in the river banks to live in through the winter. Nearly thirty vessels came to the new colony during the first year.

Penn settles Pensylvania

Although Pennsylvania was the last colony settled except Georgia, it soon became one of the most populous and one of the richest. Before the Revolution, Philadelphia had become the largest town in the thirteen colonies. This was chiefly owing to the very free government that William Penn founded in his colony. Not only English, but Welsh and Irish people, and many thousands of industrious Germans, came to Pennsylvania. People were also attracted by the care that Penn took to maintain friendly relations with the Indians, and to satisfy them for their lands. Another thing which drew people both to Pennsylvania and New Jersey was the fact that the land was not taken up in large bodies,

Rapid growth of Pennsylvania

as it was in New York and Virginia, for instance. In Pennsylvania and New Jersey the poor man could get a farm of his own.

The two
Jerseys united

By the sale and division of shares, the proprietaries of both East and West Jersey became too numerous to manage their governments well, and at length disorders arose which they were not able to suppress. In 1702 the government of both provinces was transferred to Queen Anne, and East and West Jersey were again united into the one province of New Jersey. But even to this day, in common speech, one sometimes hears the State of New Jersey spoken of as " The Jerseys " by people who do not know that two hundred years ago there were two colonies of that name. Pennsylvania remained in the hands of the Penn family, who appointed its governors until the American Revolution.

TREATY BELT GIVEN BY INDIANS TO PENN

Questions for
study

1. *To whom was the Dutch colony of New Netherland given before it was conquered by the English?*
2. *In what year was it conquered?*
3. *How was the Duke of York related to King Charles II?*
4. *What part of New Netherland did the Duke of York keep for himself?*
5. *Having retained New York, what part of his province did he give to Berkeley and Carteret?*
6. *Were there any settlements in New Jersey at this time?*
7. *How did the Dutch and Swedes come to be there before the English?*
8. *What did Berkeley and Carteret do with their interest in New Jersey?*
9. *In what year was New Jersey divided?*
10. *When it was divided in 1674, what were the two parts called?*
11. *What caused many people to come to the colonies at this time?*
12. *What promise did the proprietors of East and West Jersey make to those who should settle in their colonies?*
13. *What took place in Scotland after the Restoration?*
14. *In which of the Jersey colonies did many of the persecuted Scotch settle?*

15. From what part of America did settlers emigrate to East Jersey?
16. What religious sect was most severely persecuted at this time?
17. Where did some of these come to?
18. Who bought West Jersey?
19. When West Jersey had come into the control of some leading members of the Society of Friends, what took place?
20. What kind of a government did the Quakers establish in West Jersey?
21. What is said of the country on the other side of the Delaware River from West Jersey?
22. When had the few Swedes come to this place?
23. What famous member of the Society of Friends had a hand in the management of West Jersey?
24. Whose son was William Penn?
25. What claim did Penn have against the king? What did Charles II give to? William Penn instead of the money due to him?
26. In what year was this territory west of the Delaware given to Penn?
27. What did the king name the new province?
28. What does Pennsylvania mean?
29. In whose honor was it named?
30. Who put the country which we now call Delaware under Penn's government?
31. Tell by what ceremony Delaware was delivered to Penn.
32. In what year did William Penn send out his first settlers?
33. In what kind of houses did the settlers of Philadelphia live at first?
34. How many vessels came to the colony the first year?
35. What is said of the growth of Pennsylvania?
36. What was the largest town in the thirteen colonies some years before the Revolution?
37. What was there about the government of Pennsylvania that attracted people?
38. What people besides English came to Pennsylvania?
39. What was there in the relations of Pennsylvania with the Indians that made people like to live there?
40. What about the way the land was taken up in Pennsylvania and New Jersey?
41. How did East and West Jersey come to be managed by many proprietors?
42. What happened from this?
43. When the disorders became so great that the proprietors could not put them down, what did they do?
44. In what year was New Jersey transferred to the queen?
45. Who was Queen of England in 1702?
46. Did East and West Jersey remain apart?
47. What phrase do we sometimes hear now that reminds us of the existence of two Jerseys two hundred years ago?
48. Until what period did the Penn family govern Pennsylvania?

Tell about—
    1. The conquest of New Jersey and its division.
    2. The settlement of East Jersey by Scotch, New-Englanders, and Friends.

Study by topics

3. The coming of Friends to West Jersey.
4. William Penn and his colony.
5. The reunion of New Jersey.

New Netherland was taken from the _____ in 1664. The part of it now called _____ was given by the Duke of _____ to Lord John _____ and Sir George _____. Berkeley and Carteret afterward sold their shares to others, and New Jersey was divided into two colonies, called _____. Many persecuted Presbyterians from _____ settled in East Jersey. West Jersey was settled mostly by members of the Society of _____, often called _____. Among those who managed West Jersey was _____, the son of Admiral Penn. To him the king gave a province called _____. This province was mostly settled by _____. Besides English settlers, there were _____, and _____, and _____. Its chief city, called _____, was first settled in _____.

On the sketch-map of the middle colonies let a line be drawn, as in the subjoined map, to mark the division between East and West Jersey. Mark the site of New Castle, in Delaware. Mark the site of Philadelphia, and put in the date, 1681.

CHAPTER XII

The Settlement of Georgia, and the Coming of the Germans, Irish, and French

PENN'S settlement at Philadelphia was made, as we have seen, in 1681. This was seventy-four years after the settlement of Jamestown. In seventy-four years, which is less than a long lifetime, all the colonies were begun except one.

But after the settlement of Pennsylvania there passed fifty-one years more before another colony was begun. As the borders of Carolina were supposed to reach to the Spanish territory in Florida, and as New England touched the French territory in Canada, there appeared to be no room for any more colonies, until it was suggested to General Oglethorpe that a slice might be taken off the south side of South Carolina, and a new colony be wedged in between Carolina and the Spanish colony in Florida.

General Oglethorpe was a very benevolent man, but much given to impossible projects of different sorts. He did not propose that the new colony of Georgia should be a source of profit to anybody. He put on its seal a motto in

A GEORGIA ROAD

Latin, which meant "Not for ourselves, but for others," with a device of silkworms spinning. He wanted to provide a home for ruined debtors and a place of refuge for persecuted Protestants from other countries. He also expected to make Georgia a military barrier against the encroachments of the Spaniards from Florida, who laid claim to all of South Carolina. Besides this, he proposed to raise silkworms in Georgia, so that the English would not need to pay money to the Italians for their silk. He also resolved to keep out all slaves, and to forbid the bringing in of rum, that the people might not be idle or intemperate. Many thousands of pounds were given by benevolent people to help on this good work. Parliament also voted a donation to Georgia.

First settlement of Georgia at Savannah

In 1732 Oglethorpe took out his first company of a hundred and sixteen people, with whom he began the town of Savannah. Many others were added, among whom were a regiment of Highlanders, some Hebrews, and some persecuted Germans. Oglethorpe bore hardship with the rest, and by brilliant management defeated the Spaniards when they attacked his colony.

James Edward Oglethorpe was born in London in 1688. He was in the war of the Austrians against the Turks in 1716, and held a command under Prince Eugene in the brilliant and desperate campaign of 1717, which ended in the surrender of Belgrade. He returned to England in 1722, and served in Parliament for thirty-two years afterward. He was opposed to imprisonment for debt, and did much to improve the condition of poor debtors. He was also interested in the efforts then made to convert the black slaves in the colonies. In planting Georgia, his views were most benevolent, but the broken-down debtors that he took over at first were not the kind of men to begin a new state with. Oglethorpe was over ninety-six years old when he died.

PIPER TO A HIGHLAND REGIMENT

Oglethorpe's plans cause dissatisfaction

But the people, after a while, became dissatisfied. They were not allowed any hand in making their own laws. No man, unless he brought white servants, was permitted to own more than fifty acres of land, and this land he could not sell or rent or divide among his children. His oldest son took it at his death; if he had no son, it went back to the trustees of the colony It was thought that by this means the evils of wealth and poverty would be prevented. But, like all such attempts, this proved a failure, because the people felt that such laws interfered with their just liberties, and took away all inducements to the improvement of their property.

The complaints of the settlers became very bitter, and many of them left the colony. In 1752, twenty years after the beginning of the settlement, the trustees surrendered the government to the king. After that, Georgia was not different from the other colonies. One might own as much land as one could get, and sell or lease it at one's pleasure. Rum also came in, which certainly was no advantage. Slaves were bought, and rice and indigo plantations, like those of South Carolina, were established.

The government transferred to the king

Æ
GERMAN
COUNTRYMAN
AT THAT TIME

The Germans that came to Georgia were not by any means the first of these industrious people in the English colonies in America. There were many little sects in Germany at that time, and these suffered much persecution, from which they were glad to flee. The laws of Pennsylvania promised them freedom. Some of these sects were opposed to war, and their members emigrated to Penn's colony, where military service was not required, because the Society of Friends was also opposed to war. The tide of German emigration became greater and greater after this; thousands of Germans coming to Pennsylvania to escape the miseries brought on them by persecution and the wars which desolated their country.

The coming of the Germans

In three years, during the reign of Queen Anne, there came to England thirteen thousand poor people from that part of Germany called the Palatinate. These people were called Palatines; they were seeking to be sent to America. Some of these were dispatched to Virginia, some to the Carolinas and some to Maryland. About four thousand were sent to New York to make tar and pitch. So wretchedly were they cared for that seventeen hundred of the four thousand died at sea or soon after landing. The rest were settled on the Hudson River, where the descendants of some of

The arrival of the Palatine Germans

GERMAN COUNTRY
WOMAN OF THAT
TIME

IRISH MAN OF
THAT TIME

Irish immigrants
to the colonies

The migration to
the southward

IRISH WOMAN OF
THAT TIME

The coming of
the Huguenots

them are today. Some went to the wilderness farther west. They were badly treated in New York, and only allowed ten acres of land apiece. Three hundred of them, hearing that Germans were well received in Pennsylvania, made a bold push through the backwoods of New York, down the rivers that flowed into Pennsylvania. From that time Germans avoided New York, and thronged more than ever into Pennsylvania.

The Irish that came before the Revolution were mostly Presbyterians in belief. They had been persecuted in order to force them into the Church of England. Some of them came to New England about 1718, introducing there the spinning of flax and the planting of potatoes. There was not a colony to which they did not go, but the greatest tide of Irish immigration poured into Pennsylvania. Five thousand Irish immigrants arrived in the city of Philadelphia in the year 1729. Many of them were bold and enterprising pioneers, opening the way into unknown regions, and showing great courage in fighting with the Indians.

Pennsylvania filled up with great rapidity, and, when the later Indian wars laid waste its frontiers, many of the German and Irish settlers moved southward into the mountain-valleys of Virginia. Then, following the lines of open prairies and Indian trails, this stream of people went onward into the Carolinas. The Irish, indeed, and their children born in America, pushed southward until they had filled whole counties in North and South Carolina. They also pushed over the Alleghenies into the Western country.

The Huguenots, or French Protestants, rendered unhappy by the civil wars and persecutions of the time, came to the colonies in large numbers. They settled in almost every colony, but more largely in South Carolina than elsewhere.

Notwithstanding the multitudes of Germans, Irish, French, and Scotch that came to the colonies, those who came from England formed much the largest part of every colony.

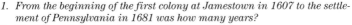

FRENCH COUNTRY MAN OF THAT DAY

1. *From the beginning of the first colony at Jamestown in 1607 to the settlement of Pennsylvania in 1681 was how many years?*
2. *Was Pennsylvania the last colony?*
3. *From the beginning of Pennsylvania—the next to the last colony—to the beginning of Georgia, the last colony, was how many years? (Subtract 1681 from 1732.)*
4. *What nation had a colony in Florida?*
5. *What nation had a colony in Canada?*
6. *Did the English colonies, as marked out, occupy all the space between?*
7. *Where did General Oglethorpe think of putting in a new colony?*
8. *What kind of a man was Oglethorpe? Did he propose to make a profit out of the new colony of Georgia?*
9. *What motto did he put on the seal of the colony?*
10. *What device?*
11. *What two classes of people did Oglethorpe expect to benefit by founding this colony?*
12. *What military purpose was the colony to serve?*
13. *What did he propose to accomplish with silkworms in Georgia?*
14. *What did he resolve concerning slaves?*
15. *What donations did the new colony receive? In what year did General Oglethorpe take out his first company?*
16. *How many people were there in it? Where did he settle these people? Among others who came afterward, what kind of people are mentioned?*
17. *What is said of Oglethorpe's endurance of hardships?*
18. *With what result did he fight with the Spaniards?*
19. *Were the people contented?*
20. *What share did they have in making their own laws?*
21. *How much land was each man allowed to own?*
22. *What could he not do with this land?*
23. *What became of the fifty acres when the man died? What became of it if he had no son? What did Oglethorpe and the other trustees hope to do by tying the land up in this way? How did the people feel about it? What resulted from the dissatisfaction of the settlers?*
24. *What disposition did the trustees make of the colony of Georgia in 1752?*
25. *What is said of the land system after that? What of rum? What of slaves? Were the Germans that came to Georgia the first of their people to settle in America?*
26. *What is said of the numerous sects in Germany at this time?*
27. *What did the laws of Pennsylvania promise to these persecuted people?*
28. *What is said about those sects that disliked war?*
29. *What miseries did thousands of Germans flee from?*

Æ
FRENCH COUNTRY WOMAN OF THAT DAY

30. What people were those that came to England in the reign of Queen Anne?
31. Why were they called Palatines?
32. What were they seeking for?
33. To what colonies were they sent?
34. How many were sent to New York?
35. How were they treated in New York Colony?
36. Where did some of them go to?
37. How did these three hundred get to Pennsylvania?
38. What effect did this have on Germans coming afterward?
39. What was the religion of most of the Irish who came before the Revolution?
40. Why did they leave Ireland?
41. In what year did the Irish come into New England?
42. What did they introduce to New England in 1718?
43. To how many of the colonies did they go?
44. To which colony did the greatest tide of Irish immigration go?
45. How many arrived at Philadelphia in 1729?
46. What was their character?
47. Where did the Germans and Irish go from Pennsylvania when the Indian wars broke out?
48. How did the Irish settlers get through the wilderness into North and South Carolina?
49. What mountains did they cross into the Western country?
50. Who were the people called Huguenots? What made them leave France? In what colonies did they settle?
51. What colony had the largest number of these settlers?
52. From what country did the largest number of settlers in every colony come?
53. What language do we speak in the United States?
54. Why do we speak English?

Study by topics

Tell about—

Part I. 1. Oglethorpe.
    2. Georgia—its location and settlement.
    3. Georgia—the objects for which it was settled.
    4. Georgia—its peculiar laws at first.

Part II. 1. The Germans—why they came.
    2. The Germans—those called Palatines.
    3. The Irish in New England.
    4. The Irish in Pennsylvania.
    5 The Southern migration of Irish and Germans.
    6. The Huguenots.

Geography

Let the pupil trace the coastline of Georgia, and mark the site of Savannah, putting down the date, 1732. Either on the sketch-map or some other, the relative po-

sition of Pennsylvania, Maryland Virginia, North Carolina, and South Carolina should be pointed out, to illustrate the migration southward from Pennsylvania.

FIRST REVIEW—DISCOVERY AND SETTLEMENT

(May be used on the blackboard)

Discovery by Columbus
- What was he looking for?
- Objections offered to his plan.
- His first voyage and return. 1492.
- His other voyages.

Other Discoveries
- North America by Cabot. 1497.
- To India by Good Hope, by Gama.
- South America by Columbus. 1498.
- Pacific Ocean by Balboa. 1513.
- Round the world by Magellan. 1520.

Raleigh's Expeditions
- Under Amidas and Barlowe. 1584.
- Under Grenville and Lane. 1585.
- Under John White. 1587.

Beginnings of Virginia
- Arrival and sickness. 1607.
- John Smith and his adventures
- The starving-time.
- Shipwreck of Gates and his arrival.
- Arrival of De la Warr.
- Dale's government.
- Pocahontas.
- The great charter. 1618.
- Division of land.
- Sending of wives.
- Indian massacre. 1622.

Pilgrims and Puritans
- Pilgrims in England and Holland.
- The Voyage in the Mayflower. 1620.
- The Pilgrims at Plymouth.
- New Hampshire and Maine. 1623.
- Coming of first Puritans to Salem. 1628.
- The bringing of the charter. 1630.
- Settlement of Connecticut and New Haven.
- Settlement of Rhode Island.

The Dutch and Swedes
- Hudson's voyage. 1609.
- Dutch settlement. 1623.
- Swedish settlement, 1638.
- Conquest of New Sweden by the Dutch. 1655.
- Conquest of New Netherland by the English. 1664.

Settlement of Maryland	{	Lord Baltimore and his colony in Newfoundland. Maryland granted. Colony begun at St. Mary's. 1634

The Carolinas settled	{	North Carolina settled as part of Virginia. 1653. Charter to eight proprietors. 1663. Beginning of settlements in South Carolina. 1670. Change of government. 1719 and 1729.

Settlement of New Jersey	{	Its conquest from the Dutch. 1664. The Jerseys divided. 1674. The Scotch come to East Jersey. New-Englanders and Friends in East Jersey. The coming of Quakers to West Jersey. The Jerseys united again. 1702.

Settlement of Pennsylvania	{	William Penn and the king. William Penn's colony. 1681.

Settlement of Georgia	{	General Oglethorpe's colony. 1732. What Oglethorpe proposed to do. Dissatisfaction of the people. Change of government.

Race Elements	{	The Germans—why they came, how, and where. The Irish—why and where. Southward movement of Irish and Germans. French Huguenots. English the most numerous.

Diagram of Emigrations on account of Persecution.

(For the blackboard.)

Pilgrims or Separatists	from	England by way of Holland	to	Plymouth Colony
Puritans	from	England	to	Massachusetts
Dissenting Puritans	from	Massachusetts	to	Rhode Island
Roman Catholics	from	England	to	Maryland
Huguenots	from	France	to	New York, South Carolina, and other colonies
Presbyterians	from	Scotland and Ireland	to	New Jersey, Pennsylvania, the Southern colonies, and elsewhere
Lutherans and other sects	from	Germany and Switzerland	to	Pennsylvania, and thence southward

CHAPTER XIII

How the Indians Lived

BEFORE the white people settled America it was inhabited by many tribes of the people we call Indians. They were called Indians because the first discoverers believed America to be a part of India. The Indian is of a brown or copper color, with black eyes and straight hair. *The Indians*

In what is now the United States the clothing of the Indians was mostly made of deerskin. A whole deerskin was *The dress of the Indians* thrown about the shoulders, a strip of the same material was hung about the loins, and the leggins worn in winter were also of deerskin. Some of the Southern Indians wore mantles woven from the fiber of a

INDIAN CHILDREN PLAYING THE GAME OF DEER AND WOLF

plant which now grows in gardens under the name of "Spanish bayonet," but which in that day was called "silk-grass." The women wore deerskin aprons. Women of the Northern tribes wore mantles of beaver skins. Shoes, or moccasins, were of deerskin, sometimes embroidered with porcupine quills or shell beads.

STRINGS OF
WAMPUM

The Indian warriors were fond of staining their faces in stripes, spots, and splashes of red, yellow, and blue. Some of the Virginia Indians wore bears' or hawks' claws, and even living snakes, dangling from their ears; and sometimes, also, the savage Indian warrior would wear the dried hand of his dead enemy in the same way. The use of such ugly adornment was to make the savages seem as fierce and terrible as possible. Both men and women decorated themselves with beads, which they made from seashells. These were called "wampum," and were worn in strings, or wrought into belts, necklaces, and bracelets. Wampum was also used among them as money, and as presents in making treaties between the tribes.

ZUÑI INDIAN WOMAN MAKING POTTERY

Indian houses   Indian houses, or wigwams, were mere tents of bark or of mats, supported by poles. Among the Indians of the Western prairies, skins of animals were used to cover the Indian houses. Indian wigwams were not divided into rooms. The inmates slept on the ground, or sometimes on raised platforms. The fire was built in the middle of the wigwam, and the smoke found its way out through an open-

INDIAN BOTTLE
OF POTTERY
FROM ARKANSAS

ing at the top. In some tribes long arbor-like houses were built of bark. In these there were fires at regular intervals. Two families lived by each fire.

MANNER OF BOILING IN AN EARTHEN POT

The Indians had very little furniture. There were a few mats and skins for bedding. Some tribes had for household use wooden vessels, which they made by burning and scraping out blocks of wood, little by little, with no other tools than shells or sharp stones.

Furniture of wigwams, and modes of cookery

These Indians cooked their food by putting water into their wooden kettles and then throwing in heated stones. When the stones had made the water hot, they put in it whatever they wished to cook. Other tribes knew how to make pots of earthenware: and yet others cut them out of soapstone. Vessels of pottery and soapstone could be set over the fire.

AN INDIAN VASE

Often fish and meat were broiled on sticks laid across above the fire; green corn was roasted under the ashes, as were also squashes, and various roots. Indian corn, put into a mortar and pounded into meal, was mixed with water and baked in the ashes, or boiled in a pot. Sometimes the meal

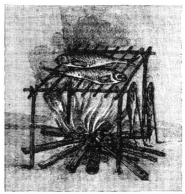

INDIAN MANNER OF BROILING IN 1585

was parched and carried in a little bag, to be eaten on a journey. A few tribes near to salt springs had salt, the rest used leaves of several sorts for seasoning.

STONE AXE

For tilling the ground the Indians had rude tools; their hoe was made by attaching to a stick a piece of deer's horn, or the shoulder-blade bone of an animal, or the shell of a turtle, a bit of wood, or a flat stone. They raised Indian corn, beans, squashes, and tobacco. They prepared the ground by girdling the trees so as to kill them; sometimes they burned the trees down. Some tribes had rude axes for cutting trees; these were made of stone.

Indian Agriculture

The handle of the stone axe was formed by tying a stick to it, or by twisting a green withe about it. Sometimes an Indian would split open a growing young tree and put the axe into the

INDIAN GIRL WITH BASKETS

The coming of the white people made great changes in the Indian life. The furs and skins, which the Indians did not value except for necessary clothing, were articles of luxury and ornament of great value in Europe. Many a half-starved Indian was clothed in furs that a European prince would have prized. The savage readily exchanged his beautiful beaver coat for a bright-colored blanket and thought he had made a good bargain, though his furs were worth to the white man the price of many blankets. The cheap glass beads and tiny bells, such as the people of old time hung about the necks of the hawks with which they hunted birds, were greatly prized by savages. Jews-harps were also much liked by them, and were sometimes used in paying them for land. The Indian who could possess himself of a copper kettle was a rich man in his tribe. The cheap iron hatchets of the trader drove out the stone axes, and knives were eagerly bought, but guns were more sought after than anything else; and, though there were many laws against selling firearms to the Indians, there were always men who were glad to enrich themselves by this lawless trade. The passion of the savage for intoxicating drinks was so great that evil men among the traders were often able to strip them of all their goods by selling them strong liquors. The white settlers generally bought the land they occupied from the Indians. As land was not worth much, the price paid was trifling. Manhattan Island, on which New York now stands, was sold to the Dutch, by the Indians, for about twenty-four dollars. The land-sales made trouble, for the lines were not well defined, and were often matters of dispute. The Indians did not understand business, and they sometimes had to be paid over and over again for a piece of land.

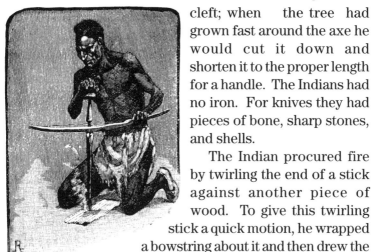

INDIAN KINDLING FIRE

cleft; when the tree had grown fast around the axe he would cut it down and shorten it to the proper length for a handle. The Indians had no iron. For knives they had pieces of bone, sharp stones, and shells.

Cutting tools

The Indian procured fire by twirling the end of a stick against another piece of wood. To give this twirling stick a quick motion, he wrapped a bowstring about it and then drew the bow swiftly to and fro.

Making fire

The most remarkable product of Indian skill was the canoe: this was made in some tribes by burning out a log, little by little, and scraping the charred parts with shells, until the "dugout" canoe was sufficiently deep and rightly shaped. Many canoes made in this way, without any other tools than shells and sharp stones, would carry from twenty to forty men. The Northern tribes constructed a more beautiful canoe, of white birch bark, stretched on slender wooden ribs, and sewed together with roots and fibers. Such canoes were made watertight by the use of gums.

Canoes

PIUTE INDIAN GIRLS WITH WATER-JARS

Division of labor   Among the Indians, the hardest work fell to the women. Hunting, gambling, and making war, were the occupations of the men. The male Indian was from childhood trained to war and the chase. Game and fish, with such fruits, nuts, and roots as grew wild in the woods and swamps, were the principal dependence of the Indians for food. As they suffered much from hunger and misery, the population of the country was always thin.

One Indian is seen scraping out the charred wood, another is fanning the fire, while a third is burning down a tree to begin a new canoe.

MAKING A CANOE

Wars between the tribes   Moreover, the continual wars waged between the various tribes, in which women and children as well as men were slain, kept the red men from increasing in numbers. Large tracts of country were left uninhabited, because tribes at war dared not live near to one another, for fear of surprise. In all the country east of the Mississippi River there were but a few hundred thousand people; hardly more than there are in one of our smallest states, and not enough, if they had all been brought together, to make a large city.

Questions for study

1. *What were the people called who lived in America before white men came?*
2. *Why were they called Indians? (Are there any of them remaining yet?) What is the color of their skin? What kind of eyes have they? What sort of hair? What material was mostly in use among them for clothing? What garments did they wear?*
3. *Of what plant did the Southern Indians make mantles?*

4. What sort of mantles were used by women in the Northern tribes?
5. How were their shoes made?
6. With what were their shoes embroidered?
7. How did the Indian " braves," or warriors, stain their faces?
8. What did they sometimes wear hanging to their ears?
9. What kind of beads did the Indians wear?
10. For what other purpose was wampum used?
11. What was the Indian house, or wigwam, made of?
12. How did the Indians sleep?
13. Where was the fire made?
14. How did the smoke get out?
15. Some tribes built long houses: what is said of these? What did the Indians have for bedding?
16. What kinds of vessels for household use? How did they hollow out their wooden vessels? How did those tribes that had only wooden vessels cook food in them?

POTTERY FROM MISSOURI

INDIAN WIGWAMS OF BARK

17. How did those that had pottery and soapstone kettles use them for cooking?
18. How were fish and meat sometimes broiled?
19. How were green corn and other vegetables roasted?
20. How was corn made into meal?
21. How was bread baked? What did the corn made into meal?
22. How was bread baked?
23. What did the Indians do for salt?
24. What can you tell about the various sorts of hoes made by the Indians?

NAVAJO INDIAN WOMAN WEAVING A BELT

25. What plants did they cultivate? How did they clear the ground?
26. Some tribes had axes: what were these made of? How did they put handles to them?
27. Had the Indians any iron? How did they commonly make knives? How did they produce fire? What was the most remarkable product of Indian industry?
28. How was the dugout canoe made without metal tools?
29. How many men would the larger of these carry?
30. Of what did the Northern tribes make their canoes? How did they sew them? How did they make them tight?
31. What was the difference between the work of the women and the occupations of the men?
32. What is said of the education of Indian boys? On what did the Indians mainly depend for food? What effect did their poverty have on the population?
33. What other cause kept the Indians from increasing in numbers?
34. What is said of the Indian population east of the Mississippi River?

Tell what you know about—
I. The appearance of the Indian.
   1. Complexion, hair, eyes.
   2. Articles of dress.
   3. Things worn for ornament.
II. The Indians' mode of living.
   1. Houses: their construction.
   2. Houses: their inside arrangements.
   3. Furniture.
   4. Cookery.
III. The Indian at work.
   1. Tools.
   2. Plants cultivated.
   3. Canoes.
IV. Men's and women's work.
V. Effect of poverty and war on the Indian population.

Study by topics

MEDICINE MAN WITH A MANTLE OF SILK GRASS. DRAWN IN 1585

Blackboard Illustration

Divide the board horizontally into three parts. Then write, from suggestions made by the pupils, in the topmost division, the various items of dress and ornaments belonging to an Indian's head; in the second, those worn on the body; in the third, those used on the feet.

Composition

Let the pupil suppose himself to be a settler in America in the early colonial times. Let him write a letter to a supposed friend in England, telling in his own words what is told in this and the two following chapters, especially about Indian customs and the trade between them and the white people.

Books

Major Powell's Reports of the Ethnological Bureau. *Century Magazine*, May, 1883, "The Aborigines and the Colonists."

CHAPTER XIV

Early Indian Wars

THERE were, between the two races, occasions enough for quarreling. Dishonest white men were sure to cheat the ignorant Indians, and the violent among the Indians were as sure to revenge themselves. If an Indian suffered wrong from one white man, he thought he had a right to take vengeance on any man, woman, or child of the white race when he found opportunity.

Dishonest traders and the Indians

We have seen how suddenly the Indians massacred the Virginians in 1622 (page 32). This led to a long war, with many treacheries and cruel surprises on both sides. After some years the Indians were subdued by the Virginians, under the lead of William Claiborne. But in 1644 the old chief Opechankano, who had led in the first massacre, planned a second. He was so old that he could not walk without assistance, and could not see, except when his eyelids were held open. He was carried to the scene of bloodshed. The Indians had by this time secured guns. By a sudden surprise they killed about five hundred white people in a single day. But they paid dearly for their victory, for the colony had grown strong enough to defeat and punish them. They were driven away from their villages. Opechankano was taken prisoner, and, while a captive, was suddenly killed by an infuriated soldier.

Early Indian massacres in Virginia

FLORIDA WARRIOR, 1585

INDIAN MASK

The Pequot
war in 1637

The Pe´-quot war in Connecticut grew out of the differences between the Dutch and the English settlers. The English brought back the Indians whom the Pequot tribe had just driven away. The Pequots began the war by killing some English traders. The attempts of the English colonists to conquer the Pequots were at first of no avail. The Indians were light of foot, and got away from men in armor. They continued to seize and torture to death such English as they could catch. In 1637, John Mason, a trained soldier, at the head of a company of Connecticut men, with some from Massachusetts, marched into the Pequot country. At Mystic, Connecticut, just before daybreak, the Connecticut men surrounded the palisaded village of Sassacus, the dreaded Pequot chief. In the first onset Mason set the village on fire. A horrible slaughter followed. Indian men, women, and children, to the number of five or six hundred, were shot down or burned in the village, or in trying to escape. In the war which followed this attack, the whole Pequot tribe was broken up, and the other Indians were so terrified that New England had peace for many years after.

SHELL AXE

About the same time cruel Indian wars raged between the Dutch of New Netherland (now New York) and the Indians in their neighborhood. At one time the Dutch colony was almost overthrown. There was also a war between the Marylanders and the Sus-que-han´-nah tribe. In 1656 the Virginians suffered a bitter defeat in a battle with the Indians at the place where Richmond now stands. The brook at this place got the name of Bloody Run.

Indian wars in
New York,
Maryland, and
Virginia

In 1675 there broke out in New England the terrible Indian war known ever since as King Philip's War. Philip was the son of Massasoit, the Indian chief who had been long a friend to the Plymouth settlers. Philip was a proud man, and thought that he was not treated with enough respect by the rulers of Plymouth Colony, who acted with imprudent boldness in their dealings with him. He was also irritated because large numbers of his people were converted to the Christian religion through the labors of John Eliot. These converted people, or "praying Indians," formed themselves into villages, and lived under the government of the Massachusetts colony.

King Philip's war, 1675

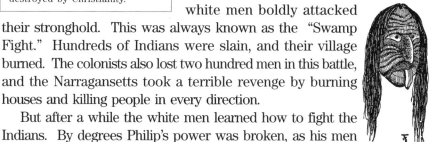

BELT OF WAMPUM

> Many of the white people sincerely desired to do the Indians good. Schools for the education of Indian children were set up in Virginia and in New England. Catholic missionaries labored among the Indians of Maryland. John Eliot, of Massachusetts, preached to thousands of Indians, and translated the whole Bible into their language. He is called the "Apostle to the Indians." But, even in trying to do the Indians good, the white men offended them. The chiefs and "medicine men" of the Indians did not like to see their ancient customs treated with contempt, and their own influence destroyed by Christianity.

Philip won some successes at first, and Indians of other tribes came to his assistance. Many New England towns were laid in ashes, and hundreds of people were killed or carried away into captivity. The powerful tribe of Narragansetts gave Philip secret aid, and in the winter the white men boldly attacked their stronghold. This was always known as the "Swamp Fight." Hundreds of Indians were slain, and their village burned. The colonists also lost two hundred men in this battle, and the Narragansetts took a terrible revenge by burning houses and killing people in every direction.

The "Swamp Fight" at the Narragansett fort

But after a while the white men learned how to fight the Indians. By degrees Philip's power was broken, as his men were most of them killed or captured. Captain Benjamin Church was the most famous fighter against the Indians in this war. Church's men surrounded Philip in a swamp and killed him. The rest of the Indians were soon subdued. Most of the captive Indians were cruelly sold into slavery in Barbados.

MASK MADE BY IROQUOIS INDIANS

Captain Church and the death of Philip

About the time of Philip's war the Doegs and Susquehannahs were ravaging the Virginia frontier, while the governor of that colony refused to allow any one to march against them. But Nathaniel Bacon, a young man of great spirit, was chosen by the people to lead them, which he did in opposition to the governor's orders. This disobedience led to "Bacon's Rebellion," as it is called, the story of which is told in Chapter XXVI.

All the colonies suffered from Indian wars. The infant settlement in South Carolina was almost ruined by a war with the Indians called Wes´-toes, ten years after the arrival of the first white men, and in the very year that Charleston was settled; that

Benjamin Church was one of the first of the Indian fighters. He knew how to manage men, and had great influence over them. He would even persuade captive Indians to join his band and lead him to the haunts of their friends. It was one of these Indians who shot Philip. Church let him take Philip's scarred hand for a trophy. This he carried about the country, making money by showing it. Captain Church was tireless, fearless, and full of expedients. He first taught the Englishmen to practice the arts of the Indian in war. When Philip was dead, only old Annawon, Philip's headman remained in the field with a party. When Church at last found him, he was sheltered under some cliffs. Church had but half a dozen men with him; Annawon ten times that number of resolute braves. But by creeping down the cliffs, while an Indian woman was making a noise by pounding corn in a mortar, Church succeeded in capturing the guns of the Indians, which were stacked at Annawon's feet. Seeing his boldness, the Indians thought that Church had surrounded them with a great many men, and they therefore surrendered. Church also performed many famous exploits in the war with the Indians of Maine.

is, in 1680. In 1711 the warlike Tuscaroras [tus-ca-ro´-rahs] ravaged the scattered settlements of North Carolina, putting people to death by horrible tortures. It was only by the help of the Virginians and South Carolinians, and the Yam-as-see´ Indians, that the settlers, after two years, finally defeated the Tuscaroras, capturing and sending many hundreds of them to be sold as slaves in the West India Islands.

But in 1715, two years after the close of this war, the Yamassees, who had helped the white people to put down the Tuscaroras, joined with the Spaniards in Florida, and with all the other Indians from Florida to Cape Fear, in an attempt to destroy the colony of South Carolina. There were six or seven thousand Indian warriors in this league, while South Carolina could only muster fifteen hundred white men and two hundred trusty Negroes. Governor Craven knew that a single defeat would ruin the colony, so he marched with the utmost caution until he brought on a great battle; and overthrew the Indians. The war lasted about three years.

The Yamassee war in South Carolina, 1715

NORTH CAROLINA WARRIOR IN 1585

1. *What followed the Indian massacre in Virginia in 1622?*
2. *What was the nature of that war?*
3. *Who led the settlers when the Indians were at length subdued?*
4. *What Indian chief conducted the massacre in 1644?*
5. *What was the condition of Opechankano in 1644?*
6. *What kind of arms did the Indians have by this time?*
7. *How many white people did they kill in the first attack?*
8. *What was the result of the war to the Indians?*
9. *What happened to the old chief Opechankano?*
10. *What was the cause of the Pequot war in Connecticut?*
11. *How did the Pequots begin it?*
12. *How did the colonists succeed in their first attempts to subdue the Pequots?*
13. *Why did they not succeed?*
14. *What did the Pequots continue to do?*
15. *Who was put in command of the Connecticut troops in 1637?*
16. *Where did he lead his men?*
17. *At what point did he attack the Indians?*
18. *Whose village did he surround?*
19. *What kind of a village was this?*
20. *(What is a palisaded village? Answer: A village surrounded with upright posts or palisades for defense.) How was the village destroyed? What became of the people in it? What do you think of this way of carrying on war?*

Questions for study

21. What is said of the wars of that day?
22. What became of the Pequots?
23. What other Indian wars were waged at this time?
24. Where did the Virginians suffer defeat in 1656?
25. What is the brook called where the battle was fought?
26. What war broke out in New England in 1675?
27. Who was Philip? What feelings inclined him to make war?
28. What is said of the converted, or praying, Indians?
29. What effect did Philip's successes have on other Indians?
30. What took place in the attack on the Narragansetts? What did the white men learn?
31. Who was especially famous in this war with the Indians?
32. How did Philip lose his life?
33. What became of the remainder of King Philip's Indians?
34. What colony was ravaged by the Doegs and Susquehannahs?
35. What did the governor of the colony do?
36. Who was chosen to lead the people?
37. By whom was he chosen?
38. To what did this lead?
39. How long after the arrival of settlers in South Carolina was it when the war with the Westoes broke out?
40. What effect did this first war have on the feeble settlements?
41. In what year did the Tuscarora war break out in North Carolina?
42. What did the Tuscaroras do with the people they captured?
43. What colonies helped to put down the Tuscaroras?
44. What Indians helped to conquer them?
45. How long did the Tuscarora war last? What was done with the captured Indians?
46. Did the Yamassees keep their peace with South Carolina?
47. With whom did they join?
48. How many Indians were against South Carolina?
49. How many white soldiers were there?
50. What would have been the result of a single defeat?
51. What was the result of Governor Craven's fight with the Indians?
52. How long did the Yamassee war last?

CALUMET OR
PEACE PIPE

Questions for study

Tell about—   1. The principal Indian war in Virginia.
          2. The Pequot and Philip's war in New England.
          3. The Indian wars in South and North Carolina.

Blackboard illustration

The three topics above may be set down and the brief mention of particulars, as drawn from the answers of the pupils, added. For example: "Pequot war: English brought back the expelled tribe. Pequots killed traders. English failed at first. Captain Mason. Attacked Sassacus' fort. Palisaded. Set fire. Six hundred men, women, and children killed. "Let the other prominent wars be treated in the same way.

MATCHLOCK GUN

CHAPTER XV

Traits of War with the Indians

THE most important weapon of the Indian, when the white men came, was the
bow and arrow. The arrow was headed
with a sharpened flint or a bit of horn.
Sometimes the spur of a wild-turkey or the
claw of an eagle was used to point the ar-

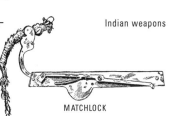

Indian weapons

MATCHLOCK

row. Next to the bow and arrow the Indian warrior depended on a war-club, which had a handle at one end and a
heavy knob at the other, or upon a tomahawk, made by
fastening a wooden handle to a round stone, or a stone axe.
But all their rude weapons were given up as soon as the
Indians could get knives, hatchets, and guns from the white
men. In some cases, it is said, they were so eager for gunpowder that they sowed what they got at first, supposing it
to be the seed of a plant. The Pequots commanded two
white girls, whom they had captured, to make some gunpowder, supposing that all white people knew how to
make it.

At the first arrival of white men, they protected themselves by wearing armor, and the Indian arrows could not
do them much hurt. But as soldiers could not get about
very fast in heavy armor and with clumsy guns, they could
not do much hurt to the Indians. Some of the guns used
were matchlocks. In order to shoot, the soldier had to place
in front of him a "rest"—a kind of forked stick or staff—
and lay his heavy gun across it. In firing, the powder on
the lock of his gun was set off with a lighted fuse or match;
and the soldier had to carry a burning fuse in his hand. If
he let his fuse go out, he could not use his gun until he got

MATCHLOCK GUN

Armor and arms of the white men

fire again, for friction matches were unknown. But the Indians would not stand still while the white men got ready to shoot. This awkward matchlock-gun was sometimes used as late as 1675, the time of Philip's war. The snaphance, or flintlock, was already coming into use when the colonies were settled. The flintlock was set off by the striking of the flint against a piece of steel, when the trigger was pulled. (Guns with percussion caps are a much later invention.) Some of the white men at first were armed with pikes or spears; but it was found to be a very dangerous business to poke an Indian out of the brush with a pike. During Philip's war the pike began to go out of use in America.

The Indians get firearms. White men change their mode of fighting

When the Indians had procured firearms, the armor which the soldiers wore, being of little use against bullets, was rather a burden than an advantage. Long after the first settlements were made, white men ceased by degrees to wear the head, and breast, and back pieces of metal, and they laid aside also the heavy buff-coats, which were made of leather and stuffed, to resist bullets. The colonists also learned to march in scattering parties, as the Indians did, in order to avoid surprise, and to lie in ambush, and to load their guns while lying down. For a long time the savages made attacks on the Northern settlements in the winter, when the snow was so deep that the soldiers could not move about; but, after stupidly suffering this for many years, the Northern colonies at length put their

PIKEMAN OF THAT TIME

soldiers on snowshoes too, and then all was changed.

The Indian did not hesitate to resort to treachery to en- Indian stratagems trap his foes. He would profess friendship in order to disarm an enemy. He gloried in ingenious tricks, such as the wearing of snowshoes with the hind part before, so as to make an enemy believe that he had gone in an opposite direction. He would sometimes imitate the cry of the wildturkey, and so tempt a white hunter into the woods, that he might destroy him. An Indian scout would dress himself up with twigs, so as to look like a bush. Many of these things the white people learned to practice also.

The Indians were very cruel; it was part of their plan to Treatment of prisoners by the Indians strike terror by their severity. This is why they tortured their prisoners to death and disfigured the dead, and why they slew women and children as well as men. They not only put their prisoners to death in the most cruel way their ingenuity could devise, but, in some tribes, they even devoured them afterward. Sometimes, however, a prisoner was adopted into an Indian family, and kindly treated. Many hundreds of white children were thus adopted, and forgot their own language. Some of them afterward engaged in war against their own people. One boy, named Thomas Rice, was carried off from Massachusetts in childhood, and became a chief of the tribe which had captured him.

SNOW SHOES

The settlers learned after a while many ways of defending themselves. They built blockhouses in every exposed settlement, for refuge in case of attack. When Indians were Defense of the settlements discovered lurking about in the night, a messenger would be sent from the blockhouse to warn the sleeping settlers. This messenger would creep up to a window and tap on it, whispering, "Indians!" Then the family within would get up, and, without speaking or making a light, gather the most necessary things and hurry away along dark paths through the woods to the blockhouse. In some of the more exposed regions the dogs were even trained not to bark unless commanded to.

BLOCKHOUSE

In some, if not all, of the colonies, the firing of three shots in succession was the

---

Escape of Prisoners—A young girl in New England, after three weeks of captivity, made a bridle out of bark, caught a horse running in the woods, and, by riding all night, reached the settlement. Two little lads named Bradley got away, but they were tracked by the Indian dogs, who came up with them while they were hidden in a hollow log. They fed the dogs part of their provisions to make them friendly. After traveling nine days the elder fell down with exhaustion, but the younger, who was the more resolute, dragged himself starving into a settlement in Maine, and sent help to his brother. Hannah Dustin, Mary Neff, and a boy were carried off from Haverhill, Massachusetts. At midnight, while encamped on an island, they got hatchets and killed ten Indians, and then escaped in a canoe down the river. This bold escape soon became famous in the colonies, and the Governor of Maryland, hearing of it, sent to the returned captives a present for their courage.

Stories of Defense—A town in Maine was attacked and almost destroyed by Indians, when one man sent his family by boat out of the back door of his fortified house, remaining there alone. By frequently changing his hat and coat, and then appearing without a hat and then without a coat, and by giving orders in a loud voice, he made the Indians believe that his house was too full of men for them to attack it. Some Swedish women, near where Philadelphia now stands, saw Indians coming, and took refuge in their fortified church, carrying with them a kettle of hot soap. They defended themselves until their husbands came by throwing the boiling soap, with a ladle, at every Indian who approached the church. A maidservant in Massachusetts, left alone with little children, drove away an Indian, who tried to enter the house, by firing a musket at him and throwing a shovelful of live coals on his head. A young girl in Maine held a door shut until thirteen women and children had time to escape by a back door into a blockhouse. The Indians, when they got in knocked the girl down but did not kill her.

---

sign of danger. Every man who heard it was required to pass the alarm to those farther away, by firing three times, and then to go in the direction in which the shots had been heard. In many places large dogs were kept and trained to hunt for Indians, as highway robbers were hunted down in that day in England. In all exposed places, a part or all of the men took their arms to church with them.

The people became very brave, and were fierce and even cruel during these long-continued Indian wars. A wounded soldier would beg to have a loaded gun put into his hands that he might, before he died, kill one more Indian. Captives often escaped from the Indians by ingenious devices, and sometimes suffered dreadful hardships in getting back to the settlements.

Courage of the people

1. *What was the Indians' chief weapon when the white men came to America?*
2. *How was the head or point of the arrow made?*
3. *What kind of a war-club was used?*
4. *What sort of a weapon was the tomahawk?*
5. *Why were these weapons abandoned?*
6. *What stories are told of the Indians' eagerness to get gunpowder?*
7. *How were the white soldiers protected from the Indian arrows at first?*
8. *Why could not the white men in armor do much harm to the Indians?*
9. *What kind of guns were some of those in use?*
10. *How did the soldier arrange his gun in order to shoot?*
11. *How did he fire his gun?*
12. *If his fuse went out, what was the result?*
13. *How late was the matchlock-gun used?*
14. *What newer gun was coming into use when the colonies were settled?*
15. *How was the flintlock fired off? How are guns made to go off in our time?*
16. *How were some of the white men armed at the time of the settlement of the colonies?*
17. *Was the pike good for Indian war? When did it go out of use in America?*
18. *When the Indians had procured guns, what difference did this make in the value of the armor that the soldiers wore?*
19. *What pieces of the armor used in this country were of metal?*
20. *What sort of a coat was worn for defense?*

Questions for study

WAR CLUB

21. What did the colonists learn from the Indians about marching?
22. What about ambush and the method of loading their guns?
23. What change took place in the mode of making war in winter?
24. What is a snowshoe?
25. What is said of Indian treachery? Tell some of the ingenious tricks to which Indians resorted.
26. Why were the Indians cruel to their prisoners, and given to disfiguring the dead?
27. Why did they kill women and children?
28. What did some tribes do with prisoners after they had put them to death?
29. When they spared a prisoner's life, what did they do with him?
30. What is said of white children adopted by the Indians?
31. What kind of buildings were constructed for the defense of the settlements?
32. How were the people warned that Indians were about?
33. What precautions were taken against discovery by the Indians?
34. What was a common mode of giving alarm in some of the colonies?
35. What must a man do who heard three shots?
36. What were dogs trained to do?
37. What precautions against surprise at church were taken?
38. What effect did the Indian wars have on the people?
39. What is said of wounded soldiers?
40. What is said of the escape of captives?

Study by topics

I. Indian weapons. 1. Their first weapons. 2. The change to those of the white men.
II. Arms of the white men. 1 Their defensive armor. 2. Their firearms. a. Matchlocks. b. Flintlocks. 3. Pikes.
III. Change of armor and tactics. 1 Defensive armor abandoned. 2. Indian tactics adopted.
IV. Character of Indian war. 1. Indian strategy. 2. Cruelty of Indian war. 3. Treatment of prisoners by the Indians.
V. Defense of the settlements. 1. Blockhouses. 2. Alarms. 3. Keeping dogs and carrying arms.
VI. Courage of the people.

Blackboard illustration

Indians change from	bow and arrow stone war club	to	firearms hatchet
White men change from	heavy armor matchlock guns pikes	to	no defensive armor flintlocks no pikes

CHAPTER XVI

Life in the Colonial Time

WHEN people first came to this country, they had to take up with such houses as they could get. In Virginia and New England, as in New York and Philadelphia, holes were dug in the ground for dwelling places by some of the first settlers. In some places bark wigwams were made, like those of the Indians. Sometimes a rude cabin was built of round logs, and without a floor. As time advanced, better houses were built. Some of these were of hewed logs, some of planks, split, or sawed out by hand. The richer people built good houses soon after they came. Most of these had in the middle a large room, called "the hall."

First houses of the colonists

CABIN OF ROUND LOGS

The chimneys were generally very large, with wide fireplaces. Sometimes there were seats inside the fireplace, and children, sitting on these seats in the evening, amused themselves by watching the stars through the top of the chimney. In the early houses most of the windows had paper instead of glass. This paper was oiled, so as to let light come through.

Chimneys and windows

Except in the houses of rich people the furniture was scant and rough. Benches, stools, and tables were home made. Beds were often filled with mistletoe, the down from cattail flags, or the feathers of wild-pigeons. People who were not rich brought their food to the table in wooden

Furniture and dishes

trenchers, or trays, and ate off wooden plates. Some used square blocks of wood instead of plates. Neither rich nor poor, in England or America, had forks when the first colonies were settled. Meat was cut with a knife and eaten from the fingers. On the tables of well-to-do people pewter dishes were much used, and a row of shining pewter in an open cupboard, called a dresser, was a sign of good housekeeping. The richest people had silverware for use on great occasions. They also had stately furniture brought from England. But carpets were hardly ever seen. The floor of the best room was strewed with sand, which was marked off in ornamental figures. There was no wallpaper until long after 1700, but rich cloths and tapestry hung on the walls of the finest houses.

How the colonists cooked their food

Cooking was done in front of fireplaces in skillets and on griddles that stood upon legs, so that coals could be put under them, and in pots and kettles that hung over the fire on a swinging crane, so that they could be drawn out or pushed back. Sometimes there was an oven, for baking, built in the side of the chimney. Meat was roasted on a spit in front of the fire. The spit was an iron rod thrust through the piece to be roasted, and turned by a crank. A whole pig or fowl was sometimes hung up before the fire and turned about while it roasted. Often pieces of meat were broiled by throwing them on the live coals.

What they ate

A mug of home-brewed beer, with bread and cheese, or a porridge of peas or beans, boiled with a little meat, constituted the breakfast of the early colonists. Neither tea nor coffee was known in England or this country until long after the first colonies were settled. When tea came in, it became a fashionable drink, and was served to company from pretty little china cups, set on lacquered tables. Mush, made of Indian corn meal, was eaten for supper.

In proportion to the population, more wine and spirits What they drank were consumed at that time than now. The very strong

A WEDDING IN NEW AMSTERDAM

Madeira wine was drunk at genteel tables. Rum, which from its destructive effects was known everywhere by the nickname of "kill-devil," was much used then. At every social gathering rum was provided. Hard cider was a common drink. There was much shameful drunkenness. Peach brandy was used in the Middle and Southern colonies, and was very ruinous to health and morals.

What they wore   People of wealth made great display in their dress. Much lace and many silver buckles and buttons were worn. Workingmen of all sorts wore leather, deerskin, or coarse canvas breeches. The stockings worn by men were long, the breeches were short, and buckled, or otherwise fastened, at the knees.

A CALASH

Our forefathers traveled about in canoes and little sailing boats called shallops. Most of the canoes would hold about six men, but some were large enough to hold forty or more. For a long time there were no roads except Indian trails and bridle paths, which could only be traveled on foot or on horseback. Goods were carried on pack horses. When roads were made, wagons came into use.

How they traveled

Their education   In a life so hard and busy as that of the early settlers, there was little time for education. The schools were few and generally poor. Boys, when taught at all, learned to read, write,

BIRCH CANOES

and "cast accounts." Girls were taught even less. Many of the children born when the colonies were new grew up unable to write their names. There were few books at first, and no newspapers until after 1700. There was little to occupy the mind except the Sunday sermon.

In all the colonies people were very fond of dancing parties. Weddings were times of great excitement and often of much drinking. In some of the colonies wedding festivities were continued for several days. Even funerals were occasions of feasting, and sometimes of excessive drinking. In the Middle and Southern colonies the people were fond of horse racing, cock fighting, and many other rude sports brought from England. New England people made their militia trainings the occasions for feasting and amusement, fighting sham battles, and playing many rough, old-fashioned games. Coasting on the snow, skating, and sleighing were first brought into America from Holland by the Dutch settlers in New York. In all the colonies there was a great deal of hunting and fishing. The woods were full of deer and wild turkeys. Flocks of pigeons often darkened the sky, and the rivers were alive with waterfowl and fish.

Their amusements

DUTCH WOMAN OF THE TIME SKATING

1. *Mention some of the houses, or other shelters, used when people first came to this country.*
2. *How were planks for houses made in the early times?*
3. *What kind of houses did the richer people build?*
4. *What sort of chimneys did they have in that time?*
5. *What is said of the seats in the fireplace?*
6. *How did the windows of the early settlers differ from ours?*
7. *What sort of furniture was there in the houses?*
8. *What is said of benches stools, and tables?*
9. *How were beds often filled?*
10. *In what kind of dishes was meat served?*

Questions for study

11. From what kind of plates did they eat?
12. What about forks?
13. How did they eat meat in that day?
14. What kind of dishes were on the tables of people better off? How was the pewter kept?
15. What kind of ware did the richest people have? What kind of furniture? What is said of carpets?
16. How was the floor of the best room ornamented?

PACK HORSES

17. What was used in fine houses in place of our wallpaper?
18. How was the cooking done?
19. Where was there sometimes an oven?
20. What was it used for?
21. How was meat roasted?
22. What was a spit? How were pigs and fowls roasted?
23. How was meat sometimes broiled?
24. What kind of a breakfast was eaten by the early colonists?
25. What is said of tea and coffee?
26. How was tea served?
27. What was much used for supper?
28. What is said of the use of wine and spirits then, as compared with the use of those drinks now?
29. What kind of wine was drunk?
30. What is said of the use of rum then?

31. What of hard cider? What of drunkenness? What kind of brandy was used?
32. With what results?
33. How did rich people dress?
34. What sort of breeches did workingmen wear?
35. What sort of stockings?
36. How were the breeches fastened at the knees?
37. How did our forefathers travel about?
38. How large were the largest canoes? What was the common size of the canoe? What kind of roads did they have at first?
39. How did they travel overland?
40. How were goods carried?
41. What change took place when roads were made?
42. Why was there not much education given to children born in the colonies at first?
43. What kind of schools did they have?
44. What were boys taught?
45. How were girls taught?
46. Did all the children get some education?
47. What is said of books and newspapers?
48. What was there to occupy the mind?
49. Of what kind of parties were people fond in all the colonies?
50. What is said of weddings? Of funerals?
51. What amusements were people fond of in the Middle and Southern colonies?
52. What was made a time for amusement in New England?
53. What kind of games were played on training-days?
54. From what country were coasting, skating, and sleighing brought to America?
55. What is said of hunting and fishing?
56. What of the abundance of game and fish?

1. Houses.
   a. Various kinds of dwellings. b. Chimneys. c. Windows.
2. Furniture.
   a. Seats, tables, and beds. b. Tableware. c. Floor and wall coverings.
3. Food,
   a. How cooked. b. Kinds of food. c. Drinks.
4. Dress.
5. Travel.
6. Education.
7. Amusements.

Study by topics

A SCHOOL SCENE IN 1740. THE MASTER AND HIS ASSISTANT WEAR HATS.

CHAPTER XVII

Farming and Shipping in the Colonies

Early experiments in silk raising, vine growing, etc.

WE have seen how the people who came first to North America expected to find either a way to India, or mines like those discovered farther southward. But when they found that they could not secure either the spices of India or the gold and silver of Peru, they turned their attention to the soil, to see what could be got by farming. But at first their plans for farming in America were as wild as their plans for getting to India. They spent much time in trying to produce silk and wine, two things which can be raised with profit only in old and well-settled countries. They also tried to raise madder, coffee, tea, olives, and the cocoa bean, from which chocolate is made.

Tobacco growing in Virginia and Maryland

John Rolfe, the husband of Pocahontas, in 1612 took a lesson from the Indian fields about him, and succeeded in growing tobacco for the English market. Before this time, English smokers and snuff-takers got their tobacco from the Spaniards. The plant was well suited to the Virginia climate, and it was easy to ship tobacco from the farms, which were all on the banks of the rivers. Gold and silver coins were scarce in those days, and, in half a dozen years after John Rolfe planted the first tobacco, it had become the only money of Virginia. Almost everything bought and sold in Virginia and Maryland, before the Revolution, was paid for in tobacco.

Rice produced in South Carolina

The colony of South Carolina maintained itself in a rather poor way, during the first twenty-six years of its existence, chiefly by shipping lumber to the West Indies, and by making tar and pitch. But there was living in Charleston, in 1696, a gentleman named Thomas Smith, who had seen rice cultivated in Madagascar. One day when a sea-captain, an old friend of Smith's, sailed into Charleston Harbor from Madagascar, Thomas Smith got from him a bag of seed-rice. This was carefully sown in a wet place in Smith's garden in Charleston. It grew, and soon Carolina was changed into a land of great rice plantations. The raising of rice spread into Georgia when that colony was settled.

In 1741 an energetic young lady, Miss Eliza Lucas, began to try experiments in growing the indigo plant in South Carolina. A frost destroyed the first crop that she planted, and a worm cut down the next. The indigo maker brought from the West Indies tried to deceive her afterward, but by 1745 this persevering young lady had proved that indigo could be grown in South Carolina, and in two years more two hundred thousand pounds of it were exported. It was a leading crop for about fifty years, but, when the growing of cotton was made profitable by the invention of the cotton gin, that crop took the place of indigo. (See Chapter LX.)

Eliza Lucas introduces Indigo-culture

Indian corn the settlers got from the Indians. It was unknown in Europe. From it was made the most of the bread eaten by Americans before the Revolution. It was also shipped to the West Indies from Virginia and North Carolina. New York, New Jersey, and Pennsylvania formed the great wheat region of the colonial time. These colonies sent wheat, flour, and "hard tack" bread in large quantities to the West Indies and the countries on the Mediterranean Sea. Many thousands of great country wagons were employed in bringing grain to Philadelphia. Potatoes had been brought to Europe probably from South America; but they were unknown to the Indians in what is now the United States. They were taken

Indian corn, wheat, and potatoes

FLAG OF NEW YORK
MERCHANT SHIPS.

to Virginia at the first settlement of Jamestown. Potatoes were not planted in New England fields until 1718.

Cattle, hogs, and horses

Cattle and hogs were brought from England very early, and were grown by thousands in the colonies. For the most part they ran in the woods, having marks on them to show to whom they belonged. Many cattle grew up without marks of ownership, and were hunted as wild. There were "cow-pens" established for raising cattle in the wilderness, something like the "ranches" in the Western country today. The horses of that day were small and hardy. When not in use they ran at large in the woods, and some of them quite escaped from their owners, so that after a while there came to be a race of wild horses. It was accounted rare sport to ride after a wild horse until he was tired out, and so to capture him.

The English plow of that time was very heavy, and drawn by six horses or as many oxen. Efforts were made to introduce this to the colonies, but it was not suited to a new country. The plow most used in the colonies was a clumsy thing, with thin plates of iron nailed over the rude wooden plowshares. There were many stumps and few plows. All the tools were heavy and awkward.

Farming implements

The middle colonies raised wheat, the colonies on Chesapeake Bay tobacco, and the Southern colonies rice and indigo; but the soil and climate of New England were not suited to any agricultural staple of great value. So the New Englanders were driven to follow the sea. They built immense numbers of ships, some of which they sold to English merchants; others they used in fishing for codfish and mackerel. These fisheries became very profitable to them. When the Long Island-

COLONIAL PLOW

The Pirates—Captain William Kidd, of New York, was sent out in 1695 to put down the pirates that infested the Indian Ocean. The expense of his outfit was borne by certain gentlemen in America and England, who were to share his spoils. Not falling in with any pirates, he took to piratical ways himself. When he came back to America he was arrested by Lord Bellemont, Governor of New York and New England, and sent to London for trial and execution. In 1717, Steed Bonnet and Richard Worley, two pirates with their crews, had taken possession of the mouth of Cape Fear River in North Carolina, whence they committed great depredations on the commerce of South Carolina. Colonel Rhett, of South Carolina, pursued Bonnet into Cape Fear River, and, after a fight, captured him and thirty of his men. They were tried and hanged at Charleston. Governor Johnson, of South Carolina, took another vessel and attacked Richard Worley and his pirates, who fought until all were dead but Worley and one man, and these were taken, desperately wounded, and hanged. Blackbeard, whose real name was Teach, had his refuge also in the shallow waters of the North Carolina coast. A little more than a year after the overthrow of Bonnet, Lieutenant Maynard sailed from Virginia and fought Blackbeard in Ocracoke Inlet. After a hand-to-hand battle all the pirates were killed or wounded, and Maynard sailed back with Blackbeard's head hanging at his bowsprit. So many of the pirates were captured in the next half-dozen years that they gave little trouble afterward.

ers discovered the art of taking whales along the coast, the New England people learned it, and became the most prosperous whalers in the world. The products of their fisheries were sent to many countries, and New England ships were seen almost all over the world. Boston and Newport were the chief New England seaports.

Fishing, whaling, and seagoing in New England

ENSIGN CARRIED BY NEW ENGLAND SHIPS

The people of New York also built many ships which were remarkable for their great size and the long voyages they made. But before the Revolution New York was not so large a town as Boston. Philadelphia, which was started later than the other leading cities, grew fast and became the greatest of all the cities in the colonies. But Philadelphia contained only about thirty thousand people when the Revolution broke out.

Trade in New York and Philadelphia

There were many pirates on the coast, who sometimes grew so numerous and bold as to interrupt trade. Some of

Pirates

PIRATE BLACKBEARD
AS SHOWN IN A
PICTURE OF THE TIME

them were caught and hanged. Captain Kidd, of New York, who was sent to put down pirates, became a pirate himself, and was taken to London and there hanged. The most noted of the pirates was a cruel desperado called Blackbeard, who was killed after a bloody fight in Ocracoke Inlet in North Carolina. Steed Bonnet, another famous pirate, was captured about the same time and executed at Charleston.

Questions for study

1. *What did those who came first to North America expect to find?*
2. *When they failed to find a way to India, or gold-mines, to what did they look for profit?*
3. *What was the character of their first plans for farming?*
4. *In what kind of countries is the raising of wine and silk profitable? What mistake did the colonists make about these things?*
5. *Mention some of the things which they tried to cultivate. What is the name of the man who first raised tobacco in Virginia to send to England?*
6. *What was the name of Rolfe's wife?*
7. *What advantages did Virginia have for raising and shipping this plant?*
8. *What was the principal money of the Virginians and Marylanders?*
9. *How did the colony of South Carolina maintain itself at first?*
10. *Where had Thomas Smith seen rice growing? How did he get his seed-rice? Where did he sow it first?*
11. *What was the result?*
12. *Who first introduced the indigo-plant into South Carolina?*
13. *What discouragements did she meet with?*
14. *What had she proved by 1745?*
15. *What was the result?*
16. *What at last drove indigo out of cultivation?*
17. *What was the chief bread of the colonists?*
18. *Where did the colonists get the Indian-corn plant?*
19. *Had it been known in Europe?*
20. *From what colonies was Indian corn sent to the West Indies?*
21. *What three colonies constituted the great wheat region?*
22. *Where were wheat and flour sent to in that time?*
23. *From what part of the world were potatoes taken to Europe?*
24. *Were they known to the natives in what is now the United States?*
25. *How early were potatoes first planted in Virginia?*
26. *In what year were they first planted in New England?*
27. *Where were the first cattle and hogs in this country brought from?*
28. *How were they raised?*
29. *Were they numerous?*
30. *What is said of wild cattle? How were cattle sometimes raised away from settlements in the wilderness?*

31. *What were these ranches called at that time?*
32. *What was the character of the horses of the time?*
33. *What kind of a plow was used in England when America was first settled?*
34. *What kind of plow was commonly used in America?*
35. *What was the general character of the tools used?*
36. *What drove the New England people to follow the sea for a living?*
37. *What did they do with the great numbers of ships built in New England?*
38. *What kinds of fish did they catch?*
39. *Who in America first learned to take whales?*
40. *What is said of the whale-fisheries of New England?*
41. *What of the trade of New England? Which were the chief seaports of New England?*
42. *What is said of the trade of New York in colony times?*
43. *What of Philadelphia?*
44. *How many people were there in Philadelphia before the Revolution?*
45. *What is said of pirates before the Revolution?*
46. *Where was Captain Kidd executed?*
47. *Where was Blackbeard killed?*
48. *Where was the pirate Steed Bonnet executed?*

1. Products. Study by topics
   a. The attempts to raise silk, wine, etc. b. Tobacco. c. Rice. d. Indigo. e. Indian corn. f. Wheat. g. Potatoes.
2. Animals.
   a. Cattle and hogs. b. Horses.
3. Implements.
   a. Plows. b. Other tools.
4. Commerce.
   a. New England fisheries and commerce. b. Trade of New York and Philadelphia. c. The pirates.

Chief wheat region	{	New York. New Jersey Pennsylvania	Blackboard
Chief tobacco region	{	Maryland Virginia, Northern part of North Carolina
Rice and indigo	{	South Carolina Southern part of North Carolina
Shipbuilding fisheries, and trade	{	New England colonies

Point out on a map the location of Madagascar and Ocracoke Inlet. Point out the chief wheat region in colony times. The chief tobacco region. The land of rice and indigo. Geography

CHAPTER XVIII

Bondservants and Slaves in the Colonies.

Tenants   WHEN the English people came to this country they brought English ways with them. In England at that time the lands of rich men were cultivated by tenants, who not only paid rent, but owed much respect and service to their "lord," as they called the owner of their lands. If these tenants did not pay their rent faithfully, they could be punished. Many of the people sent to Virginia at first were tenants, who were expected to work on other people's land in a sort of subjection. They were to pay half of all they produced to the landowner, and they were bound to stay on the land for seven years. Tenants were also sent to Maryland, and the Dutch established the same system in New York.

Bondservants   Besides tenants, there were sent to Virginia people of a poorer class, who were called "indentured servants." Those sent at first were poor boys and girls, bound to serve until they were of age. After a while there were sent to Virginia and to New England adult servants, bound to serve for seven or ten years, but afterward they were only required to serve four years to pay their passage. This way of getting laborers became very common, and many thousands were sent over in this temporary bondage. During the time of their bondage they could be bought and sold like slaves. They were often whipped and otherwise cruelly treated when they chanced to fall into the hands of hardhearted masters.

There were people in England at that time called "spirits" and "crimps." By many false stories they persuaded poor men to go to the colonies as servants. Sometimes the crimps

ENGLISH FARM
LABORER, SEVEN-
TEENTH CENTURY

entrapped a man aboard ship, where he was detained and carried off to the colonies against his will. This was called "trepanning" a man. Sometimes they kidnapped or "spirited" away children, and sold them into service in the colonies. Sometimes people who wished to inherit an estate

KIDNAPPING A MAN FOR THE COLONIES

sent away the true heir and had him sold in America. One lad, who would have been Lord Annesley, was entrapped on shipboard by his uncle and sold into Pennsylvania. He was twelve years in bondage, after which he returned to

England and proved his right to the lordship, though he died before he came into possession of it.

Great number of bondservants or "redemptioners" Bondservants were in some places called "redemptioners." About 1670 fifteen hundred of them were sold in Virginia every year. In Pennsylvania the men who took droves of redemptioners about the country and peddled them to the farmers were called "soul-drivers." Many of the bondservants, when their time was out, got land and grew rich. But the lot of the poor man was much harder in that time than in our day.

Convict-servants The English laws in old times were very severe against small crimes. A man could be hanged for stealing bread to satisfy his hunger. Many people sentenced to death for small offenses were pardoned on condition of their going to the colonies. In America convicts were sold for seven years. The Americans complained bitterly that such bad people were forced on them.

Introduction of slaves In 1619, the year that the Great Charter reached Virginia, there came a Dutch ship into James River, which sold nineteen Negroes to the planters. They were the first slaves in America. In that day it was thought right to make slaves of Negroes because they were heathens; but for a long time the number of slaves that came into the colonies was small. White bondservants did the most of the work in Maryland and Virginia until about the close of the seventeenth century, when the high price of tobacco caused a great many Negroes to be brought. About the same time the introduction of rice into South Carolina created a great demand for slaves.

There were slaves in all the colonies. But in the colonies far to the north there was no crop that would make their labor profitable. Negroes in New England were mostly kept for house servants. In New York city and in Philadelphia there were a great many, but not many in the country regions about these cities, where wheat was the chief crop, for wheat did not require much hard labor. The larger number of Negroes were taken to the colonies which raised tobacco, rice, and indigo. Negroes were especially fitted to endure a hot and malarial climate. After the Revolution, slavery was abolished in the colonies that had few Negroes. But, where almost all the labor was done by slaves, it was much harder to get rid of slavery. This led to the difference between free and slave states, and at last to our civil war.

Distribution of slaves

SIR JOHN HAWKINS, THE FIRST ENGLISH SLAVE TRADER

The slaves at first did not speak English, and they practiced many wild African customs. Some of them were fierce, and the white people were afraid of them. Great harshness was used to subdue them. The Negroes often made bloody insurrections, which were put down with great harshness. One of these was in New York city in 1712, Twenty-four Negroes were put to death on this occasion, some of them in the cruel ways used in that time. In 1740 there was an uprising of slaves in South Carolina, and a battle between them and the white people, in which the Negroes were routed. In 1741 on a bare alarm of intended insurrection, thirty-three slaves were executed in New York, thirteen of them by fire. Like severity was shown in other colonies, for people were more cruel in that day than in later times.

Character of the slaves. Insurrections

1. *What English system of cultivating land was brought to Virginia at the first?*
2. *What could be done with a tenant if he did not pay his rent?*
3. *What share of the produce of the land did the tenant pay to his lord?*
4. *How long was the tenant bound to stay on the land?*
5. *To what other English colony were tenants sent?*
6. *Where did the Dutch establish the same system?*

Questions for study

7. What other class besides tenants were sent to Virginia?
8. What were most of these at first?
9. What other servants were after a while sent to Virginia and New England?
10. What is the meaning of "adult?"
11. How long were these adult servants bound to serve?
12. Were there many or few of this sort?
13. In what respect were these servants like slaves?
14. How were they often treated?
15. What was the business of the people called "spirits" or "crimps"?
16. How did they sometimes send men against their will?
17. What was this called?
18. How did they procure children to sell to the colonists?
19. How were the heirs to estates treated in some cases?
20. Tell what happened to little Lord Annesley.
21. What were white bondservants called?
22. How many of these were yearly sold into Virginia about 1670?
23. What were the men called who took droves of redemptioners through Pennsylvania to sell?
24. What happened to many of these servants?
25. What was the character of the English laws against small crimes at this time?
26. What was done with some of the people who were sentenced to death for petty offenses?
27. How long a time were the convicts sold for?
28. What did the Americans think of this plan of sending convicts to this country?
29. In what year were Negroes first brought to Virginia?
30. By what kind of a ship?
31. What other notable event happened in Virginia in this year?
32. Why was it thought right to make slaves of Negroes?
33. Were many Negroes brought at first?
34. Who did most of the labor?
35. What caused a great many Negroes to be brought to Virginia and Maryland about the close of the seventeenth century?
36. What caused many slaves to be brought to South Carolina near the same time?
37. Why were there fewer slaves in the Northern colonies than in those farther south?
38. For what were slaves mostly kept in New England?
39. In what two cities of the middle colonies were there a great many Negro slaves?
40. Were there many slaves in the country regions of New York and Pennsylvania? Why not?
41. To what colonies were the larger number of Negroes taken?
42. Why was it easier to abolish slavery in the Northern colonies than the Southern?
43. What caused the difference between free and slave states? What war grew out of this difference?

44. *What peculiarities had the Negroes when they first came?*
45. *What was the character of some of them?*
46. *What took place among the Negroes in New York in 1712?*
47. *How many Negroes were put to death?*
48. *What happened in South Carolina in 1740?*
49. *What took place in New York in 1741?*
50. *How many were put to death?*
51. *How were some of these executed?*
52. *In what way did the people of that time differ from people in our day?*

I. White tenants and servants.
    1. Tenants.
    2. Indentured servants
    3. Trepanning and kidnapping.
    4 Redemptioners and soul-drivers.
    5. Convict-servants
II. Negro slaves.
    1. The first slaves in 1619.
    2. Increase of slaves after 1700.
    3. Negro slaves at the North and at the South.
    4 Character of the Negroes and their treatment.
    5. Negro insurrections.

Study by topics

CHAPTER XIX

Laws and Usages in the Colonies

OUR forefathers brought many curious old customs and laws from England. The laws of that time were very meddlesome. Men were punished for lying, which nowadays we think is only to be cured by good example and good teaching. A fine was imposed on profane swearing by the laws of nearly all the colonies; in New England the tongue of the swearer was sometimes pinched in the opening of a split stick. In all the colonies there were laws about keeping the Sabbath; in many of them there were punishments for not going to church. In New England the Sunday laws were rigorously enforced, and the Sabbath was made to begin at sunset on Saturday evening. The people were at first called to church by beating a drum in the streets For more than a hundred years after the

Laws against lying, profanity and sabbath-breaking

settlement of Massachusetts, people were not allowed to sit in Boston Common on Sunday, or to walk in the streets except to church, or to take a breath of air on a hot Sunday by the seashore directly in front of their own doors. Two young people were arrested in Connecticut for sitting together on Sunday under a tree in an orchard.

Laws against scolding and drunkenness

If men were punished for swearing, women were also forbidden to be too free with their tongues. In Virginia and some other colonies women, for scolding or slander, were put upon a ducking-stool and dipped in the water. In New England they were gagged and set by their own doors, "for all comers and goers to

THE DUCKING STOOL

gaze at." Drunkards were sometimes obliged to wear a red letter D about their necks, and other offenses were punished by suspending a letter, or a picture, or a halter about the neck.

Other curious punishments

Standing with the head and hands fast in the pillory, to be pelted with eggs by the crowd, and sitting with the feet fast in the stocks, were forms of punishment. In some places there were cages, in which criminals were confined in sight of the people. Punishments in the pillory and stocks, or in a cage, were inflicted on some occasion of public concourse—a lecture day or a market day—to make the shame greater. More severe than stocks or pillory were the customary punishments of whipping on the bare back, cropping or boring the ears, and branding the hand with a hot iron. There were also sometimes, for great crimes cruel punishments of burning alive. Or hanging alive in chains, but these were very rare.

THE STOCKS

Charms against witches

Our forefathers were more superstitious than people are now, and they were very much afraid of witches. This foolish belief in witchcraft prevailed both in England and America. People sometimes nailed up horse shoes, or hung up laurel-boughs in their houses, to protect themselves from magic charms. When butter would not come for churning, red-hot horseshoes were dropped into the milk to "burn the witch out." When pigs were sick and thought to be bewitched, their ears and tails were cut off and burned. There were people tried in almost every colony for witchcraft. In England and in many other countries, executions for witchcraft were more common than in any of the colonies.

Of the many excitements about witchcraft in the colonies, the one that went to the greatest extreme was that in

The Salem witchcraft excitement

Salem, Massachusetts, in 1692. So great was the agitation that the most serious people lost their self-possession, and some poor people even believed themselves to be witches, and confessed it. In the fright and indignation that prevailed, twenty people were executed, and the jails were crowded with the accused. One fourth of the inhabitants of Salem moved away, afraid either of the witches or of being charged with witchcraft. At length reason returned to the people, the prisoners were released, and there was the deepest grief that the fanaticism had gone so far. There has never been an execution for witchcraft in this country from that day to this, though there are still some ignorant people who believe in such things.

PUNISHMENT OF A DRUNKARD

In most of the colonies there was, at some time persecution for religious opinions. In Virginia, only the Church of England form of worship was allowed at first, and Catholics, Puritans, Quakers, Presbyterians and Baptists were persecuted. In Massachusetts, for a long time, only the Puritan or Congregational worship, as set up by law, was allowed. Those who advocated other doctrines were punished, and many Quakers were whipped, and some of them even put to death for coming back after they had been banished. Lord Baltimore wished to give toleration in Maryland to all who believed in Christ, but the

Religious persecution in the colonies

lawmakers of Maryland afterward made laws to annoy those who were of Lord Baltimore's own religion, the Roman Catholic. Roger Williams, who was banished from Massachusetts for his opinions, founded what is now called Rhode Island, on the plan of entire liberty in religious matters. He went further than Lord Baltimore, and gave to Hebrews and to unbelievers the same liberty with Christians. In Pennsylvania, where the Friends or Quakers were in the majority, there was toleration; and persecution ceased in all the colonies before the Revolution.

1. *What did our forefathers bring from England?*
2. *What difference was there between their treatment of lying and ours?*
3. *How was profane Swearing treated?*
4. *What kind of laws were there in all the colonies about the Sabbath?*
5. *And in nearly all about churchgoing?*
6. *At what time did the New England Sabbath begin?*
7. *What examples are given of the strictness of the Sabbath law in Boston for more than a hundred years?*
8. *What example is given of the law in Connecticut?*
9. *How were women punished in some of the colonies for scolding and slander?*
10. *How were they punished in New England?*
11. *How were drunkards punished sometimes?*
12. *How was a man punished in the pillory? In Cages?*
13. *What punishments are mentioned as more severe than the pillory or the cage?*
14. *What very cruel punishments were sometimes visited on great crimes?*
15. *What is said of the superstitiousness of our forefathers?*
16. *What did people do in former times to keep off the evil charms of witches?*
17. *When they thought that the churning of milk was bewitched what did they do?*
18. *What did they do in the case of bewitched pigs?*
19. *What is said of witchcraft trials in nearly all the colonies? In England?*
20. *Where was the worst of all the witchcraft excitements in America? In what year?*
21. *What was the effect of the agitation?*
22. *How many people were executed?*
23. *Were these all who were accused?*
24. *What was the effect on the population of Salem?*
25. *When reason returned to the people, what was done?*
26. *How did they feel about it?*
27. *Has there ever been an execution for witchcraft in this country since?*

Questions for study

28. Was religious persecution common in the colonies?
29. What form of religion was established in Virginia?
30. What denominations were persecuted there?
31. What was the established religion in Massachusetts?
32. What was done to the advocates of other doctrines?
33. What happened to Quakers in Massachusetts?
34. What did Lord Baltimore wish to do in the matter of religious toleration?
35. What did the lawmakers of Maryland afterward do?
36. From what colony was Roger Williams banished?
37. What colony did he found?
38. On what plan did he establish it?
39. How did he go further than Lord Baltimore?
40. Was there persecution in Pennsylvania?
41. What religious denomination held control there?
42. How had they been treated in the other colonies?
43. What change took place in the matter of persecution. Before the Revolution?

Study by   I. Laws against lying, swearing, Sabbath-breaking, scolding, and drunkenness.
topics   II. Old-fashioned punishments.
            III. Superstitions.
                1. The fear of witches.
                2. The Salem witchcraft delusion.
            IV. Religious persecution.
                1. Persecution in Virginia.
                2. Persecution in Massachusetts.
                3. Lord Baltimore's plan for Maryland.
                4. Roger Williams and Rhode Island.
                5. Toleration in Pennsylvania.

SECOND REVIEW—LIFE IN THE COLONIES.

First Division: The Indians and the White People.

I. Indian life. (Chapter XIII)

    1. Appearance and dress of the Indians.
    2. Their houses, furniture, and food.
    3. Their occupations and tools.
    4. Their trade with white men,

II. Their wars with the white people. (Chapter XIV)

    1. The first massacre and war in Virginia.
    2. The Pequot war.
    3. King Philip's war.
    4. Bacon's war in Virginia,
    5.Wars in South and North Carolina.

III. Methods of early Indian war. (Chapter XV)

  1. The primitive weapons of the Indians.
  2. Pikes, matchlock guns, and armor of the white man.
  3. Change of arms by Indians and white men.
  4. Indian modes of fighting.
  5. Captives among the Indians.
  6. How settlers defended themselves.

  Second Division: Life and Labor among the Colonists.

  1. Homelife in the colonies. (Chapter XVI) I. Various sorts of houses.
  2. Furniture.
  3. Food and drinks.
  4. Dress.
  5. Modes of travel and of carrying freight.
  6. Education.
  7. Amusements.

 II. Farming and commerce in the colonies. (Chapter XVII)

  1. Silk, wine, and other experiments.
  2. Tobacco raising
  3. Rice and indigo.
  4. Corn, wheat, and potatoes.
  5. Cattle, hogs, horses.
  6. Farming utensils.
  7. Commerce and fisheries.
  8. Pirates.

III. Bondservants and slaves. (Chapter XVIII)

  1. Tenants.
  2. Bondservants, crimps, etc.
  3. Convict-servants.
  4. Slaves.   a. Introduction of them, 1619.   b. Distribution of slaves.
      c. Insurrections and punishments.

IV. Laws and customs. (Chapter XIX)

  1. Sabbath laws.
  2. Curious punishments.
  3. Laws about witchcraft. The Salem excitement.
  4. Persecutions for religion.

CHAPTER XX

The Spanish in Florida and the French in Canada

The Spanish colony in Florida   THE English were not the only people who had colonies in North America. The Spaniards, who claimed the whole continent, had planted a colony at Saint Au´-gus-tine, in Florida, in 1565, forty-two years before the first permanent English colony landed at Jamestown. Saint Augustine is thus the oldest city in the United States. But the Spaniards were too busy in Mexico and in Central and South America to push their settlements farther to the north, though they were very jealous of the English colonies, and especially of South Carolina and Georgia.

Founding of Quebec by Champlain   The French laid claim also to a large part of North America. They tried to plant a colony in Canada in 1549 and afterward made some other attempts that failed. Quebec [kwe-bec´] was founded by a great French explorer, Champlain, in 1608, the very year after the English settled at Jamestown. At Quebec the real settlement of Canada was begun, and it was always the capital of the vast establishments of the French in America.

French explorations in the interior   The French, like the English, were trying to find the Pacific Ocean, and they were much more daring in their explorations than the English colonists, whose chief business was farming. A French explorer named Joliet [zhōl-yay] reached the Mississippi in 1673, and another Frenchman, La Salle [lah-sahl], explored the great country west of the Allegheny Mountains, and discovered the Ohio. After many disasters and failures, La Salle succeeded in reaching the mouth of the Mississippi. Father Hennepin, a priest, explored the upper Mississippi. The French then laid claim to all the country west of

CHAMPLAIN

the Alleghenies. Over the region they established posts and mission houses, while the English contented themselves with multiplying their farming settlements east of the mountains.

Spanish Discoveries in Florida—
Ponce de Leon [pōn´-thay day lay-ōn; commonly in English, pons deh lee´-on], an old Spanish explorer, set sail in 1513 from the island of Porto Rico, to discover a land reported to lie to the northward of Cuba, and which had somehow come to be called Bimini [bee-mee-nee]. It was said to contain a fountain, by bathing in which an old man would be made young again. On Easter Sunday Ponce discovered the mainland, which he called Florida, from Pascua Florida [pas´-kwah floree´-dah], the Spanish name for Easter Sunday. In 1521 Ponce tried to settle Florida, but his party was attacked and he was mortally wounded by the Indians. Florida was then believed to be an island. After his death, other Spanish adventurers explored the coast from Labrador southward; and even tried to find gold mines, and plant colonies in the interior of the country. The most famous of these expeditions was that of Hernando de Soto [aer-nan´-do day so´-to], a Spanish explorer, who reached Florida in 1539. He marched through Georgia, Alabama, and Mississippi. He was determined to find some land yielding gold, like Mexico and Peru. But he treated the Indians cruelly, killing some of them wantonly, and forcing others to serve him as slaves. The savages, in turn, attacked him again and again, until his party was sadly reduced. De Soto tried to descend the Mississippi River to the Gulf of Mexico, but at the mouth of the Red River he died of a fever. His body was buried in the Mississippi, to keep the Indians from disfiguring it in revenge. A few of his followers reached the Gulf and got to the Spanish settlements in Mexico.

When La Salle reached the mouth of the Mississippi, he took possession of the country in the name of Louis XIV., and called it Louisiana, in honor of that king. The settlement of Louisiana was begun in 1699. The French held the St. Lawrence and the Mississippi, the two great waterways of North America, and they controlled most of the Indian tribes by means of missionaries and traders. They endeavored to connect Canada and Louisiana by a chain of fortified posts, and so to hold for France an empire, in the heart of America, larger than France itself.

Founding of Louisiana and of French posts among the Indians

LA SALLE

But the weakness of the French in America lay in the fewness of their people.

Weakness and strength of the French in America

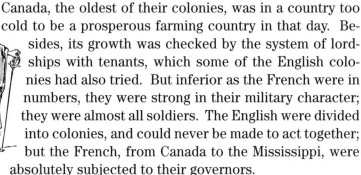

FRENCH GENTLE-
MAN OF THE TIME

Canada, the oldest of their colonies, was in a country too cold to be a prosperous farming country in that day. Besides, its growth was checked by the system of lordships with tenants, which some of the English colonies had also tried. But inferior as the French were in numbers, they were strong in their military character; they were almost all soldiers. The English were divided into colonies, and could never be made to act together; but the French, from Canada to the Mississippi, were absolutely subjected to their governors.

The French influence over the Indians

The French were also rendered terrible to the English colonies by their skill in controlling the Indians. The great business of the French in Canada was the fur trade, and this was pushed with an energy that quite left the English traders behind. The French drew furs from the shores of Lake Superior and from beyond the Mississippi. The French traders gained great influence over the Indians. The English treated the Indians as inferiors, the French lived among them on terms of equality. The French also gained control of the Indian tribes by means of missionary priests, who risked their lives and spent their days in the dirty cabins of the savages to teach them religion. The powerful Iroquois confederacy, known as the "Five Nations," and afterward as the "Six Nations," sided with the English, and hated and killed the French. They lived in what is now the State of New York. But the most of the tribes were managed by the French, who sent missionaries to convert them, ambassadors to flatter them, gunsmiths to mend their arms, and military men to teach them to fortify, and to direct their attacks against the settlements of the English.

The wars between the French colony in Canada and the English colonies in what is now the United States were

A MISSIONARY
PRIEST

caused partly by wars between France and England in Europe. But there were also causes enough for enmity in the state of affairs on this side of the ocean. First, there was always a quarrel about territory. The French claimed that part of what is now the State of Maine which lies east of the Kennebec River, while the English claimed to the St. Croix. The French also claimed all the country back of the Alleghenies. With a population not more than one twentieth of that of one of the English colonies, they spread their claim over all the country watered by the lakes and the tributaries of the Mississippi, including more than half of the present United States. Second, both France and England wished to control the fisheries of the eastern coast. Third, both the French and the English endeavored to get the entire control of the fur trade. To do this the French tried to win the Iroquois Confederacy to their interest, while the English sought to take the trade of the Western tribes away from the French. Fourth, the French were Catholics and the English mostly Protestants. In that age men were very bigoted about religion, and hated and feared those who differed from them.

Subjects of dispute between the French and English in America

COREUR DES BOIS, OR
WANDERING FUR TRADER OF
CANADA

1. *When did the Spaniards plant a colony in Florida?*
2. *Whereabouts in Florida did the Spaniards first settle?*
3. *Which is the oldest city in the United States?*
4. *How long before the settlement at Jamestown was St. Augustine settled?*
   [Subtract 1565 from 1607.]
5. *Why did the Spaniards not push their settlements farther to the north?*
6. *What feelings did they have about South Carolina and Georgia?*
7. *How much of North America did Spain claim?*

Questions for study

LONGHOUSE OF THE IROQUOIS

8. Where was the beginning of permanent French settlements in America made?
9. By whom was Quebec founded?
10. In what year?
11. How long was this after English settlement at Jamestown?
12. What was the capital and center of the French establishments in America?
13. What were the French trying to find?
14. How did their explorations compare with those of the English?
15. What was the chief business of the people in the English colonies?
16. Who discovered the Mississippi in 1673?
17. Who first explored the Ohio River?
18. Who descended the Mississippi to its mouth?
19. What large city is now situated near the mouth of the Mississippi?
20. What is the name of the priest who first explored the upper Mississippi?
21. To what part of this country did the French lay claim?
22. What did they establish here?
23. What were the English colonists doing at this time?
24. What did La Salle call the country at the mouth of the Mississippi?
25. In honor of what king did he thus call it?
26. When was the settlement of Louisiana begun?
27. What two great waterways did the French control at this time?

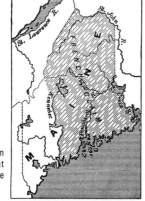

French claim to the present State of Maine

28. How did they propose to connect Canada and Louisiana?
29. What would they thus hold for France?
30. What was the weakness of the French power in America?
31. Why was Canada not a prosperous farming country?
32. What held its growth in check?
33. How were the French strong?
34. Which were the most united, the English or the French, in America?
35. What besides this rendered the French terrible to the English?
36. What was the chief business of the French in Canada?
37. From how far to the west did they get furs?
38. What difference was there in the French and the English way of treating the Indians?
39. What is said of the missionary priests?
40. What powerful Indian nation held to the English?
41. How did the French control most of the other tribes?
42. How were many of the wars between the French and English in America caused?
43. But, besides these quarrels between the two countries in Europe, there were causes of strife in America: what is the first one named?
44. What part of Maine did the French claim? (Look on the map and say about what proportion of the State lies east of the Kennebec River.)

45. What other territory did they claim in what is now the United States?
46. In what way were the fisheries a source of enmity?
47. How was the fur trade a matter of conflict?
48. How did the French try to get entire control of it?
49. How did the English seek to get it?
50. What religious ground for opposition between the two was there?
51. What was the character of religious differences in that day?

1. The Spanish colony at St. Augustine. 1565.
2. The French colony at Quebec. 1608.
3. The French explore the Mississippi.
4. Louisiana settled. 1699.
5. Weakness and strength of the French in America.
6. French influence over the Indians.
7. Causes of war between the French and English in America.

Study by topics

St. Augustine in _____ was planted by the _____ in 1565, _____ years before Jamestown was settled. The oldest city in the United States is _____. The beginning of permanent French settlement in America was made at _____ in _____, one year after Jamestown was settled. Quebec was founded by _____. The Ohio was discovered by _____. The Mississippi was explored to its mouth by _____, who called the country _____ after Louis XIV, king of France. Louisiana was settled in _____. The French controlled at this time two great waterways from the sea to the heart of the continent—the river _____ and the river _____.

Skeleton summary (of the narrative part of the chapter)

St. Augustine		Florida		Spaniards, 1565
Jamestown	in	Virginia	founded by	English, 1607
Quebec		Canada		French, 1608

Blackboard Illustration

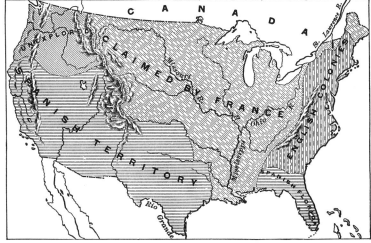

Present territory of the United States, showing by whom it was claimed before 1763

Geography   Let the pupil, on a map of the United States, point out the St. Lawrence and the Mississippi, as two roads leading to the heart of America. Let him show how the French and Spanish Territory quite surrounded the English colonies on all but their ocean side, and stopped their growth to the westward. Point out Florida and St. Augustine. Point out Quebec. Point out the mouth of the Mississippi.

Books   Parkman's *Pioneers of France in America.*

CHAPTER XXI

Colonial Wars with France and Spain

"King William's
War" begun   THERE were four wars with the French during the colonial time. The first was called "King William's War," from William III, King of England. It lasted from 1689 to 1697. In this war the first severe blow fell on the settlements of Maine, where the Indians in the French interest attacked the settlers in June, 1689, paying old grudges by torturing their victims. But the French did not escape. The Iroquois Indians were in alliance with the English, and had, besides, their own reasons for taking revenge on the French. In this same summer of 1689 they attacked the settlements about Montreal at daybreak, and killed, in their horrible way, two hundred people, and carried as many more into captivity.

French and
Indians attack
Schenectady
and other places   The French replied, not by assailing the Indians, but by carrying fire and massacre into the province of New York. In the bitter weather of January, 1690 a party of one hundred and ten, French and Indians, having traveled through frozen forests for many days, entered Schenectady [sken-ec´-ta-dy] at midnight and massacred sixty of its people. Those who escaped fled half naked through the snow to Albany, sixteen miles away. Another party, from Canada, fell on the settlement at Salmon Falls, N. H., and a third carried the like horrors to Casco Bay, in Maine. All the people on the frontier of the North-

ern colonies were now in terror.

To meet the danger, some sort of united action among the colonies was necessary. A congress of commissioners from several colonies met in New York, in 1690, and planned an invasion of Canada. In accordance with this plan, Sir William Phips took Port Royal, in Nova Scotia. Two expeditions were sent against Quebec: the one from New York and Connecticut went by Lakes George and Champlain; the other, from Boston, under Sir William Phips, was sent in a fleet of thirty-four ships. The land expedition was a failure, and never even reached Canada. The fleet reached Quebec, but failed to capture it.

First united action of the colonies

But Peter Schuyler, of Albany, a man much beloved by the Iroquois, who called him "Quider," led an expedition, in 1696, into the French settlements. He did what he could to prevent Indian cruelties. But the war was made up of barbarities and miseries without result, until peace between France and England, in 1697, brought a little welcome repose to the colonists of both nations, after eight years of war.

Colonel Schuyler's expedition against the French

In 1702 began the war known as "Queen Anne's War." In this war England fought against Spain as well as France. South Carolina was involved in a war with the Spaniards and Indians of Florida, while the Northern colonies were struggling against Canada. The Governor of South Carolina made successful inroads upon the Florida Indians, but he could not capture St. Augustine. Port

Colonel Schuyler's expedition against the French

Royal, in Nova Scotia, was again taken from the French in 1710, but the attempts made to take Quebec were once more a failure. The war was chiefly notable for the horrible onslaughts of the Canada Indians on some of the towns of the Northern frontier. Deerfield in western Massachusetts, was destroyed in 1704, and more than a hundred of its people carried into captivity. The war lasted about eleven years. A treaty was made in 1713, and there was a long peace between France and England. But the intrigues of both powers with the savages continued, and New England had many bloody engagements with the Indians of Maine, who were under the influence of the French.

QUEEN ANNE

In 1740 during a war with Spain, General Oglethorpe, the founder of Georgia, tried to conquer Florida, but the fortifications of St. Augustine were too strong for him. Two years later the Spaniards invaded Georgia, but Oglethorpe maneuvered his little force with so much skill as to lead the Spanish into ambuscades and defeated them at every point.

In 1744 the war between England and France, known as "King George's War," began. At that time many French privateers were sent out to plunder New England ships. These privateers came out of Louisbourg [loo-ee-boorg], a French stronghold on Cape Breton Island. Governor Shirley, of Massachusetts, sent against this place four thousand untrained New England militia. They were commanded by a merchant, and their officers did not know even the meaning of military terms. But they made up in courage and enthusiasm for their inexperience. The Americans had few cannon, but their favorite amusement had always been target shooting, and the deadly skill with which they used their muskets made it almost impossible for the French to work

GATEWAY AT
ST. AUGUSTINE

their guns. The excitement over this contest put a stop to almost all kinds of business in the Eastern colonies, and when at length the powerful fortress surrendered to a little army of farmers and mechanics, there was no end of joy in New England. This was the chief victory of the war, and it gave the American troops confidence in themselves. At the close of the war, in 1748, England returned the place again to the French, in exchange for advantages elsewhere. This was a bitter disappointment to the New Englanders, who called the day of its surrender a "black day, to be forever blotted out of New England calendars."

1. How many wars were there with the French during the colonial time?
2. What was the first of these called? In what year did it begin? In what year did it end?
3. Subtract 1689 from 1697: about how many years did it continue? Where was the first severe blow felt?
4. Who attacked the settlements of Maine?
5. How did the Indians of Maine pay old grudges against the settlers?
6. Who struck the first blow against the French?
7. How many people did the Iroquois kill about Montreal?
8. How many did they take prisoners?
9. How did the French reply to this blow?
10. What town did they attack in New York?
11. What became of the people of Schenectady?
12. What place was attacked by another party from Canada?
13. Where did a third party strike?
14. What were the feelings of people in the frontier towns at this time?
15. What was necessary to meet the danger?
16. Where did the commissioners from the various colonies meet?
17. In what year did the first united action take place?
18. What did the commissioners plan?
19. What place was taken from the French by Sir William Phips?
20. How many expeditions were sent against Quebec?
21. By what route did the troops from New York and Connecticut try to go?
22. How was the Massachusetts expedition sent?
23. What was the result of the expedition sent by the lakes?
24. What did the fleet do?
25. Who led an expedition into the French settlements in 1696?
26. Where did Schuyler live?
27. How was he regarded by the Iroquois?
28. What did the Indians call him?
29. What did he do with reference to Indian cruelties?
30. But what was the character of the war?
31. In what year did France and England make peace?
32. In what year did Queen Anne's War break out?
33. What other country besides France did England have war with at this time?
34. What colony was involved in a struggle with the Spaniards?
35. What did the Governor of South Carolina do?
36. What town in Nova Scotia was taken?
37. What was the result of a new attempt to take Quebec?

38. For what was the war chiefly notable?
39. What happened at the destruction of Deerfield in 1704?
40. How long did the war last? In what year was peace made?
41. Was this a long or short peace?
42. But what disturbed the repose of the colonies during this peace?
43. What did General Oglethorpe do in 1740?
44. What happened when the Spaniards attacked Georgia two years later?
45. In what year did King George's War begin?
46. From what port were French privateers sent out to destroy New England ships?
47. Where was Louisbourg?
48. Where is Cape Breton Island? How many men did governor Shirley, of Massachusetts, send against this place? What kind of men were they?
49. What kind of officers did they have?
50. How did these soldiers make up for their inexperience?
51. What had been their favorite amusement?
52. What was the effect of their marksmanship?
53. When the place surrendered, what was the feeling in New England?
54. What proportion of the New England men lost their lives?
55. What was the effect of the victory on the American troops?
56. What was the feeling in New England when *Louisbourg was returned to the French in 1748?*

OLD HOUSE AT DEERFIELD

Study by
topics

GEORGIA AND
FLORIDA AS THEY
WERE IN
OGLETHORPE'S TIME

Geography

I. King William's War. 1689 to 1697.
  1. The first blows.
  2. The attacks on Schenectady and other places.
  3. The attempt to take Quebec.
II. Queen Anne's War.
  1. Florida attacked from South Carolina.
  2. Attacks on Canada.
  3. Massacres on the Northern frontier.
III. Oglethorpe's attack on Florida.
IV. The third French war, or King George's War. 1744 to
   1748.
  1. The taking of Louisbourg.
  2. Its return to the French.

    The geographical points to be fixed in the pupil's mind
by reference to maps are—1. The French claim in Maine.
(Is the region east of the Kennebec about two thirds or
about three fourths of Maine ?) 2. The French claim to
the Mississippi Valley. (Let the pupil, after examining a map of the United States,
decide whether the portion of our country drained by rivers flowing into the Mississippi is less or more then one half.) 3. The position of Cape Breton and
Louisbourg. 4. By what course would fleets sailing from Boston have to go to
reach Quebec? 5. Let the pupil point out on a map the route to Canada and Quebec by the way of Lakes George and Champlain. 6. Relative position of Georgia
and Florida.

CHAPTER XXII

Braddock's Defeat and the Expulsion of the Acadians

Washington
sent to protest
the French forts

THE French made use of the years that intervened between the peace of 1748 and the outbreak of hostilities in
1754 to draw a line of posts along the Ohio and near to the
Allegheny Mountains, intending to confine the English to
the country east of the Alleghenies, and to secure to themselves the whole of the great interior valley. This was especially exasperating to Virginia, which claimed the western
country. George Washington, then a young man of twenty-
one, who had already spent much time on the frontier as a
surveyor, was sent into the wilderness by the Governor of
Virginia as an ambassador to urge the French to depart
peaceably. This errand the athletic and cool headed young

man accomplished, in spite of great hardships and dangers.

In the next year—1754—Washington was sent as a major at the head of some troops to dislodge the French, who had built a post at the head of the Ohio, where Pittsburgh now stands. This they called Fort Duquesne [du-ken]. Washington found the French too strong for his force, but, by surprising and defeating a skulking party of them, he brought on the war, which the French wished to postpone. Washington was himself afterward attacked by a superior force, and compelled to capitulate and retire from the disputed ground.

Washington tries to expel the French

In 1755 General Braddock, an English of ricer, marched from Virginia in command of an army of English regulars and colonial militia, to drive the French from Fort Duquesne. Braddock was brave and honest, but harsh and brutal in manners. He could not understand the nature of a war in the woods. Like other English officers of the time, he despised the American militia and their half-Indian way of fighting.

Braddock's expedition

When only eight miles from Fort Duquesne, the French and Indians attacked Braddock's army. The scarlet coats and solid ranks were a good target, and the soldiers were

Braddock attacked

mowed down by the deadly fire that came from trees and gullies where no enemy was to be seen.

The British soldiers, though brave enough, were unused to such warfare, and unable to do anything to repel the unseen foe. After standing huddled together for three hours, they broke and fled. The Virginians, whom Braddock had despised had stood their ground for a while, fighting behind trees like

GEORGE WASHINGTON
RALLYING BRADDOCK'S TROOPS

the Indians; but Braddock, esteeming this cowardly, ordered them to "come out in the open field like Englishmen," and even struck some of them with the back of his sword.

Braddock defeated and killed

General Braddock exposed himself fearlessly. He had four horses killed under him, and was on the fifth when he was mortally wounded. George Washington, who was the only officer on Braddock's staff not killed or wounded, behaved with admirable courage. He had two horses shot under him, and four bullets pierced his clothes. Nearly all the officers of Braddock's army were killed or wounded, and the soldiers who escaped the slaughter fled back to Fort Cumberland in a wild panic.

In the same summer with Braddock's defeat came the removal of the Acadians. Acadia was the name of the region now included in the provinces of Nova Scotia and New Brunswick. It had been settled by the French about one hundred years when the English conquered it in 1710, during Queen Anne's War. The people were a very ignorant peasantry, who continued to speak French and to take sides secretly with their own nation in every struggle between the two countries, though they had lived forty five years under English rule. In this war the hard resolution was taken to scatter the Acadians through the various English colonies. They were seized and put on board vessels and sent away; their houses and barns were burned, and their lands confiscated. Some of them got to Louisiana, some to Canada, and some, after great hardships, made their way back to Acadia; others were scattered in various places, and their sufferings have excited pity even to our own times, and have been made the subject of Longfellow's poem of "Evangeline."

Expulsion of the Acadians

SIR WILLIAM JOHNSON

Almost the whole of this year's operations of the British and colonial troops ended in failure. Sir William Johnson was sent to capture Crown Point, a French fort on Lake Champlain. His raw forces succeeded in beating off the French in the battle of Lake George, but Johnson, who was no soldier, did not even attempt to go farther, and Crown

Battle of Lake George. Failure of Johnson's and Shirley's expeditions

Point was not attacked. General Shirley set out to capture the French fort at Niagara, but he was out-generaled by the French, and did not reach it.

Bad management of the war

The statesmen who governed in England at this time were very incompetent. The colonies were divided by factions and jealousies, and the war in America was carried on with halfheartedness and stupidity.

Capture of Fort William Henry, and massacre of part of the garrison

Lord Loudon [low´-den] was sent, in 1756, to command the troops in America. He laid siege to Louisbourg in 1757, but failed to take it. For this movement he drew away many of the troops that had protected the New York frontier. Aware of this, the French, under Montcalm [mont-cahm], besieged and captured Fort William Henry, at the south end of Lake George. By the terms of capitulation

LORD LOUDON

the colonial troops were to be allowed to return home, but after they had surrendered the fort, the Indian allies of the French fell on them and killed a great many. Others they seized and carried off.

Questions for study

1. How did the French make use of the years of peace that followed King George's War? What did they wish to secure?
2. What colony claimed the country west of the Allegheny Mountains?
3. Who was sent into the wilderness by the Governor of Virginia?
4. What was he sent for?
5. The following year Washington was again sent into the wilderness in what capacity? What was he expected to do?
6. Where had the French built a fort? What did they call it?
7. Why did not Washington succeed in dislodging the French?
8. What did he do to a skulking party?
9. What was the effect of this?
10. Did the French wish for war at this time?
11. When the French attacked Washington, what was the result?
12. Who commanded an expedition against Fort Duquesne in 1755?
13. What kind of a man was General Braddock?
14. What kind of a war was it that he could not understand?
15. How did he regard the American militia?

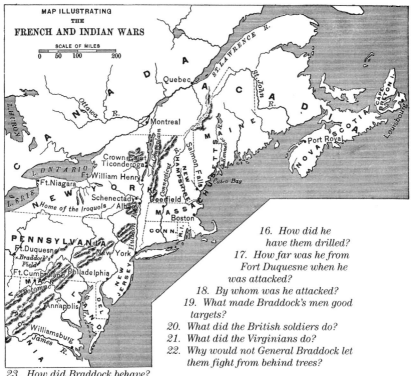

16. How did he have them drilled?
17. How far was he from Fort Duquesne when he was attacked?
18. By whom was he attacked?
19. What made Braddock's men good targets?
20. What did the British soldiers do?
21. What did the Virginians do?
22. Why would not General Braddock let them fight from behind trees?

23. How did Braddock behave?
24. What was his fate?
25. How did Washington behave?
26. What was the fate of nearly all the officers?
27. What became of the remainder of the army?
28. What region of country was called Acadia?
29. How long had the French been settled there when the English conquered it?
30. In what war was it taken from the English?
31. What sort of people were the Acadians?
32. Which side did they take secretly in the wars between the two countries?
33. How long did they live under English rule in Acadia?
34. What hard resolution was taken?
35. What was done with them?
36. What was done with their houses?
37. What disposition was made of their lands?
38. What is the meaning of the word confiscated? What became of the Acadians?

39. What poem treats of their sorrows?
40. What French post did Sir William Johnson try to capture?
41. On what lake is Crown Point?
42. In what battle did Johnson's troops beat the French?
43. Did Johnson attack Crown Point?
44. What fort did General Shirley try to capture? Did he succeed?
45. What kind of statesmen were those in power in England at this time?
46. What was the state of the colonies?
47. How as the American war carried on?
48. Who was sent to take command in 1756?
49. What French stronghold did he besiege?
50. Who had taken Louisbourg from the French before?

THE DOTTED LINE SHOWS BRADDOCK'S MARCH FROM FORT CUMBERLAND, ON THE POTOMAC TOWARD FORT DUQUESNE

51. When had it been given back? (See Chapter XXI.)
52. What advantage did the French take of the weakening of the forces on the New York frontier?
53. Who commanded the French when they took Fort William Henry?
54. What were the colonial troops to be allowed to do?
55. But what happened after the surrender?

Study by topics

Skeleton summary

What can you tell about—
1. The beginning of the war.
2. Braddock's defeat.
3. The removal of the Acadians.
4. The failure to take Crown Point and Niagara.
5. The surrender of Fort William Henry, and the treachery that followed.

A young man named _____ was sent to protest against the occupation of the country west of the Alleghenies by the _____. Washington was afterward sent to drive the French from Fort _____, at the forks of the River _____, where the city of _____ now stands, but was forced to retire. In 1755 General _____ marched against Fort Duquesne. He was attacked and his army_____. Braddock was _____. The _____ were removed from their homes in the same year. Sir William Johnson defeated the French in the battle of Lake _____, but failed to take the fort at_____. General Shirley failed to take the fort at _____. In 1757 Lord Loudon laid siege to _____, but failed to take it. The French general, Montcalm, attacked Fort _____, on Lake _____, and captured it.

The various works of Francis Parkman for a history of the French in Canada and their wars, and Irving's *Life of Washington*.

Books

CHAPTER XXIII

Fall of Canada

WILLIAM PITT

WILLIAM PITT, afterward Earl of Chatham, became Prime Minister of England. He made great changes in the conduct of the war in America. He was resolved, indeed, to take Canada, and to drive the French out of America. He chose his commanders with care, and from the time he came to power the English colonies began to feel some hope of getting rid of the enemy that had so long sent the Indians, like wolves to destroy the defenseless settlements.

Pitt conducts the war against France with vigor

In 1758 the English, under Amherst, again laid siege to Louisbourg, that great fortress which New Englanders had once captured. After a siege by sea and land, lasting nearly two months, and much hard fighting, the town surrendered.

AMHERST

Capture of Louisbourg by Amherst, 1758

In September of this same year the French fort, called Frontenac, which stood where the town of Kingston in Canada now stands, and controlled Lake Ontario, was taken by an English expedition.

Capture of Fort Frontenac

General Forbes, though so sick with a painful and mortal illness that he had to be carried on a litter, cut a road through the thick forests on the Pennsylvania mountains,

General Forbes obliges the French to abandon Fort Duquesne, Pittsburgh founded

marched to the Ohio, and forced the French to abandon Fort Duquesne. The English established a fort here and called the place Pittsburgh, in honor of the great prime minister who had turned the current of the war from defeat to victory.

Defeat of the English at Ticonderoga

The English army in America suffered one considerable defeat at Fort Ticonderoga, on Lake Champlain. General Abercromby had sailed down Lake George and marched through the woods to attack Montcalm, at Ticonderoga. The English and colonial troops tried to carry the French works by assault, but after several repulses they retreated in a panic to their boats, and sailed back to the fort at the south end of Lake George.

Decline of the French power in America

But the English successes in 1758 pushed the French in America far toward ruin. Louisbourg, the great French stronghold, from which privateers were sent

Robert Rogers and the Rangers— The perils of the frontier led to the formation of companies of rangers, who fought the Indians in their own way. Robert Rogers became very famous for his daring expeditions in the region about Lake George. He had many desperate fights with the French. He and his men journeyed on skates or snowshoes in winter, and in light whaleboats or afoot in summer. His main objects were to capture prisoners for information and to annoy the enemy. Once, with fifty men, he carried his light whaleboats six miles over a mountain gorge, from near the middle of Lake George to the waters of Lake Champlain, and then rowed with muffled oars under the French fort at Ticonderoga, so close as to hear the sentries give the watchword and then passed the fort at Crown Point in the same way. He captured and sunk two sloops laden with provisions, hid his boats, and got back afoot to Lake George. Then he returned and reconnoitred Lake Champlain in his boats, captured some prisoners, and again hid his boats. This time the French found his boats, and sent out scouts to find some water passage by which the boats could have come into Lake Champlain, not suspecting that they could have been carried over. Rogers, with five men, once walked coolly up to a sentinel near the French fort. When challenged, he answered in French. Then, when he had got near the sentinel, and the latter demanded, in amazement, "Who are you?" He answered, "Rogers," and took him prisoner. There is a tradition that, in escaping from the Indians, he threw his packs down a steep rock to the ice on Lake George, and then turned round on his snowshoes and walked away. The Indians, seeing the tracks, believed that two men had slid down the frightful slope. The place is still known as "Rogers' Slide."

out, was gone, and by the fall of Fort Duquesne and Fort Frontenac the routes from Canada to Louisiana were cut off. The fur trade of Canada was destroyed, and the Indi-

ROGERS' SLIDE, LAKE GEORGE

ans of the interior were no longer willing to come to the support of the French, seeing the English in possession of the main roads into their country.

During the siege of Louisbourg, Wolfe, a young briga- Wolfe attacks dier-general, had attracted much attention by the energy Quebec and daring of his operations. He was sent by Pitt to take Quebec, if such a thing were possible. Quebec is on a high, steep bluff, overlooking the St. Lawrence where that river is narrow, and the natural strength of the fortress is very great. All through July and August of 1759, Wolfe's army and the English fleet tried in vain to find a weak spot in the defenses of the Canadian stronghold but the fortress frowned on them from its inaccessible heights. In several attacks, made at various points, the English were repulsed. As the season of storms was coming on, and the fleet must soon leave, even Wolfe began to despond. But, in spite of sickness and pain, this heroic man roused his army to make one more attempt. Meantime Montcalm, who commanded the French forces, was extremely vigilant. He kept his horses saddled day and night to ride to any point that might be assailed, and he did not take off his clothes for nearly three months.

WOLFE

Wolfe scales the Heights of Abraham

Wolfe put his men in boats and dropped down, in the night, from the fleet above the town to a little bay, now known as Wolfe's Cove. Twenty-four volunteers climbed the steep precipice by a rough path and drove off the guard at the top. When firing was heard, the whole force landed and clambered up the rocky steep, holding by bushes. When morning came, the British soldiers were in line of battle on the "Plains of Abraham," less than a mile from Quebec, where the French must fight or have their supplies cut off.

Defeat of the French on the "Plains of Abraham." Death of Wolfe and Montcalm

Montcalm attacked immediately, but his ranks were broken by the steady English fire, and Wolfe led a charge in person. Though twice wounded by bullets, Wolfe kept on until a shot entered his breast, inflicting a mortal wound. When told that the enemy were fleeing everywhere, he said, "Now, God be praised, I die in peace!" Montcalm, who was also mortally wounded, said, "I am happy that I shall not live to see the surrender of Quebec."

MONTCALM

Quebec soon capitulated, and the fate of Canada was sealed. The French attempted to retake the city in vain.

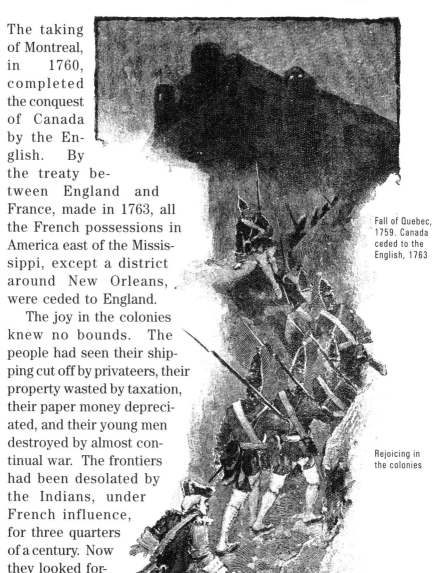

The taking of Montreal, in 1760, completed the conquest of Canada by the English. By the treaty between England and France, made in 1763, all the French possessions in America east of the Mississippi, except a district around New Orleans, were ceded to England.

Fall of Quebec, 1759. Canada ceded to the English, 1763

The joy in the colonies knew no bounds. The people had seen their shipping cut off by privateers, their property wasted by taxation, their paper money depreciated, and their young men destroyed by almost continual war. The frontiers had been desolated by the Indians, under French influence, for three quarters of a century. Now they looked forward to peace,

Rejoicing in the colonies

and the expansion of the English settlements in America into a vast empire.

OLD VIEW OF QUEBEC

Questions for study

1. What was the name of the new Prime Minister of England who made great changes in the conduct of the war in America?
2. What was he resolved to do?
3. How did he choose his commanders?
4. How did the colonists feel after he came to power?
5. In what year did the English again lay siege to Louisbourg? Under what general?
6. By what troops had it been once taken?
7. How did it come back into French hands? (See page 126.)
8. How long did the siege of Louisbourg under Amherst continue? What was the result?
9. What French fort controlled Lake Ontario?
10. What Canadian town is now situated where Fort Frontenac stood?
11. What happened to Fort Frontenac in September, 1758?
12. What general had a road cut through the forests on the Pennsylvania mountains?
13. Why was General Forbes carried on a litter? What did he force the French to do?
14. What city now stands on the site of old Fort Duquesne?
15. In whose honor was Pittsburgh named?
16. Why was Pitt honored in America?
17. Where did the English suffer defeat in 1758?
18. What English general sailed down Lake George?
19. What fort did he attack?

20. What French general commanded at Ticonderoga?
21. How did the English try to carry the French works? What was the result?
22. To what place did the English retreat?
23. What was the effect on Canada of the English successes in 1758?
24. What was the effect of the loss of Louisbourg?
25. How had the routes from Canada to Louisiana been cut off?
26. What was the effect on the fur trade?
27. Why were the Indians of the interior no longer willing to come to the support of Canada?

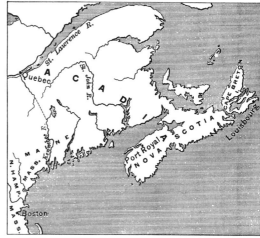

ACADIA, PORT ROYAL, AND LOUISBOURG, AND THE ROUTE BY SEA BETWEEN BOSTON AND QUEBEC

28. How had General Wolfe attracted attention?
29. What was he sent to do?
30. How is Quebec situated? What is its natural strength?
31. What did Wolfe's army and the English fleet try to find?
32. What was the result of several attacks made by the English at different points?
33. How did Wolfe feel?
34. What did he rouse his army to do?
35. How did the English get up to the top of the cliff?
36. Where did they form a line of battle?
37. How far were they from Quebec?
38. Why were the French obliged to fight?
39. What was the result of Montcalm's attack?

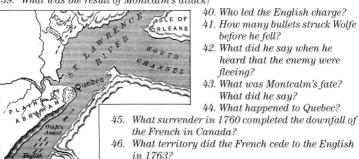

40. Who led the English charge?
41. How many bullets struck Wolfe before he fell?
42. What did he say when he heard that the enemy were fleeing?
43. What was Montcalm's fate? What did he say?
44. What happened to Quebec?
45. What surrender in 1760 completed the downfall of the French in Canada?
46. What territory did the French cede to the English in 1763?

47. *What is said of the joy in the colonies?*
48. *What calamities had come on the colonists by the continual war with France?*
49. *For how long a time had the desolation of the frontiers been going on?*
50. *To what did they now look forward?*

Study by topics

Tell about—
1. Influence of Pitt.
2. Capture of Louisbourg.
3. Fall of Frontenac.
4. Driving of the French from Duquesne and founding of Pittsburgh.
5. Defeat of the English at Ticonderoga.
6. Fall of Quebec.
7. Fall of Canada.

Geography

Let the pupil point out or describe the location of Louisbourg. Of Fort Frontenac (Kingston). Of Fort Duquesne (Pittsburgh). Of Fort Ticonderoga. Of Quebec. Of Montreal.

Books

Parkman's *Montcalm and Wolfe*, besides the general histories of Bancroft and Winsor, mentioned in earlier chapters.

CHAPTER XXIV

Characteristics of the Colonial Wars with the French

The regular soldiers

THE English and French regulars wore neat uniforms. The French were remarkable a long way off for the white, the English for the red, which predominated in their dress. The drill of regular soldiers was careful, and their discipline severe. They fought with great steadiness, standing up and facing the enemy, and they and their officers held in contempt the skulking way of fighting which prevailed among the colonial troops on both sides.

The Americans, in both the French and English colonies, had learned to fight in the woods. They loaded their guns lying on the ground, and they fired from behind trees and stumps, now running forward and now retreating and charging again. The regular troops took no definite aim, but fired at the enemy's line, while the colonists were the

A FRENCH
REGULAR

best marksmen in the world, and the man whom one of them covered with his gun was generally doomed. In the first siege of Louisbourg their deadly aim at last rendered it impossible for the French to load or fire a cannon. Though without experience, they had plenty of courage. At the battle of Lake George it was said that the American provincials fought in the morning like good boys, about noon like men, and in the afternoon like demons.

The American Troops

A CANADIAN SOLDIER

The British officers were generally incapable of getting on well with the American soldiers. They looked with contempt on men who wore little or no uniform, and sometimes carried in the same company guns of the various sorts they had used in hunting. The Americans made a bad show on parade, and refused to fight standing up in close ranks. By the side of the neatly kept red-coated British troops, the American militia looked shabby enough. The British offic-

British officers and colonial soldiers

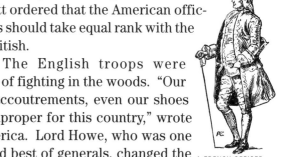

A FLINTLOCK

ers holding the king's commission assumed to command American officers of higher rank, and this caused a dislike of the English to spread through the colonies. Pitt ordered that the American officers should take equal rank with the British.

The English troops were rather unfit for the work of fighting in the woods. "Our clothes, our arms, our accoutrements, even our shoes and stockings, are all improper for this country," wrote General Wolfe from America. Lord Howe, who was one of the noblest of men and best of generals, changed the dress of his men to fit them for marching in the woods. Hair was worn long in that day, and Lord Howe cut off his own fine head of hair to persuade the men to sacrifice theirs.

A FRENCH OFFICER

A FLINTLOCK GUN

He reduced the officers' baggage, and dismissed the great company of washer women, setting a good example by washing his own linen in the brook. Lord Howe cultivated the friendship of the American officers, and treated the soldiers with great respect. He was second in command to Abercromby, and was killed in a skirmish just before the attack on Ticonderoga. The defeat of Abercromby in the battle which followed is attributed to the loss of Lord Howe, who was the real soul of the army. (See the preceding chapter.)

LORD HOWE

INDIAN MOCCASINS

It was impossible to keep troops enough in the field to protect the long frontier. No one could tell where the Indians would strike, and when they had massacred a family they escaped too swiftly for pursuit. The colonies were driven to offer rewards for the scalps of Indians as they were accustomed to pay for wolves' heads. One can see how barbarous their feelings were, however, in the offer of smaller rewards for the scalps of Indian women and children.

In many ways the French wars tended to corrupt the people of the colonies. A race of traders secretly sold arms to the Indians that were butchering their own people. Another set of men, some of whom were connected with the government, sold provisions to the French. Very many embarked in privateering—that is, they fitted out ships to capture and plunder the merchant ships of France. This was only a kind of lawful piracy. Many of the soldiers who returned from the war had learned habits of idleness and dissipation.

The sorrows inflicted on both the French and English colonists were more than can be imagined. The frontier

people lived in continual fear of sudden death by the tomahawk, or slow death by torture. Yet their courage grew
with their danger.

In 1689 captives taken in Maine were carried to Canada
and sold there. From that time forward innumerable people
captured on the frontier by the Indians were sold into
Canada, enduring horrible sufferings in their forced journeys through the woods. Many of these were ransomed by
their friends. Husbands made dangerous and sorrowful
journeys to redeem their wives, and parents went in search
of their children. Great compassion was excited in New
England for the captives, and collections were frequently
made for their redemption. Sometimes cap-
tive children were reclaimed who had been
educated in French, and had quite forgotten
the language and the religion of their parents.
The Canadians were generally
kind to the captives, and some of
the prisoners were very sorry to
return. Many of the captives remained among the savages; one
Indian village contained a
hundred white people
carried away in child-
hood. These had forgot-
ten how to
speak En-
glish. Some
of the Indian
tribes
doubled
their num-

LORD HOWE
WASHING HIS LINEN

bers in the last French war by adopting white children. Three thousand, men, women, and children, were carried into captivity from Pennsylvania and the provinces south of it in the year 1756.

Pontiac's war

The colonies did not immediately have peace. The Indians of the Western country hated the English, and the occupation of the old French forts by small English garrisons excited their jealousy. Under the lead of Pontiac, an Ottawa chief, a great conspiracy was formed in 1763, the year of the peace.

WHITE CAPTIVES DRIVEN INTO CANADA BY INDIANS

The garrisons of many of the smaller forts were massacred. Detroit and Pittsburgh were attacked, and the families on the frontier suffered horrible inroads from the savages. It became necessary to march forces into the Indian country. General Bouquet, with five hundred men, defeated a large force of Indians in a desperate two days' battle at Bushy Run, in Pennsylvania, in 1763. "Pontiac's War," as it was called, was brought to a close in 1764, and the frontiers had a brief rest. But already there were seen the beginnings of that great quarrel of the Americans with the mother country which brought on the bitter struggle of the Revolutionary War.

Captives in the French Wars—One of the first of the many thousands of captives carried to Canada was a little girl named Sarah Gerrish. An Indian girl once tried to drown her by pushing her off a precipice into the river, but she saved herself by catching hold of the bushes. Once she was so weary that she overslept, and awoke to find herself alone in the woods and covered with snow. She followed the tracks of the Indians until she overtook them. Again, the Indians built a great fire, and told her that she was to be burned, but she threw her arms around her Indian master's neck and begged him to save her. She was sold to the French in Canada, and kindly treated by them until she was returned. In the fall of 1677 two men, Waite and Jennings, set out from the Connecticut River for Canada, to redeem their wives and children carried off by Indians. Without guides they paddled through Lake Champlain and reached Canada. After seven months' absence they brought back about twenty captives in all. The people sent horses to meet them at Albany and bring them into Hatfield, where they were received with the greatest joy. One woman, when she got her children together, after captivity, found one of her sons, a lad of eleven, an Indian in habits, and not able to speak any but the Indian language; while a daughter of fifteen, who had been educated in a Canadian convent, spoke nothing but French. One Pennsylvanian got home just as the sale of his property at auction had been completed, his neighbors having supposed him dead. James Smith, having endured six years of captivity among the Indians, came home a few days after his sweetheart had married another man.

Questions for study

1. How were the English and French regulars dressed?
2. What color was conspicuous in the dress of the French?
3. What in that of the English?
4. What was the nature of the drill and discipline of the regulars? How did they fight?
5. What did they think of the mode of fighting which prevailed among the colonial troops?
6. How had the Americans learned to fight? How did they load? How did they fire?
7. What difference was there between their firing and that of the regular troops?
8. What was the effect of their fire at Louisbourg?
9. What did the French commander at the battle of Lake George say about their fighting?
10. How did the British officers get on with the colonial troops?
11. Why did they hold them in contempt?
12. What difficulty was there about the rank of American officers?
13. What effect did this have on the feelings of the Americans toward the English?
14. What order did Pitt make about the rank of the American officers?
15. What is said of the fitness of English troops for fighting in the woods?
16. What did General Wolfe write on this subject?
17. What kind of a man was Lord Howe?
18. What did he do about the dress of his men? What about their hair?
19. What about baggage and the washing of clothes?
20. How did he treat the American officers and soldiers?
21. When was Lord Howe killed?

What defeat is attributed to his death?

22. What difficulty was there in protecting the frontier?
23. What measures were taken to reward the Indian fighters of the frontier?
24. What sign of barbarous feeling do we see in the way in which rewards were offered for scalps?
25. What are some of the ways in which the French wars tended to make the Americans barbarous?
26. What kind of a secret trade was there with the Indians?
27. What kind of a secret trade with the French?
28. What kind of a business was privateering?
29. Was it much carried on at that time?
30. What effect did the war have on the soldiers engaged in it?
31. What were the sorrows inflicted on the French and English colonists?
32. What fear was continually in the minds of people on the frontier?
33. What is one of the most sorrowful chapters of the war?
34. In what year were the first captives carried to Canada?
35. Where were they taken from?
36. How were many of these ransomed?
37. What change had sometimes taken place in children carried to Canada?
38. How did some of them feel about returning?
39. Were all the captives sold to Canada?
40. How many white people were found in one Indian village?
41. Were the Indian tribes increased by the adoption of white children?
42. How many people were carried into captivity from Pennsylvania and the provinces south of it in 1756?
43. Did the peace with France bring a lasting peace with the Indians?
44. In what year was a great conspiracy of the Indians formed?
45. What was the name of the chief who was the leader in this war?
46. In what battle did Colonel Bouquet defeat the Indians?
47. In what year was Pontiac's War brought to a close?
48. What struggle was already beginning?

Study by topics

Tell about—

I.   The different kinds of soldiers.
   1. The English and French regulars.
      a. Their appearance. b. Their mode of fighting.
   2. The American militia.
      a. Their appearance. b. Their mode of fighting.
   3. The lack of agreement between English and Americans.
      a. The question of rank. b. Lord Howe's reform in the dress of the British soldiers.
II. The frontier.
   1. The reward for scalps.
   2. Captivity.
      a. In Canada. b. Among the Indians.
III. Pontiac's War.

Five kinds of soldiers in the French wars: Blackboard illustration

French regulars, Canadian militia,	on the French side.
English regulars, Colonial militia,	on the English side.
Indians,	on both sides.

Where is Pittsburgh? Where is Detroit? Geography

THIRD REVIEW—COLONIAL WARS

Chapters XX to XXIV

Review by topics

The Spaniards in Florida. (XX)	Settlement of St. Augustine.
The French in America (XX)	Planting of Quebec in 1608. Joliet reaches the Mississippi. La Salle discovers the Ohio. La Salle reaches the mouth of the Mississippi. Hennepin explores the upper Mississippi. Louisiana founded. Attempt to possess the whole interior.
French and English. (XX)	Fewness of the French in numbers. Their union and military character. Their influence with the Indians. The superiority of the English in numbers. Their lack of union. Their lack of influence with many of the Indians.
Causes of quarrel. (XX)	Disputed territory. Fisheries. Fur trade. Religious prejudices.

"King William's War," 1689-1697.   (XXI)
- Indians attack in Maine.
- Iroquois attack Montreal.
- Massacres at Schenectady, Salmon Falls, and Casco Bay.
- Congress of the colonies, 1690.
- Two expeditions against Quebec
- Peter Schuyler against the French

"Queen Anne's War," 1704-1713.   (XXI)
- The war against the Spaniards in Florida.
- Attempts to take Quebec.
- Massacres at Deerfield and elsewhere.

War with the Spaniards in Florida.   (XXI)
- Oglethorpe invades Florida, 1740
- The Spanish invade Georgia, 1742.

"King George's War," 1744-1748.   (XXI)
- The taking of Louisbourg by New Englanders.
- Louisbourg returned to the French.

Last French war begun in 1751.   English reverses.   (XXII)
- Washington begins the war, 1754.
- Braddock's defeat, 1755.
- The Acadians removed.
- Failure of English expeditions.
    - a. Against Crown Point.
    - b. Against Fort Niagara.
    - c. Against Louisbourg.
- The French capture Fort William Henry.

English conquer Canada. War concluded, 1763.   (XXIII)
- Pitt governs England.
- Second capture of Louisbourg.
- Capture of Fort Frontenac.
- General Forbes takes Fort Duquesne.
- Defeat of Abercromby at Ticonderoga.
- Wolfe takes Quebec.
- Fall of the French power in Canada.

Traits of the French wars.   (XXIV)
- Regular soldiers and militia.
- Sorrows of Indian warfare.
- "Pontiac's War."

CHAPTER XXV

How the Colonies were Governed

THE close of the French war made way for the Revolution. But, before we consider the events which led to the separation of the colonies from England, it will be best to ask, How were the colonies governed at the close of the French wars? There were three forms of government in America—"royal," "charter," and " proprietary."

Three forms of government in the colonies

The oldest colony, Virginia, was under what was called a royal government, because the king appointed the governor, and approved or disapproved of the laws that were passed. "Royal" means belonging to the king. New York had been granted to the Duke of York as a proprietary government, but when that duke became king, as James II, it became a royal, or king's province. New Jersey became a royal colony after the king bought the right of the proprietors. The two Carolinas were proprietary governments at first, but in 1729 the king bought out the proprietary rights, and they became royal governments. Georgia was first settled under a body of twenty-one trustees, but in 1752 these trustees surrendered the government to the king. In 1679 New Hampshire was separated from Massachusetts, and became a royal colony. So that, after 1752 there were seven colonies under royal governments, namely, Virginia, New York, New Jersey, North and South Carolina, Georgia, and New Hampshire.

Colonies under royal governments

Three colonies—Massachusetts, Connecticut, and Rhode Island—were under charter governments; that is, they were for the most part governed by their own people, according to charters granted by the king. Massachusetts, after it lost its first charter, had a governor appointed by

Colonies under charter governments

the king, but the power remained mostly in the hands of the Legislature. Maine was attached to Massachusetts.

Colonies under proprietary governments   Maryland had been given to Lord Baltimore, Pennsylvania to William Penn. Baltimore and Penn were called "proprietors," or "proprietaries." The heirs of these first proprietors exercised in these two colonies power somewhat similar to those of the king in the royal colonies. These were called proprietary governments. Delaware had been ceded to Penn by the Duke of York, and, though it had a separate Legislature, it was under the same governor as Pennsylvania. There were, therefore, at the close of the French wars, three proprietary governments—Maryland, Pennsylvania, and Delaware.

Colonial Legislatures   Each of the thirteen colonies had a legislative body. These were divided into two houses. There was a lower house, or Assembly, elected by the people. The members of the upper house, or Council, were generally appointed by the king in the royal colonies, and by the proprietary in the proprietary colonies. In the charter colonies governors and members of the Council were elected by the Assembly.

How laws were passed in the colonies   In order to pass a law both houses of the Legislature must vote for it and the governor must agree to it. We have kept the same rule. Our State and national laws are made in this way now. The body we call the Senate takes the place occupied by the governor's Council in the colonies. But in our time the people elect the governors and both houses of the Legislature. In nearly all of the colonies the people had no voice in choosing the governor or the upper house of the Legislature. The people could not, therefore, make laws which were not agreeable to the king or the proprietary. There was, consequently, almost a continual quarrel between the governors, acting under instructions from

England, and the representatives of the people.

All laws regulating the trade between the colonies and with other countries were made by the English Parliament. The colonies were obliged, often much against their will, to admit Negro slaves, brought in by English merchants. Commercial laws made by the English Parliament

They were forced to send nearly all their leading products to England for sale. They were not allowed to buy any European goods, except in England, and no foreign ships were allowed to enter a port in this country. Laws were made to discourage people in the colonies from making and trading in such things as were made in England. There were English laws against the manufacture of ironware and woolen goods by the Americans. The colonists had many furs, and could make hats very cheaply, but no hatter was allowed to send hats from one colony to another.

A HATTER'S SHOP IN OLD TIMES

Customhouses were established by law in all the principal ports of the colonies, and duties collected for the king. But the colonists evaded these unjust laws in every way they could, and there was a great deal of smuggling all along the coast. Customhouses and smuggling

1. *What did the close of the French war make way for?*
2. *How many kinds of governments were there in the colonies?*
3. *What were they called?*
4. *Which form of government was Virginia under?*
5. *Why was this form called "royal"?*
6. *What does the word "royal" mean?*

Questions for study

7. *To whom had New York been granted? (When? See pages 47, 48.) When did it become a royal province?*

8. *How did New Jersey, which once belonged to proprietors, become a royal colony?*

9. *What kind of governments did the two Carolinas have at first?*

10. *In what year did the king buy out the proprietors?*

11. *What kind of governments did the Carolinas have after 1729?*

12. *Under what kind of a body had Georgia been settled?*

13. *What did the trustees of Georgia do in 1752?*

14. *From what colony was New Hampshire separated in 1679?*

15. *What sort of a colony did it then become?*

16. *How many colonies were there under royal governments?*

17. *What were their names?*

18. *There were thirteen colonies in all: were the royal colonies more or less than half of them?*

19. *How many colonies were under charter governments? What three were they?*

20. *How were the charter colonies governed?*

21. *After Massachusetts had lost its first charter, who appointed its governor?*

22. *In whose hands did the power mostly remain?*

23. *Which one of our present States was at that time attached to the government of Massachusetts?*

24. *To whom had Maryland been given?*

25. *To whom had Pennsylvania been given?*

26. *What were Baltimore and Penn therefore called?*

27. *What powers did their heirs exercise in their colonies?*

28. *What were their governments called?*

29. *What colony had been ceded to Penn by the Duke of York?*

30. *What is said of the government of Delaware?*

31. *How many proprietary governments were there? Name them.*

32. *What did each of the thirteen colonies have?*

33. *How many "houses" were there in each Legislature?*

34. *How were the members of the Assembly chosen?*

35. *Who appointed the members of the Council, or upper house, in a royal colony?*

36. *Who appointed them in a proprietary colony?*

37. *How were they generally chosen in a charter colony?*

38. *What was necessary in order to pass a law in one of the colonies?*

39. *How do our ways of making laws at the present time resemble this?*

40. *But what is the difference?*

41. *Who elects the governor now?*

42. *What part of the State Legislature is elected by the people now?*

43. *Did the people of the colonies choose their own governors?*

44. *Did they choose the upper house of the Legislature?*

45. *What kind of laws could they not make?*

46. *What was the result of this arrangement?*

47. *What kind of laws were made for the colonies by the English Parliament?*

48. *What were they obliged to receive against their will?*

49. *Where were they forced to send all their leading products?*
50. *Where must they buy all European goods?*
51. *What kind of ships were forbidden to come to this country?*
52. *What kind of goods were people in the colonies discouraged from making?*
53. *What three sorts of manufacture were particularly restricted?*
54. *What were established in the colonial ports?*
55. *For whom were the duties collected?*
56. *Did the colonies willingly obey the laws made against their trade?*
57. *What is said of smuggling? (What is smuggling?)*

Tell about— Study by topics

  I. The three kinds of government in the colonies.
    1. Royal government. a. What was it ? b. What colonies were governed in this way ?
    2. Charter government. a. What kind of a government was it? b. What colonies were governed under charters?
    3. Proprietary government. a. What kind of a government was it? b. What colonies were proprietary at the close of the French wars?
  II. The colonial Legislatures.
    a. The two houses that formed the Assembly. b. The way in which laws were passed, and the difference between them and our Legislatures.
  III. The laws regulating the trade of the colonies.

Blackboard

ROYAL	CHARTER	PROPRIETARY
Virginia	Massachusetts	Maryland
New York	Connecticut	Pennsylvania
New Jersey	Rhode Island	Delaware.
North Carolina		
South Carolina		Royal 7
New Hampshire		Charter 3
Georgia		Proprietary 3

Total 13

IN THE COLONIES.

I. Governor chosen by { the king, the proprietary, or the Assembly.

II. Council chosen by { the king, the governor, or the Assembly.

III. The Assembly chosen by the people.

IN THE STATES.

I. Governor
II. Senate
III. House of Representatives
} chosen by the people.

CHAPTER XXVI

Early Struggles for Liberty in the Colonies

Love of liberty in the colonists

THE colonies were settled at a time when the English people were trying to establish the principles of liberty in their own government. Many of the colonists were driven to this country by acts of tyranny. The settlers in America brought with them the English love of liberty. They were always ready to assert their right to "the liberties of Englishmen."

Early struggles for liberty in Virginia

Free government was first established in America by the Virginia charter of 1618. (See page 30.) The king, in dissolving the Virginia Company, struck a blow at the liberty

THE PILLORY AS USED IN AMERICA

of the colony, but the people strove hard to maintain their freedom. When, in 1624, the clerk of the Virginia Council betrayed their secrets to the king's commissioners, the Virginia Assembly sent him to the pillory, and had part of his

Nathaniel Bacon belonged to a family prominent in the county of Suffolk, in England. After graduating at Cambridge he studied law. His habits, like those of other young gentlemen of the time, were extravagant, and he exceeded the allowance made him by his father. About 1673 he went to Virginia, where he had a cousin, also named Nathaniel Bacon, who was rich and childless, and who wished to make the younger Nathaniel heir to his fortune, if he could have persuaded him not to embrace the popular cause. But the generous heart of the younger Bacon was touched with the wrongs of the people, and though he had been appointed a member of the governor's council, he yielded to the request of the people and became their leader. He showed excellent ability, and he was idolized by the people who stood guard day and night over his house lest he should be assassinated. In fighting the Indians he caused his men to stand so close to their fort that they could fire through the portholes, and yet, by standing at one side, escape the fire of the Indians. When, with a little handful of men, he marched swiftly on Jamestown, which was garrisoned by five times as many, the people brought food out into the road to refresh his soldiers, and the women cried after him, "General, if you need help, send for us! "He treated his enemies with gentleness, but he pushed his measures with vigor. When he died, his body was secretly buried by his friends, by sinking it in the waters of the river, in order that his enemies might not dig up his bones. The only document to be found that appears to have been written by Bacon's own hand is signed "Nathaniel Bacon, General, by consent of the people." So that he was something of a republican, though he lived a hundred years before the Revolution.

ears cut off, to the great disgust of King James. When Sir John Harvey was governor of Virginia, he opposed the people, and the Council deposed him in 1635, and sent him to England. King Charles I was offended at their presumption in deposing a royal governor, and he sent him back again as governor. But the people succeeded in having him removed in 1639.

Sir William Berkeley, the royal governor of Virginia, opposed the people, and in 1676 refused to allow them to make war on the Indians, who were ravaging the frontiers. This he did, lest the large profits he was making out of the fur trade should be reduced. The people of the frontier put themselves under the lead of a brilliant young man, Nathaniel Bacon by name. He forced the government to give him a commission, and he got the Legislature to pass some good laws, that were much

Bacon's rebellion

needed. Then he marched against the Indians and drove them back. On his return, hearing that Berkeley had determined to arrest him, he marched straight on Jamestown, and, though his force was not a fourth part so numerous as that in the town, he laid siege to it, captured it, and burned it to the ground. Governor Berkeley fled to the Eastern Shore of Chesapeake Bay, and the people of Virginia, except the few on the eastern side of the bay, took an oath to support Bacon, hailing him as a deliverer. But Bacon was worn out by the cares and exposures of the Indian war and the Jamestown siege, and he soon died. Berkeley succeeded after a while in reducing Bacon's followers, and in confiscating for his own use much of their property. Twenty-three leading men he put to death. For this severity the king recalled him in disgrace.

Attempts to dissolve the Massachusetts charter, in the reign of Charles I

Soon after Massachusetts had been settled, under the patent or charter of the Massachusetts Company (see pages 40, 41), an attempt was made to destroy that charter by the same kind of a lawsuit that had been used to destroy the charter of the Virginia Company. But the Massachusetts charter had been carried to America, and, when the judges in England sent orders to have it brought back to be examined, the rulers of the colony made excuses until the troubles in England caused the matter to be laid aside.

Massachusetts rebels against Governor Andros

In the reign of Charles II, proceedings were again taken against the Massachusetts charter, and in 1686 it was dissolved. King James II, who had by this time come to the throne, soon after appointed Sir Edmund Andros governor of New York and New England. He was a tyrant, who tried in every way to overthrow the liberties of the colonies. The people of New England were exasperated to the highest pitch, and when they heard that the Prince of Orange had landed in England, to overthrow James II, they rose against Andros and imprisoned him, establishing a government of their own. This was in 1689.

During the time that Andros was governor of all New England, he had tried to carry off the Connecticut charter. But it is said that, when the charter was brought in and laid on the table, the lights were suddenly blown out, and when they were lighted the charter was gone. It had been taken away and hidden in the hollow of an oak tree. This tree stood for nearly a hundred and seventy years after and was always respected as "the Charter Oak."

The charter of Connecticut hidden in an oak

GOVERNOR ANDROS

Andros was supreme governor of New York as well as of New England. In New York there was also great dissatisfaction with his government, and, when the common people heard that Andros had been put in prison in Boston, they rose against his lieutenant, and set up Captain Jacob Leisler for governor. Leisler, who governed the colony for more than two years, was a plain merchant, with no knowledge of government. He was bitterly opposed by the rich men of the colony. Though a man of patriotism, he was imprudent, and, after the arrival of a royal governor, his enemies succeeded in having him executed for treason.

Leisler's rebellion in New York

In 1719 the people of South Carolina overthrew the oppressive government of the lords-proprietors and put themselves under the government of the king, who bought out all the rights of the proprietors ten years later.

Rebellion against the proprietors of South Carolina

The spirit of liberty was in all the colonies. The governors appointed in England made continual efforts to encroach on the freedom of the people. The colonial Legislatures were in a perpetual quarrel with their governors. English statesmen desired to have the governors paid a fixed

Legislative resistance to the colonial governors

salary, so that they would not be dependent on the colonies. But the colonies kept the purse strings in their own hands, as far as possible, in order to preserve their liberties.

Questions for study

1. What spirit did the settlers in America bring with them from England?
2. What right were they ever ready to assert?
3. By what charter was free government first established in America?
4. At what did King James strike a blow when he dissolved the Virginia Company?
5. What did the people strive hard to maintain?
6. What did the clerk of the Council in Virginia betray to the king's commissioners in 1624?
7. What punishment did the Virginia Assembly inflict on him?
8. What did the Virginia Council do when Sir John Harvey oppressed the colony in 1635? What did the king do? What did the people succeed in doing with him?
9. How did Sir William Berkeley govern Virginia?
10. Why did he refuse to make war on the Indians?
11. Under whose lead did the people of the frontier put themselves?
12. What kind of a man was Nathaniel Bacon?
13. What did he force the governor to do?
14. What did he get the Legislature to do?
15. Against whom did Bacon march?
16. When he got back what did he hear?
17. What did he do?
18. How did his force compare with that in Jamestown?
19. When Bacon had taken Jamestown, what did Governor Berkeley do?
20. What did the people of Virginia do?
21. What became of Bacon?
22. What did Berkeley succeed in doing after Bacon's death?
23. How many did he put to death?
24. How did the king treat him for this?
25. What kind of an attempt was made to destroy the Massachusetts charter?
26. Where was the charter?
27. What course did the rulers of Massachusetts take to protect the charter?
28. In whose reign were new proceedings begun against the Massachusetts charter?
29. In what year was it dissolved?
30. What king was on the throne in 1686?
31. Whom had he appointed to be governor of New York and New England?
32. What news from England encouraged the people to rise against Andros? What did they do with him? In what year was this?
33. What had Andros tried to do in Connecticut?
34. How did the people protect their charter?
35. Where was the charter hidden?

AMERICAN UNIFORMS IN THE REVOLUTIONARY WAR

LIGHT INFANTRY   FIRST CITY TROOP PHILA.   WASHINGTON'S BODYGUARD   PENN. LINE INFANTRY PRIVATE   CONTINENTAL ARTILLERY PRIVATE   MASS. LINE INFANTRY LIEUTENANT   N.Y. LINE INFANTRY PRIVATE   ARTILLERY CAPTAIN   S.C. LINE INFANTRY LIEUTENANT   GEN. WASHINGTON'S UNIFORM   MOYLAN'S DRAGOONS

36. *How long did the charter oak stand?*
37. *Who was supreme governor of New York at this time?*
38. *What did the New Yorkers do when they heard that Andros had been imprisoned in Boston?*
39. *Whom did the New Yorkers set up for governor?*
40. *What kind of a man was Leisler? What became of him?*
41. *Where did much of the resistance to the encroachments of the governors take place?*
42. *What did English statesmen desire?*
43. *What did the colonies wish to keep in their own hands? Why?*

Tell about—

Study by topics

   I. Early struggles for liberty in Virginia.
     1. Against King James when the Virginia Company was dissolved.
     2. Governor Harvey sent home.
     3. Bacon's rebellion.
  II. Early struggles for liberty in Massachusetts.
     1. The preservation of the charter in the time of Charles I.
     2. The overthrow of Andros.
 III. The Connecticut charter in the charter oak.
 IV. Overthrow of the Andros government in New York.
  V. Revolution of 1719 in South Carolina.
 VI. Colonial Legislatures resist the royal power.

CHAPTER XXVII

The Causes of the Revolution

LONG before the Revolution there was much dissatisfaction in the colonies. Many of the governors sent over were tyrannical and dishonest. The Americans did not like the transportation of criminals, nor the action of the British government in annulling the laws made to keep out slaves. They were also much annoyed by English laws, which prevented them from sending away woolen goods, hats, and ironwares of their own make, from one colony to another. Most of all, they disliked the "navigation laws," the object of which was to compel them to do most of their trading with England (page 153).

General causes of discontent

The enforcement of these unpopular laws was in the hands of customhouse officers. The customhouse officers

PATRICK HENRY

The writs of assistance in Boston, in 1761, asked the courts for "writs of assistance," which would give them the right to search any house, at any time, for the purpose of finding smuggled goods. This produced a great excitement, and made the navigation laws still more unpopular. The trial which took place about these writs was a kind of beginning of the quarrel which brought on the Revolution fourteen years afterward.

The Stamp Act But England and the colonies, while always carrying on a family quarrel, had little thought of separating. Separation would probably have come when the colonies grew too large to be dependent, but this might at least have been postponed for two or three generations if the men who ruled England had not tried to tax the American colonies. Parliament passed, in 1765, what was known as "The Stamp Act." This law required that all bills, notes, leases, and many other such documents used in the colonies, should

Patrick Henry was born in Hanover County, Virginia, in 1736. He was chiefly educated in a school taught by his father. He read law and began the practice of his profession. In 1763 he was engaged to plead in defense of the people against a suit of the parish clergy. It was known as "The Parsons' Cause." Before a court, in which his own father was the presiding magistrate, he pleaded the case of the people with such extraordinary eloquence and vehemence that the clergymen rose and left the room, and Henry's father wept tears of triumph, while the people carried the young lawyer about on their shoulders. Elected to the Virginia Legislature, he immediately took the lead against the Stamp Act and became famous. It was in his speech on the Stamp Act that he uttered the famous words "Caesar had his Brutus, Charles the First his Cromwell, and George the Third—" As Henry reached this point his opponents cried "Treason! treason!" But the speaker finished by saying, "—may profit by their example," and added, "If that be treason, make the most of it!" When pleading for the organization of the Virginia militia, before the Revolutionary War had begun, he closed with these memorable words: "Is life so dear, or peace so sweet, as to be purchased at the price of chains and slavery? Forbid it, Almighty God! I know not what course others may take, but as for me, give me liberty or give me death!" He was several times governor of Virginia. He died in 1799.

James Otis was born at what is now West Barnstable, on Cape Cod, in 1725. After studying in his native town he went to Harvard College, where he graduated when he was eighteen years old. But, wishing to lay a good foundation, he spent a year and a half more in general studies before he entered on the study of the law. He practiced at first in Plymouth and afterward in Boston. He rose to the highest rank in his profession. He was an honorable man, and would never take unfair advantages of an opponent. When the customhouse officers applied for "writs of assistance," which would enable them to search any house at any time, it became the duty of Otis, as advocate general, to argue in favor of the writs. But he gave up this lucrative office and took the side of liberty. He made a great speech, five hours long, against the writs, and this speech is considered by some the starting point of the Revolution. It was in this speech that he first raised the popular cry against "taxation without representation," which was the watchword of the Revolution. In the great struggle over the Stamp Act, and in the debates that followed, to 1769, he was the brilliant leader. When the bitterness of the controversy with England was at its height he became involved in an affray with several officers of the customs, and was seriously injured. Soon after this his mind, wearied by the exciting controversies in which he was engaged, became gradually deranged, and he retired from public affairs. In 1783 he was killed by a stroke of lightning.

be written on stamped paper, which should be sold by officers at such prices as should bring a revenue to the English government. All newspapers were required to be printed on stamped paper.

The American people quickly saw that, if the British Parliament could pass such an act, they could tax America in any other way. The cry was raised in all the colonies. "No taxation without representation!" Patrick Henry, a brilliant speaker, took the lead in the agitation in Virginia, and James Otis, an eloquent Boston lawyer was the principal orator in Massachusetts. The rivalries and jealousies between the various colonies died out in the new patriotic feeling, and the excitement ran like a flame of

Violent opponent to the Stamp Act

JAMES OTIS

fire from New Hampshire to Georgia. There was everywhere a call for union among the colonies. A congress of delegates from nine of the colonies met in New York in October, 1765. It is known as "The Stamp Act Congress."

But the people were too much excited to stop at orderly measures. In colony after colony violent mobs compelled the stamp officers to resign. In some places the people pulled down or rifled the houses of British officials. Not one man in all the colonies dared to sell a piece of stamped paper.

The Americans agree not to import English goods. Repeal of the Stamp Act

Though America had almost no manufactures, the merchants pledged themselves to import no English goods until the Stamp Act was repealed. As black goods came from England, the people resolved to wear no black at funerals, and they began to dress in homespun. They resolved, also, to eat no more mutton, in order to increase the home production of wool. English merchants, whose trade was hurt by these measures, now joined in the clamor for the repeal of the Stamp Act, and it was repealed in 1766, to the great joy of the colonies.

Other acts of oppression

But Parliament passed another bill at the same time, asserting its right to tax the colonies. New ways of raising a revenue in America, without the consent of the people, were tried. Troops were quartered in the colonies, and the people were required to pay the expense. This the colonies refused to do. In 1770 a collision took place between British troops and some people in Boston. Three of the people were killed. This was called " The

SAMUEL ADAMS

Samuel Adams was born in Boston in 1722. He graduated at Harvard College at twenty years of age. He was already devoted to liberty, and his oration when he received the degree of master of arts defended the right of the people to resist the supreme magistrate "if the commonwealth cannot otherwise be preserved." He was one of the first to oppose taxation by Parliament, and he early became the chief organizer and leader of the revolutionary movement in Massachusetts. He is said to have proposed the Congress of 1774. When General Gage offered pardon to the Americans, he excepted Samuel Adams and John Hancock. Adams was a member of the Continental Congress and a principal advocate of American independence. He lived a pure and incorruptible life, and, though always poor, the king could not buy him from the path of virtue. He died in 1803.

Boston Massacre. It excited deep feeling in all the colonies, and Samuel Adams, the leader of the Boston town meeting, compelled the governor to withdraw the troops from the city.

The tax was at length taken off from nearly everything except tea. By releasing a part of the English duty on tea sent to America, the government arranged it so that the Americans, after paying a tax in America, would have their tea cheaper than before. The Americans were not contending for a little money, but for a principle, and they refused to receive the tea. They began to drink tea made of sassafras roots, sage, raspberry leaves, yaupon, and other American plants. The English government sent over consignments of tea to the principal ports. At Boston a company of fifty men, disguised as Mohawk Indians, boarded the ships and emptied three hundred and forty-two chests of tea into the sea. This is known as "The Boston Tea Party." In New York the people emptied a private consignment of tea into the water, and the ships which were sent by the government they compelled to go back to England. Philadelphia also sent the tea ships home again. In Charleston the tea was landed, but purposely stored in damp cellars, where it rotted; and at Annapolis, a ship that had paid the duty on a private consignment of tea was burned in the harbor.

Opposition to the tax on tea

The English Parliament punished Boston by closing its port until the tea thrown overboard should be paid for. This act produced a great deal of distress in Boston, by ruining its business and throwing its working people out of employment. But it excited the sympathy of the other colonies, who sent aid to its people and who resolved to support it. A committee in New York immediately suggested that Massachusetts should call a congress, and thus the colonies were finally brought into a union against the mother country.

1. What was the character of many of the men sent over to America as governors?
2. What kind of people did the British government transport to be sold into service in America?
3. How did the people feel about the bringing in of criminals?
4. What did the English government do about the importation of slaves?
5. What laws were made about American manufactures?
6. What three sorts of manufacture were particularly restrained?
7. What was the object of the navigation laws?
8. In whose hands was the enforcement of the navigation laws?
9. What kind of writs did the customhouse officers ask for in 1761?
10. What right did the "writs of assistance" give to the officers?
11. How did the people feel about this?
12. Was there much thought of separation?
13. Would the colonies have separated from England when they did if the English government had been wise?
14. What act was passed in 1765? What did this law require?
15. What did the American people see in this measure?
16. What cry was raised in all the colonies?
17. Who took the lead in the agitation in Virginia?
18. Who was the chief orator in Massachusetts?
19. What effect did the excitement have on the jealousies between the colonies?
20. When did the "Stamp Act Congress" meet? Where?
21. Did the people stop with orderly measures?
22. What took place in many of the colonies? Were many stamps sold?
23. What pledge did the merchants make? What did the people refuse to wear?
24. In what kind of goods did they dress themselves?
25. Why did they refuse to eat mutton?
26. Who now joined in the clamor for the repeal of the Stamp Act?
27. Why did the merchants wish it repealed? When was it repealed?

28. *What bill did Parliament pass when it repealed the Stamp Act?*
29. *What was done about taxing America?*
30. *What was done about gathering troops? Did the colonies quarter the troops?*
31. *What took place in 1770? What is this occurrence called? What effect did it have?*
32. *When the taxes were taken off of other articles, what article was still taxed?*
33. *How did the British government seek to make this agreeable to the Americans?*
34. *Why would they not accept an arrangement which made tea cheaper?*
35. *What did the people drink instead of tea?*
36. *What happened when the government sent tea to Boston?*
37. *What is this occurrence called?*
38. *What did New York do about the tea? What did Philadelphia do?*
39. *What became of the tea sent to Charleston?*
40. *What of a consignment of tea at Annapolis?*
41. *How did the English Parliament punish Boston for her part in the tea business?*
42. *What was the effect of the closing of the port on the people of Boston?*
43. *How did the other colonies feel about it?*
44. *What did the New York committee suggest?*

I. Old causes of dissatisfaction.   Study by topics
   1. Character of the governors.
   2. Transportation of criminals and slaves.
   3. Laws about manufactures and navigation.
   4. Writs of assistance.
II. The Stamp Act of 1765.
   1. Its nature.
   2. The excitement in America.
     a. No taxation without representation. b. Patrick Henry.
     c. James Otis. d. The "Stamp Act Congress."
   3. The mobs.
   4. The agreement against English goods.
   5. Repeal of the act.
III. New measures of oppression.
   1. Parliament claims the right to tax.
   2. Imposes new taxes.
   3. Tries to quarter troops at the expense of the colonies.
   4. "The Boston Massacre."
IV. The duty on tea.
   1. The new plan of taxing tea.
   2. Substitutes used.
   3. Boston Tea Party.
   4. Tea in New York, Philadelphia, Charleston, and Annapolis.
V. The closing of the port of Boston.
   1. The effect on Boston.
   2. The sympathy of the other colonies.
   3. The calling of a congress.

CHAPTER XXVIII

The Outbreak of the Revolution and Declaration of Independence

PINE TREE FLAG USED ABOUT BOSTON AT THE BEGINNING OF THE REVOLUTION

The Congress of 1774

THOUGH the Congress of the thirteen colonies which met in Philadelphia in 1774 had no authority to make laws, the people chose to obey its recommendations and to disobey the governors sent to them from England. The Congress petitioned the king and Parliament to restore their rights. But meanwhile the colonies organized the militia, and collected military stores, that they might be ready to fight for their liberties.

British troops sent from Boston to Concord

General Gage was in command of the British forces at Boston. He resolved to check the rebellious spirit of the people. He sent out troops from Boston soon after midnight on April 19, 1775, to destroy some military stores at Concord, about twenty

> **Paul Revere**, an engraver and an active patriot, was sent to tell Adams and Hancock, who were at Lexington, that the British were coming. He waited at Charlestown until he saw a light hung in a church steeple, which was a signal to him that the British were moving. Then he rode to Lexington, warning the people of their danger. (See Longfellow's famous poem on the subject.)

miles away The Americans had formed companies ready to be called out on the minute; these were called "minutemen." At Lexington the British troops fired on the minutemen and killed eight of them. At Concord the soldiers destroyed the stores.

GENERAL GAGE

The battle of Lexington and the beginning of the Revolution

But the minutemen were now pouring in from the whole country, and the English troops beat a hasty retreat back through Lexington. The Americans swarming like maddened bees, attacked them in the rear in front and on both sides. The minutemen fired from behind trees, rocks, and

Capture of Ticonderoga—Soon after the battle of Lexington, Ethan Allen, at the head of eighty backwoodsmen from Vermont, known as "Green Mountain Boys," made a sudden descent on Fort Ticonderoga, near the south end of Lake Champlain. Entering the fort in the night, he found the commander in bed, and summoned him to surrender. "In whose name?" demanded the officer. "In the name of the great Jehovah and the Continental Congress!" replied Allen. With the fort Allen secured a supply of powder, then very much needed by the Americans.

ETHAN ALLEN

stone fences. The English retreated in a state of exhaustion, with a loss in killed and wounded of nearly three hundred men; the Americans lost about eighty-five. Messengers on horseback carried the news of the "battle of Lexington;" as it was called, all over New England and into the Middle and Southern colonies. The people now knew that the war so long threatened had begun.

After the battle of Lexington, an irregular army of New Englanders blockaded the English troops in Boston. A detachment sent to

The battle of Bunker Hill

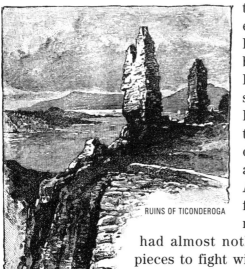

RUINS OF TICONDEROGA

encamp on Bunker Hill threw up breastworks on Breed's Hill instead. Here the British attacked them with nearly double their force and though the Americans were farmers who had never fought, and had almost nothing but fowling pieces to fight with, they twice repulsed the British regulars with great

slaughter, and, when their ammunition was exhausted, fought with the butts and barrels of their guns until compelled to retreat. One third of the British force was killed or wounded, and the result of the battle was to give great confidence to the Americans, who have always regarded the battle of Bunker Hill, as it was called more as a victory than a defeat.

Meanwhile, it fell to the Continental Congress, in session

Early life of Washington—George Washington was born in Virginia, February 22, 1732. His father was a planter, with a large landed property; his mother was a woman of great force of character, but, like many ladies of that day, she had little education. Washington got such education as the poor country schools of the time afforded, but he made the most of it. His exercise books are models of method and neatness. Besides the common branches of reading, writing, and arithmetic, he learned surveying and bookkeeping. He was a lad of great strength, and took the lead in all athletic sports, and he became one of the best horsemen of his time. He bore hardships with great resolution, he spoke the truth, he was economical, industrious, and systematic in his habits. He was, while yet hardly more than a boy, engaged in surveying wild lands for Lord Fairfax, an English nobleman, who owned a great tract of Virginia Territory, and lived in the Shenandoah Valley. He thus came to know the frontier Country and the habits of the Indians. He was made a major of the militia at nineteen, and he was but twenty-one when Governor Dinwiddie sent him on a mission to the French posts on the Ohio, as we have told in another chapter. By his prudent conduct in Braddock's and Forbes' expeditions, and in the defense of the Virginia frontier, he won the confidence of the American people. He was a member of the Continental Congress of 1774. He was not a brilliant man, but even in 1774 Patrick Henry pronounced him, for "solid information and sound judgment, unquestionably the greatest man" on the floor of the Continental Congress.

in Philadelphia, to elect a commander-in-chief for the new army. Colonel George Washington, of Virginia, who had gained distinction for zeal, courage, and prudence in the French and Indian wars, was chosen to this responsible place. He declined all pay except his expenses. He set out for Cambridge, Massachusetts, where he took command on July 3, 1775.

Washington made commander-in-chief

Washington brought his irregular army to a tolerable state of organization, and closely besieged the British in Boston until March of the next year, 1776, when he sent a strong force to occupy and fortify Dorchester Heights, which commanded the harbor and the town. This forced the English to withdraw their troops from Boston to Halifax in Nova Scotia.

The English evacuate Boston

FLAG BORNE BY AMERICAN TROOPS AT THE SOUTH AT THE BEGINNING OF THE REVOLUTION

Up to this time the Americans had been fighting for their liberties as British subjects. But now they were everywhere weaned from attachment to England. The colonies, one after another, formed constitutions inde-

RATTLESNAKE FLAG, USED AT THE BEGINNING OF THE REVOLUTION. IT SOMETIMES BORE THE MOTTO, "DON'T TREAD ON ME!"

The Declaration of Independence

pendent of England, or took steps looking toward independence. On the fourth day of July, 1776, the Continental Congress adopted the "Declaration of Independence." This act was a formal separation of the united colonies from England, whose king was no more to be king in the thirteen colonies. Thomas Jefferson, of Virginia, wrote this eloquent declaration, which will never be forgotten.

The Declaration says: "We hold these truths to be self evident: That all men are created equal; that they are endowed by their Creator with certain unalienable rights; that among these are life, liberty, and the pursuit of happiness." The Declaration of Independence lists various acts of tyranny which the colonies had suffered under the government of George III, and then says: "We therefore, the representatives of the United States of America in general Congress assembled, appeal-

Thomas Jefferson was born near Charlottesville, Va., in 1743. His father was a noted land surveyor, and one of the authors of a map of Virginia. He left an ample fortune. Thomas was an eager student. He graduated at William and Mary College, and was soon recognized as perhaps the most accomplished general scholar in the colonies. He was an excellent mathematician, and knew Greek, Latin, French, Spanish and Italian. There was almost no knowledge that he was not eager to acquire. He was not gifted as an orator, but with his eloquent pen he rendered great services to the cause of liberty in America. He wrote the Declaration of Independence, the most famous state paper in the world. He used his best endeavor to have slavery and the slave trade abolished. He took the lead in abolishing the colonial laws that gave to the oldest son the largest share of the father's property. He was also the leader in separating church and state, and giving to the people religious freedom. To him we owe the change of our money from pounds, shillings, and pence to a simple decimal system of dollars, dimes, and cents. To him, also, was due the purchase from France of the territory west of the Mississippi. He was the third President of the United States chosen in the year 1800, and was elected for a second term in 1804. He died on the 4th of July, 1826, just fifty years to a day from the adoption of the Declaration of Independence, and the aged John Adams, second President, died on the same day.

ing to the Supreme Judge of the world for the rectitude of
our intentions, do, in the name and by the authority of these
colonies, solemnly publish
and declare, that these
United Colonies are, and of
right ought to be, free and
independent States." It
closes with these words:
"And for the support of this
declaration, with a firm reliance on the protection
of Divine Providence,
we mutually pledge
to each other our
lives, our for-
t u n e s ,
a n d   o u r
s a c r e d
honor."

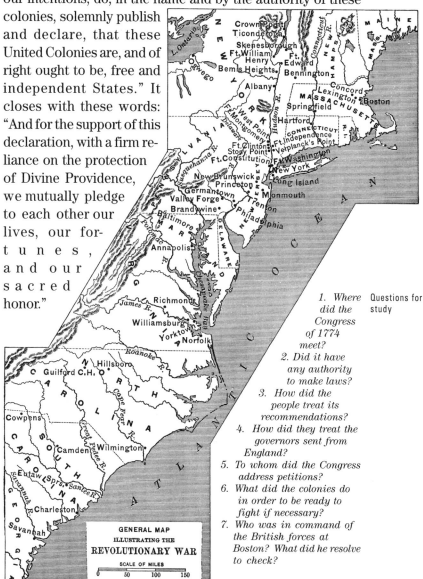

GENERAL MAP
ILLUSTRATING THE
REVOLUTIONARY WAR
SCALE OF MILES
0   50   100   150

Questions for study

1. Where did the Congress of 1774 meet?
2. Did it have any authority to make laws?
3. How did the people treat its recommendations?
4. How did they treat the governors sent from England?
5. To whom did the Congress address petitions?
6. What did the colonies do in order to be ready to fight if necessary?
7. Who was in command of the British forces at Boston? What did he resolve to check?

8. *At what time of night did he send out troops from Boston?*
9. *On what day of what month was this? In what year?*
10. *What were these troops to destroy?*
11. *Where were the military stores?*
12. *How far away is Concord from Boston?*
13. *What took place at Lexington as the troops passed through?*
14. *Who were called minutemen?*
15. *How many minutemen were killed in this first fire?*
16. *What did the British troops do at Concord?*
17. *Who were now pouring in from the whole country?*
18. *What did the English troops do?*
19. *What did the Americans do?*
20. *How many did the English lose?*
21. *How was the news carried?*
22. *What war did this battle begin?*
23. *What kind of an army blockaded the English in Boston after the battle of Lexington?*
24. *On what hill was a detachment sent to encamp?*
25. *On what hill did they throw up breastworks?*
26. *How much stronger than the Americans was the force sent to attack them?*
27. *What kind of troops were the Americans? What kind of guns did they have? How did they fight?*
28. *What did they do when their ammunition was exhausted?*
29. *What portion of the British force was killed and wounded?*
30. *What was the result of the battle?*
31. *How have the Americans always regarded it?*
32. *By whom was a commander-in-chief of the army elected?*
33. *Whom did the Congress choose for this place?*
34. *What qualities had given him distinction in the French and Indian wars?*
35. *What did Washington do about salary? Where did he go to take command of the army? On what day did he take command?*
36. *Where were the British whom Washington now besieged?*
37. *To what heights did he send a force? In what month was this?*

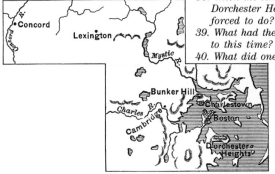

38. *When the Americans had taken possession of Dorchester Heights what were the English forced to do?*
39. *What had the Americans been fighting for up to this time?*
40. *What did one colony after another do?*
41. *What declaration did Congress adopt? On what day?*
42. *What was this act a separation from?*
43. *Who wrote the Declaration of Independence? Two truths are held to be self evident in the Declaration of Independence: what is the first one?*

50. *What unalienable rights are said to belong to all men?*
51. *Of what acts of tyranny does the Declaration give an account?*
52. *What solemn declaration is then made? What pledge is given?*
    (Give as nearly as possible the exact words of the Declaration.)

I. Preparations for the Revolution.
II. Battle of Lexington.
III. Battle of Bunker Hill.
IV. Appointment of Washington.
V. Recovery of Boston.
VI. Declaration of Independence.

Study by topics

General Gage sent out troops to destroy some military stores at _____ about _____ miles from Boston. The Americans had companies called _____. These attacked and drove in the _____ troops. This is called the battle of _____. The Americans sent a force which encamped on _____ Hill, now commonly called _____ Hill. The English attacked them and carried the works with great loss Colonel _____, of Virginia, was appointed general-in-chief of the American forces, and took command at _____. In March following he sent a force to occupy _____ Heights, commanding Boston; this obliged the _____ troops to evacuate the town.

Skeleton summary

The region about Boston. Make a diagram of, or otherwise locate with reference to Boston, Lexington, Concord, Bunker Hill, Dorchester (now South Boston) Heights.

Geography

CHAPTER XXIX

The Battle of Trenton and the Capture of Burgoyne's Army

KING GEORGE III

THE people received the Declaration with joy. Pictures of the king were destroyed; his coat-of-arms was torn down from public buildings and thrown into the patriotic bonfires. The leaden Statue of George III, which stood in Bowling Green, in New York city, was made into bullets.

Joy of the people at the news of the Declaration of Independence

But the joy of the Americans was soon turned into anxiety. About the time of the adoption of the Declaration of Independence, General Howe landed a large body of English troops on Staten Island near New York, and a few days later his brother, Admiral Lord

Arrival of an English army near New York

ADMIRAL LORD HOWE

DESTROYING THE STATUE OF GEORGE III AT THE BOWLING GREEN, IN NEW YORK CITY

Howe, came with reinforcements.

The battle of Long Island, and the evacuation of New York by the Americans

The battle of Long Island was fought near Brooklyn, on the 27th of August, 1776. In this battle the Americans were defeated, and Washington withdrew his troops from Brooklyn, and left the whole of Long Island in the hands of the British. The Americans were not strong enough to hold New York, and it was soon evacuated. Fort Washington, above New York, with two thousand Americans, was captured by the British, who soon crossed the Hudson. Washington was obliged to retreat, step by step, across New Jersey into Pennsylvania.

Washington crosses the Delaware and captures Trenton

The American cause seemed on the verge of ruin. It was necessary to strike some blow to hearten the people. The English government had hired a body of Hessian soldiers, men from that part of Germany called Hesse-Cassel [hess-cas´-sel], to assist in subduing the Americans. Fifteen hundred of these were stationed in Trenton. Washing-

ton crossed the Delaware River, above Trenton, on the
night of Christmas, with twenty-five hundred men. The
river was so full of floating ice that it took Washington all
night to get over with his men. The Hessians were, as
Washington expected, stupefied by their Christmas revel-
ries of the night before. The Americans surprised them at
eight in the morning. About a thousand prisoners were
taken.

A HESSIAN
TROOPER

THE RETREAT FROM LONG ISLAND

Battle of Princeton

AMERICAN FLAG, ADOPTED IN 1777

A little later the British advanced upon Trenton and put Washington in great danger, because he could not retreat across the river in the presence of the enemy. He saved himself by a bold move. Building up his camp fires, so as to deceive the enemy, he moved around the British force and attacked and captured Princeton, in their rear. This forced the British to fall back to New Brunswick, and left the most of New Jersey in the hands of the Americans.

Burgoynes' expedition

In 1777 General Burgoyne was sent to force his way down from Canada, through Lake Champlain and Lake George, to the Hudson. He was expected to capture Albany, and make a junction with the British forces about New York. The effect of this would have been to cut the United Colonies in two.

Fall of Ticonderoga

Burgoyne compelled General St. Clair to evacuate Ticonderoga, and captured the artillery and all the stores which St. Clair was trying to move. He then went to Skenesborough, now Whitehall, at the south end of Lake Champlain. At length he reached the Hudson at Fort Edward, having gained complete control of Lake Champlain and Lake George.

Battle of Bennington

From Fort Edward, Burgoyne sent out a force of hired German troops into what is now Vermont, to capture stores and horses. But the militia of western New England, who like almost all men in a new country were accustomed to the use of firearms from childhood, gathered under the lead of General Stark, and at the battle of Bennington utterly defeated the detachment sent out by Burgoyne.

The whole Northern country was up now. The ranks of the army under General Gates, which opposed the

HESSIAN MADE PRISONER BY MINUTEMAN

march of Burgoyne, were quickly filled by militia pouring in from New York and New England. In a hard fought battle at Bemis Heights the Americans won a decisive victory. Burgoyne was soon hemmed in on every side by the increasing American force. His retreat was cut off in every direction and on the 16th of October he signed articles of capitulation. The next day his whole army laid down their arms. This victory delivered the American cause from the greatest peril, and brought joy without measure to the people.

GENERAL GATES

1. *How did the people receive the Declaration of Independence?*
2. *How did they show their dislike to the king, George III?*
3. *What became of his leaden statue in New York?*
4. *What turned the joy of the Americans to anxiety?*
5. *What English general landed on Staten Island?*
6. *Near what city is Staten Island?*
7. *Who brought reinforcements to General Howe?*
8. *Near what city was the battle of Long Island fought? In what month?*
9. *Who were defeated in this battle?*
10. *What did Washington do after the battle?*
11. *Why did he evacuate New York?*
12. *What fort did the British capture?*
13. *What river did the British cross after capturing Fort Washington?*
14. *Across what State did Washington retreat? Into what State?*
15. *What were the prospects of the American cause at this time?*
16. *What kind of soldiers had the English hired?*
17. *Where were the Hessians from?*
18. *How many Hessians were in Trenton at this time?*
19. *What river was between Washington's army and Trenton?*
20. *At what time of the year did Washington and his troops cross?*
21. *What made it hard to get over?*
22. *By what were the Hessians stupefied?*
23. *At what time in the morning did the Americans attack them?*
24. *How many prisoners were taken?*
25. *When the British advanced against Washington, in Trenton, why was he in danger?*
26. *How did he save himself?*
27. *What effect did this have on the British?*

Questions for study

HESSIAN TROOPER'S BOOT

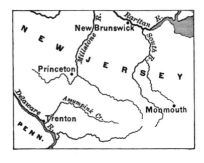

28. *In what year was Burgoyne's expedition sent from Canada?*
29. *Through what lakes did Burgoyne move?*
30. *Toward what river?*
31. *What city did he expect to capture?*
32. *With what English forces was he to make a junction?*
33. *What would have been the effect of this?*
34. *What fort did Burgoyne force General St. Clair to evacuate?*
35. *To what place did Burgoyne then go?*
36. *Where did he reach the Hudson?*
37. *Of what lakes had he gained control?*
38. *Into what region did Burgoyne send out a detachment?*
39. *For what purpose were they sent?*
40. *Under what general did the militia of New England gather?*
41. *What happened at the battle of Bennington to the detachment which Burgoyne had sent out?*
42. *In what battle was Burgoyne's army defeated?*
43. *What did he try to do?*
44. *Finding he could not retreat, what took place?*
45. *What was the effect of this victory on the Americans?*

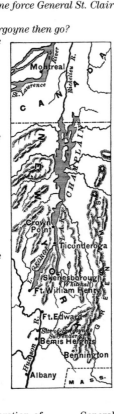

Study by topics

Tell about—

I. Events following the Declaration.
  1. Joy of the people at the Declaration of Independence.
  2. Landing of Howe.
  3. Battle of Long Island and other English successes.
  4. Battle of Trenton.
  5. Battle of Princeton.
II. Burgoyne's expedition.
  1. Its purpose.
  2. Burgoyne's successes.
  3. Battle of Bennington.
  4. Defeat of Burgoyne.
  5. Surrender of Burgoyne's army.

Skeleton summaries

1. British successes. About the time of the Declaration of _____ General Howe landed on _____ Island. The _____ were defeated in the battle of Long Island. It was fought near _____, August 27, 17 ___. Washington soon after evacuated _____ . Fort _____, above New York, was captured by the _____, and Washington was obliged to retreat into _____.

2. Washington's successes. The English had a body of hired German soldiers stationed at _____. Washington crossed the _____ on the night of _____, and attacked them at eight o'clock in the morning. He took _____ prisoners. When the English advanced to Trenton, he attacked and took _____ in their rear, and forced them to fall back, leaving nearly the whole State of _____ in his hands.

3. Burgoyne's campaign. Burgoyne's advance from Canada took place in the year 17___. He forced St. Clair to abandon Fort _____, and got possession of Lake _____ and Lake _____, and reached the _____ River at Fort Edward. He sent out an expedition into what is now the State of _____, which was defeated by American militia in the battle of _____. Burgoyne's army was defeated in the battle of _____ Heights, and surrendered on the 16th of _____, 1777.

In what direction could the English pass from Staten Island to Long Island? From Long Island to New York? From New York Island to New Jersey? In what part of New Jersey is Trenton? What direction is Princeton from Trenton? In what part of New Jersey is New Brunswick? In what direction did Burgoyne move from Canada to Ticonderoga? On what lake is Ticonderoga? By what water would one pass from Ticonderoga to Whitehall? What lake lies south of the main body of Lake Champlain? On what river is Fort Edward? In what State? In what direction from Fort Edward is Bemis Heights? From Fort Edward, in what direction is Bennington? In what State ?

Geographical inquiries

CHAPTER XXX

The Dark Period of the Revolution

GENERAL BURGOYNE

THE overthrow of Burgoyne relieved the American cause of one great danger, but it was sorely beset in other quarters. General Howe had taken his army around by sea, and landed at the head of Chesapeake Bay, in order to capture Philadelphia, which was then the seat of Congress. Washington's army was inferior to the British, and he retired behind the Brandywine River, where, on the 11th of September, 1777, was fought the battle known as "The Battle of the Brandywine." The

The battle of the Brandywine, Sept. 11, 1777

GENERAL SIR WILLIAM HOWE

Americans were forced to retreat, and the British entered Philadelphia.

Battle of Germantown, Oct. 4, 1777

On the 4th of October Washington attacked British at Germantown, near Philadelphia, but he was again defeated. The winter of 1777-'78 was the darkest season of the Revolution. Washington went into winter quarters at Valley Forge. Congress had no money. Many of the soldiers were without shoes, and in their marches over frozen ground they left blood in their tracks. Some of the poor fellows sat up by the fires at night, for want of blankets to keep them warm.

LA FAYETTE

Winter quarters at Valley Forge, 1777-'78

The war of the colonies against England had excited much sympathy in Europe. Many foreign officers had come over to assist the Americans. Some of these were mere adventurers, but others were men of ability and gener-

BARON STEUBEN

The Marquis de La Fayette was born of an illustrious French family on the 7th of September, 1757. He was but nineteen years old, with every prospect which great wealth and family influence could give, when he embraced the cause of liberty in America. Against the command of the King of France, he freighted a ship at his own expense, and landed in America in 1777, to offer his services as a simple volunteer. He quickly won the favor of Congress and the lifelong friendship of Washington. He was made major-general, and, though so young, showed considerable ability as a commander. His conduct was always prudent. He was wounded at the Brandywine, and he distinguished himself by a masterly retreat from Barren Hill and fine conduct at the battle of Monmouth. In Virginia, when Cornwallis threatened him with a superior force, and boasted that the "little boy," as he called La Fayette, could not get away from him, the young marquis avoided a battle, and prepared by his skillful movements for the final success at Yorktown. La Fayette was all his life a lover of liberty and order. He took a brave part in the French Revolution, but refused to go to extremes. He was arrested and imprisoned for years in Austria, in spite of American efforts to relieve him. At the instance of Bonaparte he was freed in 1797. He visited the United States in 1824 when he was welcomed as the guest of the nation. He made the tour of the country, rejoicing in its prosperity. He was everywhere received with enthusiasm by those whose fathers he had helped in their hour of distress. Congress voted him $200,000 and a township of land for his losses and expenses in the Revolution. Though an old man, he took part in the French Revolution of 1830, and remained the devoted friend of human liberty until his death in 1834.

PULASKI

ous spirit. Such was the young French nobleman La Fayette; Count Pulaski, Baron Steuben, and Baron De Kalb were also excellent officers.

France had from the first taken a lively interest in the fate of America, partly from a jealous dislike of England, partly from the love of liberty that was growing among the French people. The courageous persistence with which Washington attacked Howe's army at Germantown made a strong impression in France, and on the 30th of January, 1778, a treaty of alliance between France and the United States was signed. This was received in America with the greatest joy.

DE KALB

The first result of the alliance with France was the recovery of Philadelphia. Sir Henry Clinton. who had succeeded Howe in command of the British army, was afraid that the French might blockade the Delaware, and thus shut him up in Philadelphia. He therefore retreated across New Jersey to New York, pushed by Washington's army. During this retreat the battle of Monmouth was fought. The Americans gained a partial victory, the English retreating under cover of night.

When the war had lasted three or four years, the British government became convinced that it was a most difficult task to subdue the Northern and Middle States. The people could not be subdued even when the armies were beaten. But as there were more slaves, and as the white

SIR HENRY CLINTON

GENERAL MOULTRIE

population was more scattered, in the Southern States, they supposed it might be easier to overrun them. At the close of the year 1778 the British captured Savannah, and Georgia was soon subjugated. In the next year an attempt was made by the Americans, assisted by the French fleet, to capture Savannah, but it failed. In this attempt Count

Sergeant Jasper—In 1776 the British fleet attacked Fort Sullivan, in Charleston harbor, which was successfully defended by General Moultrie. During the hottest of the fire, the flag of the fort which bore the device of a crescent, was shot away. A sergeant named Jasper leaped down outside the fort and recovered the flag, which he fixed to a sponge staff. This he stuck in the sand and then returned unharmed to the fort. For this act the governor of South Carolina gave him his own sword. In 1779 he was engaged in the attack on Savannah, when the colors of his own regiment were shot away. Jasper tried to replace them on a parapet, but he was mortally wounded. In this condition he brought away his colors.

GENERAL LINCOLN, WHO
DEFENDED CHARLESTON IN 1780

Pulaski lost his life. After a regular siege a British fleet and army took Charleston in May, 1780. General Gates, who had commanded the Northern army when Burgoyne surrendered, was put in command of all the American troops at the South. But Gates was utterly beaten, and his whole army routed and dispersed, by the British under Cornwallis, at the battle of Camden, in South Carolina. There was no longer any American army worthy of the name in the whole South.

Sumter and Marion maintain a partisan warfare in South Carolina

But in the South, as in the North, the British could not gain permanent advantages. Though the Americans shrank from entering the army, which was poorly paid and badly fed, they refused

One of the most brilliant enterprises of the war was the capture of Stony Point on the Hudson. General Wayne led a force of Americans, by defiles in the mountains, to within a mile and a half of the fort on the evening of July 15, 1779. To prevent discovery, all the dogs on the road were killed. At midnight the Americans moved on the fort. The advanced guard carried empty guns with fixed bayonets, and thus faced the fire of the defenders as they rushed over the works and made the British garrison prisoners.

to be subdued. Sumter and Marion mustered considerable bodies of South Carolina militia. These men knew the country perfectly; they lurked in the forests and swamps, coming out from time to time to strike the British where they were weakest.

GENERAL MARION

1. *Where did General Howe take his army in order to capture Philadelphia?*
2. *Behind what river did Washington retire?*
3. *In what year was the battle of the Brandywine fought?*
4. *Who were forced to retreat?*
5. *What city did the British enter?*
6. *In what month in 1777 did Washington attack the British in Germantown?*
7. *Near what city is Germantown? (It is now a part of Philadelphia.)*
8. *What was the result of the battle of Germantown?*
9. *What was the state of feeling in Europe about the war in the colonies?*
10. *Who came over to assist the Americans?*
11. *What was the character of some of these officers?*
12. *What kind of men were others of them?*
13. *From what country was La Fayette?*
14. *From what country was Pulaski?*
15. *What other two officers are mentioned?*
16. *What country had from the first taken a lively interest in the American struggle?*
17. *Why was France interested?*
18. *What made a strong impression in France?*
19. *When was the treaty of alliance between France and America signed?*
20. *How was the news of this treaty received in America?*
21. *What was the first result of the treaty with France?*
22. *Of what was Clinton afraid? What did he do?*
23. *What battle was fought during his retreat from Philadelphia to New York?*
24. *After three or four years of war in the Northern and Middle States, to what conclusion did the British government come?*
25. *Why did they think it easier to conquer the Southern States?*
26. *What city did the British capture at the close of the year 1778?*
27. *What State was soon subdued?*
28. *Who assisted the Americans in the recapture of Savannah in 1779?*
29. *What was the . result?*
30. *What distinguished officer lost his life in this attack?*
31. *What city did the British fleet and army capture in 1780?*
32. *Who was put in command of the American army in the South?*

Questions for study

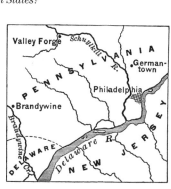

33. In what battle was Gates utterly beaten?
34. What became of his army?
35. In what State is Camden?
36. Why could the British not gain permanent advantages in the South.
37. Who mustered considerable bodies of South Carolina militia?
38. Where did they lurk?

Study by topics

Tell about—

I. The darkest hour.
  1. The battle of the Brandywine.
  2. The loss of Philadelphia.
  3. The battle of Germantown.
  4. The winter at Valley Forge.

II. Foreign aid and brighter prospects.
  1. Foreign officers..
  2. Alliance with France.
  3. Retreat of the British from Philadelphia.
  4. The battle of Monmouth.

III. The British overrun Georgia and South Carolina.
  1. Reason for attacking the South.
  2. The taking of Savannah.
  3. The Americans fail to recapture it.
  4. The siege and capture of Charleston.
  5. Defeat of Gates at Camden.
  6. The guerrilla war of Marion and Sumter

Questions in Geography

In what State was the battle of the Brandywine fought? In what direction is the battlefield from Philadelphia? On which side of Philadelphia is Germantown? In what direction from Philadelphia is Valley Forge? In what State is Monmouth, where the battle was fought? In what State is Savannah? In what State is Charleston? In what direction from Charleston is Camden?

CHAPTER XXXI

The Closing Years of the Revolution

IT was in 1780 when the affairs of the Americans were at a very low point, that there occurred the treason of Benedict Arnold. Arnold was a brave soldier and a brilliant leader, but in all the affairs of life he had proved himself something of a scoundrel. He had led an expedition against

UNIFORMS OF FRENCH
SOLDIERS IN AMERICA

BENEDICT ARNOLD

Quebec, and had shown great courage at Bemis Heights.
He had been accused of fraud in his accounts, and had been
once sentenced to be publicly reprimanded. Arnold opened
a correspondence with the British general and afterward got himself appointed to the command
of the posts in the Highlands of the Hudson in
order to betray them. Major André [an-dray], of
the British army, was sent to arrange with Arnold
the surrender of these posts. On his way back to
New York André was captured by three men, who
refused all the rewards which he offered them,
and delivered him and his papers, which were in
Arnold's handwriting, to the nearest American

officer. André was tried and hanged for a spy. Arnold had

MAJOR ANDRÉ

time to escape to the British army, in which
he fought with great vindictiveness against
the Americans. He afterward lived in England, detested by everybody as a trai-
tor.

With the coming in of the year 1781,
American prospects began to brighten.
Greene had taken command of what
was left of the ruined army at the South,

GENERAL NATHANIEL GREENE

which he immediately recruited and improved by strict
discipline. At the battle of the Cowpens, fought in South
Carolina in January, 1781, a detachment under Morgan
defeated a British force under Tarleton. Greene skill-
fully retreated for two hundred miles across North
Carolina to the border of Virginia, followed by
Cornwallis. When Cornwallis moved to Hillsboro,
Greene, reinforced, again marched southward, but
managed to avoid a battle until he had gathered new

COLONEL TARLETON

troops. In the severe battle of Guilford Court-house, Cornwallis drove the Americans from the field at the close of the day, but his army was so badly shattered that he was forced to begin a prompt retreat to the seacoast leaving his wounded in the hands of the pursuing Americans. The scene of this battle is now called Greensboro, in honor of General Greene.

ONE OF MORGAN'S RIFLEMEN

Cornwallis, who was the ablest of all the English commanders in America, made a junction with the British troops in Virginia, and Greene took advantage of this to reconquer South Carolina from the English. Though often checked and sometimes defeated, he had the satisfaction of recovering the three Southern States so far that the English held only the three chief seaports, Savannah, Charleston, and Wilmington.

Greene reconquers most of the South

LORD CORNWALLIS

Battle of York-town and surren-der of Cornwallis, October 19, 1781

Reaching Virginia, Cornwallis pushed the work of fighting and destruction with his usual vigor. La Fayette who was in command of the Americans, showed much ability in avoiding a battle. Washington now marched his forces to the southward, in company with a French army under Rochambeau [ro-sham-bo]. The French fleet blockaded the troops of Cornwallis at Yorktown, and the American and French armies, cooperating in the friendliest way, laid siege to the place. On the 19th of October, 1781, the British army under Cornwallis surrendered, prisoners of war.

The English people had grown weary of the war. The surrender of Cornwallis took

ROCHAMBEAU

ROYAL FLAG OF FRANCE

Benjamin Franklin—Franklin was the son of a tallow chandler, and was born in Boston in 1706. He learned the printer's trade in his brother's office, and also did some rude engraving for the paper. He was studious from childhood. He went to Philadelphia at seventeen and worked as a journeyman printer. After many vicissitudes he rose to the ownership of a printing office. He published an almanac, known as *Poor Richard's*, that became famous for its wise proverbs, and he printed and edited the best newspaper in the American colonies. He was postmaster-general for the colonies. He became a student of electricity, and in 1752, by means of a kite, he proved that the lightning of the clouds was electricity. This discovery, and the invention of the lightning rod, made him famous. He promoted the formation of literary institutions, and furthered the public welfare in many ways. He went to London more than once as agent for his own and other colonies, and was chiefly influential in securing the repeal of the Stamp Act. He was in London as agent for several of the colonies when the Revolution broke out, but he immediately returned to America. He was one of the committee to draft the Declaration of Independence. He went to France in 1776 as ambassador, and it was his skillful hand that negotiated the treaty with that country, without which the Revolution could hardly have succeeded. He assisted in making the treaty of peace with England in 1782, and took part in framing the Constitution of the United States in 1787. He died in Philadelphia in 1790, aged eighty-four years. It was said of him that "he wrested the thunder from the sky and the scepter from tyrants"

BENJAMIN FRANKLIN

away from England the last hope of subduing America. From this time it was certain that American independence would be granted by England. Terms of peace were at length agreed on at Paris in 1782, and a treaty was signed the following year. By this peace England recognized the independence of the United States. Among those who negotiated the peace was the venerable Dr. Franklin.

Preliminaries of the peace, 1782

AMERICAN ARTILLERY DRAWN BY OXEN

Washington retires to private life, 1783

Washington, who was the idol of the people, resigned his command of the army in 1783, bidding farewell to his troops, and returning to private life at Mount Vernon, like a good citizen. His patience, wisdom, coolness, and unselfish patriotism procured the successful end of the long struggle.

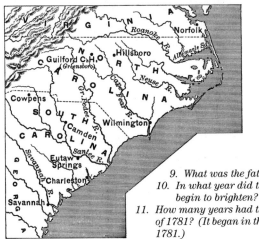

1. What kind of a soldier was Benedict Arnold?
2. What expedition had he led?
3. In what battle had he shown great courage?
4. What accusation had been made against him?
5. What posts was he in command of?
6. What British officer was sent to arrange with him for the betrayal of these Posts?
7. How was André captured?
8. What became of Arnold?
9. What was the fate of André?
10. In what year did the prospects of the American cause begin to brighten?
11. How many years had the Revolution continued in the spring of 1781? (It began in the spring of 1775—subtract 1775 from 1781.)
12. Who had taken command of what was left of the Southern army?

Questions for study

13. Who had command of it before?
14. Where was the battle of Cowpens fought?
15. In what month and year?
16. Who was beaten at Cowpens?
17. How far did Greene retreat, followed by Cornwallis?
18. When Cornwallis marched to Hillsboro, what did Greene do?
19. Where did they fight a battle?
20. Who held the ground after the battle of Guilford Courthouse?
21. But what did Cornwallis do the next morning?
22. Who followed him in this retreat?
23. What is the town of Guilford Courthouse now called?
24. Why is it called Greensboro?
25. With whom did Cornwallis now seek a junction?
26. What advantage did General Greene take of this? How successful was he?
27. What did Cornwallis do when he reached Virginia?
28. What general was in command of the Americans in Virginia?
29. How did La Fayette show ability?
30. What did Washington do?

31. Who commanded the French army that accompanied Washington?
32. What part did the French fleet take in the siege of Yorktown?
33. On what day did Cornwallis surrender?
34. How did the English people feel about the war at this time?
35. What effect did the surrender of Cornwallis have?
36. In what year was peace made?

37. What did England recognize by this peace?
38. What famous man was among those who negotiated the peace on the part of America?
39. What did Washington do when peace was made?

I. The treason of Arnold.
II. Cornwallis and Greene in North Carolina.
III. Greene reconquers the greater part of the three Southern States.
IV. Cornwallis and La Fayette in Virginia.
V. Siege and surrender of Yorktown.
VI. The peace.

In the year _____ Benedict _____ tried to betray to the English certain fortified posts on the _____ River. In the year 1781 the English under Tarleton were defeated by the Americans under _____ at _____, in South Carolina. Greene was defeated at _____ Courthouse, in North Carolina, by the English under _____. Cornwallis afterward moved into Virginia, and Greene reconquered all of the three Southern States except the three cities, _____ in North Carolina, _____ in South Carolina, and _____ in Georgia. Cornwallis was besieged by the _____ and Americans in _____ in Virginia, and surrendered in October, 17____. Peace was made at Paris in 17____.

a. The Highlands of the Hudson—their location. b. Describe the location of, or point out on the map, the Cowpens in South Carolina, and Hillsboro and Greensboro in North Carolina. c. In what general direction would Cornwallis move in going from Wilmington in North Carolina to Yorktown in Virginia? d. On what river is Yorktown? In what direction from Chesapeake Bay? From Norfolk?

Study by topics

Skeleton outline

Geographical studies

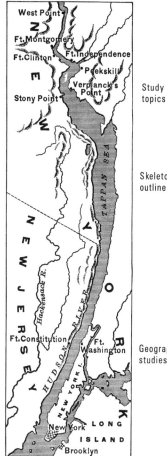

REVOLUTIONARY POSTS IN THE HIGHLANDS OF THE HUDSON AND THE LOWER PART OF THAT RIVER

CHAPTER XXXII

Traits and Incidents of the Revolutionary War

AT the outbreak of the Revolution, the American colonies had no navy. It was quite impossible for them to form a navy that could contend with that of England, which was the best in the world. But the Americans of that time were a seacoast people, who did nearly all their trading and traveling by water. They quickly fitted up some ships, that did good execution. At the outbreak of the war the American army lacked powder, arms, and clothing. While powder factories were building, daring American seamen, North and South, put to sea and captured supplies of powder from British ships. In 1776 ten thousand suits of winter uniform, on their way to Burgoyne's army, were captured. These were sent to clothe the destitute American soldiers.

ESEK HOPKINS, FIRST COMMANDER OF THE AMERICAN NAVY

Early achievements of the Americans at sea

But the little navy rendered other and more important services. Captain Nicholas Biddle gained much renown by his brilliant successes in a small ship. John Paul Jones, a Scotchman, had entered the American navy, and he soon proved himself one of the best seamen and one of the most unconquerable fighters that ever sailed the sea. He scoured the English and Irish coasts—a terror to sea and land. In the *Bonhomme Richard* [bon-om rish-ar´] he encountered the Englishman-of-war *Ser´-a-pis*, and, finding no other chance for victory, he ran alongside the enemy

AMERICAN SEA-MAN, 1776

Captain Biddle's success. Paul Jones and the battle of the Bonhomme Richard with the Serapis

JOHN PAUL JONES

and lashed the two ships together. After a bloody battle, lasting two hours, the English ship surrendered. But the *Bonhomme Richard* was so badly cut to pieces that Jones was forced to transfer his crew to the *Serapis*, leaving his own ship to sink.

AMERICAN MARINE, 1776

A great deal of destruction was done to English commerce by privateers—vessels of war fitted out by private individuals. The profits made, even by common seamen, from prizes taken in this kind of war, drew many men into it, and prevented enlistments in the army.

American Privateers

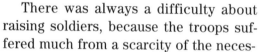

There was always a difficulty about raising soldiers, because the troops suffered much from a scarcity of the necessaries of life. Then, too, a private soldier in that day was liable to punishment by flogging and other degradations not relished by most Americans. But many of the people were always ready to fight in an irregular way. The armies were often broken, but the people were not subdued. The farmer militia usually wore brown tow-shirts and carried long fowling pieces. Their ammunition was carried in a powder horn and shot bag.

AN ENGLISH GRENADIER

The American militia

REVOLUTIONARY POWDER HORN AND CANTEEN

Bayonets were often lacking. At the battle of Saratoga, one of the divisions of the Americans had but one bayonet to every three men. It is said that they often put one bullet and two buckshot in a gun together. There were many men among the Americans whose aim was very deadly. The riflemen from the frontier were capable of incredible accuracy in shooting. Double barreled guns were almost, though not quite, unknown at that time. The percussion cap had not

Arms of the Americans and their mode of fighting

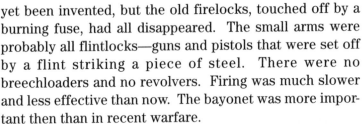

yet been invented, but the old firelocks, touched off by a burning fuse, had all disappeared. The small arms were probably all flintlocks—guns and pistols that were set off by a flint striking a piece of steel. There were no breechloaders and no revolvers. Firing was much slower and less effective than now. The bayonet was more important then than in recent warfare.

The American troops suffered extreme hardships. The paper money issued by Congress to pay the sol-diers declined in value until it was almost worthless. In more than one campaign the barefoot soldiers left blood on the ground when they marched. To relieve the necessities of the soldiers, patri-otic women collected blankets and sent them to the army.

THE AMERICAN RIFLEMAN FROM A PRINT OF THE TIME

Sufferings of the American soldiers

Weakness of the American govern-ment during the Revolution

When the Revolution broke out there were nearly three millions of people in the American colonies. During the war the population increased, and, not withstanding the interruption of business and the destruc-tion of property, the wealth also increased.

AN AMERICAN MAJOR-GENERAL. FROM A PRINT OF THE TIME

The loss of credit and the inefficiency and suffering of the army were principally due to the weakness of the govern-ment. There were, indeed, thirteen governments, bound together very loosely. Congress had no way of making each State pay its proportion of the expense of the war, and so one State waited for another. It was not until some years after the peace that a strong government was formed.

A SOLDIER OF THE CON-GRESS, FROM A DRAW-ING BY A GERMAN OFFICER AT THE TIME

REVOLUTIONARY MUSKET CALLED "BROWN BESS"

Questions for
study

1. What kind of a navy was that of England at the outbreak of the American Revolution?
2. What had the Americans to put against it?
3. Could they hope to build one that would equal it?
4. How did the Americans do their trading and traveling in that time?
5. What did they do in regard to ships?
6. What did the army lack? How was this in part supplied?
7. What is said of Captain Nicholas Biddle?
8. What kind of a seaman was John Paul Jones?
9. What was the name of the ship in which he fought with the Serapis?
10. In what position were the ships during the fight?
11. What was the result of this desperate fight?
12. What became of the Bonhomme Richard?
13. What is a privateer?

ISRAEL PUTNAM A NOTED GENERAL IN THE REVOLUTION

14. What was accomplished by the privateers during the Revolution?
15. Why did many men prefer sailing in privateers to enlisting in the army?
16. What was the chief cause of the difficulty in raising troops?
17. How were the people ready to fight?
18. What did the militia usually wear?
19. What arms did they carry?
20. How did they carry their ammunition?
21. What is said of the supply of bayonets?
22. What is said of their aim?
23. What of double barreled guns?
24. How were the guns set off at that time?
25. Were there any breechloaders and revolvers?
26. What is said of the use of the bayonet?
27. What can you tell of the hardships suffered by the troops?
28. What was done to relieve the necessities of the soldiers?
29. How many people were there in the colonies when the Revolution broke out?
30. Did the population increase during the war?
31. What was the cause of the loss of credit and the suffering of the army?
32. How many governments were there?
33. Was there any strong central government during the war?

Study by
topics

I. By sea.
    1. Capture of supplies.
    2, Captain Nicholas Biddle's brilliant successes.
    3. John Paul Jones' exploits.
    4. Privateers.
II. War on land.
    1. Irregular militia; their equipments and modes of fighting.
    2. Firearms and sharpshooting.
    3. Hardships of soldiers and their relief.
III. The government.
    1. Population.
    2. Weakness of the government.

FOURTH REVIEW—THE AMERICAN REVOLUTION

Chapters XXV to XXXII

Government of the colonies. (XXV)
- Royal governments.
- Charter governments.
- Proprietary governments.
- Colonial Legislatures.
- Commercial laws made in England.

Early struggles for liberty in the colonies. (XXVI)
- Rebellion against Harvey in Virginia, 1635.
- Bacon's rebellion, 1676.
- Massachusetts contends for its charter.
- Rebellion against Andros, 1688.
- Connecticut charter hid in an oak.
- Leisler's rebellion in New York.
- Government overthrown in South Carolina.
- Legislatures resist the governors.

Causes of the Revolution. (XXVII)
- General causes of discontent.
- The Writs of Assistance, 1761.
- The Stamp Act, 1765.
- Its repeal compelled, 1766.
- The tax on tea opposed.
- The Boston Port Bill.
- A Congress called, 1774.

The war begun. (XXVIII)
- The first collision at Lexington, 1775.
- The battle of Bunker Hill.
- Washington appointed commander.
- Boston evacuated.
- Independence declared, 1776.

Battles about New York and in New Jersey. (XXIX)
- Battle of Long Island.
- Washington retreats to Pennsylvania.
- Capture of Trenton.
- Battle of Princeton.

Burgoyne's campaign. (XXIX)
- Burgoyne comes through the lakes, 1777.
- Fall of Ticonderoga.
- Burgoyne reaches the Hudson.
- Hessians defeated at Bennington.
- Burgoyne defeated at Bemis Heights.
- Surrenders his army.

The war about Philadelphia. (XXX)
- Battle of the Brandywine, 1777.
- Battle of Germantown.
- Winter at Valley Forge.
- Arrival of La Fayette and others.
- Alliance with France, 1778.
- British retreat from Philadelphia.
- Battle of Monmouth.

Georgia and South Carolina overrun. (XXX)
- British take Savannah, 1778.
- Attempt to retake it, 1779.
- Charleston surrenders, 1780.
- Gates defeated at Camden.
- Sumter and Marion keep up resistance.

Arnold's treason and death of André. 1780. (XXXI)

Greene at the South. (XXXI)
- Battle of the Cowpens, 1781.
- Battle of Guilford Courthouse.
- Most of the South recovered.

Close of the war. (XXXI)
- Cornwallis in Virginia, 1781.
- Surrender of Cornwallis at Yorktown.
- Preliminaries of peace, 1782.
- Washington retires to Mount Vernon, 1783.

The war at seal. (XXXII)
- First captures at sea.
- Paul Jones takes the Serapis.
- Destruction by privateers.

American militia. (XXXII)
- Irregular soldiers.
- Their arms and accoutrements.
- Their mode of fighting.

Difficulties. (XXXII)
- Sufferings of American soldiers.
- Lack of money.
- Weakness of the government.

CHAPTER XXXIII

The Adoption of the Constitution

AT the beginning of the Revolution, the different colonies were governed under charters of one kind or another from the king, as we have seen in Chapter XXV. After the

New State constitutions adopted during the war

war began, the most of them adopted constitutions which established governments very much like those they had been accustomed to. The chief difference was, that the authority of the king was not recognized in the new government.

The Articles of Confederation adopted

The Congress of the Colonies was as yet only a congress of men representing thirteen different allied countries, for each State assumed to act as an independent nation. A confederation was therefore proposed, which combined all the States into one government for purposes of war and the regulation of commerce. The Articles of Confederation were not accepted by all of the colonies until 1781. This confederation left each State independent in the matter of taxes. Much of the suffering of the American army during the Revolution came from the lack of power in Congress to levy a tax without the assent of the several States. The largest States had but one vote apiece in Congress; the smallest had the same. This made a wretchedly weak government, which was soon held in contempt at home and abroad.

Meeting of the Constitutional Convention

But this weak government continued for several years after the close of the Revolution, until it became unbearable. In 1787 a convention met in Philadelphia, to form a constitution better suited to give strength to the nation. George Washington, who had retired to private life when the war was over, was chosen president of this convention.

The Constitution adopted by the States

The Constitution adopted by this convention, which, with a few amendments, is the one we now live under, was not to go into force until nine States had adopted it. There was a strong party opposed to the Constitution, and it was not until June, 1788, that the ninth State voted to adopt it. Rhode Island was the last of the thirteen to accept it, which it did in 1790.

Under the old confederation, the execution of the acts of Congress was entrusted chiefly to committees of its own members. But the new Constitution made an almost complete separation of the government into three parts, each of which is confined to its own duties. *Three departments of the Federal government*

First, the legislative, or lawmaking, department is called in the Constitution "the Congress." It includes two bodies—a House of Representatives, chosen by the people, and a Senate, chosen by the Legislatures of the several States. In the House of Representatives the States have a greater or less number of members, according to their population. In the Senate each State has two members. A bill must get a majority of votes in both the House of Representatives and the Senate, in order to become a law. It must also be approved by the President. But, if the President refuses to sign it, then two thirds of both the Senate and the House may pass it, and it becomes a law in spite of the President's veto. *The legislative department*

Second, the executive department, which consists of the President (and those appointed under him). The President is chosen for four years. He is commander-in-chief of the army and navy. He appoints all the chief executive officers, with the consent of the Senate. In case of the death of the President, the Vice-President takes his place. *The executive department*

Third, the judicial department consists of the Supreme Court of the United States and such lower courts as Congress may establish. The President appoints the judges of the United States courts, with the advice and consent of the Senate. *The judicial department*

It is a great advantage of our system of government that lawmaking for the regulation of morals and the ordinary business of life is left to the States, so that people of each region can have laws suited to their necessities. It is also a *The division of power between the several States and the United States* great source of strength that the general concerns of the whole country—the money, the foreign commerce, treaties with foreign nations, and affairs of war and peace—are settled by the central government of the whole country.

Freedom of religion, of the press, and of speech

Before the Revolution, the Episcopal Church of England was established in the Southern colonies, while the Congregational churches were supported by law in all the New England colonies except Rhode Island. During the Revolution, Thomas Jefferson led a movement in favor of religious freedom. Now there is no religious establishment in any part of the country, but all are free to worship in their own way. The Constitution provides that Congress shall not interfere with religious freedom, or with the freedom of speech or the freedom of the press.

Questions for study

1. *How were the colonies governed when the Revolutionary War broke out?*
2. *What did most of them do after the war began?*
3. *Were the new governments founded by the State Constitutions like or unlike the old ones?*
4. *What was the chief difference between the old governments under the charter and the new ones under the State constitutions?*
5. *What did the first Congress represent?*
6. *How did each State assume to act?*
7. *What was done to combine the States into one? For what purposes was this combination formed?*
8. *In what year were the Articles of Confederation accepted by the last of the colonies?*
9. *Under this confederation, how were taxes to be raised?*
10. *What was the cause of much of the suffering of the American army during the war?*
11. *How many votes did each State have in Congress?*
12. *Was there any difference in favor of the larger States?*
13. *What kind of government was the confederation? How was it regarded at home and abroad?*
14. *Did this government continue after the close of the Revolution?*
15. *In what year was a convention called to adopt a new Constitution?*
16. *In what city did the convention meet?*
17. *Who was President of the Constitutional Convention of 1787?*
18. *How many States were obliged to adopt the Constitution before it could go into force?*
19. *Was there any opposition to the Constitution? When did the ninth State adopt it?*

20. *To whom was the execution of the acts of Congress entrusted under the old confederation?*
21. *Into how many departments did the new Constitution separate the government?*
22. *What is the legislative department of the government called?*
23. *How many "houses," or separate bodies, are there in Congress? What are they called?*
24. *In which house do the States have representatives according to their population?*
25. *How many senators are allowed to each State?*
26. *How does a bill pass into a law?*
27. *After a bill has passed both houses of Congress by a majority of votes present, what is necessary to make it a law?*
28. *If the President vetoes an act by refusing to sign it, how may it still become a law?*
29. *Who is the head of the executive department of government?*
30. *For how long a term is a President chosen? What is his relation to the army and navy?*
31. *Whose consent is necessary when the President appoints important executive officers?*
32. *When the President dies, who takes his place?*
33. *What is the third department of the government called?*
34. *Of what courts does it consist?*
35. *How are the judges in these courts appointed?*
36. *How are laws relating to the ordinary business of life made under our system of government? Why is this an advantage?*
37. *Mention some of the things committed to the central government of the whole country?*
38. *What form of religious worship was established by law in the Southern colonies before the Revolution?*
39. *What form of worship was established in New England?*
40. *Who led a movement in favor of religious freedom?*
41. *Is there any religious establishment in any part of the United States now?*
42. *What does the Constitution provide regarding religious freedom?*
43. *What two things besides religion are to be free under the Constitution?*

I. The new State Constitutions.

II. A confederation formed.

III. The Federal Constitution adopted.

IV. Three departments of the government under the Constitution.
   1. The legislative department.
   2. The executive department.
   3. The judicial department.

V. The State and Federal governments.

VI. Religious freedom, free speech, and a free press.

Study by topics

The Legislative		makes	
The Executive	department	executes	laws
The Judicial		decides questions relating to	

Blackboard

GEORGE WASHINGTON

FROM A PAINTING BY GILBERT STUART

CHAPTER XXXIV

The New Republic and Its People

WHEN the Constitution was adopted, a new nation was formed out of thirteen States, which before that time had been almost independent of one another. There was now to be chosen a President of this new nation, and the whole country turned its eyes to one man. General Washington, who had been for five years living quietly on his plantation at Mount Vernon, was the only person thought of for President, and he was elected without a rival. John Adams was chosen Vice-President. Washington elected first President

Washington was inaugurated President of the United States in the city of New York, which was then the seat of government, on the 30th day of April, 1789. Washington inaugurated, 1789

The country, when Washington became President, contained less than four million of people. The single State of New York in 1888 had a larger population than the whole country had in Washington's time, and Pennsylvania also had more, while Ohio and Illinois had each nearly as many. The census of 1890, when it was tabulated, showed that in one hundred years the population had increased to more than seventy million, or to at least seventeen times as many as there were when the first census was taken in 1790. Population of the country at the beginning of Washington's administration

The three or four millions of people in America, when the Constitution made the States one nation, were settled chiefly along the Atlantic coast. The center of population was east of Baltimore, on the eastern shore of the Chesapeake Bay. This shows how closely the people clung to the sea, which was almost the only great highway of their commerce. In traveling up into the country, one found the popu- Population mostly along the seacoast lation becoming more sparse, and the houses generally mere cabins. By the time one reached the Allegheny Mountains, there was an end of settlements. All to the west of the mountains was a wilderness, filled with hostile savages and wild beasts, except the little pioneer settlements in Kentucky and Tennessee. The western line of the territory of the United States was the Mississippi River, but the unbroken forests and prairies of that region seemed about as far away as the interior of Alaska does today.

Modes of travel: sailing vessels and stagecoaches

The people of the first years of the republic had neither railroad nor steamboat. One of the commonest modes of travel from one town to another was by sailing packets. When one set out, it was impossible to foretell the length of the voyage; all depended on wind and weather. Stage wagons were also run between the larger towns. It took six days to make the journey from Boston to New York, and two or three to get from New York to Philadelphia. A journey required as many days then as it does hours now.

Travel by private vehicles. The ferries

Many travelers made journeys in their own coaches or in light two wheeled vehicles. The ferries were a terror to these. Large rivers were usually crossed in rude scows, and not without danger, but at some places it was necessary to swim the horses over and float the carriage at the stern of a canoe.

Horseback travelling. The American natural pacer

Probably the most comfortable of all modes of travel at the time was that of riding on horseback. The "natural pacer," of Virginia, and the "Narragansett pacer," of Rhode Island, were highly prized, and were matters of wonder even in Europe. Two people often traveled with one horse. The first rode ahead and tied the horse by the road; the second, when he came up, rode on

RIVER BATEAU

past his companion and in turn tied the horse and left him for the other. This was called "traveling ride and tie."

When Washington became President, all the chief towns were on the seacoast, or on the tide water of the rivers, except Lancaster, in Pennsylvania. Outside of that State, the roads were so bad that a large trading town was not possible away from water conveyance. The interior trade of Pennsylvania was carried on in great wagons, known as Conestoga wagons, each drawn by six or eight stout horses. There were ten thousand or more of these wagons running out of Philadelphia. The wagon trade with the interior made Philadelphia the chief town of North America. Trade with

Badness of the roads generally. The great wagon traffic in Pennsylvania

WAGONS AND CARRIAGES OF THAT TIME

remote districts of the country was still carried on by means of pack horses and *bateaux*, or small boats.

There was not much letter writing then, and the mails were carried mostly on horseback, with little regularity and no speed, so that news sent by mail almost became history by the time it reached the reader. The newspapers were published weekly, and were slow with their news and rather dull in their comments.

Carrying the mails

There were schools in all the leading towns and cities. In New England there were schools in almost every township. But there was no public school system like that which prevails at present. The schools were, for the most part, poor; the discipline in them was severe, and sometimes brutal. Boys were taught to read and write, and sometimes to "cast accounts." Girls learned to read, sometimes also to write. But needlework and fancy work were thought more appropriate to them. The oldest college in the country was Harvard, at Cambridge, Massachusetts. The next oldest was the college of William and Mary, at Williamsburg, then the capital of Virginia. Yale College, in New Haven, was the third in age. There was also a college in New York, one in Philadelphia, and another in Princeton, New Jersey.

SINGING WITH THE HARPSICHORD AND FLUTE

Science, Literature, and art

For a long time after the colonies were settled there had been little that one could call literature or art or science. People that are busy in cutting down forests and building new towns have no time to write books or paint pictures. The early books were almost all on politics or religion. But in the fifty years before the Revolution there came to be a considerable interest in science and literature. One American, Benjamin Franklin, became famous in Europe as well as in America by his great discovery that the lightning of the clouds was but ordinary electricity. Franklin was also an admirable thinker and writer on many subjects, and one of the greatest men of his century. Three Americans, Copley, West, and Stuart, gained reputation in England as painters, but America could furnish only a slender support to artists.

THE TERRITORY OF
THE UNITED STATES
AT THE CLOSE OF
THE REVOLUTION.

SCALE OF MILES
0   100   200   300

The Territory north of the Ohio River was claimed by Virginia; New York also claimed it; Connecticut and Massachusetts each claimed that portion of it lying directly west of their own territories. These claims were all finally yielded to the United States.

1. Who was
   chosen first
   President?
2. Was there any
   opposition to
   Washington's election?

Questions for
study

3. Who was elected Vice-President?
4. Where was Washington inaugurated? In what year?
5. How many people did the United States contain when Washington was
   inaugurated?
6. Which of the States contains more people today than the whole country did
   in Washington's time?
7. How many people will the census of 1890 doubtless show?
8. This will be how many times the population of 1790?
9. In what region were these three or four millions of people that formed the

population settled when the Constitution was adopted?
10. Where was the center of population?
11. What was almost the only great highway of commerce?
12. What did one find in traveling up into the country?
13. Where was there an end of settlements?
14. Were there any settlements west of the mountains? Where?
15. What was the western line of the territory of the United States?
16. How far away did the forests and prairies on the Mississippi seem?
17. What familiar modes of travel in our time were wanting in the first years of the republic?
18. What was one of the commonest modes of travel from one town to another?
19. On what did the length of the voyage depend?
20. How long did it take to go from Boston to New York by stage?
21. From New York to Philadelphia?
22. How did many travelers make journeys?
23. How were large rivers usually crossed?
24. But what ruder ways of getting a horse and carriage across a river prevailed in some places?
25. What was probably the most comfortable of all the modes of travel at this time?
26. To what country was the horse that ambled naturally peculiar?
27. How were these natural pacers regarded in Europe?
28. Where were the chief towns situated in Washington's time?
29. What town was an exception to this?
30. Why were large trading towns not possible away from water carriage in any State but Pennsylvania?
31. How was the interior trade of Pennsylvania carried on?
32. How many Conestoga wagons were employed in the trade of Philadelphia?
33. What made Philadelphia the chief town of North America at that time?
34. How were the mails mostly carried at that time?
35. How open were newspapers printed?
36. What was their general character?
37. Were there schools in those days?
38. What is said of schools in New England?
39. What was the character of the schools?
40. What were boys taught?
41. What education was given to girls?
42. Which was the oldest college in the country?
43. What college was next in age? Which was third?
44. Why was there little that could be called literature or art for a long time after the settlement of the colonies?
45. What were the early books mostly about?
46. At what time did there come to be a considerable interest in science and literature?
47. What American gained a worldwide fame for a great discovery?
48. What did he discover?
49. What Americans had gained fame in England as painters?

> The smaller square represents the population of the United States in 1790, 3,929,214.
>
> ———
>
> The larger square represents the population of New York in 1890, 5,997,853.

Study by topics

CHAPTER XXXV

Home and Society in Washington's Time

NOT only did the people of the United States, in the time of President Washington, have no railroads and no steamboats, but they lacked a great number of other conveniences. Telegraphs and telephones were unknown. Electric lights are an invention of a later time, but our ancestors did not even have gas or kerosene oil. Lamps of any kind were almost unknown; houses were lighted with tallow candles, though some of the people made candles of a green wax derived from the berries of the wax myrtle tree. The poorest people burned a wick in a vessel containing a little grease, or lighted pieces of pitch pine on the hearth. With such lights, it was no great virtue that they went to bed early. Even the streets of large towns were lighted with dim lanterns. Stoves for heating were almost unknown; those for cooking were not yet dreamed of. Wood was the only fuel used in houses. Blacksmiths burned charcoal.

Lack of modern conveniences

There were few mines and very few manufactures. Wool or flax was prepared and spun at home, and then woven into plain homespun cloths for men's and women's wear. The greater part of the people were farmers, and the farmer rarely spent money. What his family ate and wore was produced at home. The rough shoes worn in winter were, per-

Life among the farmers

haps, bought of a neighboring cobbler, but they were sometimes made at home. The children, and, in many cases, the parents themselves, went barefoot in summer. Many plows, wagons, and sleds were made on the farm. In many parts of the country the plow was unknown, and the pack horse or rude sledge took the place of the wagon. The farming was generally of the roughest kind, but the land was new and fertile.

Habits of the backwoodsmen

There were many backwoodsmen who had a dress of their own. They wore loose hunting shirts of deerskin or homespun, a fur cap, moccasins, and buckskin leggings. These woodsmen lived by hunting, by trapping, by poling boats and driving pack horses, by small Indian trading, and sometimes by petty farming. Until after the Revolution, mechanics and working men wore leather breeches.

Negro slaves

Of the nearly four millions of people in the United States in 1790, about one seventh were Negro slaves. These slaves were found in every State except Massachusetts and Maine, which was then a part of Massachusetts. But they were few in the Northern States. Of the Northern States New York had the most slaves—more than twenty thousand. Nearly seven eighths of all the slaves were in Maryland, Virginia, and the two Carolinas. These were the lands of tobacco, indigo, and rice culture.

Traits of life at the South

In these States country life preserved aristocratic forms. Here, until after the Revolution, the oldest son of the family usually inherited the land, according to the custom of the old English law. Some of the great planters lived like nobles. They were accustomed to manage public affairs, and from this class came some of the most eminent statesmen of the period following the Revolution. Virginia was called "the Mother of Presidents." But the poorer people at the South, like the poor in the North, had little or no chance for education. There were few towns in the Southern States, very few mechanics, and little of the shipbuilding and manufactures that were soon to make New England rich. But in Washington's time the Southern States were the richest as well as the most populous. If they had but little town life, there was much social gaiety in the plantation houses.

HAT WORN IN WASHINGTON'S TIME

The so-called cities of the United States, at the time of the adoption of the Constitution, were only what would now be counted towns of moderate size. But in each of these little capitals there was an aristocracy that affected the style and fashion of the English gentry. Gentlemen and ladies gathered at fashionable houses in the afternoon, and spent the time in talking, and sipping tea from dainty little china cups. Sometimes large parties rode down to a public garden in the country, or a tavern by the seaside, to drink tea. In most of the chief towns there were held once in two weeks "assemblies," or balls. At these assemblies there were stately minuets and country dances, and much money was lost and won at card tables in a room prepared for fashionable gambling, which was then one of the recognized amusements of good society.

Society in the cities

About the time of the Revolution gentlemen wore their hair long, and powdered it white. Ladies dressed their hair in a lofty tower. One fine lady of the time paid six hundred dollars a year to her hairdresser. Gentlemen, as well as ladies, wore bright colors and a variety of rich fabrics, so that a fashionable assembly presented a gay appearance.

Costume in Washington's time

But, with all this gaiety in the upper ranks of society, life was less comfortable then than now. The common people lived harshy, with few comforts and fewer luxuries. Even

HIGH HEADDRESS OF THE TIME

Comparative
discomfort of the
life of the time the rich, with all their loaded tables and fine show, lacked
the substantial comforts of our modern life.

1. *Name some of the conveniences for traveling about in our time which the people of Washington's time lacked.*
2. *What means of lighting our houses have we which they had not?*
3. *How did they light their houses after dark?*
4. *What kind of wax did they sometimes make candles of?*
5. *What did the poorest people have?*
6. *What is said of stoves for heating?*
7. *What of cooking stoves?*
8. *What kind of fuel did they use?*
9. *What did blacksmiths use?*
10. *What is said of mines and manufactures in that day?*
11. *Where did the people get cloth for their clothes?*
12. *What was the chief occupation of the people at that time?*
13. *Why did the farmer spend little money?*
14. *What is said of shoes?*
15. *Where did the farmer get his plows and wagons?*
16. *Was the plow everywhere in use?*
17. *What took the place of the wagon in many parts of the country?*
18. *What was the general character of farming?*
19. *How did the frontiersman dress?*
20. *What pursuits did the backwoodsman follow?*
21. *What was the peculiarity of the dress of a mechanic or working man in the days following the Revolution?*
22. *What portion of the population of the United States was composed of slaves in 1790?*
23. *Where were they found?*
24. *What Northern State had the most slaves?*
25. *In what four States were seven eighths of the slaves found?*
26. *What crops were grown in these States?*
27. *What was remarkable in the life of the four States in which were the most slaves?*
28. *How was the landed property inherited?*
29. *How did the great planters live? To what were they accustomed?*
30. *What kind of men were some who came from this class?*
31. *What was the condition of the poorer people in the Southern States?*
32. *What is said of towns in the Southern States?*
33. *Where was there much social gaiety?*
34. *What sort of places were the American cities in the time of Washington?*
35. *What is said of fashionable society in each of these towns?*
36. *What of the tea parties?*
37. *What can you tell about the assemblies?*

38. *What were the two chief amusements at these balls?*
39. *How did gentlemen wear their hair about the time of the Revolution?*
40. *How did ladies dress their hair?*
41. *What is said of the colors worn at that time?*
42. *What is said of the comfort of the modes of living at that time?*
43. *What was the State of morals as compared with the morals of our time?*

I. Lighting and warming of houses.
II. Dress and habits.
  1. Of farmers.
  2. Of backwoodsmen.
III. The prevalence of slavery.
IV. Society in the States having the most slaves
V. Society in town.
VI. Fashionable dress.

Study by topics

CHAPTER XXXVI

Washington's Presidency, from 1789 to 1797

IN 1791 the capital of the country was removed to Philadelphia, to remain there until it should be permanently fixed on the Potomac. President Washington lived in Philadelphia, and there Congress held its sessions.

Removal of the capital from New York to Philadelphia, 1791

Washington was elected by the unanimous vote of the country, and he was reelected in 1792 without opposition. He kept himself aloof from political parties, and tried to be impartial. But his preference for a strong central government attached him rather to the party called Federalist than to its opponents.

Washington not a partisan

The Federalist party had first taken its name in the struggle to secure the adoption of the Constitution which that party favored. Federalists were generally in favor of strengthening the central government. They also liked to see the government conducted with some pomp and ceremony, after the English way. The Federalist party was

The Federalist party

strong in the cities, and among people of wealth and those devoted to commerce. Such people in that day were generally aristocratic in their feelings, and leaned to English ways. In the war between England and France the sympathies of the Federalists were in favor of England and against France.

The Republican party The party opposed to the Federalists was called at first the Republican and afterward the Democratic party. (It is not to be confounded with the Republican party of our time.) The members of this party were afraid that the central government would grow too strong, and perhaps overthrow the liberties of the people. They wished to increase the power of the States and diminish that of the United States. They cherished ideas of individual liberty and equality, and were afraid of an aristocracy. The old Republican or Democratic party of that day sympathized with France, which had, in the great Revolution of 1789, overthrown the monarchy and set up a republic, and the Republicans disliked England. Many of them at one time showed their partisanship by wearing the tricolored cockade worn by republicans in France. The Republican party in America wished to bring in republican manners and simple tastes, and they objected to the stately ceremonies which Washington and the Federalists liked.

Hamilton and Jefferson the great party leaders The great leader of the Federalists was General Alexander Hamilton, who did everything in his power to strengthen the government of the United States. The Republicans were led by Thomas Jefferson, the author of the Declaration of Independence. Hamilton was Secretary of the Treasury and Jefferson was Secretary of State in Washington's first cabinet, so that both parties were represented in the cabinet at the same time, a state of things never seen nowadays.

Alexander Hamilton—This great man was born in the Island of Nevis, in the West Indies, in January, 1757. His father was poor, and he was put into a countinghouse. At fifteen years of age he wrote for the *St. Christopher's Gazette* an account of a hurricane that had just desolated the Leeward West India Islands. The remarkable ability of this description attracted the attention of the chief men of the place, and the boy was sent to the American continent to be educated. In 1774, when but seventeen years of age, while a student in King's College (now Columbia College), in New York, he made a speech on the Revolutionary side at a great meeting in the fields, which at once stamped him as a wonderful youth. He also wrote several anonymous pamphlets that attracted great attention, and were attributed to the leading men of the party. In 1776, when he was but nineteen, he took command of an artillery company, and so distinguished himself at the battle of White Plains and in the retreat across New Jersey that Washington put him on his own staff. He was employed by Washington in many delicate and confidential missions, and he distinguished himself in more than one battle. He led the assault on one of the British outworks at Yorktown. His great work lay in his efforts to persuade the American people to adopt the Federal Constitution, by which the national existence was firmly established. As the first Secretary of the Treasury, he held Congress firmly to the duty of paying every dollar of the national debt at its face. He also prevailed on Congress to adopt the debts incurred by the States in carrying on the war, and he thus established the credit of the nation. He retired from office on account of poverty, but his law practice was afterward very profitable. He was killed in a duel with Aaron Burr in 1804.

During Washington's administration there began those troubles with the Indian tribes which have plagued the government and the people of the frontiers from that day to this. The English government refused to surrender forts which it held among the Indian tribes in what is now Ohio, and encouraged the savages to hostilities. There arose in consequence a most deadly and cruel war between the white settlers in Kentucky and the tribes living on the north side of the river. More than fifteen hundred Kentucky settlers had been killed in seven years, and very many carried away into a cruel captivity. The horrible slaughters of men, women, and children in Kentucky gave that State the name of "the Dark and Bloody Ground."

General Harmer was sent against the Indians in 1790, but from carelessness on his

Indian troubles at the West

ALEXANDER
HAMILTON

Harmer's defeat, 1790

KENTUCKY CAPTIVES

GENERAL ST. CLAIR

St. Clair's
defeat, 1791

part, and a lack of discipline among his troops, the white soldiers were cut to pieces by the savages under Little Turtle.

General St. Clair was sent against these same Indians in the following year. He allowed himself to be surprised by Little Turtle and a strong force of Indians, who routed and almost ruined his army. The Indians butchered the wounded with the most brutal cruelty while St. Clair's army was in flight.

Washington was greatly distressed at this defeat. He now selected General Wayne, who had gained distinction in the Revolution, and whose courage was such that he was called "Mad Anthony Wayne." But he was as prudent as he was brave. The Indians called him "The Black Snake," and they also called him "The Chief who never Sleeps." After trying in vain to make peace with the Indians, Wayne attacked and defeated them, driving them from their hiding places by a bayonet charge. This battle was fought in 1794, on the banks of the Maumee River, in northern Ohio. It brought peace to the frontier for a while.

Wayne's victory on the Maumee, 1794

Anthony Wayne—General Wayne was born in Chester County, Pennsylvania, in 1745. He early showed a fondness for military life. He received a good education for the time, and became a land surveyor. During the troubled times of 1774 and 1775 Wayne devoted himself to drilling military companies in his own county. He entered the army as colonel in 1776, and distinguished himself in many actions. His most notable exploit, perhaps, was the storming of Stony Point, on the Hudson. This formidable work he carried at midnight by a bayonet charge, the soldiers' guns being empty. He afterward handled a small force in Georgia in such a way as to hold in check a much larger body of British troops. It was his careful organization and bold execution of various enterprises during the Revolution which caused his selection by Washington to retrieve the fortunes of the Indian war after St. Clair's defeat. When he returned from his successful expedition against the Indians he was received in Philadelphia in triumph. He was sent in 1796 to receive the surrender of the Western forts, and died in December of that year on the shore of Lake Erie.

ANTHONY WAYNE

There was about this time a rebellion in western Pennsylvania, known as "the Whisky Insurrection." The people of western Pennsylvania raised Indian corn. The roads over the mountains were such that they could not well haul this corn to market, so they fell to making it into whisky, in which shape it was less bulky and more easily carried. The new United States tax on whisky interfered with this business, and the people rose against the revenue

The Whisky Rebellion, 1794

officers. Washington sent troops to enforce the law, and the people submitted after the ringleaders of the rebellion had fled.

Retirement and death of Washington

Washington declined to be a candidate for the third time, and in September, 1796, the "Father of his Country" issued a farewell address, full of good advice. At the end of his term, in March, 1797, he retired to Mount Vernon, where he spent his closing years in peace. Washington died on the fourteenth of December, 1799. Of the many great men of the eighteenth century, he was, though not the most gifted, probably the most illustrious. The whole United States paid honor to his memory. Until recently, he and Lincoln were the only presidents whose birthdays we honored as public holidays.

Questions for study

1. *To what city was the capital removed in 1791?*
2. *Was it expected that Philadelphia would remain the capital?*
3. *Did Washington have any rival candidate when he was elected the first time?*
4. *Was there any opposition to his second election?*
5. *Did he belong to any party?*
6. *To which party did his sympathies incline?*
7. *In what struggle did the Federalist party first take that name?*
8. *Was the Federalist party in favor of or opposed to the Constitution?*
9. *How did the Federalists feel about strengthening the central government of the United States?*
10. *How did they feel about the use of dignified ceremonies in conducting the government?*
11. *Where was the Federalist party strong?*

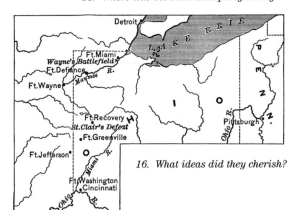

12. *Which did they prefer, England or France?*
13. *What was the party opposed to the Federalists called?*
14. *Of what were the members of this party afraid?*
15. *As between the several State governments and the government of the United States, which did the old Republicans wish to see strengthened?*

16. *What ideas did they cherish?*

17. *Of what were they afraid?*
18. *As between France and England, which did the Republicans favor?*
19. *What change had taken place in the government of France in 1789?*
20. *What kind of manners and tastes did the Republican party wish to bring in?*
21. *Who was the great reader of the Federalists?*
22. *Who was the leader of the Republicans?*
23. *What office did Hamilton hold in Washington's first Cabinet?*
24. *What was Jefferson's place in the Cabinet?*
25. *Are the two great parties represented in this way at the same time now?*
26. *What had the English government to do with the Indian troubles of Washington's time?*
27. *Where were the forts which the English refused to give up?*
28. *What name did Kentucky get on account of the horrors of Indian war?*
29. *Who was sent against the Indians in 1790?*
30. *What was the result of Harmar's expedition?*
31. *Who was sent against the savages in 1791?*
32. *What happened to St. Clair's army?*
33. *How did Washington feel about St. Clair's defeat?*
34. *Whom did Washington select to fill St. Clair's place?*
35. *What was Wayne called?*
36. *But was "Mad Anthony Wayne" reckless?*
37. *What name did the Indians give him?*
38. *What else did they call him?*
39. *Did Wayne try to make peace with the Indians?*
40. *How did he attack them?*
41. *Where was this battle of 1794 fought? What was the result?*
42. *What was the rebellion in Pennsylvania at this time called?*
43. *What did the people of this region do with their corn?*
44. *What tax interfered with their business?*
45. *What did the people do?*
46. *What did President Washington do?*
47. *What was the outcome of the rebellion?*
48. *Why was Washington not elected a third time?*
49. *What sort of an address did he issue in 1796?*
50. *To what place did he retire at the close of his term?*
51. *When did he die?*
52. *How does he compare with the many other great men of the eighteenth century?*

   I. Washington the President and Philadelphia the capital.   Study by
  II. The two political parties.   topics
     1. The Federalists and their opinions.
     2. The Republicans and their opinions.
     3. The leaders of the parties.
 III. The Indian troubles.
     1. Their causes.
     2. Harmar's expedition in 1790.

3. St. Clair's expedition in 1791.
4. Wayne's expedition in 1794.
IV. The Whisky Insurrection.
V. Retirement and death of Washington.

Geography   In what State is Philadelphia situated? In what State is the Maumee River? In what part of Ohio did Wayne fight the Indians? Into what great lake does the Maumee flow? In what direction does this lake lie from Wayne's battlefield?

CHAPTER XXXVII

Troubles with England and France—Presidency of John Adams

Grounds of complaint against England   WHEN the English government acknowledged the independence of the United States, in 1783, there remained still in the hands of English troops certain military posts in the Indian country which were within the territory of the United States. In violation of the treaty, the English government retained these posts among the Indians, and, by the encouragement given to the tribes, kept alive the Indian war. When Wayne defeated the Indians on the Maumee, as we have related in the preceding chapter, he found Canadians fighting on the side of the Indians, and he drove them before him under the very guns of a fort held by the English, who did not dare to aid the savages and their allies. There was also much anger in America against the English government on account of the illegal seizure of American vessels by British cruisers.

Jay's treaty   To prevent a new war with Great Britain, Washington sent John Jay to England in 1794 to make a treaty, "Jay's Treaty," as it was called, was very unpopular in America, especially with the members of the Republican party, who thought that it yielded too much to England. But it was confirmed by Washington and the Senate, for, according to the Constitution, every treaty made with

JOHN JAY

a foreign nation must be agreed to by the Senate. It provided for the surrender of the Western forts by England, and it prevented a war with Great Britain, which would have been a misfortune to so weak a country as ours was at that time. When a war with England came at last, in 1812, the United States had nearly twice as many people as it had when the Jay treaty was made.

This treaty with Great Britain was exasperating to the French government, which was then engaged in war with England. As France had helped the United States to gain its independence, the French expected the assistance of America in their new war with England. Washington wisely kept this country free from alliances with either of the contending nations.

France and the Jay treaty

John Adams was the son of a farmer. He was born in Braintree, Mass., in 1735. He graduated at Harvard, taught school for two years, and began the practice of law when he was twenty-three years of age. He took an active part in the Stamp Act agitations from 1765 onward. He removed to Boston in 1768, and soon became a leading lawyer and a chief of the Revolutionary party. Adams was one of the foremost men in the Congress of 1774 and 1775, and was one of the committee to prepare the Declaration of Independence. He was one of the commissioners to negotiate the treaty of peace with England, and was minister at London for three years. He was Vice-President during the whole of Washington's presidency, and in 1796 was elected to succeed Washington as President. He was an able and courageous man, honest and true to his convictions, but vain, irritable, and somewhat quarrelsome. His peculiarities had something to do with his unpopularity and his defeat when he ran for the presidency a second time. He died on the 4th of July, 1826, exactly fifty years after the Declaration of Independence.

In 1796 John Adams, the candidate of the Federalist party, was chosen President over Thomas Jefferson, who

Election of John Adams, 1796

JOHN ADAMS

CANNONEER, 1797

was the candidate of the Republicans, or Democrats.

The administration of Adams was mostly occupied with the difficulties with France. That country, after the great Revolution that overthrew the monarchy in 1789, had now fallen into the hands of a government called the "Directory." It was composed of five directors. The successes which their armies achieved under the command of the rising young general, Napoleon Bonaparte, made the Directory very overbearing. When the United States sent a new minister to Paris, the French government refused to receive him, and presently ordered him to leave the country.

Discourteous behavior of the French Directory

The Directory seek to extort money from the United States

In 1797, President Adams, who desired to avoid a war if possible, sent three envoys to France, having assurances that they would be received with honor. But the American envoys were informed that, in order to secure a peace, the United States must make a loan to the French government and pay secret bribes to the members of the Directory.

SEAMAN, 1798

The envoys refused this dishonorable demand, and, when it was known in America, the popular cry became, "Millions for defense, but not one cent for tribute!" The tricolored cockade was no longer worn, but a black cockade was put on by those in favor of a war with France. "Hail, Columbia," then a new song, became universally popular. Ships were built, an army was raised, and Washington was made commander-in-chief.

"Not one cent for tribute"

Peace made with Napoleon Bonaparte

But the French did not wish a war, and Napoleon Bonaparte, who had now overthrown the French Directory, made a new agreement with the United States in September, 1800. Thus the infant country again escaped a foreign war.

In the year 1800 the government was removed from

Philadelphia to Washington city. In 1790 Congress had re- Removal of the
solved to fix the permanent capital on the Potomac River, capital to Washington, 1800
and the selection of the site was left to Washington himself. When the government moved there, in 1800, the place
was almost a wilderness. The few people living in the new
town were scattered over the whole region, and one sometimes had to go one or two miles through a forest to see his
next door neighbor, though both were living within the "Federal City," as Washington had named it.

It was thought desirable that the national capital should The District of
not be within the jurisdiction of any State. A tract ten miles Columbia
square was given by Virginia and Maryland to form the District of Columbia. But the portion taken from Virginia was
afterward ceded back to that State. The District of Columbia is governed wholly by laws made in Congress, in which
its inhabitants have no representative.

1. *Where did the English government hold posts that were on American* Questions for
   territory? study
2. *What effect did the keeping of these posts have on the Indians?*
3. *Whom did Wayne find fighting among the Indians when he defeated them*
   on the Maumee?
4. *By whom was the fort held near which Wayne defeated the savages?*
5. *How did the American people feel toward the English government at this time?*
6. *What other cause of anger toward England was there?*
7. *Of what was there great danger?*
8. *Whom did Washington send to England in 1794?*
9. *What was Jay sent to do?*
10. *How was Jay's treaty received by the people?*
11. *What did the members of the Republican party think of it?*
12. *What did Washington and the Senate do about it?*
13. *What has the Senate to do with treaties?*
14. *What good did the treaty do?*
15. *Why would a war with England have been a great misfortune at that time?*
16. *How did the French government feel about the Jay treaty?*
17. *What was the relation between France and England at that time?*
18. *Why did France expect the United States to help her in a war with England?*
19. *What did Washington do?*
20. *How did many members of the Republican party show their sympathies*
    with France?

21. Who was chosen President in 1796?
22. Who was the candidate opposed to Adams?
23. Of what party was Adams the candidate?
24. What party supported Jefferson?
25. With what country did we have difficulty in Adams' time?
26. What was the government of France at this time called?
27. How many directors were there?
28. With whom was France at war?
29. What young general was fighting the battles of the French?
30. What did General Napoleon Bonaparte afterward become?
31. What effect did Bonaparte's victories have on the Directory?
32. How did the Directory treat the minister sent by the United States?
33. How many envoys did President Adams send to France in 1797?
34. What information was given to these envoys?
35. How did they treat this demand for money?
36. When their refusal to pay money became known in America, what was the popular cry?
37. What kind of a cockade was worn by those in favor of a war with France?
38. What song became popular?
39. What preparations for war were made?
40. Who was appointed to command the army?
41. Who had by this time overthrown the French Directory?
42. What did Napoleon do with reference to this country?
43. In what year was the government removed from Philadelphia?
44. To what place was it removed? Who had selected the site?
45. What was the condition of the place when the government was removed to it in 1800?
46. What name had Washington given it?
47. How was the District of Columbia formed? How is it Governed?

Study by topics

   I. Difficulties with England.
      1. The Western posts.
      2. Illegal seizures of American vessels.
      3. The Jay treaty.
   II. Presidential election of 1796.
  III. Difficulties with France.
      1. The Directory refuse to receive an American minister,
      2. The Directory seeks a bribe to keep the peace.
      3. Patriotic excitement against France.
      4. Measures for defense.
      5. A new agreement.
  IV. The capital removed to Washington, 1800.

Geographical studies

On what river is Washington city? Into what bay does the Potomac flow? In what direction is Washington from Philadelphia? From Baltimore? From Richmond, Va.?

THOMAS JEFFERSON

CHAPTER XXXVIII

Election of Jefferson—War with Tripoli

JEFFERSON'S SEAL

THE Federalists favored a strong government. In the excitement caused by the troubles with France, very stringent laws were passed by them. Foreigners were required to live in America fourteen years before they could be naturalized. By what was called the "Alien Law," the President was given authority to send out of the country, without trial, any "alien" or unnaturalized foreigner. By the "Sedition Law," speakers and newspaper writers were to be severely punished for "libeling" the officers of the government. Many of the people thought the alien law took away the right of trial by jury, and that the sedition law attacked free speech and a free press.

The alien and sedition laws

Defeat of the Federalist party in 1800; Services rendered by the Federalists

In the presidential election of 1800. John Adams was the Federalist candidate a second time, but he was defeated, and the Federalist party never was able to elect another President. The Federalists had secured the adoption of the Federal Constitution; they had made the national government strong; and they had begun the work of paying the national debt in full, and so making the credit of the government good. No party ever did a better work than the Federalists did in bringing a bankrupt and disorderly confederacy into a firm union.

The Republican party and its work

But the Federalists leaned too much to the English notions of government that had prevailed before the Revolution. The Republicans held more to the equality of men; they trusted the people, and believed in progress toward a larger personal liberty. The Federalist movement made us a nation; but the movement represented by the old Republican party made us republicans and Americans.

It was the intention of those who framed the Constitu- How the president was elected at first tion that the people should not vote for particular men for the presidency. They were to choose in each State a certain number of men called "electors." These were to select a President. But, instead of choosing eminent men, and leaving the choice of a President to them, the people vote for electors pledged beforehand to cast their votes for the candidates of their party. The people thus vote for the President. It was provided at first that each elector should vote for two candidates for President. The candidate who received the highest number was to be the President, the one having the next highest was to be Vice-President. The effect of this, in 1796, was to make John Adams President, and his opponent, Thomas Jefferson, Vice-President. The President and Vice-President thus belonged to opposite parties.

In 1800 the Republicans resolved to elect Jefferson Presi- Struggle between Jefferson and Burr in 1800, and the change of the Constitution that followed dent and Aaron Burr Vice-President. But, as the only way of electing a Vice-President was by voting for him as one of the two candidates for President, it happened that both Jefferson and Burr received the votes of all the Republican electors, and had, therefore, exactly the same number of electoral votes, although nobody had thought of Burr for President. The Constitution provided then, as it does now, that the choice between the two, in case of a tie vote, should be by the House of Representatives. The Federalists disliked Jefferson in particular, as the great chief of the Republicans; the most of them, therefore, voted for Burr. This produced a new tie in the House of Representatives, and there was danger that the 4th of March would

AARON BURR

AMERICAN SEAMAN IN
JEFFERSON'S TIME

arrive and find the country without a President; but, after a long struggle, some of the Federalists cast blank votes, and allowed Jefferson to be elected. This dangerous struggle led to a change in the Constitution by which the electors were to vote for but one candidate for President and one for Vice-President. This method of voting for electors still prevails.

Prosperity of American commerce

During Jefferson's time, the United States was at peace with all the great powers. The wars raging in Europe had injured the commerce of England and France. Foreign merchants, whose countries were at war, preferred to send goods in American vessels, to prevent their being captured by the enemy. In this way American commerce became very prosperous.

War with the Barbary pirates, 1800

The little Mohammedan states, along the southern coast of the Mediterranean, had long carried on a piratical warfare against the trade of Christian countries. The nations of northern Europe paid them a yearly tribute to protect their ships from robbery. The United States was obliged to redeem from slavery Americans captured by the Dey of Algiers, and also to pay tribute. But in 1801 the Pasha [pash-aw´] of Tripoli [trip´-o-ly], having been refused additional presents, broke into open war.

AMERICAN SOL-
DIERS ABOUT 1800

This war may almost be said to mark the birth of the American navy. It was a period in which Americans were fond of dangerous exploits. The officers and men of this small sea force performed acts of daring before Tripoli which have never been forgotten, and which yet serve for an example to their successors. In many actions Americans boarded the pirate ships, and fought in desperate hand-to-hand encounters, with swords, pikes, and bayonets. The frigate *Philadelphia*, having run on rocks, was captured by

Achievements of the infant American navy in this war. Peace, 1805

the Tripolitans, and the crew reduced to slavery. Lieutenant Decatur ran into the harbor at night in a ketch, boarded the frigate and burned her, escaping with his men by rowing his little boat under a storm of fire from the enemy's batteries. After four years of blockade and war, the obstinate ruler of Tripoli was brought to terms. He made a treaty of peace in 1805.

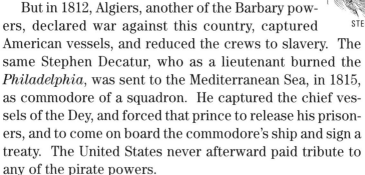

STEPHEN DECATUR

But in 1812, Algiers, another of the Barbary powers, declared war against this country, captured American vessels, and reduced the crews to slavery. The same Stephen Decatur, who as a lieutenant burned the *Philadelphia*, was sent to the Mediterranean Sea, in 1815, as commodore of a squadron. He captured the chief vessels of the Dey, and forced that prince to release his prisoners, and to come on board the commodore's ship and sign a treaty. The United States never afterward paid tribute to any of the pirate powers.

The later war with Algiers; Abolition of tribute, 1815

1. *What were the names of the two parties in the United States at this time? (See Chapter XXXVI.)*
2. *What kind of a government did the Federalists favor?*
3. *What kind of laws were passed by them?*
4. *During what excitement did the Federalists pass these stringent laws?*
5. *How long did they require foreigners to remain in the country before they could be naturalized? What is an alien?*
6. *What is an alien?*
7. *What power did the Alien Law give to the president?*
8. *What is the meaning of the word sedition? (Ans. To defame or expose to contempt by a writing or by printed matter.)*
9. *What offenses did the Sedition Law propose to punish?*
10. *What did many of the people think of the Alien Law? What of the Sedition Law?*
11. *Who was the candidate of the Federalist party in 1800?*
12. *Had John Adams been the Federalist candidate before? Had he been elected? (Chapter XXXVII)*
13. *What took place in this election?*
14. *Did the Federalist party ever again elect their candidate for President?*
15. *What party had secured the adoption of the Consitution?*
16. *What had the Federalists done about the national debt?*
17. *To what notions of government did the Federalists lean?*
18. *To what did the Republicans hold? In what kind of progress did they believe?*

Questions for study

19. *What did the Federalist movement do for us?*
20. *What did the movement represented by the old Republican party do for us?*
21. *What was the intention of those who framed the Constitution in regard to voting for a President.*
22. *What were the electors to do?*
23. *Did the people leave the choice to the electors?*
24. *Do the people really elect the President?*
25. *How were the electors to vote?*
26. *If each elector voted for two candidates for the presidency, how was the Vice-President chosen? What effect did this have in 1796?*
27. *Whom did the Republicans resolve to elect for President in 1800?*
28. *Who was their candidate for Vice-President? What was the result?*
29. *When the electors fail to make a choice, who is to elect a President?*
30. *Why did most of the Federalists in the House of Representatives vote for Aaron Burr?*
31. *Did the House of Representatives succeed in electing at first?*
32. *What danger was there?*
33. *How did the election come out at last?*
34. *What change was now made in the Consitution?*
35. *What was the character of our relations with the great powers during Jefferson's time?*
36. *What effect did the European wars have on our commerce?*
37. *Why did foreign merchants prefer to ship goods in American vessels?*
38. *What kind of warfare did the little Mohammedan states carry on?*
39. *Where were these states situated?*
40. *What did the nations of northern Europe do to protect their commerce?*
41. *To what ruler did the United States pay money to redeem captives and for tribute?*
42. *Which one of the rulers of these Barbary states broke into open war with the United States in 1801?*
43. *What relation does this war hold to the history of the navy of the United States?*
44. *How did the officers and men before Tripoli behave?*
45. *What took place when they boarded the ships of the enemy?*
46. *Relate the story of the burning of the frigate* Philadelphia.
47. *What did Decatur afterward become?*
48. *Which of the Barbary powers afterward declared war against this country?*
49. *Who commanded the expedetion against Algiers in 1815? What was the result?*

Study by topics

I. The Federalist party and its defeat.
II. The Republican party.
III. Difficulties in the presidential election.
IV. Change in the Constitution.
V. Prosperity of American commerce.
VI. Wars with the Barbary pirates.

Geography

What are the names of the four Barbary states that lie on the coast of the Mediterranean Sea? Which is the most westerly? Which the most easterly? What country in

Europe lies north from Tripoli? What country in Europe lies north from Morocco? What country lies next to Tripoli on the east? [Ans. Egypt.] What do you know about Egypt? Which of the Barbary states lies between Algiers and Tripoli? Through what strait would American ships have to pass to reach Algiers or Tripoli? [Ans. The Strait of Gibraltar.]

CHAPTER XXXIX

The Settlement of the Great Valley

BEFORE the Revolution, only a few people had gone over the Allegheny Mountains. The country to the west of this was shut off from all intercourse with the rest of the world and was infested by tribes of fierce and cruel Indians, who lived in villages for the most part widely separated, but who resisted the efforts of the white men to occupy any portion of the uninhabited wilderness west of the mountains. But, some years before the Revolution, Daniel Boone and other daring men, from North Carolina and Virginia, penetrated into the fertile lands of Tennessee and Kentucky, and formed settlements.

Pioneers before the Revolution

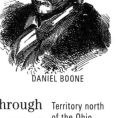

DANIEL BOONE

Some of the colonies had been chartered to run through to the Pacific Ocean, and these claimed all the territory west of them as far as the United States extended that is, to the Mississippi River. The Virginia charter, which was the oldest, made the line of that colony run " west and northwest." Under this charter Virginia claimed most of the territory north of the Ohio River, and all of that which now forms Kentucky. The territory lying north of the Ohio was ceded to the United States by Virginia and the other States claiming it.

Territory north of the Ohio River ceded to the general government

In 1787 this territory was organized as "The Northwest Territory," and its government was regulated by an act which has since become very celebrated. It is commonly known as "The Ordinance of Eighty-seven," from the year in which it was adopted. The Ordinance of Eighty-seven declared that, in the Northwest Territory, all children of a father who died without a will should inherit the estate equally, thus

The Northwest Territory established by the "Ordinance of Eighty-Seven"

doing away with the aristocratic privileges given to the oldest son under the English and colonial laws. It also forbade slavery in the territory north of the Ohio. This ordinance made Ohio, Indiana, Illinois, Michigan, and Wisconsin free States.

Great rush of emigrants to the West

Soon after the adoption of this ordinance and the purchase of the Indian title to the land, people began to pour into the Western country, now opened for settlement. A large number of Revolutionary officers and soldiers, impoverished by the war, were among these settlers. The first emigrants carried their few goods over the mountains on pack horses. At Pittsburgh or Wheeling most of them embarked in large flatboats roughly built of green lumber. In these they floated down the Ohio to one of the new settlements on its banks. The flatboat was then broken up, and its planks used in building the settler's cabin. Pennsylvania wagons, after a while, took the place of the pack horse in the journey over the mountains to Pittsburgh.

Rude and dangerous life of the first settlers west of the mountains

The people of this interior country were almost shut out from the world. They raised flax and sometimes grew wool, and spun and wove at home. Their spinning wheels and looms were made by themselves. For chairs they made rude stools, their tables and bedsteads were such as they could make, and they used wooden bowls for dishes. They tanned their own leather, and made rude shoes at home. The husks of Indian corn were used for making various articles, such as rope, horse collars, brooms, and chair bottoms. Barrels and beehives were made by sawing hollow trees into sections. By splitting one of these sections a child's cradle was constructed. For tea they drank a decoction of sassafras root or the leaves of the crop vine. Their sugar they got from the maple tree. Their small boat was a canoe made from a single log, or a pirogue [pee-rogue´], which was a canoe enlarged by splitting it in the middle lengthwise and inserting a plank. The danger from Indians was so great for many years that the settlers never went to their fields without carrying their rifles.

Whatever supplies the Western settlers got, they brought from the towns on the eastern side of the mountains, by means of pack horses and wagons. For these goods they exchanged furs, ginseng, and other light articles. The produce of Western farms was too heavy to be packed across the mountains. It could only be sold by floating it thousands of miles down the Ohio and Mississippi Rivers to New Orleans. This was done in very large flatboats, which were rowed down the river with great sweeps, but could not be brought back against the current. The flatboat men got home by taking passage on ships sailing from New Orleans to Virginia or Maryland, and then crossing the mountains to Pittsburgh.

Pack horse and flatboat trade

But, as there was a necessity for some trade up the river as well as down, there were presently used the "bargee" and the "keelboat," both of which had sharpened bows, and could be toilsomely forced up against the stream by setting poles, oars, and sails in turn, and which sometimes were towed, or "cordelled," by the boatmen walking along the shore. Four months were consumed in the voyage from New Orleans to Pittsburgh. The boatmen were rude and lawless, and navigation was rendered dangerous by the Indians and highwaymen that infested the banks of the rivers.

Boats and boatmen on the Ohio and Mississippi

Louisiana, which then included almost the whole region between the Mississippi and the Rocky Mountains, had been ceded by France to Spain in 1762. Spain wished to deny to

Purchase of Louisiana, 1803

our people the right to navigate the great river that formed our western boundary, and the people west of the Alleghenies wished our government to seize the whole of Louisiana. In 1800 Louisiana was ceded back to France. In 1803 two commissioners were sent to France by President Jefferson, with instructions to buy for the United States, if possible, a part of Louisiana, including New Orleans and the mouths of the Mississippi. But Napoleon, who then ruled France, fearing that England would seize the territory, took a sudden resolution to sell all of Louisiana to the United States. For this the United States paid fifteen million dollars. By this purchase the country acquired a great deal more territory than all she had before possessed, and there was opened to her the prospect of becoming one of the greatest nations on the earth.

Aaron Burr, who had

Louisiana Territory—The region about the mouth of the Mississippi was first explored by La Salle (see page 117), and the first settlements in that region were made by the French in 1699. In 1722 New Orleans was made the capital of the colony. In 1727 wives were sent to the planters by the government, in imitation of the plan adopted for peopling Virginia a hundred years earlier. In 1762, after the English had taken Canada (Chapter XXIII), the province of Louisiana was ceded to Spain. For a long time indigo was grown, but in 1794 sugar was successfully raised, and the colony was rendered prosperous at once. There had been much trouble between Spain and the United States about the navigation of the Mississippi, and the Western people wished to seize New Orleans and the lower Mississippi. The United States desired to buy a portion of Louisiana, but in 1800 Bonaparte procured its cession back to France. He entertained, along with other dazzling schemes, the project of rebuilding the French power in America. Monroe and Livingston were commissioned by President Jefferson to buy from France, if possible, the small portion of Louisiana so much desired by the United States, in order to secure the free navigation of the Mississippi; but Napoleon surprised the American commissioners by offering to sell the whole vast territory. French Louisiana included in whole or in part the States of Louisiana, Arkansas, Missouri, Iowa, Minnesota, Kansas, Nebraska, Colorado, and the Territories of Dakota, Montana, Wyoming, and the Indian Territory—that is to say, there are at present twelve very large States and territories almost wholly made from Louisiana as bought from France in 1803.

been Vice-President in Jefferson's first term, had not been reelected. After Louisiana was ceded to the United States, Burr formed a conspiracy to detach Louisiana and some of the Western States from the Union, and to revolutionize a part of Mexico. He enlisted soldiers in Ohio, and started down the river; but he was arrested and tried for treason. For want of evidence he was not convicted.

Aaron Burr's conspiracy

1. *What was the condition of the country west of the Allegheny Mountains before the Revolution?*
2. *By whom was it inhabited?*
3. *How did these Indians live?*
4. *How did they treat the efforts of the white men to occupy any portion of the land west of the mountains?*
5. *What daring man is particularly mentioned as having penetrated into the country west of the mountains?*
6. *Within what two of our present States did Boone and other bold men plant settlements before the Revolution?*
7. *From what States did these men emigrate?.*
8. *How far to the west did the land granted by charter to some of the colonies run?*
9. *When these colonies became States after the Revolution, what did they claim?*
10. *How was the line of Virginia to run according to its charter?*
11. *What territory did Virginia and other States cede to the United States?*
12. *What was this territory north of the Ohio River called when it was organized?*
13. *What was the act called which established the government of this territory?*
14. *Why was it called "The Ordinance of Eighty-seven"?*
15. *What provision did the Ordinance of Eighty-seven make in regard to the inheritance of property?*
16. *What privileges were thus done away with?*
17. *What did the Ordinance of Eighty-seven enact regarding slavery?*

Questions for study

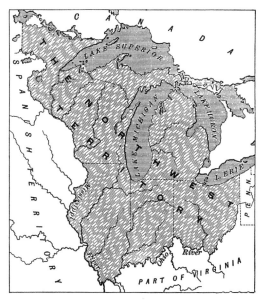

18. What five States cut out of this territory became free States—that is, States forbidding the holding of slaves?
19. What took place after the passage of the Ordinance of Eighty-seven?
20. Who were among these settlers?
21. How did the emigrants carry their goods over the mountains?
22. How did they descend the Ohio?
23. What took the place of the pack horse in crossing the mountains after a while?
24. How did the people of the interior country get clothes?
25. How did they get spinning wheels and looms to spin and weave with?
26. What sort of furniture did they have?
27. Tell how they procured leather and shoes. What did they make of corn husks?
28. How did they make barrels, beehives, and cradles?
29. What tea did they use? What sugar?
30. What was their small boat?
31. How was a larger boat, or pirogue, made?
32. What is said of danger from Indians?
33. How did the settlers get supplies from elsewhere?
34. How did they sell their produce?
35. How did the flatboat men get home again?
36. What kinds of boats were introduced that could get up stream?
37. By what means were these boats forced upward against the current?
38. What kind of men were the boatmen?
39. By what dangerous enemies were the shores infested?

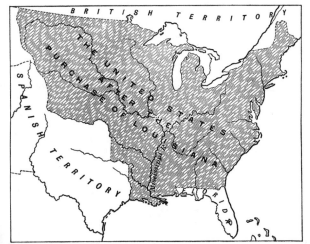

40. Who had explored the country about the mouth of the Mississippi? (Page 117.) To what nation did France cede Louisiana in 1762?
41. What region did Louisiana cover at this time?
42. What right did Spain wish to deny to our people?
43. What did the Western people wish our people to do?

44. *To whom did Spain cede Louisiana in 1800?*
45. *For what purpose did President Jefferson send two commissioners to France in 1803?*
46. *Why did Napoleon resolve to sell Louisiana to the United States?*
47. *How much did the United States pay for Louisiana?*
48. *Was Louisiana as then bounded larger or smaller than the rest of the country?*
49. *What high office had Aaron Burr held in Jefferson's first term?*
50. *What conspiracy did he form after he ceased to be Vice-President?*
51. *What did he hope to detach from the Union?*
52. *What other country did he hope to revolutionize in part?*
53. *What happened to him?*
54. *Why was he not convicted?*

I. The pioneers.   Study by topics
II. The Northwest Territory.
III. The Ordinance of Eighty-seven.
IV. The great emigration after 1787.
V. How the people lived.
VI. Flatboat, keelboat, and bargee
VII. The purchase of Louisiana.
VIII. Burr's treason.

Through what States do the Allegheny Mountains run? In what direction? On   Geography
which side of the Alleghenies is the Ohio? In what direction does it flow? Into
what river does it empty? In what general direction does the Mississippi flow?
What large city near its mouth? What large city is at the head of the Ohio? In
descending the Ohio from Pittsburgh to New Orleans, in what direction would a
boat sail? What States and territories have been in whole or in part cut out of
Louisiana as it was when the United States bought it?

FIFTH REVIEW—FROM THE CLOSE OF THE REVOLUTION TO THE LOUISIANA PURCHASE.

Formation of the Constitution.
(XXXIII)
{
The new State Constitutions.
The Articles of Confederation, 1781.
The Constitutional Convention, 1787.
The Constitution ratified in 1788.
}

Government under the
Constitution. (XXXIII)
{
Three divisions of government.
Legislative.
Executive.
Judicial.
The Federal system.
State governments.
United States government.
Freedom of religion, of the press, and of
speech.
}

Population in Washington's time. (XXXIV)
- Washington inaugurated, 1789.
- Population in 1790.
- Increase in one hundred years.
- Settlements chiefly on the coast.
- Westward movement of population.

Civilization in Washington's time. (XXXIV)
- Modes of travel.
- Freight carried by wagons, pack horses, and small boats.
- The mails and newspapers.
- Education, science, literature, and art.

Home life in Washington's time. (XXXV)
- Absence of modern conveniences.
- Farm life in that time.
- Backwoodsmen.
- Negro slaves North and South.

Society in Washington's time. (XXXV)
- Society at the South.
- Society in the cities.
- Tea parties, country excursions, and balls.
- Dress of gentlemen and ladies.
- Life less comfortable and refined than in our time.

Washington President. (XXXVI)
- Capital removed from New York to Philadelphia, 1791.
- Washington twice elected without opposition.

The old political parties. (XXXVI)
- The Federalist party.
- Its rise.
- Its policy.
- Its inclination to England.
- The Republican or Democratic party.
- Its policy.
- Its sympathy with France.
- Hamilton and Jefferson the party leaders.

Military events in Washington's time. (XXXVI)
- Indian troubles at the West.
- Harmer's defeat, 1790.
- St. Clair's defeat, 1791.
- Wayne's victory, 1794.
- The Whisky Rebellion, 1794.

Troubles with England. (XXXVII) { Causes of dissatisfaction.
The Jay treaty.

Close of Washington's career. (XXXVI and XXXVII) { Washington retires, 1797.
John Adams succeeds him.
Washington's death, 1799.

Troubles with France. (XXXVII) { France annoyed by the Jay treaty.
French "Directory" seek to extort money.
War with France threatened.
New treaty with France, 1800.

The new capital. (XXXVII) { Washington city.
The District of Columbia

Overthrow of the Federalists. (XXXVIII) { Alien and sedition laws.
Defeat of the Federalist party, 1800.
Services rendered by the Federalists.
The old Republican party and its work.

Jefferson elected, 1800. (XXXVIII) { Old system of electing the President.
The struggle between Jefferson and Burr.
Change in the mode of electing Presidents.

War with Barbary pirates. (XXXVIII) { Tribute paid to the pirates.
War with Tripoli, 1801-1805.
Brilliant success of the navy.
War with Algiers, 1815.

The opening of the West. (XXXIX) { Pioneers before the Revolution.
Ownership of Western territory disputed
by different States.
Northwest Territory ceded to the United
States,
The Ordinance of 1787.
Emigrants descend the Ohio.
Rude life of first settlers.
Trade by boat and pack horse.

Purchase of Louisiana.   (XXXIX) { France cedes Louisiana to Spain, 1752.
Spain recedes Louisiana to France, 1800.
Louisiana sold to the United States, 1803

Aaron Burr's conspiracy. (XXXIX)

CHAPTER XL

Beginning of the Second War with England

Search of ships and impressment of American seamen

During Jefferson's administration the English government was involved in a long war with Napoleon, who had made himself Emperor of the French, and had conquered a great part of western Europe. During this war England was in need of seamen for the navy. The officers of the English navy were allowed to impress British seamen from merchant vessels—that is, to force them to serve on men-of-war. But England had also long claimed the right to impress her own subjects when found on ships of other nations. Every man born in Great Britain who sailed before the mast in an American vessel was liable to be seized by an English man-of-war. More than this, English naval officers were allowed to judge whether a man was a native of England or not, and thousands of natives of America were impressed on British ships. It was very exasperating to Americans to have their ships stopped on the high seas and searched, and their citizens forced to serve in the navy of a foreign power. But England was all-powerful on the sea, and the United States had to bear with such insults or give up sailing ships.

Interference with our commerce

During this war between England and France, which shook the whole civilized world, our country tried to be neutral. But England wished to interrupt our trade with the countries under control of France, while Bonaparte issued orders to check our trade with England. The decrees which these two powers issued one after the other became so severe at last that our ships could not sail to any port without the greatest danger of being seized by the cruisers of one or the other power. As the English were much stronger at sea than the French, they did us the more harm.

If our country had been strong, it would not have borne The embargo of 1807 such outrages, but it was then far from being prepared for a war with England. President Jefferson was very anxious to avoid war, and to go on paying off the debt of the country, which was his leading purpose. The President thought that the United States might get the offensive decrees repealed by stopping all its trade with the outside world. An act was therefore passed in December, 1807, forbidding the departure of vessels from American ports. This was known as "The Embargo of 1807," or " Jefferson's Embargo." The embargo was the only very unfortunate act of Jefferson's administration, which, up to this time, had been most popular. It was like destroying our own commerce to keep others from ruining it. While our ships rotted in port, English ships got the trade we had lost. New England and New York suffered heavily by the destruction of their commerce, and there were even some hotheaded people in the Eastern States who talked of dissolving the Union. The embargo was called a "terrapin policy," as though the country had pulled its head and feet into its shell, as a terrapin does when frightened. The embargo lasted about fourteen months. The law was repealed in 1809.

Election of Madison, 1808

In 1808, James Madison, of Virginia, was elected to succeed Jefferson. He was the candidate of the Republican, or Democratic, party, for, notwithstanding the unpopularity of the embargo, the Federalist party was now so much in the minority that it carried but a little over one fourth of the electoral vote. George Clinton, of New York, was elected Vice-President.

In 1811 the irritation of the American people against England was increased by the outbreak of an Indian

GEORGE CLINTON

"THE PROPHET"

war in the Northwest. It was believed that English agents furnished arms to the Indians and encouraged their hostility to the settlers. The Indians were at this time under the control of the great Shawnee chief Tecumseh and his brother, who was called "the Prophet," and who pretended to speak by inspiration. In July, 1811, General Harrison. Governor of Indiana Territory, fought a battle with the Indians at Tippecanoe and defeated them. Tecumseh, who was absent when this defeat took place, afterward entered the British service.

In June, 1812, the United States declared war against England. Preparations were immediately made for invading Canada; but the Americans had rushed into war without being ready, and they met nothing but disaster at first.

Tecumseh and "the Prophet"— These two Indians were brothers, born at the same time, and of the Shawnee tribe. Tecumseh was a warrior, while his brother wrought upon the superstitions of the Indians by falling into trances and pretending to be a prophet. He carried about a string of sacred beans and other objects of reverence. He and Tecumseh deserted their own tribe and settled on the Wabash, where the fame of the prophet's visions drew multitudes of Indians from various tribes to him. When any chief or other influential man opposed the schemes of the brothers, the Prophet had influence enough to have him put to death for witchcraft. Tecumseh took the extreme ground that all the country belonged to all the tribes in common, and that the tribes who had sold their lands to the white men had done what they had no right to do. He wished to force the government to give up all lands north of the Ohio. He traveled from tribe to tribe, trying to form a confederacy of all. The battle of Tippecanoe was fought in his absence and the defeat of the Indians there deranged his plans. But the successes of the British in the Northwest revived his scheme. He was made a brigadier-general in the British army, and at the surrender of Detroit the British general Brock put his own scarf on Tecumseh as a mark of distinction. The wily Shawnee, though fond of this decoration, put the scarf on Round Head, an older warrior of the Wyandott tribe. Tecumseh was killed at the battle of the Thames in Canada, in 1813. He was one of the ablest men produced by the Indian race, and it is to his credit that he never countenanced the barbarous custom of torturing prisoners.

The Canadian authorities, on the other hand, had taken every precaution against invasion. The first blow was struck by them in the far-off wilderness. Fort Mackinaw, on an island in the straits between Lake Michigan and Lake Huron, was captured by a force of English and Indians before the American commander there had heard of the declaration of war. This removed all restraint from the already hostile savages of the upper country, and gave to the English the support of the Indian tribes.

Declaration of war, 1812; English successes

General Hull, who had been sent to invade Canada by way of Detroit, was now an old man, unfit to command. He showed dullness and timidity, and when attacked in Detroit by a force of English, Canadians, and Indians, he surrendered that post on the 16th of August, to the great grief of his troops and the indignation of the whole country.

Surrender of Detroit by General Hull

1. *In what war was the English government involved during Jefferson's administration?*
2. *What had Napoleon made himself?*
3. *What had he conquered?*
4. *What had England great need of?*
5. *How did the English navy get sailors?*
6. *Could an English seaman escape by embarking on the ships of another nation?*
7. *Did he escape if he was naturalized in another country?*
8. *Who was allowed to judge whether a seaman was an Englishman or not?*
9. *What happened to many American seamen?*
10. *Why could not our country resist such insults to its flag?*
11. *What part did the United States wish to take in this war that shook the civilized world?*
12. *What did England do against our trade? What did France do?*
13. *Which nation did us the more harm, England or France?*
14. *Why did England hurt us the more?*
15. *What was Jefferson's favorite purpose at this time?*

Questions for study

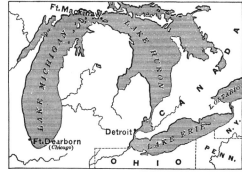

16. How did he think the country should proceed to get the decrees of England and France repealed?
17. How was all our trade with the outside world to be stopped?
18. What was this Embargo Act called?
19. What was the effect of the embargo in regard to our trade?
20. What was its effect on New York and New England?
21. What kind of a policy was it called?
22. Why a terrapin policy?
23. How long did the embargo of 1807 last?
24. Who was chosen President in the election which took place in 1808?
25. From what State did Madison come?
26. What party elected Madison?
27. Who was chosen Vice-President?
28. What increased the irritation of the American people against England in 1811?
29. What connection had the Indian war with our quarrel with England?
30. Who controlled the hostile Indians at this time?
31. To what tribe did Tecumseh originally belong?
32. What was his brother called?
33. Why was he called "the Prophet"?
34. Who fought a battle with the Indians at Tippecanoe?
35. In what year did the United States declare war against England?

36. How well were the Americans prepared for this war?
37. What befell them at first?
38. What had the Canadian authorities done with respect to the war?
39. Where did they strike the first blow?
40. What effect did the capture of Mackinaw by the British have on the Indian tribes?
41. What general was sent to invade Canada by way of Detroit?
42. What kind of a man was he?
43. What did he do when attacked?
44. How did his troops feel about the surrender?
45. How did the country feel?

I. The search of American ships and the impressment of sailors.
II. The interruption of our trade by unjust decrees.
III. Jefferson's embargo, 1807 1809.
IV. Election of Madison.
V. War with Tecumseh.
VI. Declaration of war with England.
VII. Fall of Fort Mackinaw.
VIII. Surrender of Detroit.

Study by topics

Geography   Where is Tippecanoe? In what direction from Louisville? Where is Detroit? In what direction is Mackinaw from Detroit?

Books   Schouler's *History of the United States.* Hildreth's *History of the United States.* McMaster's *History of the American People.* Mrs. Seelye's *Tecumseh.*

CHAPTER XLI

The Navy in the War of 1812

PRESIDENT MADISON was really averse to the war, and he was a vacillating leader. The generals appointed at first were mostly Revolutionary officers, too old to be good commanders. They were selected for political reasons. The soldiers were high-spirited, but undisciplined. They sometimes refused to obey a disagreeable order, or to follow an unpopular commander; sometimes they turned about and went home. They even threatened the life of a general whom they thought guilty of cowardice.

JAMES MADISON

Bad state of the army

The main purpose of the government at the beginning of the war had been to invade Canada. But the old General Dearborn, who had command of the army on the Canadian frontier was inefficient. The troops were brave, and some of the officers distinguished themselves in various battles, but the conquest of Canada proved a difficult task. Old General Hull, as we have seen, contrived to lose Detroit and the whole Northwest.

Attempt to invade Canada

James Madison—Madison, the fourth President, was born in Virginia in 1751. During the Revolution he was a member of the Virginia Legislature, and later a member of Congress. He was a member of the convention that framed the Constitution of the United States, and one of the ablest advocates of its adoption. He was Secretary of State in Jefferson's administration, and succeeded Jefferson as President, serving two terms. He retired from the presidency in 1817, and died in 1836.

The old Republican party of that day, which was the party advocating the war, had always professed a dislike for a navy. In preparing for war, the whole reliance

Neglect of the Navy at the beginning of the war

had been upon the army, and the little navy had been neglected. The success of our soldiers was not doubted, but it seemed folly for a few ships to encounter the navy of Great Britain, which was then completely "mistress of the seas." Yet in the first year of the war the failures of the army under weak officers were overwhelming, and the country was only saved from complete discouragement by the bold triumphs of the daring little navy.

CONSTITUTION AND *GUERRIERE*

Naval victories over the *Guerriere*, the *Frolic*, the *Macedonian* and the *Java*

The powerful English frigate *Guerriere* [geh-re-air] was utterly disabled and captured in an hour and ten minutes after she had engaged the American frigate *Constitution*. This gave the greatest pleasure, because the defeat of an English man-of-war on the ocean was up to that time almost unheard of. Quickly after this triumph came that of the sloop-of-war *Wasp* over the English sloop *Frolic*. One of the most notable captures was that of the *Macedonian*

When the frigate *United States* captured the British frigate *Macedonian*, a young officer, who bore the official report of the victory to the capital, entered a large public assembly, escorted by two other officers, and presented the ensign of the *Macedonian* to Mrs. Madison, the wife of the President The assembled guests cheered and wept with enthusiasm, while the young officer's mother and sisters, who were present, embraced him, delighted that he had come safely out of the battle.

by the frigate *United States*, under command of Stephen Decatur, the same who, as a young man, had captured and set fire to the *Philadelphia*, under the batteries of Tripoli (page 229). The year was closed by the capture of a fourth man-of-war, the frigate *Java*.

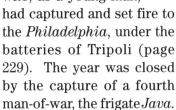

BRITISH FLAG

This was effected by the *Constitution*, which was nicknamed "*Old Ironsides*." Under three different commanders this ship won brilliant victories in the war.

There were other victories than these we have mentioned, and some defeats, but the prowess of American seamen excited admiration everywhere. It was a war for sailors' rights, and the sailors were deeply interested in it. The adventurous character of American life in that day had developed a spirit of personal daring well suited to naval warfare. Such was the emulation of officers that in boarding an enemy's ship they actually pulled one another back in some instances, so eager was every one to get over the side of the hostile vessel first. One American seaman on the *Constitution*, in her battle with the *Java*, remained on deck in a dying condition until the enemy surrendered, when the poor fellow raised himself with one hand and gave three cheers, and, falling back, expired.

Courage of American seamen in battle

SEAMAN, 1815

There were many affecting examples of courage in these contests. In the losing fight of the *Chesapeake* with the *Shannon*, when Captain Lawrence was carried below mortally wounded, he said, "Don't give up the ship!" These

Death of Lawrence

LAWRENCE

Admiration for the navy

words became a battle cry in the navy, and a watchword for brave men in difficult circumstances from that time to this.

The exploits of a little navy, pitted against the greatest maritime power the world had ever seen, set the people wild. When the commanders of successful vessels returned to port, cities welcomed them with banquets, State Legislatures voted them swords, and the general government struck medals in their honor.

Battle of Lake Erie, 1813

A little fleet was launched on Lake Erie in 1813, and its officers and men were anxious to rival the glory of the American ships at sea. In the battle of Lake Erie, fought this year, Commodore Perry hung up for his signal "Don't give up the ship!" the dying words of Lawrence. When his flagship was riddled and disabled by the enemy, he got into a small boat and was rowed to another vessel, standing upright while the enemy was raining shot about him. Reaching the ship *Niagara*, he sailed down on the British line and broke it, and at length compelled the whole fleet to surrender. "We have met the enemy, and they are ours—two ships, two brigs, one schooner, and one sloop," Perry wrote to General Harrison at the close of the battle.

PERRY

Battle of Lake Champlain, 1814

A similar engagement took place on Lake Champlain. While the battle of Plattsburg was raging on the land, the British squadron, superior in men and guns, attacked the American ships under Macdonough. The battle lasted two hours and twenty minutes, and resulted in the surrender of the English ships. So severe was the fight, that not a sound mast was left in either squadron—the masts were splinters and the sails were rags.

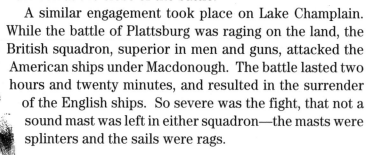

MACDONOUGH

Many private vessels were fitted out under authority of the government as privateers. These scoured the seas, and captured or destroyed above sixteen hundred British ships. The seamen on them fought with the same splendid courage as their brethren in the navy. The swiftest of these privateers were "Baltimore clippers."

1. *How was the country prepared for the War of 1812?*
2. *What kind of a leader was President Madison?*
3. *Of what sort were the generals selected at first?*
4. *For what reasons were they chosen?*
5. *What was the character of the soldiers?*
6. *In what way did they show their lack of discipline?*
7. *What was the main purpose of our government at the beginning of the war?*
8. *Who was in chief command of our troops on the Canadian frontier?*
9. *What kind of a general was he?*
10. *What had General Hull contrived to do?*
11. *How did the old Republican party of that day feel about a navy?*
12. *What was thought of the chance for success with our little navy?*
13. *How was the country saved from discouragement in the first year of the war?*
14. *What ship of ours captured the* Guerriere?
15. *Why did this victory excite pleasure and surprise in America?*
16. *What commander captured the* Macedonian?
17. *How had he distinguished himself when he was young?*
18. *What victory closed the year?*
19. *What nickname was given to the frigate* Constitution?
20. *What is said of the prowess of American seamen?*
21. *Why were sailors interested in the War of 1812?*
22. *What effect had the adventurous nature of American life in that day on the character of Americans?*
23. *How did officers show their eagerness for distinction in boarding an enemy's ship?*
24. *What anecdote is told of a dying seaman?*
25. *What did Captain Lawrence, of the* Chesapeake, *say when he was mortally wounded?*
26. *What effect did these words have on the navy?*
27. *Have they been of use to others since that time?*
28. *What kind of a maritime power was Great Britain at this time?*
29. *What was the effect of the naval victories on the American people?*
30. *How were the successful commanders treated?*

31. What motto did Commodore Perry show on his ship in the battle of Lake Erie?
32. What did he do when his flagship was disabled?
33. What did he write to General Harrison when the battle was over?
34. Who commanded the American ships in the battle of Lake Champlain?
35. What battle was raging on the land at the same time?
36. What was the result of the fight on the water?
37. What was the condition of the ships at its close?
38. How many British ships were destroyed during this war by privateers?
39. What is the difference between a privateer and a ship of war?
40. What sort of ships were the fastest of these vessels?

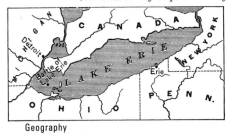

I.   Failures of the army at first.
II.   Successes of the navy on the seas.
III.   Courage of American seamen.
IV.   Exultation at naval victories.
V.   The battle of Lake Erie.
VI.   The battle of Lake Champlain.

Describe Lake Erie. What States touch it? Describe Lake Champlain. What is west of it? What State on its eastern shore? What province at its northern end?

Geography

Books   Cooper's *History of the United States Navy*. Schouler's *History of the United States*. Hildreth's *History of the United States*.

CHAPTER XLII

The Army in the War of 1812

Harrison appointed to command the Northwestern Army

GENERAL WINCHESTER, also a veteran of the Revolution, was appointed to succeed General Hull, after the latter had surrendered Detroit. But the Kentuckians, who formed the most important element in the Northwestern army, were unwilling to serve under anybody but Harrison, the hero of Tippecanoe, and the government yielded to their wishes.

Defeat of Winchester on the river Raisin, 1813

General Winchester, who commanded a part of Harrison's army, was defeated on the river Raisin, in Michigan. He surrendered his men to the British general, Proctor, a very brutal man, who, to his eternal infamy, left the

INFANTRYMAN,
1812-1834

wounded Americans to be massacred and plundered by the Indians of his army. The Americans were roused to revenge, and the war cry of the enraged Western troops became, "Remember the river Raisin!"

> When Proctor, whose force was much stronger than Harrison's, sent a demand for the surrender of the fort, Harrison answered, "Tell General Proctor that, if he shall take the fort, it will be under circumstances that will do him more honor than a thousand surrenders."

In the spring of 1813, General Proctor, with a great force of English soldiers and Indians under Tecumseh, laid siege to Harrison's little army in Fort Meigs. Harrison and his troops contrived to thwart every endeavor to capture the fort until reinforcements arrived, when the enemy gave up the siege and retired.

Siege of Fort Meigs by Proctor and Tecumseh, 1813

> **Croghan** was only twenty-one years old, and Harrison wished him to abandon the post. The English tried to persuade Croghan to surrender to avoid a massacre, but the answer was that when the fort should be given up there would not be found a man alive in it. Croghan shifted his six-pounder from one angle to another, to give the impression that he had several heavy guns. When the fort was assaulted at its weakest part, the Kentucky riflemen opened a deadly fire. But the brave English soldiers at length reached the ditch, and began to chop down the stockade. The six pounder, which had been double loaded with grapeshot and slugs, and concealed where it covered the whole ditch, was suddenly fired. Hardly a man of the assailing party escaped, and the English army retreated the next morning. During the night which followed, Croghan's men, not daring to open the gate, let down water to the wounded Englishmen outside, and at length, by means of a trench, brought them in and cared for them.

In the summer following, Fort Stephenson, a weak stockade with a single six-pound gun, was brilliantly defended by a young Kentucky officer named Croghan, with only a hundred and sixty men, against a force many times as strong, commanded by General Proctor.

Croghan's gallant defense of Fort Stephenson, 1813

In September, 1813, Perry's victory on Lake Erie was won (see page 248). This turned the scale, and opened the way for a forward movement by General Harrison's army. Harrison retook Detroit, crossed into

Battle of the Thames; death of Tecumseh, October 1813

DRESS OF A FRENCH
CANADIAN ABOUT
THAT TIME

Canada, and pursued Proctor's army, which he overtook at length on the river Thames. In a short and sharp battle, fought here on the 5th of October,

> In Harrison's general orders in starting for Canada after Perry's victory he said: "Kentuckians, remember the river Raisin! but remember it only while victory is suspended. The revenge of a soldier can not be gratified upon a fallen enemy."

1813, Harrison defeated Proctor and his Indian allies. The brave chief Tecumseh was killed in this battle, and the English army was utterly routed. Proctor, dreading the revenge of the Americans for his cruelties, ran away in a carriage. The battle of the Thames, and the death of the warlike Tecumseh, broke up the confederacy of the Indian tribes, and brought peace to the frontier.

Attempts to conquer Canada not successful; Battle of Lundy's Lane, 1814

Though Harrison and his Westerners succeeded so well, the attempted invasion of Canada to the eastward proved a failure under the lead of the feeble old generals who had survived from the Revolution. But the rise of young generals—Brown, Scott, and Ripley—to command changed the aspect of affairs, and an invasion of Canada was made in the summer of 1814. Fort Erie was taken, and the battle of the Chippewa was won by the Americans early in July. The battle of Lundy's Lane was stubbornly contested, and lasted till midnight. The Americans were left in possession of the field, but the next day they retreated. Before winter set in, the Americans retired to their own side of the Niagara River.

FRENCH CANADIAN
WOMAN

English attempt to invade the United States, 1814

The English, having now peace in Europe, had been able to send reinforcements to Canada, and in this same summer of 1814 they attempted an invasion of the United States, by Lake Champlain, the way so often traveled before by French and English expeditions. But the naval victory won near Plattsburg by Commodore Macdonough (see the preceding chapter), and the resistance made by the Americans in the battle of Plattsburg, fought at the same time, turned the British back again.

But the British invasion, by way of Chesapeake Bay, was more successful. In August, 1814, the British landed in Maryland an army stronger than any that could be brought to meet it. On the 24th of August a battle was fought at Bladensburg [blaa´-dens-burg], in Maryland, which resulted in a victory for the English, who entered Washington, and burned the Capitol and most of the public buildings. The same force that had taken Washington attacked Baltimore by land and water, but the vigorous defense of that place forced the British to retire. It was during this conflict that the song called "The Star Spangled Banner" was written.

THE STAR SPANGLED BANNER OF 1814. AFTER 1795 THE FLAG HAD FIFTEEN STARS AND AS MANY STRIPES, UNTIL 1818, WHEN THE STRIPES WERE REDUCED TO THIRTEEN AGAIN, WITH AS MANY STARS AS STATES

The persuasions of Tecumseh and his brother, the Prophet, had raised up a war party among the Creek Indians, who dwelt mostly in southern Alabama. A large part of the nation, under the lead of a half-breed chief named Weathersford, or "Red Eagle," made war on their white neighbors and on the Indians of their own tribe who were disposed to be friendly to the United States. British agents supplied these Indians with arms. Weathersford, like Tecumseh, had a prophet to help him, who had been initiated into the office by Tecumseh's brother. This chief, also, discouraged the barbarities of the Indians, but he could not restrain them, and cruel outrages of torture and massacre took place.

General Jackson, then an officer of the Tennessee militia, led a force into southern Alabama, and, after conquering the greatest difficulties and fighting many bloody battles, he broke the power of the Creeks, so that Weathersford himself entered Jackson's tent and surrendered. This was in April, 1814. Jackson, from being a commander of volunteers, was now made a major-general, and put in command of the troops in the Southwest.

Jackson seizes Pensacola   Florida was at this time in the possession of Spain, which was at peace with the United States. But that power was secretly in sympathy with England, and English troops made Pensacola, in Florida, a base of operations against Mobile. With his usual fiery zeal, Jackson marched into Spanish Territory, captured Pensacola, and dislodged the British. He then retired.

MAJOR-GENERAL, 1812

Jackson hastened to New Orleans, which was soon threatened by a large British force. With an energy unsurpassed perhaps in modern history, he formed an army out of the men and material within his reach, and built defenses against the British approach. He formed companies of free colored men, and he even took the convicts out of prison to make soldiers of them. After several preliminary battles, the English endeavored to carry Jackson's works by storm

Jackson's victory at New Orleans, January 8, 1815   on the 8th of January, 1815. But Jackson's preparations were so thorough, that the enemy was repulsed with a frightful loss of twenty-six hundred men. The Americans lost but eight killed and thirteen wounded. Sir Edward Pakenham, the British commander, was killed and the attack on New Orleans was abandoned.

Peace of Ghent, 1814   When this battle was fought, peace had already been made, but the news had not yet reached this country. The treaty of peace was signed at Ghent [pronounce G hard], in Belgium, on the 24th of December, 1814. By the terms of this treaty, neither Great Britain nor the United States gained anything. The right of searching American vessels was not mentioned in the treaty; but the war had shown Great Britain that the right to search could no longer be maintained against a spirited nation, and American ships have never been searched from that time to this.

The war had caused a great deal of suffering and misery in this country, by the derangement of business, the destruction of property, and the loss of life. The news of the peace was hailed with the greatest delight.

Suffering caused by the war

1. *Who was appointed to succeed Hull in command of the Northwestern army?*
2. *What post had Hull surrendered?*
3. *Were the soldiers willing to serve under Winchester?*
4. *Whom did the Kentuckians desire to have for commander?*
5. *Of what battle was Harrison the hero?*
6. *Against whom was the battle of Tippecanoe fought? In what State is the battleground of Tippecanoe?*
7. *Where was General Winchester defeated?*
8. *In which of the States as since formed is the river Raisin?*
9. *To what British general did Winchester's troops surrender?*
10. *What took place after the surrender?*
11. *What was the war cry of the Western troops after this?*
12. *To what fort did General Proctor lay siege in the spring of 1813?*
13. *Who commanded the Indians in this siege? What was the result of this siege?*
14. *Who defended Fort Stephenson?*
15. *What was the result of this defense?*
16. *What did Harrison do after Perry's victory?*
17. *Where did Harrison overtake Proctor's army?*
18. *What was the result of the battle of the Thames?*
19. *What chief was killed here?*
20. *What effect on the Indians did the defeat of the English and the death of Tecumseh have?*
21. *How did the attempted invasion of Canada to the eastward succeed?*
22. *What effect did the rise of younger generals have?*
23. *What battle lasted until midnight? Who held possession of the field?*
24. *Did the Americans remain in Canada?*
25. *By what road did the English attempt to invade the United States?*
26. *Had this road been used before for invasion? (see pages 123 and 178).*
27. *What naval officer commanded in the battle of Lake Champlain during this invasion? (see the preceding chapter).*
28. *What was the result of the defeat on the water and the resistance offered at the same time in the battle of Plattsburg?*

Questions for Study

29. What British invasion was more successful?
30. What battle was fought during this invasion?
31. In what State is Bladensburg? Who won the victory in this battle?
32. What happened in Washington afterward?
33. What other city was attacked during this invasion? Was it taken?
34. What well known song was written during this attack?
35. What had raised a war party among the Creek Indians?
36. What chief led them?
37. Where did they get supplies of arms?
38. In what respects was Weathersford like Tecumseh?
39. Did he succeed in restraining his savages?
40. Who led a force against the Creeks?
41. Where were the Creeks settled?
42. What came of Jackson's war with them?
43. What nation possessed Florida at this time?
44. What led Jackson to march on Pensacola?
45. What did he accomplish by this?
46. When New Orleans was threatened, what did Jackson do?
47. What happened on the 8th of January, 1815, when the British attacked Jackson's works?
48. Where was the treaty of peace made?
49. What is said of the terms of this treaty?
50. What is said of the claim to search American vessels?
51. What was the effect of the war in America?
52. How was the news of the peace received?

Study by topics

I. Harrison and the war in the Northwest.
   1. Harrison put in command.
   2. The defeat and massacre on the river Raisin.
   3. The siege of Fort Meigs.
   4. The defense of Fort Stephenson by Croghan.
   5. The invasion of Canada and the battle of the Thames.I
II. The war on the Niagara frontier and eastward.
   1. Failure of old generals.
   2. Invasion of Canada under new officers.
   3. Invasion of the United States by way of Champlain.
III. Invasion by way of the Chesapeake.
   a. Bladensburg. b. Washington. c. Baltimore,
IV. Jackson and the war in the Southwest.
   1. War with the Creeks.
   2. Invasion of Florida.
   3. Defense of New Orleans.
V. The peace.

   1. Harrison's campaign: In what States and what part of each State are the sites of—the battle on the river Raisin;

Fort Meigs; Fort Stephenson; Detroit? Where is the site of the battle of the Thames? 2. Campaign on the Niagara frontier: Where was Fort Erie? Lundy's Lane ? 3. The Eastern campaign: Where is Plattsburg? 4. In what State is Bladensburg? What direction from Washington? By what bay would ships approach Baltimore? 5. Jackson's campaign: Where is Pensacola? In what direction from New Orleans? On what river is New Orleans? By what sheet of water did the British approach it?

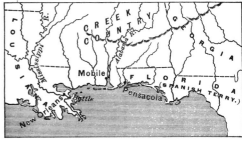

Geography

Hall's *Life of Harrison.* Mrs. Seelye's *Life of Tecumseh.* Lossing's *War of* Books *1812.* Parton's *Life of Jackson.* G. C. Eggleston's *Red Eagle.*

CHAPTER XLIII

Expansion of the Union

LET US now go back to the period immediately following the adoption of the Constitution, and trace the birth of new States. The first State admitted was Vermont. The territory which now forms Vermont was claimed by New Hampshire, which granted the land to settlers. For this reason it was called "The New Hampshire Grants." New York claimed it also, and tried to make the people buy their lands over again. But the "Green Mountain Boys" kept up an independent government of their own throughout the Revolution. In 1791 the State was admitted under the name of Vermont, a word of French derivation meaning "Green Mountain."

Kentucky was a part of Virginia, and was settled by Virginians, who took with them their slaves, their agricultural habits, and their military spirit. With the consent of Virginia, Kentucky was separated from that State and admit-

Vermont admitted as the fourteenth State, 1791

GENTLEMAN'S RIDING DRESS, EARLY PART OF THE CENTURY

Kentucky, the fifteenth State, 1792. Tennessee, the sixteenth, 1796

ted to the Union in 1792. The people of this country have generally emigrated in pretty straight lines to the westward. As Virginians broke over the mountains into Kentucky, so North Carolinians crossed into the valleys of Tennessee. North Carolina gave up her right to the territory west of the mountains soon after the Constitution was formed, and what is now Tennessee was part of the Southwestern Territory, until it was admitted to the Union in 1796.

Ohio, the seventeenth, 1803

HAIR DRESSED LIKE A HELMET, ABOUT 1806

These two States, Kentucky and Tennessee, had slaves. But the Ordinance of 1787, as we have seen on page 231, did not allow slave holding in the territory north of the Ohio River; so that all the States formed out of that territory were free States from the beginning. In the two years following the passage of this ordinance, twenty thousand people made their way down the Ohio River. But the Indian wars checked the settlement of the country until after Wayne's victory (see page 217). Ohio was admitted to the Union February 19, 1803.*

Louisiana, the eighteenth, 1812

It was more than nine years before another State was admitted. In 1812 the southern part of the great territory bought from France was admitted, under the name of Louisiana—the name at first given to the whole. Thus, when the War of 1812 began, the old Union of thirteen States had increased to eighteen.

TURBAN HEAD-DRESS WORN EARLY IN THIS CENTURY

The second war with England, and particularly the naval battles and the crushing defeat which Jackson inflicted on the British troops at New Orleans, made the United States respected in Europe as it had never been before. Emigrants began to flock to America. The peace with the Indians caused the Mississippi Valley, then called "The Far West," to fill up rapidly. In more than thirty years after the Revolu-

---

* This is the correct date, according to late investigations.

tion, only five States were added to the Union; but the next six States were admitted in six successive years—Indiana, next west of Ohio, in 1816. The defeat of the Creeks had opened the Southwest; and the new State of Mississippi, between Tennessee and Louisiana, was admitted in 1817. Illinois, west of Indiana, was admitted in 1818; and Alabama filled the gap between Mississippi and Georgia in 1819. In 1820 the District of Maine, long attached to Massachusetts, though separated from it geographically, was admitted as an independent State.

Rapid expansion after the war. Indiana, the nineteenth, 1816. Mississippi, the twentieth, 1817. Illinois, the twenty-first, 1818; Alabama, the twenty-second, 1819; Maine, the twenty-third, 1820.

By 1820, therefore, all the territory east of the Mississippi except the extreme northern portion, now included in Michigan and Wisconsin, had been made into States, and the State of Louisiana had been made out of the territory which had been bought from France. But, by this time, a new State on the west of the Mississippi River was knocking at the door of the Union. This was Missouri. Over the admission of this State there was a great debate, lasting through three sessions of Congress.

OPERA HEAD-
DRESS, EARLY IN
THE CENTURY

Debate over the application of Missouri

The cause of this debate was the fact that Missouri proposed to come in as a slave State. The bringing of slaves into the United States had been forbidden in 1808. The States north of the southern line of Pennsylvania had all, before 1820, taken measures to free their slaves. The States south of the southern line of Pennsylvania, having much of their wealth in slaves, and cultivating crops that seemed to require their labor, had by this time mostly given up the thought of freeing their slaves. So that there were now two classes of States in the Union: free States and States having slaves. Each of these divisions of the Union was afraid that the other would get control of the country. It had usually been the custom, in admitting new States, to bring in one

State of the slavery question

EVENING DRESS
IN JEFFERSON'S
TIME

from the North and one from the South, to keep the balance good.

But Missouri brought up a new question. According to the Ordinance of 1787, the States north of the Ohio had all come in as free States; but those to the south of that river had been allowed to enter as slaveholding States. Louisiana had been purchased as slaveholding territory, and was admitted as a slave State. But now the question arose whether all the great region bought from France was to be added to the Southern side of the scale. Missouri was west of the Mississippi, and so far north as to seem to break into the line of free States.

Most of the people at the North wished all the new territory made into free States; most of the people at the South wished to have it all open to settlement by Southern people with slaves. The question was finally decided by letting Missouri come in as a slave State, but slavery was at the same time forever forbidden in the rest of the territory north of the southern line of Missouri. Thus all the territory to the north and west of that State would be free. This was known as the Missouri Compromise. It was adopted in 1820, and Missouri was finally admitted in 1821. Henry Clay, the most famous of the orators and political leaders of the day, was very active in promoting this measure.

The "Old Thirteen" had now grown to twenty-four. The expansion of the nation in population and wealth was very rapid. In 1820 there were more than nine and a half million people in America. This was about three times as many as there were when the Revolutionary War was ended.

1. Which was the first State admitted to the Union after the adoption of the Federal Constitution?
2. What was Vermont called before it became a State?
3. Why was it called the New Hampshire Grants?
4. What State besides New Hampshire claimed Vermont?
5. Why are the people of Vermont called the "Green Mountain Boys"?
6. What mountains are there in Vermont?
7. Why was the State called Vermont when it was admitted to the Union in 1791?
8. Of what State was Kentucky a part? By whom was it settled?
9. What did Virginians take with them when they went to Kentucky?
10. How could Congress admit a part of a State into the Union as a new State?
11. Whose consent was given to it?
12. In what direction have the people of this country generally moved when they emigrated?
13. From what State did most of the first settlers in Tennessee come?
14. When did North Carolina give up its right to what is now Tennessee?
15. Was it formed into a State before 1800?
16. What was the difference between the States on the south side of the Ohio River and those on the north?
17. Why were there no slaves on the north side of the Ohio River?
18. What is said of the emigration to the Western country in the years following the famous Ordinance of 1787?
19. Was Ohio admitted to the Union before or after 1800?
20. What was the next State admitted after Ohio?
21. How did Louisiana come to belong to the United States?
22. What part of the old French province of that name was admitted as Louisiana?
23. In what year was Louisiana admitted?
24. What happened to the country in that year?
25. How many States were there in the Union when the War of 1812 broke out?
26. What impression did the War of 1812 make in Europe?
27. What battle of that war excited particular attention in Europe?
28. What effect did this have on emigration?
29. What caused the Mississippi Valley to fill up rapidly?
30. How many States were added to the Union in the space of one generation after the Revolution, if we count a little more than thirty years as representing a generation of people?
31. In 1816 and afterward for a number of years one State was admitted each year: for how many years did this happen?
32. Of all the territory that had belonged to the United States at the close of the Revolution—that is, of all the territory east of the Mississippi River—how much remained to be formed into States in 1820?
33. What was the first State, lying mostly west of the Mississippi, to be admitted to the Union?
34. Was Louisiana admitted before the War of 1812 or afterward?
35. What was the next State west of the Mississippi to ask for a place in the Union?

Questions for study

36. *From what country did we get the territory out of which Missouri is formed? Through how many sessions of Congress did the debate over the admission of Missouri last?*
37. *What was the cause of this debate?*
38. *At what time had the bringing of slaves into the United States been forbidden?*
39. *What had Pennsylvania and the States north of it done about slavery before 1820?*
40. *Why had the States to the southward retained their slaves?*
41. *How did the two divisions in the Union feel about each other?*
42. *In bringing States into the Union, how had the balance been kept good?*
43. *How did the new States north of the Ohio differ from those south of that river?*
44. *Were there slaves in Louisiana before the United States bought it?*
45. *What new question arose when Missouri offered to come in?*
46. *Was the greater part of Missouri north or south of the line between the free States and the slave States?*
47. *What did the Northern people wish regarding the new territory?*
48. *How did most of the Southern people feel about it?*
49. *How was the question decided?*
50. *What was this decision called?*
51. *In what year was the Missouri Compromise made?*
52. *What statesman took a leading part in promoting it?*
53. *What had he advocated in 1812?*
54. *To what number had the States increased by this time?*
55. *How many people were there in the United States in 1820?*
56. *How many times as many as the people at the close of the Revolution, less than forty years before?*

Study by topics

I. States admitted between the adoption of the Constitution in 1787 and the War of 1812.
    1. Vermont, 1791. 2. Kentucky, 1792. 3. Tennessee, 1796. 4. Ohio, 1803. 5. Louisiana, 1812.

II. States admitted between the second war with England and the Missouri Compromise.
    1. Indiana, 1816. 2. Mississippi, 1817. 3. Illinois, 1818. 4. Alabama, 1819. 5. Maine, 1820.

II. Missouri Compromise.
    1. The abolition of the slave trade, 1808. 2. The abolition of slavery in the Northern States. 3. Division of the States into two classes.
    4. A new question raised regarding slavery in the territory bought from France. 5. How the question was decided.

III. Expansion of population by 1820.

Blackboard illustration

On the blackboard, or on a large sheet of manila paper, draw a map of the Union as it was in 1787, shading the old thirteen States, or tinting them with colored crayons. Let the new States mentioned in this chapter be put in outline. Then, as each State is reached in topical recitation, let it be shaded or tinted like the rest, and the growth of the Union, step by step, will be represented.

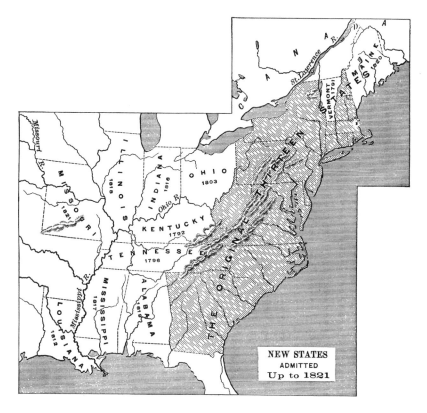

NEW STATES
ADMITTED
Up to 1821

The geographical study with reference to this chapter should have for its first   Geography
object the acquiring of a definite knowledge of the relative location of each of the
new States mentioned in the chapter. For this purpose consult the list in the topics above, and let a description of the location of each State and its surroundings
accompany the topical recitation. Fix in the mind by reference to the map the
great east and west line between the free and slave States in 1820, and the great
north and south line mostly along the Mississippi, between the territory possessed
by the United States after the peace with England in 1783 and the territory purchased from France in 1803.

CHAPTER XLIV

From Monroe to Van Buren—Rise of Whigs and Democrats

JAMES MONROE

A GREAT part of the expansion of the Union by the admission of new States, described in the preceding chapter, took place in the presidency of James Monroe, who was chosen to that office in 1816. Monroe was a man of even temper, with very little party feeling, and with the greatest desire to be just and to act wisely. He was very popular, and his

Monroe's presidency; the era of good feeling

> **James Monroe**, fifth President, was born in Virginia in 1754. As soon as he had graduated at William and Mary College, in 1776, he joined the Revolutionary army. He distinguished himself in several battles. He was minister to France and to England, and was Secretary of State when Madison was President. He was inaugurated President March 4, 1817, and served eight years. After leaving the presidency he was very poor. He died in New York on the 4th day of July, 1831. He was the third President to die on the 4th of July.

administration was called "the era of good-feeling." The Federal party being now almost extinct, Monroe was re-elected in 1820 without any opposing candidate.

Purchase of Florida from Spain, 1821

Next to the Missouri Compromise, of which we have spoken in the preceding chapter, the most remarkable event of Monroe's administration was the purchase of the Peninsula of Florida from Spain. This was completed in 1821. and General Jackson, who had seized part of Florida during the War of 1812, and again in the Seminole War of 1818, having both times to relinquish

> **Florida**—(For the early discovery and exploration of Florida, see page 116.) French Protestants made a settlement in Florida in 1564, but they were nearly all cruelly put to death by Spaniards in 1565. In this year the Spaniards founded St. Augustine, the oldest town in the present United States. In the treaty of 1763, Spain ceded Florida to England. In 1783 it was ceded back to Spain. In 1821 it was conveyed to the United States by Spain, and in 1845 it was admitted to the Union as the twenty-seventh State.

SPANISH STANDARD

it again, was now sent to receive the new province from the Spanish governor.

In 1823 the countries in America to the south of us, which had been colonies of Spain, were striving to establish themselves as independent republics, and it was feared that an alliance of European nations would help Spain to subdue them. President Monroe, therefore, sent a message to Congress, in which he announced what has always since been known as "The Monroe Doctrine." This doctrine was, that the United States would object to any attempt on the part of European powers to "extend their system" of interference to "any part of this hemisphere." This was a declaration of independence for the whole of America. The United States still maintains the principle as stated by Monroe.

Announcement of the "Monroe Doctrine," 1823

Monroe, who went out of office in 1825, was the last President connected with the Revolution.

For want of any issue between them, both the old parties had gone to pieces, and new ones were not yet formed. There were four candidates for the presidency in 1824: Crawford, Jackson, Adams, and Clay. No one of these got a majority of the electoral votes, and the duty of electing a president devolved on the House of Representatives. John Quincy Adams, of Massachu-

John Quincy Adams elected by the House of Representatives in 1824

John Quincy Adams, the sixth President, was the son of John Adams, the second President. He was born in Braintree, Mass., in 1767. He studied in France and Holland, and spent some time in Sweden, Denmark, Russia, and England while yet a boy. He graduated at Harvard College when he was twenty years old, and studied law. He was at various times American minister at the courts of Holland, England, Prussia, and Russia, and was one of the commissioners to negotiate the treaty with England at the close of the War of 1812. He was Secretary of State in Monroe's Cabinet, and President of the United States from 1825 to 1829. When he quitted the presidency he did not leave public life, but sat in the lower house of Congress from 1831 to 1848, and this was the most brilliant part of his career. At eighty years of age he was still called "The old man eloquent" He died in the Capitol at Washington in 1848.

JOHN QUINCY ADAMS

setts, was chosen. The administration of Adams was a stormy and unpopular one. He was extremely honest and faithful, but, like his father, John Adams, he had no gift for winning friends. He could not bend to the people: his cold manners and his disregard for the opinions of others made him enemies, who succeeded in preventing his re-election.

Election of Andrew Jackson in 1828

In 1828 Andrew Jackson, of Tennessee, was chosen President, taking office in March, 1829. He was re-elected in 1832, and held office in all for eight years. Jackson was a man sincerely patriotic

Andrew Jackson, the seventh President, was born in North Carolina in 1767. He joined the Revolutionary army in South Carolina when he was but fourteen years old. He studied law and settled in Nashville, Tenn. He was a member of the United States Senate and judge of the Supreme Court of Tennessee before he became distinguished as a soldier. His military achievements are told in Chapter XLII. He was President from 1829 to 1837. As the first President that had risen from the ranks of the common people, he was very popular, and was supposed to represent the American ideas of the time. He was called " Old Hickory" by his admirers. He died in 1845.

and honest, but self-willed and of a violent temper.

He was the first President who turned out of government office the men who were opposed to him, appointing his own friends in their places. He vetoed a great many acts of Congress. He succeeded in breaking down the United States Bank, which, up to that time, had kept the public moneys. He vetoed almost all the measures proposed for the promotion of

ANDREW JACKSON

roads and other "internal improvements" by the general government. Jackson set his face against the doctrine advanced by John C. Calhoun, of South Carolina, in his time, that a State could "nullify" a law of the United States. The business of the United States with other nations was conducted during Jackson's administration with great spirit and ability, and the country was respected abroad.

Character of Jackson's administration

As the moderate and peaceful administration of Monroe caused the dissolution of the old Federal and Republican parties, so the administration of a man of strong party feeling and of stormy temper like Jackson made new party divisions. Jackson loved his friends and hated all opponents. The country came to be divided into Jackson men and anti-Jackson men. The Jackson men claimed to succeed to the old Democratic-Republican party, and, retaining one of the names by which it was known, they were called "Democrats." Those who were opposed to Jackson were called "Whigs," a name formerly applied in England to the party opposed to the arbitrary power of the king. The principal feature of American politics for about twenty years was the rivalry of the Whig and Democratic parties.

Rise of the Whig and Democratic Parties

The main differences between the Whig party and the Democratic were: 1. That the Whigs advocated the reestablishment of the United States Bank; the Democrats opposed it. 2. The Whigs were in favor of the building of roads and canals at the expense of the United States. The Democrats did not believe that the government of the

JOHN C. CALHOUN

Differences between the parties

Union should undertake "internal improvements," as roads and canals were then called. 3. The Whigs generally wished to increase the power of the United States government; the Democrats were more in favor of what were called States' rights. The Democrats thought that, whatever power the Constitution did not expressly give to the general government, could only be exercised by the States.

The great party leaders, Clay, Webster, and Calhoun

The great leaders of the Whig party were Henry Clay, of Kentucky, and Daniel Webster, of Massachusetts. These were two of the greatest orators the country has ever known. Another orator of the first rank, John C. Calhoun, of South Carolina,

Election of Van Buren, 1836

Clay, Calhoun, and Webster are often spoken of together. They were the three great statesmen of what is sometimes known as "the compromise period" of American history. Henry Clay was born in Virginia in 1777. He was a poor boy, and gained his education with difficulty. He settled in Kentucky as a young man; and long represented that State in the House of Representatives and the Senate. John C. Calhoun was born in South Carolina in 1782, and graduated at Yale College. Clay and Calhoun were both bold advocates of the war with England in 1812. Webster, who was born in the same year with Calhoun, entered Congress in 1813, during the war. From this time these three men gradually came to the front as the greatest masters of the art of debate the country had known. Calhoun was a member of Monroe's Cabinet, Clay of John Quincy Adams', Webster of Harrison's and Fillmore's. But they were all three greatest in Congress. Each of them desired to be President, but all were disappointed. Calhoun was Vice President for eight years, from 1825 to 1833. Clay was active in bringing about the Missouri Compromise, which Calhoun favored. Later than this Calhoun became the chief advocate of the doctrine that the States were sovereign, and that the Union was a compact of sovereign States. Clay and Webster, on the other hand, were advocates of the authority of the Union. Clay was the author of the Compromise of 1850, which Webster favored. Calhoun died in 1850; Clay and Webster in 1852.

HENRY CLAY

was on the Democratic side. He believed in the power of a State to "nullify" a law of the nation. But the Democratic party generally agreed with Jackson, that the laws of the United States were supreme until the courts decided them unconstitutional.

In 1836 Martin Van Buren, of New York, was nominated by the Democrats and elected President. He followed the policy of Jackson, but in a gentler way. He did not veto any bills passed by Congress.

DANIEL WEBSTER

1. *What President took office in 1816?*
2. *What kind of a man was Monroe?*
3. *How was he liked by the people?*
4. *What was his administration called?*
5. *What was remarkable about his second election in 1820?*
6. *What territory did the United States acquire during Monroe's presidency?*
7. *From what country did we get it?*
8. *Who was sent to take possession of Florida in 1821?*
9. *Had he ever been there before?*
10. *Under what circumstances?*
11. *What colonies were trying to establish themselves as independent republics?*
12. *What declaration did Monroe make in 1823 regarding the interference of European nations with the affairs of America?*
13. *What is this declaration called?*
14. *Who was the last of the Revolutionary Presidents?*
15. *How many candidates were there for President in 1824?*
16. *What happened in this election?*
17. *Who was chosen by House of Representatives?*
18. *How did the administration of Adams differ from that of Monroe?*
19. *What was John Quincy Adams' character?*
20. *Was he reelected?*
21. *Was his father elected a second time? (See page 226.)*
22. *Who was elected in 1828?*
23. *What had Jackson done before this? (See page 254.)*
24. *What kind of a man was Jackson?*

Questions for study

MARTIN VAN BUREN

25. *What did he do in regard to the officeholders who were opposed to him?*
26. *What was his course regarding acts of Congress?*
27. *What influence did he have on the United States Bank?*
28. *What course did he take regarding roads and canals?*
29. *What doctrine did Calhoun and others advocate?*
30. *How did Jackson treat this doctrine of "nullification"?*
31. *How did he conduct the business of the country with foreign nations?*
32. *What effect did Jackson's administration have on political parties?*
33. *What were Jackson's friends called?*
34. *What were those opposed to Jackson called?*
35. *For about how many years did the struggle between Democratic and Whig parties occupy the field of American politics?*
36. *Give an account of the differences between the two parties in regard to the Bank of the United States.*
37. *In regard to internal improvement. Which party favored States rights as opposed to the power of the general government?*
38. *What did the Democrats think about the Constitution?*
39. *Who were the great leaders of the Whig party?*
40. *What great orator of the time was on the Democratic side?*
41. *How did the Democrats generally feel about Calhoun's theory of the right of a State to "nullify" the acts of Congress?*
42. *Who was chosen President in 1836? By what party?*
43. *What policy did he follow?*
44. *How did he differ from Jackson?*

DRESS OF A LADY IN
JACKSON'S TIME

    I. Monroe's administration. 1."The era of good feeling."
      2. The acquisition of Florida. 3. The "Monroe doctrine."
    II. John Quincy Adams' administration. 1. Election of J. Q.: Adams. 2. His character.
III.Jackson's administration. 1. Jackson's election and character.
      2. His course with regard to—a. Office-holders.b. Vetoes. e. United States Bank. d. Internal improvements. e. Nullification. f. Foreign affairs.
    IV. New parties. 1. Their formation. 2. Their differences. 3. Their leaders.
    V. Van Buren's administration.

Geography   The location of Florida with reference to Georgia and Alabama with reference to the Spanish possessions in Cuba.

CHAPTER XLV

The Steamboat, the Railroad, and the Telegraph

SOON after 1800, certain changes began in ways of travel that have made life different from that of our forefathers. We have seen in previous chapters that travel in old times was very slow. Men jogged along day after day and week after week to make a journey of hundreds of miles on horseback, or they were jolted over bad roads in stage-wagons or carriages. Pack horses or heavy wagons carried

ROBERT FULTON

all the freight that went by land. Boats, rowed or pushed with poles, went slowly up and down the rivers, carrying passengers and freight. Periaugers, with oars and sails, and other small vessels, plied up and down the coast, and all the ships at sea were propelled by sails.

Modes of travel at the beginning of the 19th century

In ships our people made great improvements. The "Baltimore clipper," a schooner with raking masts—that is; masts that slanted backward—was famous for its speed. Our frigates gained advantages in the War of 1812 by being better sailers than the English men-of-war. At a later period the American "clipper-built ships" were the swiftest sailing vessels in the world. This superiority in building and sailing swift ships has remained with America to the present time, as recent yacht races have shown.

Improvement in ships made by Americans. The Baltimore clippers

After the invention of the steam engine in England, attempts were made in France, Scotland, and America to build

Fulton's first steamboat, 1807

BALTIMORE CLIPPER

boats that would go by steam, but Robert Fulton, an American, built the first really successful steamboat. She was launched in 1807 and ran between New York and Albany, to the great wonder of all who saw her. Steamboats soon after took the place of keelboats (page 233) on the Western rivers, and they greatly aided in the rapid development of the new country.

The Erie and other canals

Steamboats served for commerce and travel where there were rivers and lakes. But how should the traffic on the Western rivers and the Great Lakes be connected with the rivers east of the Allegheny Mountains and the sea? Canals, long used in Europe, were thought of for this purpose, and Washington was much interested in a proposed canal from the Potomac to the Ohio River. But the first

FULTON'S FIRST STEAMBOAT

great canal in this country was that from the Hudson River to Lake Erie. The chief promoter of this work was De Witt Clinton, governor of New York. It was eight years in construction. It was begun on the 4th of July, 1817, and in 1825 its completion was celebrated by a procession of boats from Lake Erie to the ocean, where Governor De Witt Clinton poured a keg of Lake Erie water into the sea, as a sign of their union. This canal, by opening a trade with the West, made New York the greatest city of the United States.

But, for the more mountainous country of the Middle States, a great "National Road" for wagons was planned and built from western Maryland as far as the western part of Indiana. The extension of railroads soon rendered it of no importance as a national work.

The "National Road"

But the greatest change of all, in the life of Americans, was made by the railway, which was introduced from England. The first railroads were merely tracks of iron bars, on which little cars, loaded with coal, were drawn from the mines. The first railway in the United States was but two miles long, and was used only for hauling stone. The cars were drawn by horses. The first passenger train in America was run on the Baltimore and Ohio Railroad in 1830, but the cars were drawn by horses the first year. The extension of rail ways was very rapid; they changed America more than any other country, because here the distances are so great. We have almost as many miles of railway as all the world besides.

Railroads introduced about 1830

THE WAY THAT LITTLE GIRLS DRESSED IN THE EARLY 1800S

The first passenger cars were merely stagecoaches on the rails, and in other countries they still keep something of this form. In America large, airy cars for passengers were early introduced, and the parlor car, the sleeping car, the hotel car, and the dining car are all of American origin, and are little used elsewhere. The street tramway, or horse-railroad, and the elevated railways for rapid travel in cities, were first used in this country.

American improvements in railroads

The electric telegraph, in its present practical shape, was the invention of an American artist, S. F. B. Morse. In old times people sent messages by objects shown on high ground, by lights displayed at night, or by bonfires kindled on the hills. Even the wild Indians sent intelligence across

A BONNET OF 1880

FIRST STEAM PASSEN-GER TRAIN IN AMERICA

Invention of the electric telegraph

the Plains by waving a blanket over a fire and thus making a "smoke signal" In 1835 Morse set up and worked a telegraphic wire. But it was nine years later before he could persuade Congress to appropriate money to set up the first

S. F. B. MORSE

line. In 1844 the first message was sent from Washington to Baltimore.

Morse had gone to his lodgings in despair on the last night of the session of Congress. There were a large number of bills in advance of the one for promoting the telegraph. But the next morning the daughter of Commissioner Ellsworth called at his lodgings and informed him that a bill had passed granting $30,000 to build an experimental telegraph line. When the line was built from Washington to Baltimore, this young lady was allowed to dictate the first dispatch, which she did, sending the words, "What hath God wrought!" The first public news dispatch brought to Washington the intelligence that James K. Polk had been nominated for President.

Change in modes of living produced by railroad and telegraph

The introduction of the railway and the invention of the telegraph have completely changed the conditions of our life. In former times it was weeks after a presidential election before the result could be generally known. So wide is our country today that, if intelligence had to be carried, as formerly, by stagecoaches and post-boys on horseback, it would take months for an important event to be known in remote regions of the country. Now, every important bit of news is known from end to end of the country in a few hours. Railroads, too, have made distant places seem near together, and distributed the comforts of civilization to the most remote parts of the country.

1. What changes began to take place soon after 1800?
2. How did our forefathers travel by land?
3. How was freight carried over land?
4. What means of conveyance was there on the rivers?
5. What kind of vessels sailed along the coast?
6. How were all the ships at sea propelled?
7. What kind of improved ships did the Americans build?
8. What advantage did the Baltimore clipper have over other vessels?
9. How were its masts arranged?
10. What advantage did our frigates have in the War of 1812?
11. What is said of the relative speed of some of our sailing-vessels at the present time compared with those of other countries?
12. In what country was the steam engine invented?
13. In what countries were attempts made to build steamboats?
14. Who built the first really successful steamboat?
15. To what country did Fulton belong?
16. Between what places did his first steamboat run in 1807?
17. What water would a boat sail on from New York to Albany?
18. What effect did the invention of steamboats have on the new country west of the Alleghenies?
19. What plan was thought of for connecting the steamboat commerce and travel on the Western rivers and Great Lakes with the commerce of the Eastern rivers and the sea?
20. What canal project was Washington interested in?
21. What was the first great canal in this country?
22. Who was the chief promoter of this work?
23. How long did it take to build the Erie Canal?
24. How was its completion celebrated in 1825?
25. What effect did the Erie Canal have on New York city?
26. What plan was adopted for travel and conveyance of freight across the Allegheny Mountains?
27. In what State did the National Road begin?
28. To what State did it extend?
29. In what country did the railway originate?
30. For what were the first railroads used?
31. On what railway was the first passenger train in the United States used?
32. How were the cars drawn on this road in 1830?
33. Why did railroads work a greater change in American life than in that of any other people?
34. What country has the most miles of railway?
35. What were the first passenger cars like?
36. How do our cars differ from most of those in other countries?
37. What forms of the railway car were first used in America?
38. In what country was the electric telegraph invented?
39. How were messages sent in former times?
40. How do the wild Indians telegraph?
41. Who invented our present system of telegraphing?

Questions for study

42. How long was it after he began to work at it before he got a line established?
43. Between what places was his first line set up?
44. How long would it take for an important event to become known in remote parts of our great country if we had only the stagecoach and post-boy on horseback?
45. What were the effects of railroad and telegraph on our life?

<table>
<tr><td>Study by topics</td><td>I. The old modes of travel.
  1. By land. 2. By water.
II. Improvements in navigation.
  1. Swift ships. 2. The steamboat. 3. The Erie Canal.
III. Land travel.
  1. The National Road. 2. The railroad.
IV. The telegraph.
  1. Old methods of signaling. 2. Morse's invention.
V. Effects of the railroad and telegraph on our life.</td></tr>
</table>

CHAPTER XLVI

Annexation of Texas—Beginning of the Mexican War

The "hard times" of 1837

DURING the administration of Van Buren, various causes brought on severe financial distress in 1837. The "hard times" were attributed by the people to the hostility of Van Buren to the banks.

Harrison elected President, 1840. His death

In 1840 General William H. Harrison was nominated by the Whigs against Van Buren. The canvass of that year was one of wild excitement. The Whigs, to please the popular feeling of the time, boasted that their candidate lived in a log cabin and drank hard cider. They drew log cabins on wheels in their processions. It is known in the history of American politics as

> **William Henry Harrison,** ninth President, was born in Charles City County, Virginia, in 1773. His father was Benjamin Harrison, Governor of Virginia. He was educated at Hampden-Sidney College. He entered the army an ensign in 1791, and was aide-de-camp to General Wayne in his campaign in Ohio (see page 217). He was afterward Secretary of the Northwest Territory, delegate in Congress, the first Governor of Indiana Territory, and Superintendent of Indian Affairs. His military life is told in Chapters XL and XLII of this book. His death took place in 1841.

MEXICAN FLAG

the "Log cabin and Hard cider Campaign." Harrison was triumphantly elected, and was inaugurated amid wild rejoicings. But he died in one month after the beginning of his term.

John Tyler, of Virginia, who had been elected Vice-President in the "Hard cider Campaign," became President on the death of Harrison. He did not sympathize with his party in their views regarding the

Tyler President

WILLIAM H. HARRISON

> **John Tyler**, born in Virginia, 1790. He was a member of Congress and Governor of Virginia. Died 1862.

bank question, and when Congress passed a bill for its reestablishment he vetoed the measure. This act brought on him the anger of the Whigs and a suspicion of bad faith. His whole administration was passed in dissension with his party, and when he left office he was very unpopular.

In 1844 the Whigs nominated the eloquent Henry Clay for President: the Democrats nominated James K. Polk; of Tennessee. Polk who advocated the annexation of Texas, was elected.

The most important event of Tyler's administration was

JOHN TYLER

JAMES K. POLK

the passage of a bill for the annexation of Texas, which was accomplished just before Tyler gave up office to Polk. Texas had been one of the States of the Republic of Mexico. A large number of Americans had settled on grants of land there. These came into collision with the Mexican government, which was arbitrary and oppressive, and an armed revolution broke out in Texas in 1835. The Texans were commanded by General Sam Houston, and after several defeats achieved their independence. For about ten years Texas was an independent country, and was treated as such by several

Texas becomes an independent country, and is annexed to the United States European nations as well as by the United States. It was annexed to the United States by treaty, and admitted to the Union in 1845. In territory it is about the size of France.

Opposition to the annexation of Texas The annexation of Texas was strongly opposed by many people in the United States because its laws allowed slavery, and it would be an addition to the power of the slave holding States. Its annexation was also opposed by many of the Whigs, who feared a war with Mexico, for Mexico had never given up its hope of reconquering Texas.

Grounds of quarrel with Mexico There were already other grounds of quarrel with Mexico. In its violent revolutions American citizens had been robbed of a great deal of property by those claiming authority. As one

> **James K. Polk**, born in North Carolina in 1795. He was Speaker of the House of Representatives at one time, and was nominated for the presidency in preference to Martin Van Buren, because the latter was opposed to the immediate annexation of Texas. Polk died in 1849.

Mexican government quickly overthrew another, the United States tried in vain to get a payment of what was due to our citizens. And even if Mexico had consented to the annexation of Texas, there would have remained a dispute about its true boundary. Our government supported the claim of Texas, that the Rio Grande [ree´-o grand´-deh] was the true border, while Mexico would not allow that the State of Texas extended farther to the west than the Nueces [noo-eth´-ez] River.

General Taylor marched through this disputed territory to the Rio Grande in 1846. The Mexicans attacked his troops, and thus hostilities began. With a force much inferior to that of the Mexicans, Taylor fought and won the battle of Palo Alto [pah´-lo ahl´-to], and afterward attacked and defeated them in a strong position at Resaca de la Palma [ray-sac´ ah day lah pal´-mah].

Beginning of the Mexican War

These defeats drove the Mexicans across the Rio Grande. In May Taylor crossed the river and took possession of the city of Matamoros. But the Mexicans showed no disposition to make peace. Having re-

Capture of Monterey

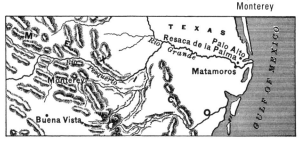

ceived reinforcements, Taylor marched on the fortified city of Monterey [mon-teh-ray´], which was defended by more than ten thousand Mexicans. Taylor's force was smaller. The place was captured on the 24th of September, 1846, after several days of hard fighting.

General Taylor now advanced farther into Mexico, but the United States government changed its plans, and orders were sent to Taylor to detach all but five thousand of his troops to the assistance of General Scott, who was to

Battle of Buena Vista

command in a new campaign, which was to be made into Mexico by way of Vera Cruz [vay-rah crooth´]. Thus weakened, General Taylor took up a strong position at Buena Vista [bway´-nah vees´-tah], where he was attacked by twenty thousand Mexicans under Santa Anna. After two days of the most courageous fighting, and after running the greatest risk of an overwhelming defeat, the little American army achieved the most brilliant victory of the war.

Character of the American troops

By this time the war had shown the immense superiority of the American troops, the most of whom were volunteers. The Mexicans often fought bravely, but the frequent revolutions and petty civil wars in Mexico had demoralized officers and soldiers. The arms of the Mexicans were also out of date. The Americans of that time were brave and enterprising, and a little too fond of military glory. They fought with great boldness and steadiness, and their early victories made them expect success.

Questions for study

1. What happened in 1837?
2. Who was President during the "hard times of thirty-seven"?
3. To what did the people attribute this financial distress?
4. Who was nominated against Van Buren in 1840?
5. What was the character of the canvass?
6. What boast did the Whigs make about Harrison?
7. What did they display in their processions?
8. What was the political campaign of 1840 called?
9. Which was elected, Harrison or Van Buren?
10. How long did Harrison live after his inauguration?
11. What battle had Harrison fought in Indiana?
12. What fort did he defend in Ohio?
13. What decisive battle did he fight in Canada? (See pages 251, 252.)
14. Who succeeded to the presidency when Harrison died?
15. In what regard did he differ from the Whig party which had elected him?
16. What did he do when they passed a bill to establish the bank again?
17. What did the Whigs think of this act?
18. How was his administration passed?
19. Who was elected to succeed Tyler in 1844?
20. What was the most important measure of Tyler's administration?
21. To what country had Texas belonged?

22. How did a revolution rise in Texas in 1835?
23. Who commanded the Texans?
24. What was the result of the rebellion in Texas?
25. How long did Texas remain an independent nation?
26. How was it annexed to the United States in 1845?
27. How does it compare with France in size?
28. Why was the annexation of Texas opposed in the United States?
29. What was feared in regard to Mexico?
30. What did Mexico claim regarding Texas?
31. What other cause for quarrel with Mexico was there?
32. Why could not the United States get a settlement of the claims of our citizens against Mexico?

33. What dispute was there between Mexico and Texas?
34. What did our government claim as the western border of Texas?
35. What river did the Mexicans claim was the border?
36. What did General Taylor do in 1846?
37. What battle did he fight?
38. What strong position did he attack and carry?
39. What effect did these defeats have?
40. What city did Taylor take in May?

TEXAS
265,780 Square Miles

FRANCE
204,178 Square Miles

41. On which side of the Rio Grande is Matamoros?
42. What city did Taylor now march against?
43. Which army had the more troops?
44. What was the result of Taylor's attack on Monterey?
45. What did Taylor do after taking Monterey?
46. Why was a great part of Taylor's troops taken away from him?
47. What battle did Taylor fight with five thousand men?
48. How many Mexicans were there against him? What was the result?
49. How did the American troops compare with the Mexicans?
50. What had demoralized the Mexicans?
51. What kind of arms did they have?

52. What was the character of the Americans of that time?
53. How did they fight?

Study by
topics

I. Political events.
    1. The effect of the hard times.
    2. The log cabin campaign.
    3. Death of Harrison.
    4. Tyler's break with the Whigs.
    5. Polk's election.
II. Texas.
    1. As a Mexican State.
    2. As an independent country.
    3. Its annexation.
III. Mexican War.
    1. Causes of the war.
        a. Mexican claim to Texas.
        b. Damage done to citizens of the United States
        c. The boundary of Texas.
    2. Taylor's invasion of Mexico.
        a. East of the Rio Grande.
        b. Matamoros and Monterey.
        c. Buena Vista.
IV. Superiority of the American soldiers.
    1. Mexicans and their arms.
    2. Character of the Americans.

Geography

The pupil should be required to describe the location of Texas with reference to Mexico, to the United States, to Louisiana, and to the Gulf of Mexico. Describe the position of Palo Alto, Resaca de la Palma, and Matamoros to one another, and to the Rio Grande. In what direction is Monterey from Matamoros? Buena Vista from Monterey? In what part of Mexico were Taylor's operations carried on? The teacher may draw an outline map on the blackboard and the location of each battlefield, without writing any name. Then let the pupils in turn each write the name of some battle opposite the mark of its location. Or the pupil may be required to make outline maps on paper, as directed in Chapter II and some others.

Ripley's *History of the Mexican War.*

Books

SHOWING RELATION BETWEEN TAYLOR'S
CAMPAIGN AND SCOTT'S

CHAPTER XLVII

The Close of the Mexican War and the Annexation of New Territory.

IT is probable that the government of the United States expected at first to conclude the war after one or two battles by Taylor on the east side of the Rio Grande. But if the Mexicans proved themselves as soldiers inferior to the troops which marched against them, they showed themselves stubborn in their refusal to treat for peace after repeated defeats. Mexico was so filled with factions, and one Mexican government was so soon turned out by another, that no government felt itself strong enough to take the responsibility of making a humiliating peace.

SANTA ANA

Persistence of the Mexicans

The war had been begun for the purpose of securing, Texas, and of enforcing the claim of Texas to the territory east of the Rio Grande. But many of the American people at that time were eager for more territory, and the object of the war was changed. Soon after the war was declared, Colonel Kearny was sent to conquer the thinly settled northern portion of Mexico and Upper California. New Mexico was surrendered to the United States without resistance in August, 1846. A civil government, subject to the United States, was immediately established there.

Conquest of New Mexico

In California matters were hurried up by the presence of an adventurous lieutenant, John C. Fremont, who was at the head of an exploring party. Under his lead the few American settlers there established an independent government. The United States ships of war on the coast seized the California ports, and the whole country was thus annexed to

Conquest of California

the United States. It now became the main object with the United States to close the war in such a way as not to surrender the great territory thus acquired.

Scott's expedition planned

When it became evident that General Taylor's victories in northern Mexico only wounded the vanity of the Mexicans without subduing them, it was resolved to land a force at Vera Cruz and march into the interior. It was thought that the Mexicans would readily make peace when their capital was threatened.

Vera Cruz taken

General Scott, at that time commander-in-chief of the American armies, took charge of this expedition. He landed on the 9th of March, 1847, and immediately laid siege to Vera Cruz. The city surrendered on the 27th of the same month.

Battle of Cerro Gordo

Marching into the interior, General Scott found the Mexican general, Santa Anna, opposing him at a strongly fortified position. On the 18th and 19th of April, 1847, Scott fought the battle of Cerro

California—The name of this State while it belonged to Mexico was Alta California, or, in English, Upper California; Lower California still remains a part of Mexico. Upper California was first visited by the Spaniards in 1542. Sir Francis Drake, the same who took Raleigh's colony back to England in 1585, visited Upper California in 1579 calling it New Albion, which means New England. It was nearly two hundred years later, in 1769, when Catholic missionaries from Spain made the first settlement of white people in that country. There were only about ten thousand white inhabitants in the whole province when it was seized by the United States in 1846. In the summer of that year California settlers from the United States set up a movement for independence, and tried to establish a government, known now as "The Bear Flag Republic." They were aided by Captain Fremont (afterward a general), who was in the province as the leader of an exploring expedition. United States naval officers on the coast, expecting a war between the United States and Mexico, raised the American flag on shore, and after some fighting, the province remained in American hands, and was definitely annexed at the close of the Mexican War. In 1848 gold was discovered in California, and the next year many thousands of people from the Eastern States sailed around Cape Horn to seek their fortunes in the richest gold mines in the world. In 1849 the people formed a State government, and the State was admitted to the Union in 1850. At first its chief interest was gold-mining, but now it is a State of very great agricultural resources, especially in fruit growing.

Gordo [ther´-ro gor´-do] completely defeating and dispersing the Mexican army. But the more the Mexicans were defeated, the more unwilling were they to make peace with an invading army.

One of the most difficult undertakings that ever fell to the lot of an army now became necessary. The American army of ten thousand men had advanced into the very heart of Mexico. It had to subsist on the country, and to attack the Mexicans, now rallying in great numbers, in strongly fortified positions.

WINFIELD SCOTT

Difficulty of Scott's march

Arrived in the region of the capital, General Scott fought and won the battle of Contreras [con-tray´-ras] on August 20, 1847, and the battle of Churubusco [choo-roo-boos´-co] on the same day. After this battle there was an armistice, but attempts at negotiation failed, and on the 8th of September Scott defeated the Mexicans at Molino del Rey [mo-lee´-no del ray]. On the morning of September 13th the

Battles about the capital. Surrender of the city of Mexico

Winfield Scott was born in Petersburg, Va., in 1786. He entered the army m 1808. His brilliant services in various battles during the War of 1812 had raised him by the close of the war to the rank of major general. In 1841 he became general-in-chief of the army. His conquering march from Vera Cruz to the city of Mexico has been described in the text. He ran for President in 1852 and was defeated. When the Civil War began, he was seventy-five years old, and he was obliged, by his infirmities, to yield the chief command to younger men. He died in 1866, at the age of eighty.

American troops carried the fortress of Chapultepec [chah-pool-ta-pec´] by storm, going over the works with scaling-ladders and fighting a hand-to-hand battle within the castle walls. The city of Mexico was attacked at the same time and the next day it was evacuated by the Mexicans and occupied by General Scott.

Peace concluded,
February, 1848

Although the Mexicans had lost every considerable battle from the beginning of the war to the conquest of the capital, their national pride made them very loath to make peace. In February, 1848, nearly five months after the capture of the capital, a peace was signed, by which all the territory of New Mexico, as then constituted, and Upper California became United States territory. Our government, however, agreed to pay fifteen million dollars to Mexico, and to pay the claims of our own citizens against Mexico.

Opinions about
the war

There has always been a difference of opinion in the United States about the Mexican War. Even at the present time opinions are divided as to whether it might not have been wisely avoided. It cost us the lives of thousands of brave men who fell in fighting on a foreign soil, or perished by the heat of the climate and the diseases of the country, and it caused much misery to innocent people in Mexico. No doubt, the ignorance and prejudice prevailing in Mexico at that time, and the frequent overthrow of one government and the setting up of another, made it difficult to treat with that country without war.

The territory
acquired from
Mexico

The territory acquired from Mexico, first and last, was larger than the United States at the close of the Revolutionary War. It comprised all the territory now included in Texas, California, Nevada, Arizona, Utah, the greater part of Colorado, and a part of Wyoming.

Dispute about
the Oregon
country

When the Mexican War broke out, we were engaged in a dispute with England about our claim to the country on the Pacific Ocean to the north of California. This had been settled in 1846 in such a way as to give us what is now the State of Oregon and the Territory of Washington. Our claim to this country was chiefly founded on the discoveries made there by a Boston sea captain in 1792, and by an expedition sent out by President Jefferson in 1804.

After the admission of Missouri in 1821, no new States were taken into the Union for fifteen years. Arkansas was admitted as a slave State in 1836, and was balanced by Michigan, which came in as a free State in the following year. Two States in the extreme South were admitted in 1845— Florida, which we had acquired from Spain (page 264), and Texas, which had been a part of Mexico and then an independent republic (page 278). But in 1846 Iowa was admitted, and in 1848 the extreme northern State of Wisconsin. In 1850 Congress admitted California, the first State on the Pacific coast, which was then like a new world to Americans.

Admission of Arkansas, 1836; Michigan, 1837; Florida and Texas, 1845; Iowa, 1846; Wisconsin, 1848; and California, 1850

SCOTT'S CAMPAIGN FROM VERA CRUZ TO THE CITY OF MEXICO

1. *What did our government expect at the beginning of the war with Mexico?*
2. *Why was Mexico stubborn in its refusal to treat for peace?*
3. *For what objects had the war been begun?*
4. *How did many of our people feel at that time about the acquisition of new territory?*
5. *What was Colonel Kearny sent to do?*
6. *What were the northern parts of Mexico as it then existed called?*
7. *When New Mexico surrendered to the United States in 1846, what was done about its government?*
8. *What hurried up the conquest of California?*
9. *What was Fremont doing there?*
10. *What did the American settlers there do?*
11. *What part did United States ships of war take in the conquest?*
12. *What now became the main object of the war?*
13. *What new expedition against Mexico was planned?*
14. *What was it expected to accomplish?*
15. *Who took charge of this new expedition?*
16. *Where did Scott land? In what year? What month?*

Questions for study

17. What city did he besiege? With what result?
18. What Mexican general did he find opposing him when he marched into the interior?
19. What battle did he fight?
20. What was the result to the Mexican army?
21. How did this affect the Mexicans as to peace?
22. What kind of a task was now before the soldiers under Scott?
23. Why was the undertaking difficult?
24. What two battles were fought on the 20th of August, 1847?
25. How did attempts to treat for peace after these battles result?
26. What is the name of the battle fought on the 8th of September?
27. What fortress was carried by storm on the 13th of September?
28. What now befell the capital of Mexico?
29. Had the Mexicans won any battle?
30. What made them loath to conclude a treaty of peace?
31. How long was it after the city of Mexico was captured when the Mexicans consented to make peace?
32. What provinces were ceded to the United States?
33. How much money did our government agree to pay to Mexico?
34. How did the most of the Whigs feel about the Mexican War?
35. Why did antislavery men oppose it?
36. What opinions are held about it today?
37. What is said of the amount of territory received from Mexico?
38. What States and Territories have been made from it?
39. On what was our claim to the country now included in Oregon and Washington Territory founded?
40. With what country did the United States have a dispute about it?
41. How was it settled in 1846?

42. What new slave State was admitted in 1836?
43. What free State in the next year?

MAP SHOWING
Territory Acquired from Mexico
SCALE OF MILES
0   100   200   300   400

44. *What two extreme Southern States were admitted in 1845?*
45. *What two Northern States were admitted in 1846 and 1848?*
46. *What extreme Western State came into the Union?*

I. Object of the war changed.   Study by
    1. Stubborn resistance of the Mexicans.   topics
    2. Factious divisions of the Mexicans.
    3. Desire for new territory.
II. Conquest of the northern provinces.
    1. New Mexico.
    2. California.
    3. Desire to retain this territory.
II. General Scott's campaign.
    1. Its plan.
    2. Capture of Vera Cruz.
    3. Battle of Cerro Gordo.
    4. Battles near the city of Mexico.
        a. Contreras and Churubusco. b. The armistice. c. Molino del Rey.
        d. Occupation of the capital.
IV. The peace. February, 1848.
V. Differences of opinion about the war.

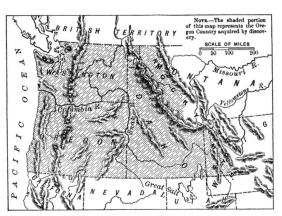

NOTE.—The shaded portion of this map represents the Oregon Country acquired by discovery.

SCALE OF MILES
0   50   100   200

    1. The opposition of the Whigs at the beginning
    2. The opposition of antislavery men.
    3. Losses by the war.
    4. Difficulty of dealing with Mexico without a war.
VI. New territory and new States
    1. The territory annexed from Mexico
    2. The Oregon country.
    3. New States.

The location of the several battles of Scott's expedition may be learned in the   Geography
way used for those of Taylor's campaign in the previous chapter. Describe the
location of the territory acquired from Mexico and its present division into States
and Territories. What great river borders Arkansas on the east? What State is
north of it?

What State is south of it? What lakes border Michigan? By what waters is Florida
bound? How does it compare with other States in the matter of seacoast? What great
river is on the east of Iowa? What on the west? What State between Iowa and Arkansas?
Between what river and lake is Wisconsin? Where is California?

SIXTH REVIEW—FROM THE BEGINNING OF THE WAR OF 1812 TO THE CLOSE OF THE MEXICAN WAR

Chapters XL to XLVII

Events preceding the second war with England. (XL)
{
Impressment of sailors.
Decrees against our trade.
The embargo of 1807.
The election of Madison.
War with Tecumseh.
}

Beginning of the war. (XL and XLI)
{
Declaration of war.
Fall of Mackinaw and Detroit.
General failure of American armies.
}

The successes of the navy. (XLI)
{
Naval victories at sea.
Naval victories on the lakes.
}

War in the Northwest. (XLII)
{
Harrison put in command.
Defeat on river Raisin.
Fort Meigs and Fort Stephenson.
Battle of the Thames.
}

Campaigns at the North and East. (XLII)
{
Failure of attempts to invade Canada.
English invasion by Lake Champlain.
Battle of Bladensburg: burning of Washington.
}

Jackson's campaign at the South. (XLII)
{
War with the Creeks.
Jackson invades Florida.
Battle of New Orleans.
}

The peace. (XLII.)

First ten States admitted. (XLIII)
{
Five States admitted before the War of 1812.
Five States admitted between the war and the Missouri Compromise.
}

The Missouri Compromise. (XLIII)
{
Abolition of the slave trade, 1808.
Gradual abolition of slavery at the North.
Missouri raises a new question.
Admission of Missouri, 1821.
}

The increase of population to 1820.   (XLIII)

Presidency of Monroe.   (XLIV) {
Decline of parties.
Purchase of Florida.
The Monroe doctrine.

Character and administration of John Quincy Adams.   (XLIV)

Jackson's presidency.   (XLIV) {
Jackson's election and character.
Traits of his administration.

New parties formed.   (XLIV) {
Differences between the Whigs and Democrats
Their leaders.

Presidency of Martin Van Buren.   (XLIV)

New modes of travel.   (XLV) {
Swift ships.
Steamboats.
Canals.
The National Road,
Railroads.

The telegraph.   (XLV) {
Morse's invention,
Effect of the railroad and telegraph on life.

Struggles of the Whigs and Democrats.   (XLVI) {
Political effects of the hard times.
Election and death of Harrison,
Tyler's presidency.
Polk's election,

Annexation of Texas.   (XLVI) {
Its history.
Admitted to the Union.

Mexican War.   (XLVI and XLVII) {
Causes of the war.
Taylor's campaign.
Conquest of the northern provinces,
Scott's campaign,
The peace.

Traits Of the war.   (XLVI and XLVII) {
Mexicans and their arms.
Character of American troops.
Opposition to the war,

New territory and new States   (XLVII) {
The territory taken from Mexico,
The Oregon Territory.
New States.

CHAPTER XLVIII

The Question of Slavery In Politics

The annexation of Texas sets in motion a chain of events that end in the Civil War

THE annexation of Texas opened a new chapter in our history. It brought on the Mexican War that brought a large addition to our territory. It was necessary to settle the question of slavery in the annexed territory, and this opened the slavery question anew. Both of the old parties were after a while split asunder by the debate, and the question of slavery or no slavery in the Territories became the leading issue in our politics. In sixteen years from the annexation of Texas, this chain of causes had plunged the country into the most tremendous civil war in the history of the world. In just twenty years the war had ended in the entire abolition of slavery in the United States. Thus, the annexation of Texas brought about unforeseen results, and changed the history of the continent.

Antislavery agitation opposed

After the Missouri Compromise in 1820 (page 260), it had been an accepted maxim in our politics that the slavery discussion should not be reopened. The antislavery men who persisted in agitating the question were thought unpatriotic. They were severely persecuted even by Northern people, who feared that their agitation of the subject might destroy the Union of the States.

The Wilmot proviso

But, when the arrangement made by the Missouri Compromise was once disturbed by annexing Texas and other Mexican territory, the political struggle between the free and slave States began anew. In 1846, during the Mexican War, a bill was introduced in Congress looking to a peace with Mexico, to be made by a purchase of territory. Mr. Wilmot, of Pennsylvania, moved to add a proviso that slavery should never exist in the territory thus acquired. This was known as "the Wilmot Proviso." The proviso was finally rejected, but it opened the question of freedom or slavery in the new territory before the Mexican War was ended.

The first effect of the excitement was to render certain the defeat of the Democratic party in the election of 1848. A large number of Democrats and a smaller number of Whigs seceded from the old parties and formed the Free Soil party, which desired to shut slavery out of the Territories. The Democrats nominated General Cass; the Whigs nominated General Zachary Taylor,

ZACHARY TAYLOR

the hero of Buena Vista, for President. The Free Soilers nominated ex-President Martin Van Buren. Taylor was elected. After serving for a year and four months, President Taylor died, and was succeeded by Millard Fillmore, the Vice-President.

Election and death of President Taylor. Fillmore succeeds to the presidency

Zachary Taylor—General Taylor was the twelfth President of the United States, and of these first twelve Presidents seven were born in Virginia,, which got the name of "the Mother of Presidents" from that fact. Zachary Taylor was born in Virginia in 1784, but he was carried to Kentucky in his infancy. He got a commission in the army when he was twenty-four years old. He gained his first distinction by his gallant defense of Fort Harrison in the war against Tecumseh's Indians. (Chapter XL.) In a war waged against the Seminole Indians in Florida he defeated the savages in a severe battle at Okeechobee. His fame rests on his achievements in the Mexican War, which we have related in Chapter XLVI.

But while the country was excited over the presidential election, an event took place in the newly annexed Territory of California that gave new violence to the slavery debate. Particles of gold were discovered in the Sacramento River in California in 1848. The California mines proved to be the richest in the world. A great rush of people to the new Territory set in. Ships loaded

Discovery of gold in California

with passengers sailed around Cape Horn, and trains of ox-carts went across the plains, then occupied only by Indians. In 1849 the people of California set up a State government without authority from Congress, and asked to be immediately admitted to the Union. As part of the new State was south of the Mis-

> **Millard Fillmore**, born in New York, 1800. He secured his education with difficulty, and rose to prominence in his profession. In his own State he secured the passage of a law abolishing imprisonment for debt. Died 1874.

souri Compromise line, and as its Constitution forbade slavery, the slave States were opposed to this addition to the number of free States.

Fugitive slaves and the slave-trade in the District of Columbia

Meantime the growing antislavery sentiment at the North made it harder to reclaim runaway slaves, who escaped in large number to the free States. The Southern States complained of this as a violation of the Constitution, which provided that all such fugitives should be sent back. The Northern States complained that the public traffic in slaves in the city of Washington was highly improper in the capital of a free country.

The veteran statesman Henry Clay had always been a skillful compromiser of difficulties. He now arranged and carried, with the help of Webster and others, the measures which have since been known as "The Compromise of 1850." By this compromise slavery was to be continued in the District of Columbia, but the buying and selling of slaves there was to be abolished. At the same time a new and severe law was made for the return of fugitive slaves,

MILLARD FILLMORE

which was no longer left to the States, but entrusted to United States officers. California was admitted as a free State, and New Mexico organized as a Territory without slavery. The leading statesmen of the country imagined that these measures, which gave something to each side, would forever put to rest this dangerous question.

The Compromise of 1850

There was indeed a lull in the excitement. The little Free Soil party, which had helped to defeat the Democrats in 1848, cast fewer votes in 1852 for its candidate, John P. Hale, than it had cast for Van Buren in 1848. The Whigs nominated General Winfield Scott, the conqueror of the city of Mexico, but divisions on the slavery question had broken the power of that party, and Franklin Pierce, of New Hampshire, the Democratic candidate, was elected by a large majority.

FRANKLIN PIERCE

Election of Franklin Pierce

The Compromise of 1850 did not prove to be, what its promoters called it, "a finality;" that is, an end of the debate. The fugitive slave law exasperated the Northern people. Every Negro claimed under it excited the sympathy of the people and awakened opposition.

Opposition to the fugitive slave law

> **Franklin Pierce**, fourteenth President, born in New Hampshire, 1804. He was a lawyer, a member of the House of Representatives, and a United States senator. He served in the Mexican War as brigadier-general under Scott. He was a man of correct life, but of mediocre ability. Died 1869.

The antislavery sentiment at the North was quickened and diffused at this time by the publication of the novel entitled *Uncle Tom's Cabin*. It was calculated to excite sympathy for slaves, and it at once reached a circulation that has hardly an equal in the history of literature.

Effect of Uncle Tom's Cabin

The South was equally dissatisfied. The violent censures of antislavery speakers and writers excited bitter feelings.

Dissatisfaction at the South

It soon became evident also that about all of the territory remaining to be admitted into the Union would, in the nature of things, come in as free States. It was seen that this would put the slave States in the minority, and destroy what was called "the balance of power" between the two sections.

Efforts to secure new territory at the South. The filibusters

Attempts were therefore made to purchase the Island of Cuba, in order to make new States from it. But Spain refused to sell Cuba. The desire of our people for new territory had been greatly inflamed by their recent acquisitions, and threats were made to seize Cuba by force. Expeditions were secretly fitted out in the United States to promote insurrections in the island, but they came to nothing. Several attempts were made by filibusters to seize territory from the weak states in Central America. These were continued until 1860, when the chief filibuster, William Walker, was captured and executed by Central American authorities.

Questions for study

1. *What war immediately followed the annexation of Texas?*
2. *How did the Mexican War lead to the reopening of the controversy about slavery?*
3. *How did this bring about at last a great change in the history of America?*
4. *How did the people of this country feel about the slavery question after the adoption of the Missouri Compromise in 1820?*
5. *How were the antislavery men regarded?*
6. *Why was the discussion of the subject thought to be unpatriotic?*
7. *What disturbed the arrangement made by the Missouri Compromise?*
8. *What was "the Wilmot Provision"?*
9. *Was it introduced before or after the close of the Mexican War?*
10. *Was it adopted or rejected?*
11. *What effect did it have?*
12. *How was the Free Soil party formed?*
13. *What did the Free Soilers wish to do?*
14. *Who was nominated by the Democrats in 1848? Who by the Whigs?*
15. *Who by the Free Soilers?*
16. *What was the result?*
17. *What had brought General Taylor into fame?*
18. *How long was he President?*

19. Who succeeded him?
20. What happened in California during the presidential Canvass of 1848?
21. What followed this discovery?
22. How did emigrants get to California in that day?
23. What did the people do for government?
24. Why were the people of the Southern States opposed to the admission of California as a free State?
25. What complaint did the Southern people make against the Northern States?
26. What did the Constitution provide in this regard?
27. What did the Northern people complain of?
28. Who arranged the Compromise of 1850?
29. What provisions were made by this compromise in regard to slavery in the District of Columbia?
30. What was done about the sale of slaves there?
31. What was done about fugitive slaves?
32. What did the leading statesmen of the country imagine in regard to these measures?
33. What was the first effect of the compromise?
34. What three candidates ran for President in 1852?
35. For what was Scott celebrated?
36. Mention some of his battles (See preceding chapter).
37. Which candidate was elected?
38. Which of the compromise measures of 1850 excited ill feeling at the North? Why?
39. What book published at this time increased the antislavery feeling?
40. What is said of the popularity of this book?
41. Why was the South dissatisfied?
42. What attempt to purchase new territory was made.?
43. With what success?
44. What is said of filibustering expeditions?
45. What was the fate of William Walker?

I. From the annexation to the Civil War.   Study by
   1. Admission of Texas led to   topics
   2. Mexican War led to
   3. Acquisition of new territory led to
   4. New shivery agitation led to
   5. Civil war.
II. The slavery agitation.
   1. The Wilmot Proviso.
   2. The admission of California
   3. The Compromise of 1850..
   4. Return of fugitive slaves.
   5. Effect of *Uncle Tom's Cabin.*
   6. Attempts to restore the balance of power.
      a. By the purchase of Cuba.
      b. By filibustering expeditions.

Geography   In what direction is the Island of Cuba from the United States? Which one of our States lies nearest to Cuba? What country lies between the United States and Central America?

CHAPTER XLIX

Breakup of Old Parties—Approach of the Civil War

Decay of the Whig party

THE Whig party was passing into decrepitude. The measures it had advocated—the United States Bank, the tariff, and internal improvements—were no longer of the highest importance in the eyes of the people.

The American, or Know-Nothing Party

The Whigs had been badly beaten in 1852. Those opposed to the Democratic party felt obliged to take new ground. A party was founded in 1853, which proposed to keep foreigners out of office and to make them wait a longer term before becoming citizens. This new party was the "American party." Its members were organized in secret lodges, and it carried many elections by surprise. To all questions about its doings the members of this order answered, "I don't know." From this arose the name "Know-Nothing," which was commonly applied to the party. It spread rapidly for two or three years, but died as quickly as it had come into life, for the slavery question took a new form. which left no room for any other debate.

STEPHEN A. DOUGLAS

The Kansas-Nebraska Bill

This new form was brought about by the bill organizing the Territories of Nebraska and Kansas, introduced in 1854 by Senator Douglas, of Illinois. This bill repealed the Missouri Compromise, which had been adopted in 1820. By that compromise slavery had been forbidden in all new territory north of latitude thirty-six degrees and a half. Kansas and Nebraska were on the north side of this line. The

"Nebraska Bill," as it was called, repealed this restriction, and left it for the settlers in the new territory to decide the question of slavery for themselves. This was called "Squatter Sovereignty " in the discussions of the time.

The excitement over the repeal of the Missouri Compromise exceeded any ever before known in this country. Many people in the North regarded it as an act of bad faith. People in the South claimed that they had an equal right with free State people to take their property of every kind to the new Territories. Both sides became exceedingly violent. As President Pierce favored the Nebraska Bill, those Whigs who took the same side generally went over to the Democratic party, while those opposed to the repeal of the Missouri Compromise, whether Whigs or Democrats, united, and, with the old Free Soil party, formed an "Anti-Nebraska party." This presently took the name "Republican," but it is not to be confounded with the old Republican party of the days of Jefferson.

Formation of the Free Soil and then of the Republican party

Meantime the great struggle between the two sections had been transferred to the new Territory of Kansas. This lay directly west of Missouri, and a strong effort was made to secure it, both by the North and the South. Emigrants poured in from both sides of the line between the free and the slave States. Societies were formed at the North to promote emigration, and in Missouri to keep emigrants from the free States away. Many free State men were stopped and turned back on the Missouri River. The free State people and the slave State people now came into collision on the Kansas prairies. Men from Missouri assisted the Southern party. Rival governments were formed. Kansas soon became the scene of a violent struggle. Midnight assassinations and mobs were common, and something like

Violent collisions in Kansas

open war broke out from time to time. The men from the Northern States soon had a majority, and asked admission to the Union. The bloody feud in Kansas by this time produced the greatest excitement in Congress and convulsed the whole country.

Buchanan elected President, 1856

While the people were in this State of passionate excitement about the struggle in Kansas, the presidential canvass of 1856 came on. The Democrats nominated James Buchanan, of Pennsylvania; the new Republican party nominated John C. Fremont, who had become known as a daring explorer in the Western plains, and who had taken part in the conquest of California. The American, or Know-Nothing, party nominated ex-President Millard Fillmore. Buchanan, the Democratic candidate, was elected. Fillmore got but eight electoral votes, Fremont one hundred and fourteen, and Buchanan one hundred and seventy-four. The election showed that the people were interested in nothing but the settlement of the slavery question. No Presidential election had ever before turned wholly or chiefly on this question.

James Buchanan, fifteenth President, born in Pennsylvania, 1791. He was a successful lawyer, a member of Congress, United States minister to Russia, member of the Senate, and Secretary of State in the Cabinet of President Polk. He was minister to England during the administration of Pierce. In 1854 he was one of the signers of a document known as the "Ostend Manifesto," by which three foreign ambassadors of the United States assembled at Ostend, in Belgium, advised their government to seize the Island of Cuba by force, if it could not be purchased from Spain. Died 1868.

The Dred Scott decision

The Supreme Court of the United States now attempted to settle the question of slavery in the Territories and thus take it out of politics. In the spring of 1857, in the case of a Negro named Dred Scott, who sued for his freedom on the ground that his master had taken him to a free State, the Supreme Court decided that the African whose ancestors had been slaves had no rights under the Constitution, and that Congress had no power to forbid slavery in the Territories. So, far from settling the question, this decision proved to be oil on the fire. The North now feared that slavery would be made national by a decision of the Supreme Court.

JAMES BUCHANAN

In 1859 John Brown, who had borne a conspicuous part as a free State man in the murderous feuds of the Kansas struggle, seized the United States armory at Harper's Ferry, in the mountains of Virginia, and undertook to liberate the slaves. As he had but eighteen men under his command, he was soon overcome. He was tried and executed, but this raid alarmed the South more than the Dred Scott decision had the North. People at the South began to fear that the Northern people were trying to arm the slaves for the murder of their masters.

John Brown's raid, 1859

The excitement over the subject of slavery had already divided into two parts nearly all the great religious denominations, and had destroyed the Whig party. In 1860 it divided the Democratic party. The majority in the convention of the party nominated Stephen A. Douglas, of Illinois, the author of the Kansas-Nebraska Bill. The Democrats who adhered most strongly to the South put forward John C. Breckinridge, of Kentucky. The Republicans nominated Abraham Lincoln, of Illinois. The Constitutional Union party, as it was called, which desired to make peace between the angry sections, nominated John Bell, of Tennessee. Lincoln was elected. We have now reached the point where the angry debate be-

Lincoln elected President, 1860

tween the North and the South was at last about to break
into a long and terrible war.

Increase in the
number of free
States, Minne-
sota admitted,
1858; Oregon,
1859; and
Kansas, 1861
One element in the political jealousies of this excited
time was the increase of free States. Minnesota was admitted in 1858, Oregon in 1859, and Kansas soon after the election of Lincoln, in 1861. These were all free States. There
was now no territory left at the South from which new slave
States could be made.

Questions for
study

1. What great party was badly beaten in 1852?
2. What measures did the Whigs advocate?
3. What new party was founded to take its place in 1853?
4. What did the American party propose to do regarding those who came from foreign countries?
5. How were its members organized?
6. Why were they called Know-nothings? Did the party last long?
7. What brought up the slavery question in a new form?
8. By whom was the "Nebraska Bill" introduced?
9. What did this bill repeal?
10. What can you tell about the Missouri Compromise?
11. Why called Missouri Compromise? (See pages 260, 261.)
12. How long had this compromise lasted in 1854? (Subtract 1821 from 1854.)
13. On which side of the Missouri Compromise line were Kansas and Nebraska—that in which slavery was allowed or that in which it was forbidden?
14. How was slavery to be settled in these Territories according to the Nebraska Bill?
15. What effect did this act have?
16. How did the people in the North regard it?
17. What view did the people of the South take of it?
18. What ground did President Pierce take?
19. What became of the Whigs who were divided by this question?
20. What name was given at first to those who opposed the Nebraska Bill?
21. What name was finally given to this party?
22. Had there been any other party called Republican?
23. What took place in Kansas?
24. How was Kansas situated with regard to Missouri?
25. What measures were taken at the North?
26. What was done to check emigration from the free States?
27. What form did the struggle in Kansas take?
28. What effect did the struggle have on Congress and the country?
29. Who was the candidate of the Democratic party in 1856?
30. Who was nominated by the new Republican party?

31. Who was the candidate of the Know-Nothing party?
32. Which was elected? What did the election show?
33. How did the Supreme Court try to settle the question?
34. In what case did they render their decision?
35. What did they decide about slavery in the Territories?
36. What effect did their plan for settling the dispute have?
37. Who was John Brown? What armory did he seize?
38. Where is Harper's Ferry?
39. How many men did he have?
40. What effect did his raid have upon the South?
41. What effect had the slavery question had on most of the religious denominations?
42. What effect had it had on the Whig party?
43. What took place in the Democratic party in 1860?
44. Who was nominated by the majority of that party?
45. Who by those that adhered most strongly to the South?
46. Whom did the Republicans nominate?
47. There was a fourth party: what was it called?
48. Whom did the Constitutional Union party nominate?
49. Who was elected?
50. What State was admitted in 1858? What in the next year?
51. When was Kansas admitted?
52. Why was it that no more slave States were formed?

Some of these topics are treated in the preceding chapter, and are here reviewed for the sake of completeness.

I. Rise and fall of new parties after the Mexican War.   Study by
   1. The Free Soil party, nicknamed "Barn-burners."   topics
   2. Decay of the Whig party.
   3. The American party, called also " Know-Nothings."
   4. The Republican party, at first " Anti-Nebraska."
   5. The Constitutional party in 1860.
II. The question of slavery in the Territories.
   1. The Wilmot Proviso.
   2. The Compromise of 1850 and the admission of California.
   3. Repeal of the Missouri Compromise.
   4. The struggle in Kansas.
   5. The Dred Scott decision.
   6. The John Brown raid.
   7. The election of Lincoln.

It would be a good exercise for a pupil to write a paper on "The Causes of the   Composition
Civil War." Let him use his own words and express his own opinions, prejudices, and sympathies, whatever they may be.

What large river rises in Minnesota? On what large lake does a part of Minne-   Geography
sota lie? What States lie to the south and east of it? How is Oregon situated with reference to California? What ocean on its western border? What State on the eastern border of Kansas?

CHAPTER L

How the Great Civil War Began

The movement of secession   THE excitement at the South had reached a pitch that rendered an effort to break up the Union inevitable. From the moment that Lincoln's election was known, active preparations were made in what were called the "cotton States"—South Carolina, Georgia, Florida, Alabama, Mississippi, Louisiana, and Texas—to dissolve the Union of States.

Difference of opinion about State sovereignty   From the beginning of the government there were two opinions in regard to the power of a State under the Constitution. The Federalists thought that nearly all the powers of government were vested in the United States authorities, but the Jefferson Republicans held that a State retained a considerable share of independence. At a later period the chief advocate for the sovereignty of the State had been John C. Calhoun, of South Carolina (page 268), who thought a State could declare an act of Congress null—that is, not valid within its bounds. In 1832 the State of South Carolina declared the tariff law null, and forbade its citizens to pay the duties. This was called nullification; but President Jackson, who did not believe in the doctrine, threatened the nullifiers with the army and navy of the United States.

The seven "cotton States" pass ordinance of secession, 1861   The States rights doctrine—as the belief in the right of a State to act independently was called—had found a good many adherents in the South, and in the present excitement the extreme Southern States claimed that, by exercising the right of the individual State, they might lawfully secede from the Union. South Carolina first passed an ordinance of secession on December 20, 1860. By the 1st of February each of the seven "cotton States" had declared itself separated from the Union and independent.

Meantime the recollection of the success of the Missouri Compromise in 1820 (page 260), and of the Compromise of 1850 (page 294), led some members of Congress to try to settle the troubles once more by compromise. Many plans for changes in the Constitution and laws were proposed in Congress, but all without avail. A "Peace Convention," suggested by Virginia, assembled in Washington on the 4th of February, 1861. There were delegates from all but the seceded States. John Tyler, ex-President of the United States, was president of this convention. But the plan of compromise suggested by the Peace Convention failed, like all others. The time for compromises had gone by, and it was beyond the ingenuity of man to prevent a collision between the two sections which had opposed each other in politics, and were now about to try their strength and endurance in the deadly struggles of the battlefield.

The Peace conference meets in vain

It was a time of great trouble and division. Many people at the North sympathized with the secession movement; many people at the South were in favor of maintaining the Union. Part of the Cabinet of President Buchanan desired to help the seceding States, to which they belonged; the other Secretaries considered secession rebellion, and urged him to use force to suppress it. The President, for his part, did not believe that the States had a right to go out of the Union, but he also did not believe that he had any authority to compel them to stay in. So everything was in confusion, debate, and perplexity in that awful winter, during which a storm was gathering, the force and extent of which nobody could foresee.

The period of confusion

All eyes were turned to Charleston harbor, where thousands of excited Southerners faced a little garrison under

Anderson in Fort Sumter

command of Major Robert Anderson. On the evening of the day after Christmas, Anderson suddenly moved his garrison in the dark from the weak Fort Moultrie into the stronger Fort Sumter. A ship sent with supplies and reinforcements was fired on by the South Carolina batteries and turned back.

Confederate government formed

On the 4th of February, the day that the Peace Convention met in Washington, there assembled in Montgomery, Ala., a convention of delegates from the seceded States. This convention proceeded to form a new government, under the title of "The Confederate States of America." Jefferson Davis, of Mississippi, was elected President.

The bombardment of Fort Sumter

On the 4th of March Abraham Lincoln was inaugurated President of the United States. Measures were soon taken to reinforce and supply the garrison of Fort Sumter. But the ships sent were detained outside the bar by a storm, and, as soon as their coming was known, all the Confederate batteries about the harbor opened on Fort Sumter, which, after a while, replied. For thirty-six hours the bombardment continued, setting fire to the woodwork of the fort and pounding its walls to pieces. At the end of this time Major Anderson, whose provisions were nearly exhausted, agreed to evacuate the fort.

Jefferson Davis was born in Kentucky, June 3, 1808. He graduated at West Point in 1828. He left the Army in 1835, and became a member of Congress ten years later. In the Mexican War he was colonel of a Mississippi regiment, and was distinguished for courage and coolness in action. He served several years as United States Senator from Mississippi, and was Secretary of War in President Pierce's Cabinet. He again entered the Senate in 1857, from which he resigned when Mississippi seceded in 1861. He was President of the Confederate States during the entire war.

The war begun

Curiously enough, nobody was killed on either side in this bombardment. But the bombardment of Sumter changed the whole situation. Doubt was at an end on both

CONFEDERATE UNIFORMS

NORTH CAROLINA MILITIA — REG. INFANTRY PRIVATE — WASHINGTON ARTILLERY — MONTGOMERY TRUE BLUE — FIELD OFFICER OF INFANTRY — GEN. LEE'S UNIFORM — REG. CAVALRY PRIVATE — LOUISIANA TIGER — LOUISIANA ZOUAVE — REG. ARTILLERY PRIVATE

sides. Virginia, North Carolina, Tennessee, and Arkansas, forced now to
take one side or the other, soon joined
the Confederacy. On the other hand,
the Sunday morning on which Major
Anderson marched out of Fort Sumter
saw the Northern States also almost
of one mind. Men were wild with excitement, and political parties were
forgotten. It was not for Congress or
the President to decide on peace or
war—the war burst uncontrollably
from the pent-up feelings of the people.

In response to a call from the President, nearly a

JEFFERSON DAVIS

hundred thousand men enlisted in The rush to
the Northern States in three days. arms
Trains loaded with volunteers began
to move toward Washington. Money
and ships without stint were offered
to the government by the rich. The
Southern people were equally en-

CONFEDERATE FLAG
OF 1861

thusiastic and unanimous. Thousands of the young men of
the South eagerly poured into Virginia. The great Civil War
had burst upon the country in all its fury.

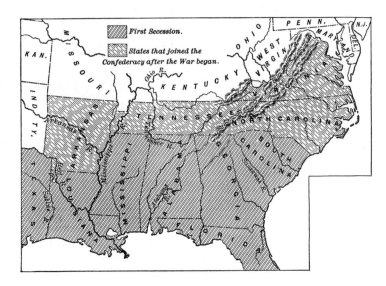

Questions for
study

1. How many States were called "cotton States"? What were they?
2. What took place in the cotton States when Lincoln's election became known?
3. What difference of opinion had there been from the beginning of the government about the power of a State?
4. What did the Federalists hold?
5. What was the opinion of the Republican party of Jefferson's time?
6. Who had been the chief advocate for State sovereignty in later times?
7. What can you tell about the nullification movement in South Carolina?
8. How did President Jackson regard the doctrine of nullification?
9. In what part of the country had the States rights doctrine found adherents?
10. How did the Southern States propose to leave the Union?
11. What State seceded first?
12. How many States had seceded by February 1st?
13. What two celebrated compromises were remembered at this time?
14. What did this recollection lead to?
15. What plans were formed in Congress? With what result?
16. What State suggested the "Peace Convention"?
17. Where did it meet?
18. Who was its president?
19. What was the result of this plan of compromise suggested by the Peace Convention?
20. Was there any way to avoid war?
21. Were the people at the North unanimous at this time?
22. Were the people of the South all agreed?
23. What division of opinion was there in the President's Cabinet?

24. *What opinions did President Buchanan hold?*
25. *To what fort in the South were all eyes turned? Who commanded this fort?*
26. *What did Anderson do on the evening of the day after Christmas?*
27. *What happened to the ship sent with supplies?*
28. *What convention assembled at the South in February?*
29. *What did this convention proceed to form?*
30. *What was this new government called?*
31. *Who was chosen President of the Confederate States?*
32. *When Lincoln was inaugurated, what was done about Fort Sumter?*
33. *What happened to the ships sent to relieve it?*
34. *What took place when the ships were discovered?*
35. *How long did the bombardment last? What effect did it have?*
36. *What did Major Anderson do at the end of this time?*
37. *What effect did the bombardment of Sumter have on the Southern States?*
38. *What new States joined the Confederacy?*
39. *What effect did it have at the North?*
40. *What is said of enlistments at the North? Of money and ships given to the government?*
41. *What is said of the excitement at the South?*
42. *Into what State did thousands of Southern young men hasten?*

I. Movements at the South.   Study by
  1. Secession.   topics
      a. The "States rights doctrine."
      b. Seven States secede.
  2. The "Confederate States"
        formed.
  3. The war begun.
      a. The capture of Fort Sumter.
      b. Four more States join the Confederacy.
      c. Troops pushed into Virginia.
II. Movements at Washington and in the North.
  1. Efforts at compromise.
      a. Plans proposed in Congress.
      b. The Peace Convention.
  2. The inauguration of Lincoln.
  3. The war begun.
      a. Effort to relieve Sumter.
      b. Effect of the attack on Sumter.

1. The situation of the seven "cotton States": How many are on the Gulf of   Geography
Mexico? How many touch the Atlantic Ocean? Which lies on both the gulf and
the ocean? Which of the cotton States border on the Mississippi River? Which one
is next to Mexico? a. The situation of the four additional States which seceded
after the war began, viz., Virginia, North Carolina, Tennessee, and Arkansas: How
many and which lie on the Atlantic? How many are on the Mississippi River?
3. The location of Fort Sumter: In what harbor? In what State is Charleston?

CHAPTER LI

Confederate Victory at Bull Run—The First Western Campaign

The question of Union or secession

WE are to remember that, though the war was caused by slavery, it was not at first about slavery, but about secession. "Our States are sovereign, and have a right to secede when they think they have reason," was the Southern view of the matter." You are a part of the Union, which forms but one nation, and to break up the Union is rebellion," was the Northern view. But the passions excited by the bitter debate over questions relating to slavery lay at the bottom of the struggle. Neither side dreamed of the long and bloody conflict that was to follow. Each expected to settle the matter in two or three battles. Both of them found out what stubborn work it was to fight against Americans.

Advantages and disadvantages

The Southerners were naturally more military than the Northern people; they were generally accustomed to the saddle and the use of firearms. Many of the Northern men, especially those of the Eastern States, had to learn to load and fire a gun after they went into the army. For a long war the North had several advantages. Money, trade, and the mechanical facilities for producing arms, ships, clothing, and other military necessities, belonged in a superior degree to the North. The North had also the advantage of numbers; the South the advantage of fighting in defense of its own ground.

The prompt movement from the North secures the border region

The divided sympathies of the people in the border States, and the quick sending forward of volunteers from the North by many railroads, prevented Maryland, Kentucky, and Missouri from seceding. In the western part of Virginia, where the slaves were few, the Union sentiment was

The Struggle for Missouri—The battles in Missouri and Arkansas proved a side campaign that had for its aim the securing of this State, in which opinion was much divided for the Union or the Confederacy. The Governor of Missouri took sides with the Confederacy. In the hard-fought battle of Wilson's Creek, August 10, 1861, General Lyon, of the United States army, was killed, and his army retreated after the fight. The Confederate general Price attacked Lexington, Missouri, on the 18th of September following, and captured nearly three thousand Union soldiers. In November following, General Pope, of the United States army, by several skillful movements, intercepted and captured large bodies of recruits on their way to join the Confederate army. A severe battle fought at Pea Ridge, in northwestern Arkansas, on the 6th of March, 1862, finally secured Missouri to the Union, by preventing the Confederate forces from reentering that State.

strong, and this region, after a while, separated itself from Virginia and formed a new State, which took the name of West Virginia. The failure to secure the border region was a serious loss to the Confederacy, for this was a land of Indian corn, most valuable for the feeding of armies. The South thus lost also the Ohio and Potomac rivers—the best line of defense.

The war opened with several small actions, such as the seizure of ports and navy yards by the Confederates, the attack on Union troops by a mob in Baltimore, several skirmishes in different parts of the country, and battles in the mountains of Virginia. The Confederates had moved their capital from Montgomery, Ala., to Richmond, Va., and the first important battleground would lie between the two capitals. So sure were the people of a short war, that most of the Northern volunteers had been called out for only three months, and it was thought necessary to fight a battle before their time should expire. The people and newspapers at the North were

Opening movements

Campaign in West Virginia—Several battles, though of no great magnitude, were fought to secure control of West Virginia. The Union armies here were commanded by General George B. McClellan. A small battle at Philippi was won by the Union troops, and a more considerable engagement at Rich Mountain (June 11, 1861), lasting about an hour and a half, gave the possession of West Virginia to the Federal government.

IRVIN MCDOWELL

Confederates
win the first
battle

Grant takes Fort
Henry and Fort
Donelson

G.T. BEAUREGARD

clamoring for a forward movement.

General McDowell moved toward Richmond, and on the 21st of July, 1861, the battle of Bull Run or Manassas, was fought, chiefly by raw troops on both sides. Generals Joseph E. Johnston and Beauregard commanded the Confederates. The battle was a severe one and the losses were heavy, but the Confederates were reinforced at the right moment, and the Union army was at length entirely routed, and fled back to Washington in confusion.

The first important movement after Bull Run was the campaign which broke the Confederate line at the West, and gave the Mississippi River above Vicksburg to the control of the Federal Government. Ulysses S. Grant,

Early Battles in Kentucky—The early struggle in eastern Kentucky was a little war by itself. Besides minor skirmishes, Colonel Garfield, afterward President, defeated the Confederate leader Humphrey Marshall in the little battle of Prestonburg on the 17th of January, 1862. Another sharp conflict took place at Mill Spring two days later, in which General George H. Thomas was victorious over the Confederate general Zollikoffer.

who had already begun to show good military abilities, moved against Fort Henry, on the Tennessee River, in cooperation with the gunboat fleet under Commodore Foote. Grant and Foote captured Fort Henry February 6. 1862. The Tennessee River here runs near to the Cumberland River. On the Cumberland River, only about twelve miles from Fort Henry, was the Confederate Fort Donelson. After a stubborn battle, in which the Union loss was twenty-three hundred men, this fort was also surrendered, and with it fifteen thousand Confederate troops. This broke the center of the Confederate line of defense in the West, and forced them to fall back from Nashville and other points.

ANDREW H. FOOTE

CHARGING AN EARTHWORK

Fall of
Island No. 10

JOHN POPE

General Pope, supported by gunboats, now moved against the Confederates who blocked the Mississippi at New Madrid and Island No. 10. New Madrid was evacuated, but, in order to capture Island No. 10, Pope, who was on the west side of the river, must cross below the island and cut off its supplies. As the batteries on the island blocked the river, he had to dig a canal across a bend in the river in order to get transport boats below the island, so as to ferry across the Mississippi. It took nineteen days to cut this canal. Gunboats could not get through it, and the transports could not cross without their protection. Two gunboats were run past the batteries of the island at night. Cut off on all sides, the island was compelled to surrender, with nearly seven thousand men.

Grant moves
toward Corinth

The object of the Union troops in attacking Island No. 10 had been to take a step toward getting possession of the Mississippi River, so as to get the use of this great highway, and thus separate the Confederacy into two parts. For the same purpose the forces under Grant, after taking Fort Donelson, pushed southward up the Tennessee River, and a movement was planned to take Corinth, in the northern part of Mississippi. Many railroads centered at this place. The Union army, under General Grant, was gathered near Corinth, at Pittsburgh Landing, in Tennessee, on the banks of the Tennessee River. Grant had from thirty to forty thousand men, and had no thought of a powerful enemy near at hand. The Confederate general, Albert Sidney Johnston rapidly collected a strong army, and determined to crush the force at the Land-

A. S. JOHNSTON

ing before Grant could be reinforced by the arrival of another army under General Buell.

The battle of Shiloh, or Pittsburg Landing, began on Sunday morning, April 6, 1862. Johnston undertook to attack in such a way as to surprise and drive Grant's army back between the river and a creek. The loss on that dreadful Sunday was great on both sides. The Confederates, with desperate energy, drove Grant's men back until Pittsburg Landing was almost in their possession. But their general, Albert Sidney Johnston, was killed. Buell's army began to arrive, and the Union troops were reformed in the night. The second day's fighting was also extremely severe. The exhausted Confederates under Beauregard at length retired from the field. This was the first great battle of the war.

The great battle of Shiloh, or Pittsburg Landing

D. C. BUELL

The Union army, when it had a little recovered from the terrible shock and had been recruited, moved forward against Corinth, which, after a siege, was evacuated by Beauregard on the 30th of May. The consequence of this success was, that the whole Mississippi River, as far down as Vicksburg, came into possession of the Federal authorities.

Corinth evacuated by the Confederates

1. *What was the war caused by?*
2. *What was the war about?*
3. *How could the war be caused by slavery, and not be about slavery?*
4. *What was the Southern claim in the matter of secession?*
5. *What was the position of the North?*
6. *Was a long war expected on either side?*
7. *Which were naturally the more military, the Southern or the Northern people?*
8. *Which knew the more in general about firearms?*
9. *What advantages had the North for a long war?*
10. *Which had the advantage of numbers?*
11. *What advantage had the Southern troops?*

Questions for study

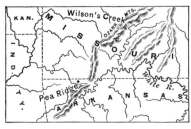

12. What prevented Maryland, Kentucky, and Missouri from seceding?
13. What part of Virginia remained in the Union? How was this managed?
14. What advantage did the North get from holding the four border States?
15. What good line of defense did the South lose in losing the border?
16. With what kind of actions did the war begin?
17. To what place did the Confederates move their capital?
18. Where would the first great battleground naturally be?
19. Why was it necessary to the Union army to fight a battle at once?
20. What movement did McDowell make?
21. What battle was fought on the 21st of July, 1861?
22. Who commanded the Confederate army at this battle?
23. Which won the battle?
24. What was the first important movement after Bull Run?
25. What fort did Grant attack first?
26. Who commanded the gun boat fleet that helped him?
27. How far away from the Cumberland is the Tennessee River at this place?
28. What fort had the Confederates on the Cumberland River?
29. What took place at Fort Donelson?
30. What was the result to the Confederates of the loss of this fort?
31. Against what two places did General Pope begin operations?
32. What happened at New Madrid?
33. What did Pope have to do to take Island No. 10? How many days did it take?
34. How did gunboats get past the island?
35. How did Pope compel the island to surrender?
36. What object was in view in the attack on Island No. 10?
37. What place did Grant now propose to seize?
38. Why was Corinth deemed important?

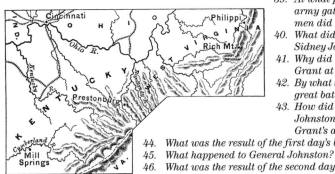

39. At what place was Grant's army gathered? How many men did he have?
40. What did General Albert Sidney Johnston resolve to do?
41. Why did he wish to defeat Grant at once?
42. By what two names is the first great battle of the war called?
43. How did Albert Sidney Johnston undertake to crush Grant's army?
44. What was the result of the first day's battle?
45. What happened to General Johnston?
46. What was the result of the second day's battle?

47. What place was taken by the Union troops after this?
48. What was the result of the capture of Corinth?

  I. The conditions of the war.
    1. The war about secession.
    2. Relation of slavery to the war.
    3. Advantages of each side.
    4. The border States.
    5. First actions.
    6. The two capitals.
  II. Bull Run and its effects.
 III. Campaign for opening the Mississippi River.
    1. Fort Henry.
    2. Fort Donelson.
    3. Island No. 10.
    4. Shiloh.
    5. Corinth.

Study by
topics

1. Relation of Washington to Richmond: In what State is Richmond? On what Geography
river? In what direction is Washington from Richmond? On what river is Washington? Is Bull Run, or Manassas, battleground nearer to Washington or to Richmond? In marching from Washington to Bull Run, what course would an army take? In marching from Richmond to Manassas, what direction would be taken?

2. Island No. 10: What State lies on the eastern side of the Mississippi at Island No. 10? What State on the west? In what river is this island situated? What is the largest river in the United States (except Alaska)? 3. In what State is Pittsburg Landing? On what river? Is it above or below Fort Henry on the same river? In what State is Corinth? What direction from Pittsburg Landing? In what direction is the city of Memphis, Tenn., from Corinth?

On the war generally: *Battles and Leaders of the Civil War*, and Dodge's Books
Bird's-Eye View of the Civil War.

CHAPTER LII

The War at the East—From Bull Run to Gettysburg

GENERAL SCOTT, who was commander-in-chief of the McClellan commander-in-chief armies of the United States at the beginning of the war, was old and infirm, and he soon retired. McClellan, by his well-planned battle at Rich Mountain, in western Virginia, had shown capacity, and he was now called to command the forces in front of Washington. He spent eight months in organizing and disciplining his army.

Peninsula
campaign begun.
Battle of
Williamsburg
Instead of moving directly against the Confederate forces lying in front of him, McClellan thought best to take his army by water to Fortress Monroe, and from there to go up between York River and James River toward Richmond. The land between these two rivers forms a peninsula; this is therefore known as the Peninsular campaign. From the

GEORGE B. MCCLELLAN

beginning, the campaign was unfortunate in many ways. Part of the troops which McClellan expected to receive were detained for the defense of Washington. The Confederates forced him to spend a month in the siege of Yorktown. Yorktown was evacuated on the 5th of May. McClellan's troops pursued the retiring Confederates, and fought the battle of Williamsburg that day. The Confederates retreated at night toward Richmond.

But the Confederate general, Thomas J. Jackson, who had got the nickname of "Stonewall" Jackson in the first battle of

Battle of
Fair Oaks
Bull Run, and who was operating in the Valley of Virginia, now made a series of rapid maneuvers, by which he defeated or confused several bodies of Union troops and frightened the authorities at Washington, so that McDowell's troops at Fredericksburg were held back from joining McClellan before Richmond. Meantime the Confederate army defending Richmond, under General Joseph E. Johnston. fought the battle of Fair Oaks, by attacking one wing of McClellan's army while it was divided into two parts by the Chickahominy River, and won a partial success. Johnston having been wounded in this battle, General Robert E. Lee succeeded him. Stonewall Jackson now slipped

away from the Valley of Virginia and suddenly brought his army down by rail to assist Lee in the struggle against McClellan.

Thomas Jonathan Jackson, called "Stonewall Jackson," was born in Virginia, January 21, 1824. He graduated at West Point in 1846. In the Mexican War he was twice brevetted for meritorious conduct. He resigned from the army in 1852, and became a professor in the Virginia Military Institute. He entered the Confederate service at the beginning of the war. During the first battle of Bull Run he resisted a charge with so much steadfastness that he gained the title of "Stonewall Jackson," by which name he will be known in history. The promptness and rapidity of his marches, and the obstinate courage he showed on the battlefield, made him an important factor in the war. He was shot by mistake by his own men, May 2, 1863, and died on the 10th.

McClellan withdrew his forces to the James River. About this time the two armies were engaged every day; these conflicts are known as the Seven Days' battles. For a whole week the Confederates beat upon McClellan's army. Its months of discipline and drill enabled it to fall back slowly before Lee's furious onslaught.

The Seven Days' battles

"STONEWALL" JACKSON

But McClellan's first plan had failed. The President had lost confidence in McClellan's ability to overmatch such generals as Lee and Jackson. A new general must be found. Pope, whose energy and success at Island No. 10 had given him reputation, was put in command of the army in front of Washington, and the army on the James River was brought back by degrees to reinforce him.

Pope in command at Washington

But Pope proved not to be equal to the Confederate generals in his front. Jackson made a great circuit around through Thoroughfare Gap, and cut off Pope's communications with Washington. The Federal army fought bravely on the old Bull Run battlefield (August 29 and 30, 1862), and Pope showed his usual energy, but his enemy had beaten him in skillful maneuvers, and his army fell back

Second Battle of Bull Run, or Manassas

disheartened to the neighborhood of Washington again, where it was a year before.

McClellan, who, in spite of the unfortunate outcome of his campaign, had won the confidence of the men in the Eastern army, was now again put in command of it. Lee followed up his advantages by crossing the Potomac. Meantime he sent a force and captured Harper's Ferry, with eleven thousand Union soldiers. On the 16th and 17th of September McClellan and Lee fought one of the severest battles of the war at Antietam Creek, near Sharpsburg, in Maryland. On the 18th Lee withdrew across the Potomac, and McClellan followed slowly, and again made the Rappahannock his line.

But McClellan had lost the confidence of his superiors, and he was now finally removed. General Burnside was next put in command of this unlucky army. McClellan had been thought too cautious, but Burnside was rash. He crossed the Rappahannock at Fredericksburg, and assailed the Confederate works on the heights back of the town on December 13, 1862. His army was defeated with great slaughter.

A. E. BURNSIDE

Burnside was relieved and General Hooker was

tried. In the spring of 1863 General Hooker fought what was called the Chancellorsville campaign, where, like those who had gone before him, he was out maneuvered by Lee's generalship and Jackson's marching qualities. On May 6th Hooker recrossed the Rappahannock.

Lee soon after crossed the Potomac, and pushed his veteran army into Pennsylvania, striking for Harrisburg. Hooker was relieved from commanding the army opposed to Lee, and General George G. Meade succeeded him. Near Gettysburg, in Pennsylvania, the vanguards of the two great armies met on the 1st day of July, 1863. The people of the North and those of the South were filled with fear and anxiety as this battle approached. The courage of the troops on both sides was simply marvelous. On the second day of the battle the Confederates carried works at both ends of the Union line. The next day the Union army recovered the lost ground on its right. The Confederates then made a tremendous assault and broke through the center of the Federal army, but they were soon driven

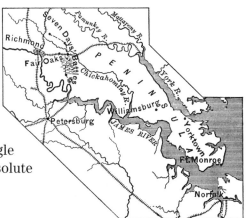

GEORGE D. MEADE

back defeated. Lee's army rested a day and then retreated. Lee had lost about one third of his men; Meade had lost a good deal more than a fourth of his. In all, about forty-eight thousand had been killed, wounded, or captured in this awful struggle between two veteran and resolute armies.

1. What was the chief trouble with the Federal armies?
2. What is said of Scott?
3. Where had McClellan distinguished himself?
4. What did McClellan do for the Army of the Potomac?
5. How long was it after he took command before he made any forward movement?
6. When he moved, what road to Richmond did he take?
7. Between what two rivers did he march?
8. Why is this called "The Peninsular Campaign"?
9. What disappointments and detentions did McClellan meet with?
10. After Yorktown was evacuated, what battle was fought?
11. What name was commonly given to the Confederate general Jackson?
12. In what valley was he operating?
13. What maneuvers did he now make?
14. What effect did these have in Washington?
15. What was the result with reference to reinforcing McClellan's army?

Questions for study

16. How was McClellan's army attacked at the battle of Fair Oaks?
17. By what river was the army divided?
18. What did Stonewall Jackson do?
19. To what river was McClellan now withdrawing?
20. What are the battles that took place at this time called?
21. What effect did the seven days' battles have on McClellan's army?
22. What had been the result of McClellan's plan?
23. How did the President regard him?
24. What general was now brought from the West?
25. In what operation had Pope shown energy and skill?
26. Of what army was he now given the command?

27. What was done with McClellan's army?
28. How did Pope compare in ability with the Confederate generals opposed to him?
29. What did Stonewall Jackson do?
30. Where did the armies fight in August, 1862? What was the result?
31. Who was again put in command of the army after Pope's failure?
32. What did Lee do?
33. What place did he capture?
34. Where was a battle fought between McClellan and Lee?
35. What kind of a battle was that of Antietam, or Sharpsburg?
36. What did General Lee do after two days' fighting?
37. What did McClellan do?
38. Who was put in place of McClellan?
39. What was Burnside's character?
40. What disastrous movement did Burnside make?
41. Who succeeded Burnside?
42. What campaign did Hooker fight? With what result?
43. What did Lee do after the campaign of Chancellorsville?
44. Who succeeded Hooker in command of the Union army?
45. Near what town did the two great armies meet on the 1st of July, 1863? In what State?
46. How did the people feel about this battle?
47. How did the soldiers fight at Gettysburg?
48. What successes did the Confederates gain the first day?
49. What took place on the second day?
50. What did Lee do after the battle?
51. What proportion of his troops did Lee lose?
52. What proportion of his whole force did Meade lose?
53. How many were lost in both armies?

I. The Peninsula.
   1. McClellan in command.
   2. The forward movement.
      a. Yorktown.
      b. Williamsburg.
   3. McClellan's reverses.
      a. Jackson in the Valley.
      b. Battle of Fair Oaks.
      c. Jackson reinforces Lee.
      d. Seven days' battles.
II. Pope's campaign.
   1. Pope called to Washington.
   2. Second battle of Manassas, or Bull Run.
III. Lee enters Maryland.
   1. Lee takes Harper's Ferry.
   2. Crosses the Potomac.
   3. Fights with McClellan at Antietam.
   4. Retreats to Virginia.
IV. Burnside and Hooker.
   1. Burnside at Fredericksburg.
   2. Hooker at Chancellorsville.
V. Lee invades Pennsylvania.
   1. Meade in command of the Union army.
   2. Confederate success the first day at Gettysburg.
   3. Confederates driven back the second day.
   4. Lee retreats.
   5. Losses.

Study by topics

I. The Peninsula: Describe the position of Fortress Monroe with reference to it. The rivers on the north and south of the Peninsula. Situation of the Peninsula with relation to Chesapeake say. 2. James River: Its relation to Richmond and to the Peninsula. 3. Position of the Valley of Virginia with reference to the Potomac River, to Washington, to eastern Virginia. Mountains on the east of the Valley; on the west. 4. Position of Antietam with reference to Washington; to the Potomac. 5. Gettysburg: In what State? In what direction from Harrisburg? From Baltimore? From Washington?

Geography

CHAPTER LIII

Various Operations in 1862 and 1863

IN order to give a clear account of the campaigns about Washington and Richmond, down to the battle of Gettysburg, we have put that branch of the war into one continuous story in the preceding chapter. Many things of the highest importance were happening elsewhere, while McClellan and the generals who came after him were wrestling with Johnston, Lee, and Jackson for Washington and Richmond.

Battle of the ironclads at Fortress Monroe

At the very moment that McClellan was getting ready to move his army to the Peninsula, there took place a famous naval battle in the waters of Hampton Roads, near Fortress Monroe. The Confederates, having seized the Norfolk Navy Yard, had changed the hull of the steam frigate *Merrimac* into an iron plated steam-ram, and named it the "*Virginia*." On the 8th of March, the *Virginia*, or, as she is generally spoken of, the *Merrimac*, came out from Norfolk into Hampton Roads, and after a battle sank the sloop-of-war *Cumberland*. The frigate *Congress* was next disabled and afterward burned, for nothing built of wood could make any impression on this iron monster, whose sloping sides resisted cannon balls as a bird's feathers shed the rain. The loss of life on both the vessels that were destroyed was great. The steam frigate *Minnesota*, which was aground, was only saved from destruction by the coming of night. It was expected that, with the morning, the iron ship would complete the sinking of the shipping in Hampton Roads, and then go to the Potomac and attack Washington city. But, at midnight, there arrived from New York, all unexpected, a little iron vessel, named the *Monitor* of a new

pattern, invented by John Ericsson. The next morning, when the *Merrimac* came out again, the *Monitor*
successfully defended the *Minnesota*, until the Confederate ram, having met its match, retired. This
battle in Hampton Roads changed the construction
of warships the world over, for it was proved that
wooden ships were of no use against iron ones.

JOHN ERICSSON

At the beginning, many of the Northern people,
who were very much in favor of the war to preserve the
Union, had been opposed to the abolition of slavery. But,
as the struggle went on, the feeling at the North against

Emancipation
proclamation

THE *MONITOR* AND THE *MERRIMAC*

slavery increased. On the 22d of September, 1862, President Lincoln announced that, if any portion of the country
should remain in arms against the government, he would
declare the slaves in that part of the country free. On the
1st of January, 1863, a proclamation declared the slaves free
in those regions yet in arms against the United States, "as a fit
and necessary war-measure for suppressing said rebellion."

Capture of New Orleans   We have seen that the first object of the Union armies in the West was to wrest the Mississippi River from the Confederate forces who held it by powerful works at Vicksburg and by forts below New Orleans. While the armies were operating above, the river was attacked from below. On the 18th of April, 1862, the bombardment of the forts below New Orleans was begun by a fleet of gunboats, and the

FARRAGUT

firing lasted for five days, but the forts held out. At ten o'clock on the morning of the 24th, Farragut, in command of the fleet, took the bold course of running his ships past the forts. The Confederates resisted by a tremendous fire from the forts and from their ships. They also tried to burn the United States vessels by floating down upon them fire rafts and burning steamboats loaded with cotton, and they attacked them also with an ironclad ram, named the *Manassas*. But, notwithstanding this resolute defense, Farragut got by the forts, with some loss, and captured the city. The forts afterward surrendered.

Bragg at Chattanooga   While Halleck dallied after taking Corinth, the Confederate general Bragg took thirty-five thousand men by rail to Mobile, and thence northward on another line and seized Chattanooga. We shall see that it afterward cost the Union troops some of the most desperate battles of the war to dislodge the Confederates from this stronghold.

Bragg and Buell in Kentucky, 1862   From Chattanooga Bragg moved north and invaded Kentucky, and tried to reach Louisville, on the Ohio. A footrace took place between the two armies, but Buell and the Union troops reached Louisville first. After a severe battle at Perryville, October 8, 1862, Bragg retreated to Chattanooga once more.

Part of the Union army was yet at Corinth. While Bragg and Buell were maneuvering in Kentucky, the Confederates, under General Van Dorn, attacked this place on the 3d and 4th of October, 1862, and by the most desperate fighting drove the Union army from line to line until a part of the attacking force actually gained the town. But the resistance of the troops under Rosecrans was as stubborn as the attack was resolute, and Van Dorn's assaults were repulsed.

Battle of Corinth

BRAXTON BRAGG

Hitherto in many operations the Confederates had the advantage in generalship. They were especially strong in this regard in the Virginia campaigns. But the Union armies at the West were gradually coming under the control of General Grant, a man of restless vigor and tremendous power of endurance under difficulty and repulse. All his first attempts to take Vicksburg failed. Plan after plan was tried. A ditch was dug across the bend of the river opposite Vicksburg, in the hope that the river would change its bed, but this failed. Grant tried to open other channels to reach the watercourses in the rear of the city. From time to time, when one plan failed, he resorted to a new device.

Grant tries many devices against Vicksburg

At last gunboats and transports were run past the Vicksburg batteries. Crossing the Mississippi at Bruinsburg, below Vicksburg, Grant got in the rear of that stronghold. He took Jackson, the capital of Mississippi, and by a series movements and successive battles he at last shut up the Confederate general Pemberton in the fortifications of Vicksburg. Grant twice tried to carry the fortifications by assault, but the Confederate soldiers were well-seasoned veterans behind strong works, and the assaults were costly failures. The Union army, therefore, settled down to a regu-

Siege and surrender of Vicksburg, 1863

lar siege of the place. On the 4th of July, 1863, the day after the battle of Gettysburg in Pennsylvania, the half-starved garrison of Vicksburg, numbering about thirty-two thousand, surrendered to General Grant.

Surrender of Port Hudson

While Grant was operating against Vicksburg, General Banks, who had taken an army of the Federal troops by sea to New Orleans, was trying to capture Port Hudson, farther down the river. Here, as at Vicksburg, two assaults were repulsed. But, when Vicksburg surrendered, Port Hudson was obliged to yield. This gave the Union armies possession of the whole of the Mississippi River, and cut off the western States of the Confederacy from the eastern.

Questions for study

1. What took place in Hampton Roads when McClellan was about to move his army to the Peninsula?
2. How was the ram Virginia, or Merrimac, built? What ships did she destroy?
3. What unexpected opponent arrived during the night?
4. What was the result of the second day's battle?
5. What effect did this battle have on the building of warships in this and other countries?
6. What change of feeling about slavery took place at the North during the war?
7. What proclamation did President Lincoln issue on the 22d of September, 1862?
8. What proclamation was made on the 1st of January, 1863?
9. What was the first object of the Union armies in the West?
10. By what fortifications did the Confederates hold the Mississippi River?
11. How did the Union forces attack the river from below?
12. For how many days were the forts below New Orleans bombarded?
13. Did they yield to the fire?
14. How did Farragut reach the city?
15. What attempts were made to destroy his fleet?
16. What became of the forts below New Orleans?
17. Were the Federal armies in the West at this time under the command of a general of great ability?
18. What advantage did the Confederate general Bragg take of General Halleck's slowness after the capture of Corinth? (For the capture of Corinth, see page 315.)

19. What route did Bragg take to get to Chattanooga from near Corinth? Is this a very direct route?
20. What movement did Bragg make from Chattanooga?
21. What city was he aiming for?
22. Who reached it before him?
23. What did he do after the battle of Perryville?
24. After what great battle was Corinth taken from the Confederates?
25. What took place at Corinth on October 3 and 4, 1862?
26. What was the result of Van Dorn's attack on the place?
27. In what regard had the Confederates been the stronger in many operations?
28. What general in the Union army was now rising into control of the Western armies?

29. What is said of him?
30. What success did his first plans for taking Vicksburg meet with?
31. What were some of his plans?
32. When gunboats had been run past the Vicksburg batteries, what did General Grant do?
33. What town did he capture to the eastward of Vicksburg?
34. Of what State is Jackson the capital?
35. What did he at last succeed in doing?
36. When he had shut up General Pemberton in Vicksburg, what did he try to do?
37. What was the result of these assaults?
38. What course was then taken to reduce Vicksburg? With what result?
39. Who was operating against Port Hudson while Grant was besieging Vicksburg?
40. Did General Banks succeed in carrying the works by assault?
41. What led to the surrender of Port Hudson?
42. What was now the condition of the Mississippi River?

I. Battle in Hampton Roads.   Study by
    1. The *Merrimac.*   topics
    2 Her first successes.
    3. The *Monitor.*
    4. Her defense and its results.
II. Emancipation Proclamation.
    1. Increase of feeling at the North against slavery.
    2. Preliminary proclamation.
    3. Final proclamation, January I, 1863.
III. The campaign against New Orleans.
    1. The effort to secure the Mississippi.
    2. Bombardment of the forts below New Orleans.
    3. Farragut runs past the forts.
    4. Capture of the city and forts.

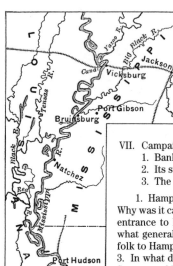

IV. Bragg and Buell.
  1. Bragg goes to Chattanooga.
  2. Bragg invades Kentucky.
  3. Battle of Perryville.
V. Battle of Corinth.
VI. The Vicksburg campaign.
  1. Rise and military character of Grant.
  2. His failures at Vicksburg.
  3. His campaign back of Vicksburg.
  4. Attempt to carry the works by storm.
  5. Siege and surrender.
VII. Campaign against Port Hudson.
  1. Banks tries to Carry it by assault.
  2. Its surrender.
  3. The conquest of the Mississippi.

1. Hampton Roads: What great river comes in at Hampton Roads? Why was it called the James River? (Page 20.) What fortress guards the entrance to Hampton Roads? On what river is Norfolk situated? In what general direction would the *Merrimac* sail in passing from Norfolk to Hampton Roads? 2. How did Farragut approach New Orleans? 3. In what direction is Louisville from Chattanooga? Across what two States would Bragg have to pass to reach Louisville from Chattanooga? In what State is Chattanooga? On what river is Louisville? 4. On what

Geography river is Vicksburg? In what direction is Jackson from Vicksburg? In what State are Vicksburg and Jackson? What direction is Port Hudson from Vicksburg? From New Orleans? What is the general course of the Mississippi River?

CHAPTER LIV

The Campaign between Nashville and Atlanta

The war in central Tennessee

THE Western part of the war had become divided into two main parts. The Union armies won their first object when they gained control of the Mississippi. But another long and bitter contest was fought out before they could secure the strongholds of central Tennessee and northern Georgia.

Battle of Stone River, or Murfreesboro

The first great battle on this line was that of Stone River, or Murfreesboro, fought on the last day of the year 1862, about the time that Grant was beginning operations against

Vicksburg. The conflict was marked by the brilliant charges made by the Confederates under Bragg, which at length broke to pieces the whole right wing of the Union army. General Rosecrans had succeeded Buell in command of the Union troops. The result of the day's fighting was very favorable to the Confederates. But in the latter part of the day the half-defeated Union soldiers, under the immediate command of General Thomas, made the most determined resistance to the dashes which the Confederates continued to make. Some of the generals wished to retreat, but Rosecrans, who had defended Corinth with so much stubbornness, announced his intention to "fight or die here." On the next day, which was the first day of 1863, neither of the shattered armies was in a condition to make a serious attack. On the third day of the battle the Confederates, by a tremendous charge, drove back part of the left wing of Rosecrans' army, but they were soon cut to pieces and themselves driven back. After the two armies had bravely held their ground with varying fortunes for three days, Bragg retreated, and Rosecrans entered Murfreesboro. Each army had lost about nine thousand in killed and wounded, besides those captured.

W.S. ROSECRANS

In the summer and autumn of 1863, Rosecrans, by some well-planned maneuvers, put Bragg at such disadvantage that he was forced to fall back from time to time until he had left Chattanooga in the hands of the Union troops. But Bragg received reinforcements, and the great battle of Chickamauga was fought on the 19th and 20th of September, 1863. It was a battle of charge and countercharge. On the first day the Union army won considerable advantage; but on the second day the right half of Rosecrans' army was broken, and it retreated in confusion toward Chatta-

The battle of Chickamauga

HOLDING THE LINE

nooga. The utter rout of the Union army was prevented by General Thomas, whose division had also saved the army at Murfreesboro. With extraordinary coolness he held the left wing against repeated assaults, and, when ammunition failed, his men used their bayonets to repel the Confederate charges. Though Bragg's troops, by splendid fighting, had gained a great victory, Thomas, by the most brilliant defense of the war, kept them back long enough to enable Rosecrans to prepare for the defense of Chattanooga, to which place the Union troops retreated.

GEORGE H. THOMAS

Grant, who had gained great reputation by his Vicksburg campaign, was now given command of all the forces west of the mountains. Rosecrans was relieved, and Thomas, who was called "the Rock of Chickamauga," was put in his place. Grant took immediate command of the besieged troops in Chattanooga, with Thomas next.

Grant in command at Chattanooga

Bragg having sent away a part of his army to attack Burnside in East Tennessee, Grant took advantage of this weakening of his force to attack Bragg's army in his front. The main body of Bragg's army was entrenched in Chattanooga Valley. Bragg also held Missionary Ridge, in his rear, and Lookout Mountain, to the southwest. Hooker attacked and carried Lookout Mountain on the morning of November 25, 1863, while a mist shut out the summit from the valley. This is sometimes called "The Battle above the Clouds." But Sherman, who had previously carried an outlying hill at the north end of Missionary Ridge, was checked in his attempt to advance by the obstinate resistance of the Confederates under Hardee. Grant, therefore, sent the army under Thomas out of Chattanooga to attack the Confederates in front, with instructions to carry the first line and lie

Bragg at Chattanooga

down. By a swift charge, under a severe fire, they carried the line at the foot of the mountain; but the guns of the Confederates on the top of Missionary Ridge sent a galling fire upon them. Without orders one impatient regiment after another rushed up the hill. Bragg's troops made a vigorous resistance, but the eager assailants carried the line in six places, and the Confederate army was forced to retreat.

Sherman against Johnston. Kenesaw Mountain

Grant was now put in command of all the Union armies, and he took charge in person of the army in front of Washington, while Sherman was left to command the Western army. Sherman, a man of incessant activity and ability of many kinds, was confronted by the Confederate general Joseph E. Johnston, who had been appointed to succeed Bragg. Johnston also was a man of military genius and extremely prudent. Sherman, by skillful maneuvers, tried to force Johnston to fight in the open field; but Johnston preferred to draw Sherman farther south, so as to increase the difficulty of supplying his army, and to compel Sherman to attack him behind breastworks. Many severe engagements were fought, but Johnston avoided a general battle. At length Sherman attacked

J. E. JOHNSTON

Joseph Eggleston Johnston was born in Virginia in 1807. He graduated at West Point in 1829. He distinguished himself as an engineer and in active service during the Mexican War. He resigned in 1861, and entered the Confederate army, where he always displayed the greatest prudence and ability.

Johnston at Kenesaw Mountain, but the Confederates repulsed him.

Hood succeeds Johnston. Sherman takes Atlanta

The Confederate government, dissatisfied with Johnston's long and cautious retreat before Sherman, removed him, and General Hood took his place. Hood believed in sharp fighting, and several battles took place at various points about Atlanta, but they generally resulted in favor of the Union army. At length, Sherman got a considerable part of his army south of Atlanta, so that Hood was compelled to abandon that city or be shut up in it.

J. B. HOOD

Questions for study

1. *Into what two main parts had the war west of the Alleghenies become divided?*
2. *What object did the Union armies secure with the fall of Vicksburg?*
3. *What strongholds were to be won by another contest?*
4. *What was the first great battle on the line of central Tennessee and northern Georgia?*
5. *What was Grant doing at the time the battle of Murfreesboro was fought?*
6. *In what part of the year 1862 did this battle near Murfreesboro take place?*
7. *How did the Confederate soldiers carry on the battle?*
8. *What effect did their charges have?*
9. *Who commanded the Union troops? What was the general result of the day's fighting?*
10. *What did Rosecrans say that night?*
11. *What was the condition of the two armies on New Year's day, 1863?*
12. *What did the Confederates do on the following day?*
13. *What was the result of this charge?*
14. *What course did Bragg then take?*
15. *What is said of the losses in this battle?*
16. *How did Rosecrans force Bragg to fall back in the summer of 1863?*
17. *What now became of Chattanooga?*
18. *What battle did Bragg fight in September, 1863, to recover Chattanooga?*
19. *What kind of a battle was it?*
20. *Which army won advantages on the first day?*
21. *What took place on the second day?*
22. *What prevented the destruction of the Union army?*
23. *What other battle had Thomas saved?*
24. *What name did Thomas get from his defense on this occasion?*
25. *Which army gained a great victory?*
26. *What did "the Rock of Chickamauga" secure by his defense?*
27. *Who was put in command of all the forces west of the Alleghenies?*
28. *Who now took the place of Rosecrans?*
29. *By what success had Grant won a great reputation?*
30. *Of what army did Grant now take immediate command?*
31. *How did Bragg at this time weaken his army?*

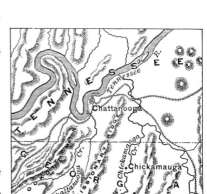

32. Where was the main body of his army?
33. What two mountains did he hold?
34. What did Hooker attack and carry?
35. What is the battle on Lookout Mountain sometimes called?
36. How did Sherman's attack on the other extreme of Bragg's defense get on?
37. What did Grant order Thomas' men to do?
38. Did they stay long at the first line? Why?
39. What was the result of this charge up the ridge?
40. What change was now made in the position of General Grant?
41. Who was left chief in command of the Western armies?
42. What kind of a man was Sherman?
43. Who had succeeded Bragg?
44. What kind of a man was Joseph E. Johnston?
45. What did Sherman try to do?
46. What did Johnston wish to do?
47. What was the result of the battle of Kenesaw Mountain?
48. Why did the Confederate government remove Johnston?
49. Whom did they put in his place?
50. What was the general result of the fighting about Atlanta?
51. How did Sherman force Hood to abandon Atlanta?

Study by topics

1. The war in the West divided into two parts.
II. Rosecrans and Bragg.
   1. The battle of Stone River, or Murfreesboro. 2. Battle of Chickamauga.
  III. Grant and Bragg.
    1. Grant in command. 2. Bragg weakens his army. 3. Battle of Chattanooga.
     a. Hooker takes Lookout Mountain. b. Sherman partly successful at Missionary Ridge. c. The volunteer charge of Thomas' troops gains the victory.
    IV. Sherman and Johnston.
     1. Sherman in command: his character.
     2. Johnston succeeds Bragg: his character. 3 Sherman and Johnston maneuvering. 4. Confederate victory at Kenesaw Mountain. 5. Johnston removed.
     V. Sherman and Hood.
      1. Hood tries sharp fighting without success. 2. Hood abandons Atlanta.

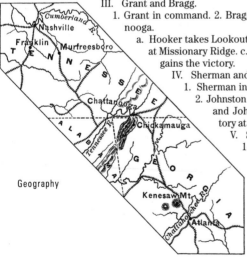

Geography

In what general direction is Murfreesboro from Nashville? In about what direction is Chattanooga from Nashville? In what direction is Atlanta from Nashville? Atlanta from Chattanooga?

CHAPTER LV

From the Wilderness to Petersburg—The War in the Valley

IN the spring of 1864 General Grant, who had taken Vicksburg and won the battle of Chattanooga, was put in

Grant confronts Lee

Ulysses S. Grant was born in Point Pleasant, Ohio, April 27, 1822. He spent his boyhood on a farm. In 1839 he was appointed a cadet at West Point, from which he graduated about the middle of his class in rank. As a lieutenant in the Mexican War, he was conspicuous for bravery, taking part in the battles of Palo Alto, Resaca de la Palma, and the assault on Monterey. He also took part in the siege of Vera Cruz, and the succeeding battles of Scott's campaign. He resigned from the army in 1854 and engaged in farming, but was not successful. When the Civil War broke out he was a clerk in the leather store of his father in Galena, Ill., on a small salary. He then became mustering officer for the State of Illinois, was appointed colonel of the Twenty-first Regiment from that State, and thus entered on his great military career, the outlines of which will be found in the text. After serving two terms as President, he retired to private life, and made a journey round the world, receiving honors wherever he went. He died on Mount McGregor, N. Y., on the 23d of July, 1885.

ULYSSES S. GRANT

command of all the armies of the Union. He left Sherman, as we have seen, to command in the West, while he took up his headquarters with Meade in front of Washington. The veteran Eastern armies that had fought so long against each other, between Washington and Richmond, were now to fight to the death, each under the most famous general on its side.

Under Grant and Meade, the Army of the Potomac moved forward toward Richmond. It encountered Lee's army in a region of dense woods, full of undergrowth, known as "The Wilderness." Grant's army was much the more numerous, for by this time the South, which had put forth nearly its whole strength from the beginning was becoming somewhat exhausted. On the other hand, Lee fought behind entrenchments, and, in changing his position, moved on shorter lines than his opponent. For sixteen days, in the Wilderness and about Spottsylvania Courthouse, the armies were so close to each other in the thick brush that the men had to be continually on guard, and so they got little chance for sleep. When they changed positions, the marching was generally done in the night, while the days witnessed the most tremendous fighting that had been seen since the battles of the great Napoleon. In sixteen days the Union army lost 37,500 men, and Lee's losses, though much less, were severe.

Lee was not crushed, but Grant got nearer to Richmond from time to time by secretly moving a part of the army from his right and marching it around to the rear of his other troops, and then pushing it as far ahead on his left as possible. By thus outflanking Lee, Grant compelled him to fall back, that he might not be cut off from Richmond and his sup-

Robert Edward Lee was born in Virginia, June 19, 1807. He graduated at West Point in 1829, second in his class. He distinguished himself as an engineer in the siege of Vera Cruz. He was for three years in command of the Military Academy at West Point. When his own State of Virginia seceded, he thought himself bound to go with it. He resigned his commission on the 20th of April, 1861, and was made commander-in-chief of the Virginia State forces, and later a Confederate general. To his great ability was mostly due the stubbornness of the struggle carried on by the Confederates between Richmond and Washington. After the war was over, General Lee accepted the result manfully, and devoted himself to his duties as President of Washington-Lee University, at Lexington, Va., where he died on the 12th of October, 1870.

plies. But Lee always managed to fall back in time to be again between Grant's army and Richmond. The two great generals and the two veteran armies were well matched, and neither could gain a complete victory.

This fighting and this moving to the eastward and around Lee's flank were kept up with varying success until Grant got near to Richmond, when, on the 2d of June, 1864, at Cold Harbor, Grant attacked the Confederate works along the whole line. The Union army was repulsed with a loss of nearly six thousand men in an hour.

On the 13th of June, 1864, by another rapid march to the left, General Grant's

ROBERT E. LEE

army began to cross the James River. As soon as over, they made an attempt to capture Petersburg, in order to cut off one source of supplies and reinforcements for Richmond. The outer works near Petersburg were carried, but the Confederates fell back to new lines, and received reinforcements. The attempt to drive them out of these by assault failed. The Union troops now built trenches close up to the Confederate works, and the two armies held these frowning lines, face to face, for nine months, until within a few days of the close of the war.

Attempt to take Petersburg

Soon after the siege began, a mine was dug from the trenches of the Union army under an angle of the Confederate works. By this mine a part of the works was blown up on the 30th of July. An attack was made immediately after, but it was badly managed, and only resulted in the loss of a great many Union soldiers.

Explosion of the mine. Attack repulsed

Hunter marches up the Valley, and tries to take Lynchburg

In all the years of the war there had been a smaller campaign carried on in the Valley of Virginia. This fertile valley lies between two ranges of mountains. Its northern end reaches the Potomac not very far away from Washington. In this valley the Confederate general Breckinridge defeated General Sigel at New Market on the 15th of May, 1864. General Hunter, who took command of the Union troops, defeated the Confederate general Imboden at Piedmont twenty days later. Hunter, with eighteen thousand men, pushed for Lynchburg, which was a place of the greatest importance. He destroyed railroads and worked much damage, but Lynchburg was reinforced in time to save it. Finding his retreat down the Valley cut off, Hunter saved his starving army by making his way into the Kanawha Valley. This took him to the west of the Allegheny Mountains, and quite out of the Valley.

Early marches down the Valley, and tries to take Washington

The Valley was thus left open to Early, who marched a Confederate force down to Harper's Ferry and across into Maryland. Early defeated a small force under General Lew Wallace at Monocacy on the 7th of July, and pushed straight for Washington, which he might have captured at a dash had he been a little quicker; but reinforcements from Grant's army marched into the works as the assault began, and he was repulsed. He retreated again up the Valley, pursued by a strong force. But, when a part of the Union troops was withdrawn and sent back to Grant, Early attacked

JUBAL EARLY

and defeated those under Crook at Kernstown, and threw his cavalry across the Potomac again, and into Pennsylvania, where they burned Chambersburg. In getting back into Virginia, this cavalry force was attacked and defeated. General Sheridan was now given charge of the Union troops on this line. Sheridan was for a long time very wary, Sheridan in the Valley. Battles at Winchester and Fisher's Hill determined not to risk a battle against an experienced general like Early without a good chance for success. When Early's force had been weakened by the sending of part of it to Petersburg, Sheridan attacked him and won the battle of Opequon, or Winchester, on the 19th of September, 1864. Three days later, Sheridan attacked Early in his trenches at Fisher's Hill, having sent a force around to suddenly assail him on one side or flank, while the rest of the Union troops charged the works in front. Early's men, attacked on two sides, were routed and driven farther up the Valley to the south.

PHILIP H. SHERIDAN

Sheridan burned all the barns filled with grain, and carried off all the stock in the Valley, to prevent the Confederates from returning. But when Destruction in the Valley. Battle of Cedar Creek. Sheridan's ride Sheridan went back toward the Potomac, Early, largely reinforced, followed him through this land of starvation. While Sheridan was absent from his troops, a part of Early's army, leaving behind their swords, canteens, and everything that could make a noise, moved in the night along a lonely path until they got around on the flank and behind the Union army, and surprised them while they were asleep. Early, at the same time, with

Philip Henry Sheridan was born in Albany, N. Y., March 6, 1831 . He graduated at West Point in 1853. He first gained distinction as a cavalry commander, then he showed great qualities at Perryville and Murfreesboro, after which he was made a major-general. At Chickamauga and in the battles about Chattanooga he further distinguished himself. His campaign in the Valley of Virginia and the part he played in the closing scenes made him one of the most famous generals of the war. He succeeded Sherman at the head of the army, and in 1888 he was made a full general. Only Grant and Sherman bad attained that rank in the United States army before him. He died at Nonquitt, Mass., Aug. 5, 1888.

the rest of his troops, attacked Sheridan's army in front. This was the beginning of the battle of Cedar Creek. The Confederates defeated and drove back the Union troops for four miles, capturing many prisoners. Sheridan, hearing the firing, put spurs to his horse, and rode up the Valley, calling to his fleeing soldiers, "Come, boys, we're going back!" His presence turned the tide, and by night he had defeated Early once more. A few smaller actions ended the campaign, for most of the troops on both sides were needed at Petersburg, where the last struggle of all was to take place.

COLD COMFORT

Questions for study

1. *Who was put in command of all the Union armies in the spring of 1864?*
2. *Whom did Grant leave in command of the Western armies?*
3. *Where did he make his own headquarters?*
4. *Where did Grant's army encounter the army of Lee?*
5. *What kind of a region was the Wilderness?*
6. *Which army contained the more men?*
7. *What was the state of the South at this time?*
8. *What advantage did Lee have?*
9. *For sixteen days after the armies came together, what was the character of the struggle?*

10. When was the marching done?
11. What is said of the fighting? What can you tell about the losses?
12. What was the result of all this fighting and moving?
13. How did Grant move his army nearer to Richmond?
14. How did Lee fall back?
15. What took place at Cold Harbor on the 2d of June, 1864?
16. What did Grant do on the 13th of June?
17. When his army was across, what did they try to do?
18. Did they meet with any success?
19. Did they capture Petersburg by assault?
20. Seeing that Petersburg could not be carried by assault, what did the Union troops do?
21. What measure was taken for blowing up the Confederate works? What was the result?
22. Why did it end badly?
23. What is said of the campaigns in the Valley of Virginia?
24. Which side won the battle of New Market in May, 1864?
25. What took place at Piedmont twenty days later?
26. What did Hunter do after defeating the Confederates?
27. Why did he not capture Lynchburg?
28. How did Hunter escape?
29. What advantage did the Confederate general Early take of Hunter's absence from the Valley?
30. What was the result of the battle of Monocacy?
31. Against what place did Early afterward march?
32. Why did he not capture Washington? Where did he go?
33. Where did he defeat Crook? What did he do afterward?
34. What town in Pennsylvania was burned by Confederate cavalry?
35. What happened to this force in getting back into Virginia?
36. Who now took charge of the Union troops in the Valley?
37. What led Sheridan to attack Early?
38. What was the result of the battle of Opequon, or Winchester?
39. What battle was fought three days later?
40. How was the attack made?
41. What was the result of the battle of Fisher's Hill?
42. What did Sheridan do to keep Early's troops from occupying the Valley again?
43. Did Early come down the Valley again?
44. How did he begin the battle of Cedar Creek? What did he accomplish?
45. What turned the tide?
46. What did Sheridan say as he came back?
47. What was the result?
48. Why did not the war in the Valley continue?
49. Where was the last struggle of all to take place?

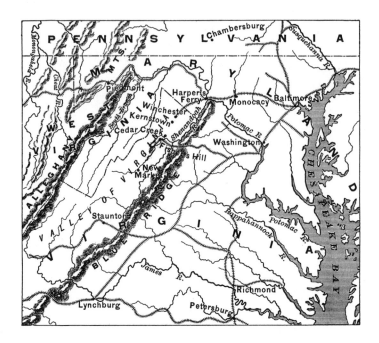

5. Early's retreat.
6. Early's cavalry cross again. Burning of Chambersburg, in Pennsylvania.
V. Sheridan against Early.
   1. Sheridan cautious.
   2. Battle of Winchester, or Opequon.
   3. Battle of Fisher's Hill.
   4. Destruction in the Valley.
   5. Battle of Cedar Creek.
   6. Close of the campaign.

1. Direction of the "Wilderness" from Washington. Location of Spottsylvania Geography
Courthouse with reference to the Wilderness. In what direction from Richmond is
Cold Harbor? On which side of the James River is Cold Harbor? On which side is
Richmond? What direction from the James River is Petersburg? Is Petersburg on
the James River? In what direction is Petersburg from Richmond? 2. What Mountains on the eastern side of the Valley of Virginia? What on the western? Where is
the Potomac River with reference to the Valley? What place is on the Potomac at
the mouth of the Shenandoah River? In what direction from Washington is Harper's
Ferry? Is Washington on the Virginia or on the Maryland bank of the Potomac? 3.
On which side of the Allegheny Mountains is the Kanawha River? Into what river
does it flow?

CHAPTER LVI

Close of the Civil War

IN Chapter LIV we have seen that Sherman captured Sherman's
Atlanta, having in opposition to him the Confederate gen- march begun
eral Hood. The latter was a bold man, and he determined
to force Sherman to fall back into Tennessee again, by going to his rear and cutting off his supplies from the North.
But Sherman, knowing that the resources of the South were
almost exhausted, concluded to risk a blow that might end
the war. Leaving the troops in Tennessee under command
of General Thomas, he set out from Atlanta with the rest of
his army, to march southward through the heart of the Confederacy.

Hood, refusing to follow Sherman into Georgia, pushed Hood in Ten-
northward into Tennessee, resolved to strike Thomas be- nessee. Battle
fore he could get his forces together. Hood attacked a part of Franklin

GENERAL SCHOFIELD

of General Thomas' troops, under General Schofield, at Franklin in Tennessee. The Confederates made the most desperate charges, carrying, at first, a portion of the Union lines, but Schofield succeeded in holding his works long enough to get safely across the Harpeth River. He then fell back, and joined Thomas at Nashville.

Battle of Nashville

Hood soon encamped before Nashville, where he was attacked on the morning of December 15th by Thomas' whole army. A two days' battle ensued, which resulted in the utter defeat of Hood's army. This was a blow from which the exhausted Confederacy could not recover.

Sherman destroying in Georgia. Savannah taken

While Hood and Thomas were maneuvering in Tennessee, Sherman and his army were marching through the Confederacy. His men were consuming supplies that would otherwise have sustained Lee in Richmond. Railroads of the greatest military value were utterly destroyed, by making fires of the crossties and then heating and twisting the rails. Nothing could have tended more to bring the war to an end than the breaking of the railways, on which food and soldiers must be moved. Just before the battle of Nashville was fought, Sherman reached Savannah and laid siege to it, having been about a month without communication with the North. On the 20th of December the Confederates evacuated Savannah, and Sherman occupied it.

Capture of Fort Fisher and Wilmington

In order to give Sherman, when he should move northward, a new base of supplies from the sea, and in order to stop blockade running, an expedition was sent to capture Wilmington, in North Carolina. Fort Fisher, which guarded the entrance to this place, was bombarded by a fleet and then carried by assault, on January 15, 1865. By way of Wilmington, General Schofield, with a part of Thomas' army from Tennessee, now pushed up to Goldsboro, in North Carolina, to meet Sherman when he should reach that place.

On the 1st of February, 1865, Sherman's tough veterans left Savannah and moved northward through the Caroli- Sherman's march northward nas, in rain and through overflowing swamps. Columbia, the capital of South Carolina, was taken. During its occupation the city was burned. The Union army pushed on northward in two columns. Johnston did not give battle till Sherman had reached

> William Tecumseh Sherman was born in Ohio in 1820. He graduated at West Point in 1840. He resigned from the army in 1853, and engaged in the banking business in San Francisco. Later he practiced law in Kansas. When the war broke out, he was superintendent of the military school in Louisiana. He was reappointed to the army in 1861. At the close of the war he was next in rank to General Grant, and he became general of the army when Grant became President.

Averysboro, in North Carolina. Here the Confederates were defeated; but at Bentonville, on the 19th of March, General Joseph E. Johnston came near to defeating one column of Sherman's army before reinforcements could reach it.

Sherman, by his marches, had broken to pieces the interior lines of travel in the Southern States, and greatly added Movements about Petersburg to the troubles of Lee in Richmond. Neither reinforcements nor supplies could be had without difficulty. The Southern people, who had bravely suffered the greatest hardships, were now disheartened. Lee began to consider how he could retreat. But Grant, whose force was more than twice as large as Lee's, moved Sheridan's part of the army around to the south of the Confederate works, in order, if possible, to prevent Lee's dwindling army from getting away.

Lee was everywhere outnumbered, and his men were beaten and captured, espe-

WILLIAM TECUMSEH SHERMAN

Battle of Five Forks. Lee's works carried

cially in the battle of Five Forks, on the 1st of April. Lee had weakened his force in front of Grant, by drawing out troops to keep Sheridan from cutting the railroads that brought him supplies, and while the battle of Five Forks was taking place, some of the Confederate works at Petersburg were carried by assault, and others were taken the next day.

Lee's retreat and surrender, April 9, 1865

The night following, that is, the 2d of April, Lee began his retreat from Richmond. His first object was to reach Danville, Va., and from that place to unite with Johnston. But, finding a Union force between him and Danville, his now starving army was turned toward Lynchburg. Sheridan's cavalry cut him off from Lynchburg, and on the 9th of April, 1865, Lee surrendered his army to General Grant, at Appomattox Courthouse.

Johnston surrenders. Close of the war

Johnston could make no stand alone, and sixteen days later he surrendered to General Sherman. The smaller bodies of Confederate troops yielded soon after, and the four terrible years of war were at last ended. The soldiers on both sides returned to their homes. No war so vast had ever been seen in modern times, and no braver men had ever fought. The impressions left by the sufferings of the Civil War have produced a strong sentiment in favor of peace.

Questions for study

1. What was Hood's plan for forcing Sherman to fall back into Tennessee again?
2. When Hood moved around to his rear, did Sherman follow?
3. What kind of a blow did he meditate?
4. Under whose command did he put the troops which he left in Tennessee?
5. What did he do with the rest of his army?
6. Did Hood follow Sherman?
7. Where did he go?
8. What portion of Thomas' troops did Hood first attack? Where?
9. What was the result of the battle of Franklin?

10. To what place did Schofield fall back?
11. Where was the next battle fought?
12. How long did the battle of Nashville last? With what result?
13. While Hood and Thomas were maneuvering in Tennessee, where was Sherman's army?
14. What was Sherman doing to injure the power of the Confederacy?
15. At what point on the coast did Sherman come out?
16. Was this before or after Hood's defeat at Nashville?
17. How long had Sherman's army been without communication with the North?
18. What happened at Savannah?
19. What fort on the coast of North Carolina was captured?
20. What city was near to Fort Fisher?
21. What general was sent to enter North Carolina by Wilmington?
22. What battle had Schofield fought in Tennessee? (See above.)
23. In what direction did Sherman move from Savannah?
24. What was the result of the fight at Averysboro?
25. Where did Johnston almost defeat one of Sherman's columns?
26. What effect had Sherman's marches produced on Lee's operations?
27. What was Lee considering? What was Grant trying to prevent? How?
28. What was the result of the battle of Five Forks on April I, 1865?
29. What happened at Petersburg while the battle of Five Forks was taking place?
30. What did Lee do when his works were carried?
31. What was Lee's first object in his retreat? Did he succeed?
32. Toward what point did he next turn?
33. How was he prevented from reaching Lynchburg?
34. What was the result?
35. What did Johnston do?
36. What is said of the end of the war?
37. What impressions did the sufferings of the Civil War make on the country?

I. Sherman and Hood.
   1. Hood in Sherman's rear.
   2. Sherman to go southward.
II. Hood and Thomas.
   1. The battle of Franklin. 2. Battle of Nashville.
III. Sherman's march to the sea.
   1. Destroying railroads. 2. Savannah captured.
IV. The move
   ment into
   North Caro-
   lina.
   1. Wilmington
   taken.
   2. Schofield
   moves to
   Goldsboro.

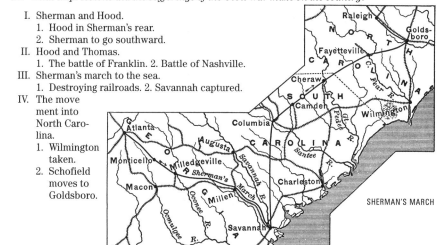

SHERMAN'S MARCH

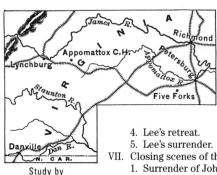

Study by
topics

Geography

What State on the Atlantic coast lies northeastward of Georgia? What State next to South Carolina on the north? What State lies on the north of North Carolina? In marching from Savannah, in Georgia, to Columbia, in what direction did Sherman go? In moving from Columbia, in South Carolina, to Goldsboro, in North Carolina, in what general direction did he march? In what direction is Goldsboro from Wilmington? Schofield's troops were moved from Nashville to Washington and thence by water to Wilmington: in what direction is Nashville from Wilmington? In what direction is Washington from Wilmington? In what State is Wilmington? What is the capital of North Carolina?

CHAPTER LVII

Traits and Results of the War—Death of Lincoln

The *Trent* affair,
Danger of war
with England

THE war led to some complications in the foreign relations of the United States. Both in England and France there were statesmen who were jealous of the rapid growth of this country. They were afraid that the United States would become more powerful than their own countries, and they would have been pleased to see it divided. In 1861 this hostile feeling in England was very much increased by what is called "the *Trent* affair." Mason and Slidell were sent as ambassadors from the Confederate States—Mason to England, and Slidell to France. They ran the blockade, getting out of the harbor of Charleston during a dark night, and reached Havana. From Havana they sailed in the *Trent*, an English steamer. Captain Wilkes, of an American man-of-war, stopped the *Trent* and took Mason and Slidell from it, carrying them prisoners to the United States. This act produced great excitement in England, and for a while war seemed imminent between the two countries. But, on the demand of Great Britain, the United States surrendered the ambassadors, as improperly captured.

The United States Navy had been rapidly enlarged after the war began. One of its principal duties was to blockade the Southern ports to keep the Confederates from getting arms and other supplies from foreign countries. Many fast-sailing English ships were engaged in running this blockade. These, by the law of nations, were subject to capture by the Union ships, and many were taken, but the high prices paid for the commodities that were got in, justified the risk. These blockade runners generally entered the Southern ports at night. But, when the chief Southern ports were captured one after another by the navy and the land forces of the Union, blockade running was gradually stopped. *Blockade of the Southern coast*

The Confederate government could not get much of a navy afloat from ports so well blockaded, but ships were built in England and secretly sent to sea. These received Confederate commissions, and almost succeeded in ruining American commerce. The most famous of these ships, called the "*Alabama*," was commanded by Captain Raphael Semmes. It was built in England, and it captured in all sixty-seven merchant and whaling ships. In a fight with the United States man-of-war *Kearsarge*, the *Alabama* was sunk in the English Channel, June 19, 1864. After the war the United States set up claims against the British government on account of the damages done to American com- *Confederate navy. The Alabama and "the Alabama claims"* merce by the *Alabama* and other Confederate cruisers built in England. The "*Alabama* claims," as they were called, after years of discussion, were submitted to a court of arbitration which sat in Geneva, Switzerland, in 1872, and condemned England to pay to the United States $15,500,000.

Legal tender paper money, or "greenbacks" The expenses of the war can never be fully estimated. The United States government borrowed money on interest, by giving bonds to pay after a certain number of years. A large part of this debt has now been paid. But, as another means of borrowing money, "legal tender notes" were issued; that is, paper bills, which by law could be used to pay debts and taxes, instead of coins. These legal tender notes were printed on a peculiar green paper, and got the name of " greenbacks." When a great quantity of them had been issued, and the dangers to the government increased, the value of this paper money decreased, until at one time a dollar of it was really worth but half a dollar. However, as the greenbacks were by law good for the payment of debts, they were used instead of the more valuable silver and gold, which for seventeen years disappeared entirely from general use. Long after the war closed, in 1879, the government began to redeem these legal tender bills in silver and gold. This was called "the resumption of specie payments." But the fact that gold or silver was to be paid for them had made greenbacks worth as much as coin, and people generally preferred to keep the paper money.

Confederate money The Confederate government also resorted to loans, which, however, became almost valueless when the success of the Confederacy became doubtful. It also issued a great deal of legal tender money, which took the place of coin, and declined in value until twenty dollars of it would not buy one of gold. When the Confederacy was over-

UNITED STATES UNIFORMS IN THE CIVIL WAR

REG. CAVALRY PRIVATE   GEN. GRANT'S UNIFORM   ARTILLERY LINE OFFICER   DURYEA'S ZOUAVE   HAWKIN'S ZOUAVE   REG. INFANTRY PRIVATE   DURYEA'S ZOUAVE LINE OFFICER   CAMPAIGN UNIFORM INFANTRY   REG. ARTILLERY PRIVATE   INFANTRY OVERCOAT

thrown, this money became of no value. The decline in the value of its paper money was one of the greatest difficulties the Confederate government had to contend with in its last years.

To avoid confusion, we have preferred to tell the story of the military operations of the war without mentioning the political affairs of the time. In 1864 the Republican party nominated President Lincoln for reelection, and Andrew Johnson, of Tennessee, a Southern Union man, for Vice-President. The Democratic party nominated General George B. McClellan, and for a time it seemed that the discouragement of the Northern people with the long continuance of the war might elect McClellan. But the success of Sherman in taking Atlanta, the capture of the forts near Mobile by the fleet under Farragut, and the successes of the Union armies under Sheridan in the Valley of Virginia, removed all doubt about the result, and Lincoln received all the electoral votes cast except those of Kentucky, Delaware, and New Jersey. Second election of Lincoln, 1864

Lincoln began his second term of office in March, 1865, when Sherman was already marching northward through the Carolinas, and when the close of the war was already in sight. When Lee surrendered, Lincoln's mind was already revolving plans for conciliating those who had been opposed to him, and for restoring the government at the South. But, while the President was sitting with his family in a box at the theatre, John Wilkes Booth, one of a band of conspirators, approached him from behind and shot him, and then leaped to the stage, crying, "*Sic semper tyrannis!*" which means, "Thus always with tyrants," and escaped. Booth was afterward overtaken, and killed in resisting arrest. Lincoln died on the 15th of April, the day after he was Assassination of President Lincoln, 1865

ABRAHAM LINCOLN

Abraham Lincoln was born in Kentucky, February 12, 1809. His father removed to Indiana when he was a little boy, and while that country was exceedingly wild and rough. The family lived in a half-faced camp—that is, a cabin with one side left out and the fire built out-of-doors, in front of the open side. Abraham endured many privations, and struggled hard to get an education. The schools were few and the teachers ignorant, but Lincoln trained his own mind by carefully thinking out every subject that puzzled him, and he spent his spare time in reading. He worked on a farm, went to New Orleans on a flatboat, was clerk in a country store, learned and practiced surveying, and then studied law. He served several terms in the Legislature of Illinois, and was a member of Congress. He became a leading lawyer and politician in his State, and gained a national fame by a series of debates, in which he was enraged with Senator Douglas in 1858. His integrity, his moderation, and his strong speeches brought him the nomination for President, and the rest of his history is that of the country. His death took place on the 15th of April, 1865.

shot; he was deeply mourned, because he had shown himself a man of great wisdom and goodness. Lincoln's assassination was sincerely regretted at the South, also, where his kindliness was coming to be known, and where the people, newly conquered, feared that his death might lead to measures of retaliation.

Release of Jefferson Davis

But the war was closed without acts of mere revenge, and nobody was put to death for a political offense. Jefferson Davis, the President of the Confederacy, who had been captured in Georgia at the close of the war, was arraigned before a court on a charge of high treason. He was confined in Fortress Monroe for two years, when he was released without being tried.

Questions for study

1. *Why did certain English and French statesmen feel jealous of this country?*
2. *What affair increased this hostile feeling in England?*
3. *What were the names of the ambassadors sent from the Confederate States in 1861?*
4. *To what countries were they going?*
5. *How did they get out of Charleston?*
6. *At what port did they take passage on the* Trent?
7. *To what country did the* Trent *belong?*
8. *How were Mason and Slidell taken from the* Trent?
9. *What effect did this have in England?*
10. *How was war with England avoided?*
11. *How was the navy of the Union employed in keeping supplies out of the Confederacy?*
12. *How did English ships get in with supplies?*
13. *What prevented the Confederate government from sending ships out of the Southern ports?*
14. *Where were ships built for it?*
15. *What effect did the cruisers have on the commerce of the United States?*
16. *What was the name of the most famous of these vessels?*
17. *How many ships did the* Alabama *destroy? In what year was she destroyed? How and where?*
18. *What claims did the United States set up?*
19. *To what kind of a court were the* Alabama *claims submitted?*
20. *Where did this court meet?*
21. *What was the decision of the court of arbitration?*
22. *How did the United States borrow money to pay the expenses of the war?*
23. *Has all of the debt been paid?*
24. *What are "legal tender notes"? Why were they called greenbacks?*
25. *What caused the paper money to lose value? Why was it still used?*
26. *What effect did the use of greenbacks have on the circulation of gold and silver?*
27. *For how many years was there no gold or silver in general circulation?*
28. *What is meant by the resumption of specie payment?*
29. *In what year did the United States begin to pay specie for greenbacks?*
30. *What effect did this have on the value of greenbacks?*
31. *How did the Confederate government raise money?*
32. *What is said of the decline in the value of its legal tender money?*
33. *Who was nominated for President by the Republicans in 1864?*
34. *Who was put up for Vice President on the same ticket?*
35. *Whom did the Democratic party nominate for President?*
36. *What victories removed all doubts about Lincoln's election?*
37. *Where was General Sherman when Lincoln began his second term?*
38. *What was the prospect of the close of the war?*
39. *When Lee surrendered, what plans was Lincoln revolving?*
40. *How was Lincoln assassinated? By whom?*
41. *What was the feeling regarding the death of President Lincoln?*
42. *What kind of a man had he shown himself to be?*
43. *What was the feeling at the South regarding it?*

44. *Was any one put to death after the war on account of political offenses?*
45. *What was done about Jefferson Davis?*

Study by
topics

 I. The *Trent* affair.
 II. The blockade and blockade-running.
 III. The Confederate ships.
  1. Building of ships in England.
  2. The *Alabama*.
  3. The *Alabama* claims.
 IV. Money during the war.
  1. How the United States borrowed money.
  2. The greenbacks.
  3. Confederate bonds.
  4. Confederate money.
 V. The election of 1864.
  1. Nominations.
  2. Election of Lincoln
 VI. Death of Lincoln.
  1. The shooting.
  2. The feeling in regard to his death.
 VII. Arrest and release of Jefferson Davis.

SEVENTH REVIEW—FROM THE CLOSE OF THE MEXICAN WAR TO THE END OF THE CIVIL WAR

Chapters XLVIII to LVII

Events following the Mexican War.
(XLVIII)
{ Election of Taylor, 1848.
{ Discovery of gold in California. 1848.

Slavery question in the new territory.
(XLVIII)
{ The Wilmot Proviso.
{ The admission of California.
{ Runaway slaves in the free States.
{ Compromise of 1850

Pierce elected, 1852. (XLVIII)

Renewed excitement. (XLVIII)
- Fugitive slave law unpopular.
- Excitement produced by *Uncle Tom's Cabin.*
- The South also dissatisfied.
- Attempts to annex territory.

Change in political parties. (XLIX)
- Decay of the Whig party.
- American (or Know-Nothing) party.
- Kansas-Nebraska Bill.
- The Republican party.

Slavery becomes the main issue. (XLIX)
- Collisions in Kansas.
- Buchanan elected, 1856.
- The Dred Scott decision.
- John Brown's raid.
- Lincoln elected. 1860.
- New free States admitted.

The rising storm. (L)
- The doctrine of State sovereignty.
- Seven States secede.
- Failure of the Peace Convention.
- Dissensions in the Cabinet.

The storm breaks. (L, LI)
- "Confederate States" government formed.
- Lincoln inaugurated.
- Fort Sumter bombarded.
- The rush to arms.
- The question at issue.
- The States take sides.

First campaigns. (LI)
- Bull Run, or Manassas.
- Fort Henry and Fort Donelson.
- Island No. 10.
- Shiloh, or Pittsburg Landing.
- Corinth evacuated.

The struggles for Washington and Richmond. (LII)
- In the Peninsula.
- The second Bull Run.
- Antietam.
- Fredericksburg.
- Chancellorsville.
- Gettysburg.

Monitor and *Merrimac*.   (LIII)

The Emancipation Proclamation.
(LIII)

Struggle for the Mississippi. (LIII)
- Fall of New Orleans.
- Movements in Kentucky, 1862.
- Battle of Corinth.
- The Vicksburg campaign.

Between Nashville and Atlanta.
(LIV)
- Murfreesboro, or Stone River.
- Chickamauga.
- Chattanooga battles.
- The struggle for Atlanta.

The Wilderness Campaign. (LV)
- Battles in the Wilderness.
- Movement by the flank.
- Cold Harbor.
- Petersburg besieged.

The war in the Valley of Virginia.
(LV)
- Hunter moves on Lynchburg.
- Early moves on Washington.
- Sheridan in the Valley.

Sherman's marches. (LVI)
- Battle of Nashville.
- Sherman's march to the sea.
- Savannah.
- Sherman's march northward.

Close of the war. (LVI)
- Lee's retreat.
- Surrender of Lee's army.
- Surrender of Johnston's army.

Naval affairs. (LVII)
- Stoppage of the Trent.
- Blockade-running.
- Confederate cruisers.
- Alabama claims.

Financial affairs. (LVII)
- Government bonds.
- Greenback notes.
- Confederate notes.

Reelection and death of Lincoln.
(LVII)
- Lincoln reelected, 1864.
- Lincoln assassinated, 1865.

Arrest and release of Davis. (LVII)

CHAPTER LVIII

Political Events since the Civil War

THE war settled two questions long debated in this country, that of State sovereignty and that of slavery. From the beginning of the government it had been disputed whether or not a State might act in a sovereign way in opposition to the United States government. The war answered "No" to this question.

The question of State independence settled

The Emancipation Proclamation had only abolished slavery in those States and districts at that time resisting the United States government. But the thirteenth amendment to the Constitution, which was adopted at the close of the war, and ratified in December, 1865, forbade slavery in all parts of the country forever.

The question of slavery disappears

A great question of history was also decided by the war. It was settled that the heart of North America is to be occupied by but one great power. Had there been more than one, the resources of the people might have been wasted and their advancement checked by standing armies, and wars happening from time to time.

But one great power in North America

Andrew Johnson, the Vice-President, succeeded to the presidency on the death of Lincoln. There soon grew up a difference between Johnson and the Republican Congress in regard to the measures to be adopted for the reconstruction of government in the Southern States. Congress required, among other things, that every State which had seceded should admit the Negroes to vote, before the representatives of the State should be again admitted to Congress. President Johnson did not think that Congress had a right to refuse admission to lawfully elected representatives.

Andrew Johnson President

President
Johnson
impeached
The difference between President Johnson and Congress, on several points in regard to reconstruction resulted in an effort by Congress to limit the power of the President to remove officers. The Republicans were more than two thirds of each House, so that they could make laws in spite of the veto of the President. They passed a law forbidding him to make removals from office except by consent of the Senate. This law Johnson refused to obey. The House of Representatives voted to impeach the President; that is, to bring him to trial in order to have him removed as unfit to be President. Such a charge must

ANDREW JOHNSON

be made by the House of Representatives, and the Senate is the court which has to decide the case. As less than two thirds of the Senate voted to remove him, Johnson remained President to the end of his term.

Grant elected
President, 1868
In 1868 General Grant was elected President, as the candidate of the Republicans. The Democratic candidate was Horatio Seymour, of New York. The election turned on the dispute over measures for reconstructing the Southern States.

The seceded
States readmitted to Congress,
Negro suffrage
established
During Grant's first administration, in 1870, the last of the States that had belonged to the Confederacy complied with the conditions demanded by Congress. All the States were now represented in Congress for the first time since South Carolina had seceded in 1860. In this same year, 1870, the fifteenth amendment to the Constitution was ratified. This gave to the Negroes the right to vote.

Disorders at
the South
Various causes produced in the South disorder and bad government for some years. The war, too, had wasted the resources of the country and left the people in poverty. But a better state of things has ensued, and the Southern people

have gradually entered on a career of peace and great prosperity.

In 1872 a portion of the Republicans, dissatisfied with Grant's administration of the government, formed a new party, which they called the "Liberal Republican" party. They nominated Horace Greeley for President. The Democratic party accepted Greeley as its candidate also, but Grant was reelected by a large majority.

Reelection of Grant, 1872

In 1876 the Republicans nominated Rutherford B. Hayes, of Ohio, for President. The Democrats nominated Samuel J. Tilden, of New York. The election was a close one, and the country came near to being thrown into a distressing confusion by the condition of the Southern State governments. In some of these were "returning boards," committees which had the right to revise the election returns, and throw out such as they thought had been affected by fraud or violence. By the votes cast, Louisiana had given a majority for Tilden. But the Republicans claimed that certain districts had been carried by intimidating the Negroes and by fraud. The returns from these were thrown out by the returning board, and the vote of the State was given to Hayes. This gave a majority of one. The most exciting debates ensued in Congress, which had finally to decide the matter.

Disputed election of 1876 decided in favor of Hayes

RUTHERFORD B. HAYES

As the Republicans had a majority in the Senate and the Democrats a majority in the House, the two bodies could not agree. The question was at length referred to fifteen commissioners, eight of whom voted to give the election to Hayes.

In 1880 General W. S. Hancock, who had won renown as a brilliant division commander in the Army of the Potomac,

Election of Garfield, 1880. His assassination, 1881

was nominated for President by the Democrats. General James A. Garfield, of Ohio, whose distinction was due to

JAMES A. GARFIELD

the ability he had shown in debate on the floor of Congress, was nominated by the Republicans and elected. Three months after President Garfield was inaugurated, on the 2d of July, 1881, he was shot and mortally wounded by a disappointed office seeker. Garfield lived eighty days after he was shot and died on September 19, 1881. His assassin was tried for murder and hanged.

Chester A. Arthur, of New York, had been elected as Vice-President when Garfield was chosen Presi-

Arthur President

dent. On the death of Garfield, Arthur succeeded to the presidency, as prescribed by the Constitution, and filled out the unexpired term for which Garfield had been elected.

In 1884 the Republicans nominated James G. Blaine for President. His distinction had been gained chiefly as Speaker of the House of Representatives and Senator from Maine. The Democrats nominated Grover Cleveland, then popular as Governor of New York. After an unusually severe struggle and a very close election, Cleveland was chosen. The Democratic party thus returned to power for the first time since the election of Lincoln in 1860.

The question of the tariff

The question which most agitated politics in Cleveland's administration was that of the tariff. Very early in the history of the government there were two opinions on this subject. One class of statesmen has maintained that American manufactures should be protected by levying high duties on articles made abroad, in order that the American market may be kept chiefly for the products of American labor. The other class maintains that high protective duties are unjust to the American consumer, and of little, if any, benefit to the manufacturer. They propose that the tariff should be used chiefly to raise the money needed to support the government. This was a main point of division between the Whigs and Democrats before the rise of the great antislavery agitation. As the ques-

CHESTER A. ARTHUR

tions which grew out of the Civil War have become less engrossing, those relating to tariff revision have again become the most prominent.

GROVER CLEVELAND

The election of 1888 turned upon questions of revenue, the Democrats proposing to reduce the duties on imports in certain particulars, which movement was opposed by the Republicans. Grover Cleveland was nominated for reelection by the Democrats. The Republicans nominated General Benjamin Harrison, of Indiana,

Election of Benjamin Harrison

who had been a United States Senator and who was a grandson of President W. H. Harrison. Benjamin Harrison was elected, and was inaugurated March 4, 1889.

BENJAMIN HARRISON

Questions for study

1. *What two great political questions did the war decide?*
2. *How long had the question of the right of a State to act independently been debated?*
3. *What answer did the war give to this question?*
4. *How far did the Emancipation Proclamation settle the slavery question?*
5. *What was the effect of the thirteenth amendment to the Constitution?*
6. *What great question of history was answered by the war?*
7. *If there had been more than one nation in the heart of North America, what evil result might have followed?*
8. *Who became President when Lincoln died?*
9. *On what subject did President Johnson differ with Congress?*
10. *What did Congress require of the States which had seceded?*
11. *What ground did the President take in regard to the admission of the seceded States to Congress?*
12. *What kind of laws did Congress pass regarding the President? Did Johnson obey these acts?*
13. *What did the House of Representatives do?*
14. *What court has to decide on the question when a President is impeached?*
15. *What did the Senate do with regard to the removal of President Johnson?*
16. *Who was elected President in 1868?*
17. *Of what party was Grant the candidate?*
18. *Who was the Democratic candidate?*
19. *On what question did the election turn?*
20. *What is said of the readmission in 1870 of the States that had seceded?*
21. *How long was this after the first State had seceded? (Subtract 1860 from 1870.)*
22. *What amendment to the Constitution was ratified by the States in 1870?*
23. *What did this give to the Negroes?*
24. *What effect did the war have upon the resources of the South?*
25. *What is said of the state of things that has followed?*
26. *What did the Republicans, who were dissatisfied with Grant's government, do in 1872?*
27. *Whom did the Liberal Republicans nominate for President?*
28. *Whom did the Democrats support?*

29. *What was the result of the election?*
30. *Who was the Republican candidate in 1876?*
31. *Who the Democratic candidate?*
32. *What came near to throwing the country into confusion?*
33. *What power did some of the Southern returning-boards have?*
34. *What changes were made in the returns from Louisiana?*
35. *How large a majority did this give to Hayes?*
36. *What was the nature of the debate in Congress on this matter?*
37. *Why could not the two houses of Congress agree?*
38. *To whom was the matter referred?*
39. *How was it decided?*
40. *Whom did the Democrats nominate for President in 1880?*
41. *Whom did the Republicans nominate?*
42. *Which was elected?*
43. *What happened to Garfield?*
44. *What was the fate of the assassin?*
45. *Who became President when Garfield died?*
46. *Who was the Republican candidate for President in 1884?*
47. *Who was the Democratic candidate?*
48. *What is said of the struggle and the election?*
49. *What was the uppermost political question in Cleveland's administration?*
50. *What opinions on this subject have been held by statesmen in favor of a high protective tariff?*
51. *What do those opposed to such a tariff maintain?*
52. *What old parties were once divided on this subject?*
53. *Who was elected President in 1888?*

I. Political questions settled by the war.   Study by
   1. That a State may not secede.   topics
   2. That there shall be no slavery.
   3. That there will be but one great power on this continent.
II. The reconstruction period.
   1. Johnson's administration. a. His dispute with Congress. b. His impeachment and trial.
   2. Grant's administration. a. His election. b. All the States readmitted. c. The fifteenth amendment. d. The disorders at the South. e. The reelection of Grant.
   3. Hayes' election. a. The returning boards. b. The Louisiana returns. e. The decision.
III. Later administrations.
   1. Garfield. 2. Arthur succeeds Garfield. 3. Cleveland elected. 4. The tariff question. 5. Harrison elected.

CHAPTER LIX

Later Developments of the Country

Additions of territory before the Civil War

WE have seen how the United States, which was at first limited by the Mississippi River on the west and by Florida on the south, received before the Civil War five great additions to its territory: 1. The old French province of Louisiana, a vast region west of the Mississippi. 2. Oregon (including Washington Territory), by exploration and discovery. 3. Florida, by purchase from Spain. 4. Texas, by the annexation of an independent republic, once a part of Mexico. 5. The Mexican cessions after the Mexican War.

Purchase of Alaska, 1867

To these must be added Alaska, which was purchased from Russia in 1867 for a little more than seven million dollars ($7,200,000). This was the only territory we had that did not lie adjoining to the rest of the country. It is partly in the arctic regions, but the climate of Alaska on the Pacific coast is not severe. The killing of seals for their furs was the chief business interest in Alaska.

West Virginia admitted, 1863; Nevada, 1864

The number of States at the beginning of the Civil War was thirty-four. By 1876, the hundredth year of the American Republic, the number had increased to thirty-eight. Two States had been admitted during the war. The people of the western part of Virginia were mostly on the side of the Union. This part of the State separated itself from eastern Virginia, which was acting with the Confederacy. It obtained admission to the Union in 1863, as a separate State, under the name of West Virginia. Nevada, just east of California, and a part of the territory ceded to us by Mexico, was admitted in 1864. It is a land of silver mining.

In 1867 Nebraska was admitted. It is one of the most fertile of farming States. In the centennial year, Colorado came into the Union. This State lies in the Rocky Mountain region, and has gold and silver mines. Cattle raising is one of its chief industries. In 1889 an Act of Congress was passed for the admission of four new States, raising the whole number to forty-two. They were North Dakota, South Dakota, Montana, and Washington.

Nebraska, 1867; Colorado, 1876; North Dakota, South Dakota, Montana, and Washington, 1889

Utah had now population enough for a State. It was settled by people professing the Mormon religion. This religion allows the practice of polygamy, and some of the Mormons have more than one wife apiece. For this reason, Congress had hitherto been unwilling to admit Utah to the Union. Most of the rest of the Territories are in mountain regions, and their increase in population is rather slow. It is probable, however, that soon after the close of the 19th century we shall have about fifty States in the Union. In 1889 the new Territory of Oklahoma was cut off from the Indian Territory and occupied by a large population in a day or two.

The Territories

The settlement of the Western States and Territories had brought the white people into conflict with the fierce and warlike Indians of the plains. In the summer of 1862 the eastern bands of the Sioux [soo] nation fell suddenly upon the defenseless settlements of Minnesota, and killed nearly five hundred people. In the war which followed, the Sioux were driven out of the State, and thirty eight of those captured were convicted of murdering women and children, and hanged.

Later Indian war. The Sioux massacre in Minnesota, 1862

Though there were no horses in America when the white men came, the Indians of the plains now had a race of small ponies, acquired long ago from the early Spanish conquerors of Mexico. The plains Indians fought on horseback, and were said to have been "the best light cavalry in the world."

Custer attacks the Indians in the winter

CUSTER

They were in the habit of committing their outrages on the settlements in the summer, when there was grass for the ponies. In the winter, when the ponies were almost starved, they took shelter in remote valleys, and counted themselves safe from attack, on account of the difficulty the white men found in moving wagon trains.

But, in November, 1868, General Sheridan sent General Custer, after the snow had fallen, to attack the hostile Indians in their villages. Custer, carrying his provisions on mules, followed the trail of a war party, under the chief Black Kettle, to their town on the Washita [wau´-she-taw] River, in the Indian Territory and fell upon the sleeping savages at daybreak, defeating them with great slaughter. This Battle terrified and subdued the Indians of the Southern plains, who no longer felt safe from punishment in their winter retreats.

Custer killed in battle

But, in a later war with the Sioux of the Northern Plains in 1876, Custer, having attacked a force outnumbering his own, was surrounded and killed, with all the men under his immediate command. In this fight the Sioux were led by Sitting Bull. The Indians were afterward attacked by fresh troops and driven into Canadian territory. They have since been allowed to return.

There have been other Indian wars, but, of course, the rash tribes are always worsted in the long run. The irresistible march of civilized man has destroyed the buffaloes, or bisons,

INDIAN WATCHING FOR BUFFALOES

BATTLE OF WASHITA

Condition of the Indians   and broken down the old life of the Indians, to which they were so much attached. All the hunting grounds were soon occupied by farms, mines, and cities. There was nothing left for the Indians but to become civilized or to perish. Good men tried to protect them from wrong, and to persuade them to have their children taught to live the lives of civilized people, on farms, owned not by the tribes, but by individuals. Many Indian children were taught at the expense of the government. Some of the tribes located in the Indian Territory have attained considerable civilization.

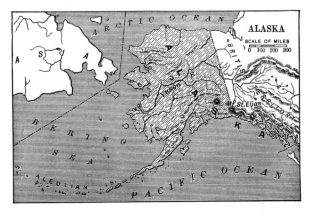

Questions for study

1. By what river was the United States bounded on the west at the close of the Revolution?
2. How many great additions were made to its territory before the Civil War?
3. What was the first?
4. On which bank of the Mississippi did the province of Louisiana chiefly lie?
5. By what claim do we own Oregon and the Territory of Washington?
6. From what country did we purchase Florida?
7. How did Texas come into the Union?
8. What other large cession was made to the United States?
9. What was the sixth great addition to the territory of the United States?
10. How much did the United States pay for Alaska?
11. Was this purchase made before or after the Civil War?
12. How does Alaska differ from other additions to our territory?
13. What is the nature of its climate?

14. *What was the chief business interest in Alaska?*
15. *How many States are there in the Union today?*
16. *How many have been added since the Civil War began?*
17. *What two were added during the war?*
18. *What were the circumstances under which West Virginia was taken into the Union?*
19. *What State was admitted in 1864?*
20. *What kind of mines are there in Nevada?*
21. *In what year was Nebraska admitted?*
22. *What kind of a State is Nebraska?*
23. *In what year was Colorado made a State?*
24. *In what mountain region is Colorado situated?*
25. *What kind of mines has Colorado?*
26. *What other principal business?*
27. *What four new States were admitted by Act of Congress in 1889?*
28. *How many States are there now in the Union?*
29. *How many more than three times the original thirteen?*
30. *Why had Utah not been admitted?*
31. *What is said of the rest of the Territories?*
32. *About how many States will there be when all are admitted (some of the present Territories having been divided)?*
33. *What is said of Oklahoma?*
34. *What has been the effect of the settlement of the newer States and Territories, with reference to the Indians?*
35. *What Indian nation attacked the people of Minnesota in 1862?*
36. *How many did they kill?*
37. *What took place in the war that followed?*
38. *What was done with those convicted of killing women and children?*
39. *What difference was there between the mode of Indian fighting on the plains and that of the Indians formerly encountered at the East?*
40. *How did the Indians get horses? What kind of horses did they have?*
41. *What kind of soldiers were they said to be?*
42. *At what time of the year did the Indians of the plains attack the settlements? Why in the summer? What did they do in the winter?*
43. *What change in the mode of war did Sheridan introduce?*
44. *What can you tell of the battle of the Washita?*
45. *What effect did this battle have on the Indians of the Southern plains?*
46. *Who commanded the troops in this battle?*
47. *What happened to Custer in 1876?*
48. *Against what tribe of Indians was he fighting when he was killed?*
49. *What chief commanded the Indians?*
50. *What happened when the Indians were attacked by fresh troops?*
51. *What changes compelled the Indians to settle on farms or perish?*
52. *What was being done for them?*

   I. Additions to the area of the United States.   Study by
      1. Recapitulation of five additions to the area of the United States.   topics
      2. The sixth addition, Alaska.

II. New States since the beginning of the Civil War.
    1. West Virginia. 2. Nevada. 3. Nebraska. 4. Colorado. 5. North Dakota, South Dakota, Montana, and Washington.

III. The Territories.
    1. Utah. 2. The other Territories.

IV. Later Indian wars.
    1. The Minnesota massacre. 2. The mounted Indians. 3. The battle of the Washita. 4. The battle with Sitting Bull, and death of Custer. 5. Efforts to improve the condition of the Indians.

Composition   Let the pupil, by reference to the index, examine all the passages in this book relating to the additions of territory to the United States. Then he will have material for an essay on "The Growth of the United States in Territory." This should be written from his own notes in his own words, and with the book closed, except when a date or other such fact is needed. Another subject that may be worked in the same way is "Indian Wars."

Geography   In what part of America is Alaska situated? What foreign country lies between the main territory of the United States and Alaska? On what ocean is Alaska? What State lies west of West Virginia? What river forms its northwestern boundary? What State is between Nevada and the Pacific ocean? What river forms the eastern boundary of Nebraska? What State south of Nebraska? How does Colorado lie with reference to Nebraska? Where does South Dakota lie with reference to Nebraska? Where does North Dakota lie with reference to Minnesota? How is Montana situated with reference to North Dakota? On what ocean is Washington? What foreign province to the north of it?

CHAPTER LX

Population, Wealth, and Modes of Living

FLAG OF 1888

THE first census was taken in 1790. There were then less than four million people (3,929,214). In 1880 there were over fifty million (50,155,783). By the end of the 1890s, there were between sixty and seventy million, say sixteen or seventeen times as many as there were one hundred years before. The population of this country was at that time very much larger than that of any of the nations of Europe except Russia. **Increase of population** It is, perhaps, safe to assume that before the close of the 20th century there will be over two hundred fifty million people in the United States.

The increase of wealth has been yet more remarkable. This is due to the resources of the country, as well as to the enterprise of the people. Wheat from the rich farms of the great interior valley, and meat from the cattle ranges of the Western States and Territories, are sent across the sea in vast quantities. Gold and silver from the Rocky Mountains and the Pacific coast, petroleum from the neighborhood of the Allegheny Mountains, and inexhaustible supplies of coal and iron in various regions are great sources of wealth. Manufactures of many kinds also enrich the people. The United States by the turn of the century was already the richest nation.

Increase of wealth

In a new country men become inventive, because they have to find out how to do things that they have never seen anybody do before. Americans are, perhaps, the most inventive people in the world. Before the Revolution, Thomas Godfrey, of Philadelphia, invented the quadrant, an instrument to help a navigator to find his whereabouts at sea. About the same time, Franklin invented the lightning rod. There was also a valuable machine invented in South Carolina for doing the hard labor of taking the hull off of the grains of rice. This was run by the ebbing and flowing of the tide. In the middle colonies, flour mills were improved, and little elevating machines invented, so that wheat did not have to be carried to the top of the mill on a man's back.

Early American inventions

America has since become celebrated for what are called labor saving machines. One of the most remarkable of these is the cotton gin. It took so much time and toil to pick the seeds out of cotton that only small quantities were raised for home use. Long before the Revolution, a "gin" for cleaning the cotton of seed had been invented, but it did not come into general use. But, when machines for spinning cotton thread and weaving cotton cloth by steam power were in-

Whitney's cotton gin

vented in England there sprang up a great demand for raw cotton. In 1794 Eli Whitney invented a "saw gin" for taking the seeds out of cotton. This made cotton raising profitable, and caused the Southern States to grow rapidly in population and wealth. After the invention of the gin, indigo culture was quite driven out by cotton raising.

Some other remarkable inventions

The cotton gin was the first of a great family of labor saving machines, partly or wholly invented in this country. Reaping and mowing machines were first made successful by American inventors. Thrashing machines were improved here. All the agricultural machines now used have practically been introduced in the last fifty years of the 19th century. The first really successful sewing machine was introduced by Elias Howe in 1845. Morse's telegraph (Chapter XLV) came into use at about the same time. The telephone enables people to hold conversations when far apart. The phonograph first recorded speech on a cylinder, which may be sealed up and kept for a thousand years, when it can be made to repeat the very tones of the voice that spoke the words.

Change made by inventions

More inventions of great importance have been made in the lifetime of people now living than in all the ages before. We live in a different world from that of our forefathers, who had only saddle horses or wagons for land conveyance, and slow-sailing ships or rowboats for water journeys. We can go around the world in a great deal less time than some of the first emigrants took to sail from England to America. Our ancestors had neither kerosene-oil, gas, nor electric light. Stoves were practically unknown; for warming themselves and cooking their food, people in old times had only wood fires in wide, open fire places, which often chilled the room with draughts of air or filled it with smoke.

They carded, spun, wove, and dyed, by hand, wool or flax for their own clothing. At the end of the 19th century, steam was made to do most of the work in spinning and weaving, in making hats and shoes, in planing boards, and in turning wood. Even delicate little things like watches were made mostly by steam machinery.

OLD FIREPLACE

Out of the use of machinery has grown up the factory system, which gathers working people into towns and sets them to work together in factories. Many people are able in this way to labor on the same piece of work, each doing his own part. This saves time, and makes each man's toil more productive. The building and running of these factories require a great deal of money: so that work is now carried on by two classes: First, the capitalists, who furnish the factory and its machines; second, the workingmen, who receive wages and do the labor. This has led to great discussions of the rights of the working people, and those who furnish the money or capital.

The factory system

THE PENNSYLVANIA FIREPLACE, INVENTED BY FRANKLIN

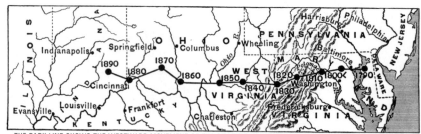

THE DARK LINE SHOWS THE WESTWARD MOVEMENT OF THE CENTER OF POPULATION IN THE UNITED STATES SINCE 1790

Questions for study

1. In what year was the first census taken?
2. How long ago is that?
3. Who was President of the United States in 1790? (Chapter XXXVI)
4. About how many millions of people were there in the country at that time?
5. How many were there in 1880?
6. How many millions were there, in 1890?
7. How does the population of the United States compare with that of the nations of Europe?
8. What European nation has a population larger than that of the United States?
9. How many people is it safe to suppose there will be in this country before the close of this century?
10. What is said of the increase of wealth in this country?
11. What articles of food do we send to Europe?
12. In what part of the country are they raised?
13. From what part of the country are gold and silver sent to Europe?
14. In the neighborhood of what mountains do we get petroleum?
15. What is said of the supplies of coal and iron? Of manufactures?
16. What cause is given for the inventiveness of the American people?
17. What did Godfrey invent in colony times?
18. What is the use of a quadrant?
19. What did Franklin invent?
20. Where was there invented a machine for taking the hull from rice?
21. What improvements were made in the middle colonies?
22. For what has America since become celebrated?
23. Who invented the cotton gin in 1794? Explain the necessity for such a machine?
24. What was the effect of its introduction?
25. What farming machines were first made successful by American inventors?
26. Within what period have all our present farming machines been introduced?
27. When was the first really successful sewing machine brought out?
28. How long ago is 1845?
29. What is the telephone used for?
30. What did the phonograph accomplish?
31. What light has been made generally useful in cities and factories?
32. How do the inventions of our time compare in number and importance

with those made before?

33. *Tell some of the differences between the life of our forefathers and ours: in regard to means of travel by land; travel by water; means of lighting; mode of cooking and of warming their houses; method of making wool and flax into clothing. Mention some of the things that steam was made to do. What system of work has grown out of the use of machinery?*

34. *How does this divide labor and save time?*

35. *What two classes of men now carry on work together?*

36. *What do we mean by a capitalist?*

37. *What discussions about rights have grown out of this system?*

I.   Growth of the country.
   1. In population.
   2. In wealth.

II. Inventions and machines.
   1.   Inventiveness of Americans.
   2.   Inventions before the Revolution.
   3.   Labor saving machines of the late 19th century.
      a. The cotton gin. b. Other farm machines. c. The sewing machine. d. Telegraph and telephone. e. Phonograph. f. Electric light.

III. Change in mode of life.
   1.   Different appliances of the late 19th century.
      a. For travel. b. For home life. c. For manufacturers.
   2.   The factory system and its effects.

Study by topics

CHAPTER LXI

Literature and Art in the United States

WE have seen, in Chapter XXXIV, that there was little that could be called literature in the United States before the last century. Franklin's writings, mostly on practical subjects, and the essays of Jefferson, Madison, and Hamilton, on political subjects, were almost the only works of permanent value written in the first two centuries after the beginning of American settlement. Great writers can be produced only where there is a community of educated and thoughtful people, such as one cannot find in a young country. Washington Irving, who is sometimes called the father of American literature, was born in New York in 1783.

The first two centuries

Irving

WASHINGTON IRVING

His first important book was a burlesque, called *Knickerbocker's History of New York*, which is very amusing, and won praise for its author on both sides of the Atlantic. But Irving's most famous work is the *Sketch Book*, in which appear the charming tales of "Rip Van Winkle" and "The Legend of Sleepy Hollow." His *Life of Washington* is still a standard biography. Among his biographical works are a delightful *Life of Christopher Columbus* and a *Life of Goldsmith*. His style is graceful and wittily playful, and his charming books did much to produce a taste for literary pursuits in this country.

Bryant

William Cullen Bryant, born in western Massachusetts in 1794, was the first American who became widely known as a poet. Though he lived to be very old, his greatest poem, "Thanatopsis," was written when he was not yet nineteen years of age. His almost equally famous poem called "Lines to a Waterfowl" was written before he was twenty.

WILLIAM CULLEN BRYANT

Longfellow

Henry Wadsworth Longfellow, the most popular and the most widely celebrated of our poets, was born in Portland, Maine, in 1807. Of his shorter pieces, "Excelsior" and "The Psalm of Life" are best known. His

HENRY W. LONGFELLOW

"Hiawatha" is an epic poem of Indian life, and his "Evangeline" is a narrative poem founded on the story of the expulsion of the Acadians (page 131).

John Greenleaf Whittier, Whittier sometimes called "the Quaker poet," was born in Massachusetts, in the same year with Longfellow (1807). Many of his poems describe simple, rural life. Others relate to slavery and the Civil War. One of the most charming is "Snow-Bound," a description of winter scenes in New England.

Oliver Wendell Holmes was born in 1809. He is famous Holmes for his witty poems, of which "The Last Leaf" and "The One-Hoss Shay" are two of the best known. His prose work, *The Autocrat of the Breakfast Table* is thought to be one of the brightest books in our literature.

Edgar Allan Poe, born in 1809, wrote some poems that have achieved a world-wide fame. Of these, "The Raven" is the best known. His weird and marvelous short stories have also a permanent place in literature. Poe's writings appeal powerfully to the imagination.

EDGAR A. POE

Ralph Waldo Emerson was born in 1803, in Boston. Some of his poems are greatly admired by literary readers; they can hardly be called popular. He is more widely known by his essays Emerson as a profound thinker and a writer of genius and poetic inspiration. His essays on *The Conduct of Life* are filled

with wise and wholesome suggestions.

Lowell   James Russell Lowell was born
in 1819. He is best known to general readers by his poems in the
New England dialect, called the
Biglow Papers. He is also a great
critic and essayist.

Cooper and   Two American writers of fic-
Hawthorne   tion in the period before the Civil
War attained a worldwide fame.
James Fenimore Cooper was born
in New Jersey in 1783. His novels are

RALPH WALDO EMERSON

mostly stories, full of action and adventure. The most famous are those known as *The Leather Stocking Tales.* A
very different writer is Nathaniel Hawthorne, who was a
rare genius, and wrote stories of a weird and subtle kind.
Of these, *The Scarlet Letter* and *The House of the Seven
Gables* are general favorites.

Our most famous historians were
George Bancroft, John Lothrop
Motley, William H. Prescott, and
Francis Parkman.

Literature since   After the Civil War there arose
the Civil War   a new group of writers. They differed from those who came be-
fore them as American life dif-
fers from the life before the war:
1. The writers of this later period were not chiefly a group of
men about New York or Boston.
Every great natural division of

JAMES FENIMORE COOPER

the country was represented in this school of writers. 2. They were not chiefly poets and essayists, like Longfellow and Emerson, Poe and Irving. This group of authors gave themselves mainly to prose fiction and to humoristic writing. 3. They were remarkable for the zeal and faithfulness with which they studied our own life. The manners and feelings of the American people in city and country were described with fullness, and the dialect of every region of the United States was reproduced in the pages of these authors.

NATHANIEL HAWTHORNE

American art had its rise in a group of portrait painters, of whom Gilbert Stuart was the chief. The conditions of our life were formerly unfavorable to the production of a great school of painters and sculptors, but there has been a large advance in late years, and some very notable work has been done in several departments of art. In the matter of book and magazine illustrations some of our artists have taken a very high rank.

American art

1. What was the character of our literature before the last century?
2. What great writer in the 18th century left literary work of permanent value?
3. What writers on political subjects produced important works?
4. Why were there no great writers in the pioneer period of the country?
5. What is Washington Irving sometimes called? What was his first important work? What is his most famous book?
6. What tales are mentioned as having appeared in the Sketch Book?
7. What biography written by Irving is still a standard work?
8. Who was the first American that became widely known as a poet?
9. How old was he when he wrote his best poem?
10. Who is spoken of as the most widely celebrated of our poets? Mention the two best known of his short pieces.
11. What kind of a poem is "Hiawatha?"
12. What is the story of "Evangeline" founded on?

Questions for study

13. *What is Whittier sometimes called? What is the character of his poems?*
14. *Which one is mentioned in particular?*
15. *Of what is "Snow Bound" a description?*
16. *What kind of poetry did Holmes write?*
17. *What two poems of his are mentioned?*
18. *What is thought of his* Autocrat of the Breakfast Table?
19. *Is the* Autocrat *in prose or verse?*
20. *Where was Poe born? What is said of his poetry?*
21. *By what is he most widely known?*
22. *What is said of him as a thinker and writer?*
23. *By what is Lowell best known to general readers?*
24. *In what other departments of authorship is he great?*
25. *What two very famous writers of fiction lived in the period before the civil war?*
26. *Were Cooper and Hawthorne alike in their writings?*
27. *What kind of novels did Cooper write?*
28. *Which are the most famous of his novels?*
29. *What kind of stories did Hawthorne write?*
30. *What two are mentioned?*
31. *What four famous American historical writers are named?*
32. *What is the first particular in which the writers since the Civil War differ from those whose fame was made before?*
33. *To what kinds of writing did these writers usually give themselves?*
34. *For what are they remarkable?*
35. *In what did American art have its rise?*
36. *What is said of American art?*
37. *What of book and magazine illustration in this country?*

Study by topics

I. The lack of literature before the last century.
II. Some of the older writers.
    1. Irving. 2. Bryant. 3. Longfellow. 4. Whittier. 5. Holmes.
    6. Poe. 7. Emerson. 8. Lowell. 9. Cooper. 10. Hawthorne. 11. Historians.
III. The new school of writers.
    1. Their representative character.
    2. Their devotion to fictitious and humorous literature.
    3. Their attention to details of manners and speech.
IV. American art.

Books

The best way to study literature is in the literature itself. If the teacher can persuade the pupil to read some of the works mentioned in this chapter, and to seek for the charm there is in them, it will tend to develop a taste for good literature, and education can render no higher service than this. For literature of the colonial period, Tyler's *History of American Literature.* For literature of the period since the Revolution, Richardson's *History of American Literature.*

EIGHTH REVIEW—FINAL CHAPTERS

Results of the war.   (LVIII)
{
Questions of the right of a State to secede settled.
Slavery abolished.
The existence of but one great power in North America settled.
}

Johnson's administration.   (LVIII)
{
Andrew Johnson President.
Question of Negro suffrage.
Johnson impeached.
}

Grant's administration.   (LVIII)
{
Grant elected, 1868.
Reconstruction of the South.
Grant reelected, 1872.
}

The election of 1876.   (LVIII)
{
The disputed election.
Settled in favor of Hayes.
}

Garfield and Arthur.   (LVIII)
{
Garfield elected, 1880.
Garfield killed, 1881.
Arthur President.
}

Cleveland's presidency.   (LVIII)
{
Cleveland elected, 1884.
Revival of tariff questions.
}

The purchase of Russian territory.   (LIX)
{
Review of the first five additions of territory.
The purchase of Alaska, 1867.
}

New States since the Civil War.   (LIX)
{
West Virginia, 1863.
Nevada, 1864.
Nebraska, 1867.
Colorado, 1876.
North Dakota, South Dakota, Montana, and Washington, 1889.
}

Population and wealth.   (LX)
{
Indian war in Minnesota, 1862.
Custer's winter campaign, 1868.
Death of Custer, 1876.
Prospects of the Indians.
}

Later Indian wars.   (LIX)
{
Increase of population since 1790.
Sources and increase of wealth.
}

Inventions. (LX)
{
Early American inventions.
The cotton gin and its effects.
Other agricultural machines.
Sewing machines.
Telegraph, telephone, and phonograph.
}

New modes of life. (LX)
{
Changes made by new inventions.
The factory system.
}

Literature. (LXI)
{
The first two centuries.
Irving.
The group of poets: Bryant, Longfellow
Whittier, Holmes, and Poe.
Emerson, essayist and poet.
Lowell, poet, critic, and essayist.
Two great novelists: Cooper and
Hawthorne.
Historians.
Later writers.
}

INDEX

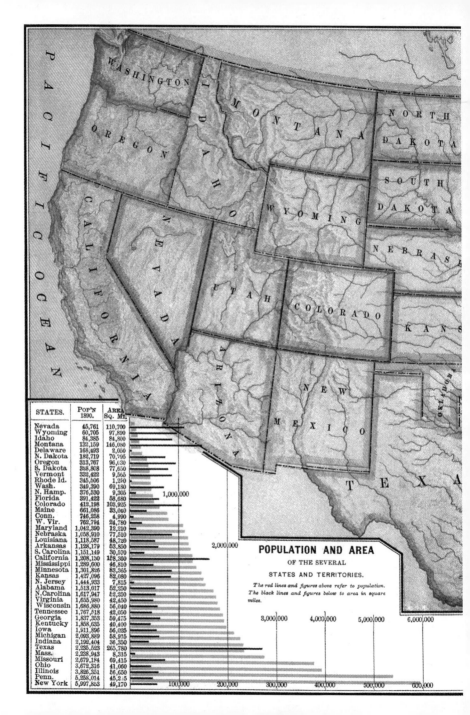

STATES.	POP'N 1890.	AREA SQ. MI.
Nevada	45,761	110,700
Wyoming	60,705	97,890
Idaho	84,385	84,800
Montana	132,159	146,080
Delaware	168,493	2,050
N. Dakota	182,719	70,795
Oregon	313,767	96,030
S. Dakota	328,808	77,650
Vermont	332,422	9,565
Rhode Id.	345,506	1,250
Wash.	349,390	69,180
N. Hamp.	376,530	9,305
Florida	391,422	58,680
Colorado	412,198	103,925
Maine	661,086	33,040
Conn.	746,258	4,990
W. Vir.	762,794	24,780
Maryland	1,042,390	12,210
Nebraska	1,058,910	77,510
Louisiana	1,118,587	48,720
Arkansas	1,128,179	53,850
S. Carolina	1,151,149	30,570
California	1,208,130	158,360
Mississippi	1,289,600	46,810
Minnesota	1,301,826	83,365
Kansas	1,427,096	82,080
N. Jersey	1,444,933	7,815
Alabama	1,513,017	52,250
N.Carolina	1,617,947	52,250
Virginia	1,655,980	42,450
Wisconsin	1,686,880	56,040
Tennessee	1,767,518	42,050
Georgia	1,837,353	59,475
Kentucky	1,858,635	40,400
Iowa	1,911,896	56,025
Michigan	2,093,889	58,915
Indiana	2,192,404	36,350
Texas	2,235,523	265,780
Mass.	2,238,943	8,315
Missouri	2,679,184	69,415
Ohio	3,672,316	41,060
Illinois	3,826,351	56,650
Penn.	5,258,014	45,215
New York	5,997,853	49,170

POPULATION AND AREA

OF THE SEVERAL

STATES AND TERRITORIES.

The red lines and figures above refer to population.
The black lines and figures below to area in square
miles.

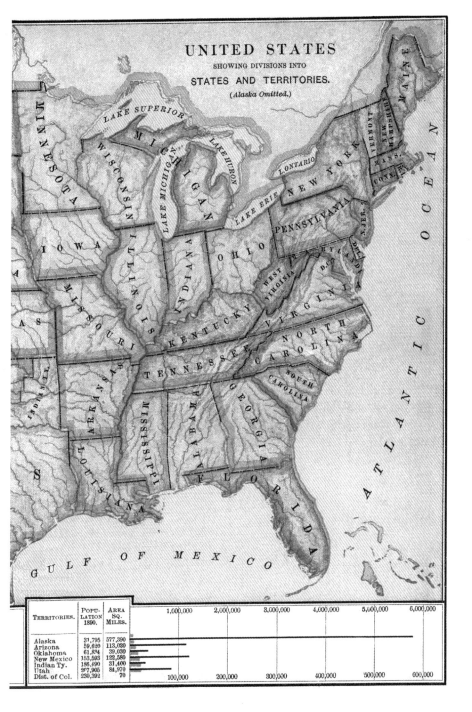

UNITED STATES

SHOWING DIVISIONS INTO

STATES AND TERRITORIES.

(Alaska Omitted.)

TERRITORIES.	POPU- LATION 1890.	AREA SQ. MILES.	1,000,000	2,000,000	3,000,000	4,000,000	5,000,000	6,000,000
Alaska	31,795	577,390						
Arizona	59,620	113,020						
Oklahoma	61,834	39,030						
New Mexico	153,593	122,580						
Indian Ty.	186,490	31,400						
Utah	207,905	84,970						
Dist. of Col.	230,392	70						
			100,000	200,000	300,000	400,000	500,000	600,000